NO BATTLE WITHOUT HIM

Charalampos Seiradakis, 1886–1970

Charis Xirouchakis

Preface by
Sir Michael Llewellyn-Smith

Helion & Company Limited

Helion & Company Limited
Unit 8 Amherst Business Centre Budbrooke Road
Warwick
CV34 5WE
England
Tel. 01926 499619
Email: info@helion.co.uk
Website: www.helion.co.uk
X (formerly Twitter): @Helionbooks
Facebook: @HelionBooks
Visit our blog at helionbooks.wordpress.com

Published by Helion & Company 2025
Designed and typeset by Mach 3 Solutions (www.mach3solutions.co.uk)
Cover designed by Paul Hewitt, Battlefield Design (www.battlefield-design.co.uk)

ISBN 978-1-804519-34-9

British Library Cataloguing-in-Publication Data.
A catalogue record for this book is available from the British Library.

For details of other military history titles published by Helion & Company Limited, contact the above address, or visit our website: http://www.helion.co.uk

We always welcome receiving book proposals from prospective authors.

Contents

To my sons Nikolaos and Alexios
and my nephew Michael
to get to know their great-grandfather

Tout homme qui écrit, écrit un livre;
Ce livre, c'est lui.
[Every man who writes, writes a book.
This book is himself.]

Victor Hugo
Œuvres complètes, Poésie I
Paris, 20 February 1880

Table of comparative military ranks

Greek ranks have been used throughout but using the Latin alphabet. The ranks using the Greek alphabet, along with their British equivalent are given below.

Rank in Greek (Latin Alphabet)	Rank in Greek (Greek Aphabet)	British Equivalent Rank
Archistratigos	Αρχιστράτηγος	Commander-in-Chief
Stratarchis	Στρατάρχης	Field Marshal
Stratigos	Στρατηγός	General
Navarchos	Ναύαρχος	Admiral
Antistratigos	Αντιστράτηγος	Lieutenant General
Ypostratigos	Υποστράτηγος	Major General
Yponavarchos	Υποναύαρχος	Rear Admiral
Taxiarchos	Ταξίαρχος	Brigadier General
Antinavarchos	Αντιναύαρχος	Vice Admiral
Syntagmatarchis	Συνταγματάρχης	Colonel
Antisyntagmatachis	Αντισυνταγματάρχης	Lieutenant Colonel
Dioikitis	Διοικητής	Commander
Tagmatarchis	Ταγματάρχης	Major
Ypodioikitis	Υποδιοικητής	Lieutenant Commander
Lochagos	Λοχαγός	Captain
Moirarchos (Gendarmerie)	Μοίραρχος (Gendarmerie)	'Squadron Leader' (Gendarmerie)
Anthypaspistis	Ανθυπασπιστής	Lieutenant
Ypolochagos	Υπολοχαγός	Second Lieutenant
Anthypolochagos	Ανθυπολοχαγός	Sub Lieutenant
Ypaxiomatikos	Υπαξιωματικός	Petty Officer
Ypaspistis	Υπασπιστής	Adjutant
Epilochias	Επιλοχίας	Staff Sergeant
Lochias	Λοχίας	Sergeant
Dekaneas	Δεκανέας	Corporal
Dekaneas Aggelioforos	Δεκανέας Αγγελιοφόρος	Corporal-messenger
Stratiotis / Fantaros	Στρατιώτης	Private
Frourarchos	Φρούραρχος	Fortress Commander
Archigos Epiteleiou	Αρχηγός Επιτελείου	Chief of Staff
Epitelarchis	Επιτελάρχης	Staff Officer

Foreword

Charalampos Seiradakis (1886–1970) a Cretan from the Selino area of the west of Crete whose long career in the Greek military ended with his appointment in 1947 as *nomarch*, or Prefect, of Chania, has been lucky in his chronicler, Charis Xirouchakis. The writer prefaces his book with words from Victor Hugo: '*Tout homme qui écrit, écrit un livre: ce livre, c'est lui.*' A good motto!

Seiradakis seems from his youth to have seen his future as a military one. He started at the bottom, enlisting as a *stratiotis* in the Greek Army in February 1911, and gradually made his way upwards through the ranks, finally leaving the army in 1947 with the rank of colonel. There were hiccups on the way. For example, he was obliged to leave the army in 1935 as a result of taking part in the failed Venizelist coup d'état, but was readmitted in 1941, before the Battle of Crete, in the rank of Lt Colonel. Other Venizelists will have trodden a similar path.

The background to Seiradakis' military career was the turbulent conditions of Ottoman Crete, of Greek uprisings met by Ottoman repression in the late nineteenth and early twentieth centuries. The army was his first loyalty. The second was the Cretan politician and leader, Eleftherios Venizelos. The author of this biographical account, who lives in Chania, is well placed by family connections and personal interests to tell this story. It starts in the small town of Kandanos in the west of Crete, and moves on to the Greek Army, where Seiradakis takes part in succession in the Balkan Wars (1912–1913); in Lorraine with the French in the Great War; in Gallipoli, again with the French; and after several other assignments, in the Middle East with the Greek forces in the Second World War and in the Battle of Crete. The early part of the book rests on good foundations in existing Greek literature (Ventiris, Mavrogordatos et cetera) but other parts are relatively unknown, and the book adds significantly to the body of knowledge. Throughout this story, during which Seiradakis was several times wounded, he remained faithful to the Venizelist liberal cause and to his military honour and upbringing.

Back in his native Crete, he married a much younger girl, became *Nomarch* of Chania, and settled down in his mature years, with so many things to remember, like Shakespeare's 'old men' who look back on a soldier's life.

The author deals with his subject's long career meticulously, drawing on an archive left by the subject himself, and on a wide range of sources which are set out in a useful bibliography. It is a complex story, reflecting the changing circumstances of the Greek armed forces of the first half of the twentieth century. In this period the army moved from triumph in the Balkan Wars, which established the geography of the modern Greek state, to periods in which the Greek Army itself was divided into hostile and fractious forces, some loyal to King Constantine, others to Venizelos. It seems from the book that throughout, Seiradakis, while retaining his allegiance to Venizelos, managed to avoid involvement in the petty politics of factions in the army.

This is a carefully written account which draws on many sources, some well-known, others relatively obscure, and of course on the notes and documents in the Seiradakis archive which Mr Xirouchakis has used. The book has clearly been a labour of love. Charis Xirouchakis is to be congratulated on bringing this long and detailed account to a successful conclusion.

Sir Michael Llewellyn-Smith

Preface to English Edition

During the twentieth century Greece has often been at war. There have been wars to throw off the foreign yoke, wars in the Balkans, and most of all the two world wars. Although fortunes were mixed, at the end of the Second World War Greece came out largely a winner, doubling its size and population compared to a century earlier.

This war epic has bred a generation of Greek soldiers with special virtues. Inspired by age-old traditions, they were brave in battle, endured tough hardships and never abandoned the struggle in adversity. They showed chivalry to opponents and remained fixed on purpose. Perhaps their worst enemy was their own opposing fractionising which often led to losing what was gained in battle. But their patriotism and ethos remained impeccable throughout.

I always thought it would be fascinating to give an account of these wars through the eyes of an eyewitness soldier who took part in them. In this I was fortunate to draw on the adventures of my own maternal grandfather, an officer of the Greek Army, Charalampos Seiradakis, who fought in almost all Greek wars between 1897 and 1947. Throughout his life he remained loyal to the army and to the liberal politician and statesman Eleftherios Venizelos. Although several times wounded, he had survived with so many things to remember like Shakespeare's 'old men' who look back on a soldier's life, as Sir Michael Llewellyn-Smith has written in the forward to the book.

The war experiences of Charalampos Seiradakis are not without interest to the British reader. In his campaigns he often fought next to British, French, Australian, New Zealand and Allied troops in his native Crete, in Northern Greece, and in France, Bulgaria, Albania, Egypt and Turkey. When I sat down to write his story, I was amazed to find out that his name is often mentioned in several historians' accounts. His personal memoirs and the military archives in the Greek, French and British Armies revealed some unknown pages of modern military history, for example the presence of a Greek contingent in Lorraine and at Gallipoli during the First World War. Through his eyes the wars of the twentieth century come to life, like an exciting adventure.

The book was originally published in Greece by Epikentro in Thessaloniki, a tribute to Seiradakis' long military service in Greece. The idea to publish it in English came up in discussions with my dear friend Charles Duckworth, who was married to my late cousin, Rena Kassimatis Duckworth, and with our common friend, Paul Watkins, editor of the *Anglo-Hellenic Review* published by the Anglo-Hellenic League. They considered that Seiradakis' military adventures together with the British Army over half a century could be of general interest and thus encouraged me to publish the book in English.

For the translation I relied initially on DeepL, a language translation engine. The text, however, had to be meticulously edited and for this I am indebted to my friend Mrs Lucy Stambouzou and her husband Michael Stambouzos who have succeeded in coming up with a fascinating narrative in English. My companion Andrea Dahmen, to whom I owe the title of the book, provided useful advice throughout the process of adapting the text in English. My thanks also to Ms Niki Xifantaraki who worked tirelessly to give the text a proper form.

But my special thanks go to Duncan Rogers, who from the outset recognised the originality of the book and agreed to publish it through Helion & Co. Ltd, a military publications specialist. His colleagues, Ms Vicky Powell and Mr Stephen Ede-Borrett, have been very helpful advising me on the present publication.

To my dear friend and mentor Sir Michael Llewellyn-Smith, who possesses a deep insight into Greek history, I will always owe gratitude. His objective comments during our discussions have been a guide in approaching the tragic epic of the twentieth century wars and the brave men who fought them.

Charis Xirouchakis
Korakies, Crete
17 July 2025

A Note on Charalampos Seiradakis's Military Career

Charalampos Seiradakis enrolled as soldier in the Greek Army on February 1911 at the age of 25. After the siege at Bizani in 1913, where he was wounded, he was promoted to *lochias*, and the following year to *epilochias*. During WW1 in 1915 he served in the expeditionary force of the *Clan Crétois* in Lorraine, France, where he was promoted to *ypaspistis*.

Upon his return to the Greek Army in 1917 he was promoted to *anthypolochagos*; three years later to *ypolochagos*; in 1923 to *lochagos*; and in October 1933 to *Tagmatarchis* on grounds of merit.

After taking part in the failed coup of 1935, he was dismissed from the army, but was called back in May 1941, on the eve of the Battle of Crete, with the rank of *Antisyntagmatachis*.

He left the army in 1947 with the rank of *Syntagmatarchis*. That same year he was appointed as *Nomarch* of Chania.

Transcript:
To the descendants of the Seiradakis family

Our family has provided invaluable national and social service over the centuries. It has history and glory, but it is precisely this wonderful past that is a heavy burden for today's generation and those to come. Those of us with such a family past are not allowed to fall into humiliation or shame, and this will happen if we do not prove ourselves worthy of our ancestors, constantly adapting ourselves to the national and social needs of our country; otherwise this glorious past with its glorious and historic sacrifices, instead of being a crown of honour for the descendants, will be turned into a tombstone which will fall inexorably on the decaying body of our national heritage.

We must never forget that we have inherited great and glorious historical traditions, but precisely for this reason, by respecting the memory of our ancestors, we also have a corresponding responsibility towards their memory.

Signed at Athens, on 15 May 1961

[Signature] *Charalampos Seiradakis*

Πρός
τούς ἐπιγενομένους τῆς Οἰκογενείας τῶν Σειράδων
Ἡ οἰκογένειά μας ἔχει προσφέρει εἰς τήν δια-
δρομήν τῶν αἰώνων ἀναντιρρήτως ἐθνικάς ἀλλά καί
κοινωνικάς ὑπηρεσίας. Ἔχει ἱστορίαν καί δόξαν, ἀλλά
αὐτό ἀκριβῶς τό θαυμαστόν παρελθόν ἀποτελεῖ διά
τάς σημερινάς γενεάς, ἀλλά καί τάς ἐπερχομένας κλη-
ρονομίαν βαρυτάτην. Δέν ἐπιτρέπεται εἰς ἡμᾶς
μέ τοιοῦτον οἰκογενειακόν παρελθόν νά πε-
ριπέσωμεν εἰς ταπείνωσιν ἤ κατασχύνην καί ἀ-
φάνειαν· τοῦτο θά συμβῇ ἐάν δέν ἀναδειχθῶμεν
ἀντάξιοι τῶν προγόνων μας, ἀνα προσαρμοζόμενοι
δημιουργικῶς μέ τάς [illegible] ἐθνικάς ἀλλά καί κοι-
F [illegible] νωνικάς ἀνάγκας,F ὅπως ἡ ἔνδοξος ἱστορική [illegible]
[illegible] τῶν Δυσικῶν κ.λ.π. οἰκογενειακῶς [illegible] αὐτή καί [illegible]
[illegible] [illegible] διά τούς ἐπιγενομένους, τό ἄδοξον
αὐτό παρελθόν, θά [illegible] εἰς [illegible]
ἡ ὁποία θά [illegible] [illegible] ἐπί τοῦ [illegible]
[illegible] οὔτε [illegible] τῇ Ἐθνικῇ μας Κληρονομιᾷ.
Δέν [illegible] νά λησμονῶμεν ὅτι
ἔχομεν κληρονομήσει μεγάλας καί λαμπράς ἱστορικάς
παραδόσεις ἀλλά ἀκριβῶς γι' αὐτό [illegible] τὴν μνή-
μην τῶν προγόνων μας ἔχομεν καί [illegible] ἔναντι τῆς μνή-
μης αὐτῶν εὐθύνας.—
Ἔγραψα ἰδιοχείρως ἐν Ἀθή- [signature] Σειραδάκης
ναις τῇ 15ῃ Μαΐου ~~1964~~ 1961

Handwritten letter by Charalampos Seiradakis.

Introduction

Since the beginning of the nineteenth century Crete had been fighting constantly to throw off the Turkish yoke. The first rebellion of Daskalogiannis had taken place in 1770 in the Orloff Uprising, the so-called *Orlofika*, but it was a bloodbath. The Cretans participated in the national uprising of 1821, but Crete was not included in the newly established Greek state. Since then, the Cretans had rebelled continuously almost every 10 years. But each failed uprising was followed by persecution and repression that decimated the Cretan population. The countryside was almost deserted and living conditions on the island were miserable.

Charalampos Seiradakis grew up in this gloomy atmosphere. He was born in 1886 in the mountainous village of Livadas, which is now East Selino, and which used to belong to the province of Sfakia. Nature has a wild beauty in these areas where he grew up. On one side are the snow-covered White Mountains, or Madares, and on the other the turquoise waters of Sougia. Forests of olive trees cover the mountains. Although the family of the Seirades were farmers, the family tradition was war, as was the case with most people in the Cretan mountains. The Turkish occupation had accentuated their militancy and from generation to generation they all participated in the wars of independence.

Indeed, the independence of Crete was approaching. When Charalampos Seiradakis was 11 years old, in 1897, the Cretans rose up again against the Turks. The siege of Kandanos was his baptism of fire. This time, developments were positive for the rebels, and the following year the European naval leaders of the Great Powers sailing to Crete forced the Turkish Army to evacuate the island after the brutal murder of British soldiers. Crete was declared an autonomous state. This first experience sealed the life of Charalampos Seiradakis who, on the eve of the Balkan Wars, joined the Greek Army. From then on, he never stopped fighting.

Charalampos Seiradakis was a fierce and active army officer. Although he did not rise to the highest ranks of the hierarchy, having joined the army at the age of 25, he was promoted to the rank of *Syntagmatarchis*. His presence was continuous in most of the wars fought by Greece and beyond.

Firstly, in the two Balkan Wars as a *Bizanomachos*, fighter at Bizani, then as a volunteer on the French front of Lorraine and in the Gallipoli campaign, and immediately afterwards on the Thessaloniki Front during the First World War. He rejoined the army after the failed coup of 1935 and took part in the Battle of Crete before moving to the Middle East where he participated in the organisation of the exiled Greek Army. He was repeatedly wounded but survived. In a way, he was one of the unsung heroes of the Greek wars. He was always present, though not one of the primary protagonists.

Two elements of his war record deserve special mention. The first is his participation in the Hellenocretan Legion on the Lorraine Front in 1915. This is a relatively unknown page in Greek military history, although not in French history, which acknowledged the contribution of the *Clan Crétois*, the Cretan Volunteer Corps, in the battles of Bois-le-Prêtre in North-Western France. In addition to the commemoration of their heroism by the military, a memorial has been erected at the battle site to pay tribute to the 'Cretan volunteers' (*volontaires Crétois*).

Even less known is the presence of the Hellenocretan Legion in the Gallipoli Campaign in the Dardanelles. Immediately after the Lorraine Front, the legion landed at Xeros Bay and took part in commando operations against the Turkish Army in August 1915. It is only recently that British and French historians have referred to the role of the *Clan Crétois* in the bloody battles of Gallipoli. In command of the legion in both campaigns was *Lochagos* Pavlis Gyparis, whose officers included Charalampos Seiradakis, Andreas Gyparakis and Kostas Giannakakis.

The second element is the participation of Charalampos Seiradakis in the Battle of Crete in May 1941. Although this epic battle is well documented by Greek, British, Australian, New Zealand and German historians, the Battle of Floria and of the Kandanos Gorge has not been analysed as much as it deserves. This battle delayed the German advance south and contributed to the early withdrawal of the Allied Army to Egypt to avoid capture. At the same time, however, it was the cause of harsh reprisals and Kandanos was razed to the ground by the Nazis. The battles of Kandanos, from Voukolies to Floria, of 22 to 25 May 1945, were led by *Antisyntagmatachis* Seiradakis.

Of course, Charalampos Seiradakis was not uninvolved in the political conflicts that marked the first half of the twentieth century. He was a Venizelist, which is to be expected for a young patriot who grew up in Crete at a time when Eleftherios Venizelos was leading the campaign for union with Greece. For the Cretans, Venizelos was not only a revolutionary but also a leader, a *homme d'état*. It is doubtful that the sacrifices of the Cretans made for their freedom would have had the same happy outcome if his political activity had not intervened.

At the same time, Venizelos' liberal ideas represented democratic Crete. But not only Crete. In 1909, the Military League in Athens had invited Venizelos to govern Greece. For the next 35 years he played a leading political role and was the moderniser of the country. It was only natural for Seiradakis, along with a large majority of progressive society, to stand at Venizelos' side. As long as Greece remained united, as in the Balkan Wars, they succeeded in incorporating territories historically inhabited by Greek people. But the disagreement between Prime Minister Venizelos and King Constantine in 1915 led to a national division and forced Greek society to take a stand – and Seiradakis was no exception. His loyalty to Venizelos remained firm until the end of his life.

Seiradakis was first and foremost a patriot. This was evident when he left Crete for the Middle East in the middle of the Second World War. It was the time when mutinies in the Greek Army in the Middle East became manifest. Faced with the danger of the Greek Army being disbanded in wartime, Greek officers were called upon to show unity and overcome old rivalries. Seiradakis was the first to set an example. He did not hesitate to contact officers who were divided by old differences to reconcile extreme behaviour in the army.

He believed that the common interest should be the restoration of the Greek Army's military prowess. But the result was not what he expected.

After his retirement, Seiradakis continued to be involved in public affairs. His last public service was his term as *Nomarch* of Chania in 1947.

* * *

I first encountered the military archives of my grandfather Charalampos Seiradakis when studying in Athens in the late 1960s. Although the economics I was studying had nothing to do with the military, the war memorabilia – mainly documents that testified to battles and exploits – had fascinated me.

Moreover, the recital of war stories by my grandfather was frequent and many of them stuck in my memory. At that time, many of Seiradakis' comrades-in-arms and friends came to visit him. I was present at a lot of discussions that were revealing of a long period of Greek history – from before 1900 to after 1950, almost a century. Even in his 80s, Seiradakis' memory was vivid about people and events that shaped the course of Greek history. When I later found time to study his archives, I was greatly helped by my aunt Helen-Ellas Seiradakis-Kourakos, the younger daughter of Charalampos Seiradakis. I will always be grateful to her for her help. I would also like to thank Mrs Fotini Pipi for her thorough linguistic editing, which greatly improved the text, and Mrs Andrea Dahmen for the inspiration of the title of the book. With my brother Nikos Xirouchakis we shared common memories. My versatile friend Kyriakos Naxakis read original texts and helped me in shaping the Appendices. With my friend and historian Manolis Manousakas we travelled back in time in Chania during the period of Eleftherios Venizelos and even earlier. Warm thanks to my dear friend military historian Tasos Sakellaropoulos for valuable comments during the writing process. I certainly could not fail to express my gratitude to Sir Michael Llewellyn-Smith for willingly accepting to write the Foreword to the book. And, of course, my sincere thanks to Mr Petros Papasarantopoulos and 'Epikentro' Publications for publishing the book, and to Mr. Thomas Siomos for putting me in touch with them.

This biography, although not a history book *Stricto Sensu*, is based on historically verified sources. First, the personal archives of Seiradakis, which include correspondence, war reports and rare documents – although others were lost in the bombing of 1941. Much of what survived is coming to light for the first time and reveals unknown aspects of our history. Seiradakis' records in the archives of the Greek Army number 175 pages and were kindly provided to me in CD format by the recruitment office in Goudi, Athens. Additionally, his records in the French Army, numbering 21 pages, were also sent to me electronically, by the corresponding department of the French Army.

It is noteworthy that the name of Charalampos Seiradakis appears in books, studies and memoirs in many countries and languages. Apart from Greek authors, he is also mentioned by British, Australian, New Zealand, French and German authors – most of them military historians. For the writing of this biography, I visited several of the places where Seiradakis fought. The most moving experience was in France, near the town of Pont-à-Mousson in Lorraine, where the *Clan Crétois* fought alongside the heroic *Loups* ('Wolves') in the forests of Bois-le-Prêtre. I am grateful to the French historian Mr Eric Ebelmann who showed me around the areas where the battles took place and proudly showed me the monument where the Cretan volunteers, *les volontaires Crétois*, are mentioned. On a visit to Epirus, in Northern Greece, I was impressed by the fortifications at Bizani, outside Ioannina, where the *Bizanomachoi* suffered terribly before they came out victorious. In nearby Metsovo, they have a story to tell about the Cretan *Lochagos* Kleidis who sacrificed himself to drive the Turks away.

Closer to where Seiradakis was born, I used to visit my relatives in Livadas from a young age. I walked the Gorge of Kandanos many times, trying to locate the place where he resisted the Germans. But I have not yet been able to visit Xeros Bay in Gallipoli, the hills of Skra and Raviné in Macedonia, Tobruk and the desert of Ismailia in Egypt – all places where Seiradakis was active and fought.

It is encouraging that more young researchers are analysing unknown aspects of our war history. On the internet I am constantly discovering interesting studies. Although in this publication I mention those I know of, there are surely others that I have missed. Just as there are dozens or hundreds of names of fighters, fellow combatants and even relatives that I have not included. I apologise in advance for all these omissions, for which I alone am responsible. I would like to be able to tell those stories too, at some point in the future

A few words about the arrangement of the material:

Chapter 2 is a brief review of the history of Crete up to the nineteenth century.
Chapters 3 and 4 refer to the early and teenage years of Charalampos Seiradakis with references to the Cretan revolutions.
Chapters 5, 6 and 7 deal with the Balkan Wars, in which Seiradakis fought and was wounded.
Chapters 8 and 9 tell of his participation in the Lorraine and Gallipoli campaigns.
Chapters 10 and 11 of the First World War and the consequences of the National Schism.
Chapter 12 is about the aftermath of the Asia Minor catastrophe and the marriage of Charalampos Seiradakis and Fani Louka.
Chapter 13 tells of the failed military coup of 1935.
Chapter 14 covers the Battle of Crete in Floria and the Kandanos Gorge.
Chapters 15 and 17 are about Seiradakis' participation in the exiled army in the Middle East.
Chapter 16 tells of the destruction of the village of Livadas in 1943.
Chapter 18, the final chapter, describes the post-war situation in Crete and Seiradakis' tenure as *Nomarch* of Chania.

The bibliography on which I based the biography is at the end of the book. In addition, some selected extracts from historical and other documents are shown in Appendices I and II, while selected photos appear in Appendix III.

1

Tobruk, May 1943

On Board to Tobruk

As the British warship HMS *Hedgehog*[1] was quietly departing on 8 May 1943 from the southern shores of Crete and heading in the darkness towards Tobruk, Libya, *Antisyntagmatachis* Charalampos Seiradakis was lost in thought. He was thinking about all the battles he had taken part in up to that point. He was already 57 years old and since the age of 11, when he had first picked up a rifle while chasing the Turks in Kandanos, he had not stopped fighting for a moment. Nor was there any prospect of his stopping any time soon. The Second World War, which had been going on for three years and had bloodied Europe and the whole world, was not about to end.

Two years had passed since the German paratroopers under the command of *Generalleutenant* Kurt Student had succeeded, against all predictions and after a bloody struggle, in capturing Crete. The German paratroopers had attacked on 20 May 1941. After the campaign of Operation *Marita*, with which they invaded mainland Greece, the Axis forces launched Operation *Merkur* for the capture of Crete. It was a Pyrrhic victory. The hundreds of dead in this historic battle included British, Australians, New Zealanders and Greeks who had been assigned to defend the island, and – more numerously – German paratroopers.

After the Battle of Crete, the elite *fallschirmjäger* corps was virtually nonexistent. Significantly, it was never used again during the Second World War, while Student himself fell from grace and was considered to have failed in his mission. As it became clear later in the war, the occupation of Crete offered no strategic advantage to the Germans since the Middle East front had moved west, and the German Army was supplied from Sicily rather than Crete.

Seiradakis had taken part in the Battle of Crete at Floria and in the Battle of the Kandanos Canyon. In the deadly battles that took place from 22 to 25 May 1941 he had tried to intercept the advance of German paratroopers from Maleme Airfield to Paleochora in Southern Crete. He had had no luck. The Germans had called in reinforcements and the Cretan fighters had retreated. The memory of those who fought in

1 The *Hedgehog* was a small P-class destroyer used by the British for raiding operations in the Middle East. Like its twin, *Porcupine*, it was equipped with anti-aircraft guns and radar.

the Battle of Crete was imprinted with the violence of the fighting from 20 to 29 May. In many cases there had been combat using bayonets, reminiscent of the trenches of the First World War.

Charalampos Seiradakis had his own experience of such battles, having participated 26 years ago in the Great War against the Germans, on the Lorraine Front. He recalled that in February 1915 he had taken part as a volunteer in the Hellenocretan Legion organised by *Lochagos* Pavlis Gyparis when they had fought alongside the French on the Western Front in the deadly battles of Bois-le-Prêtre[2] near Verdun. In August of the same year, the legion was ordered to depart to take part in the Gallipoli Campaign in the Dardanelles, where British, French, New Zealanders and Australians were trying without success to break through the Turkish defences that had been fortified by German officers. Before them were the Balkan Wars, the Aetorachi, Emin Aga, Bizani, Thessaloniki, Macedonia. Immediately after the Macedonian Front, the battles against the Bulgarians. It was as if not a day had passed. How many had he taken part in? The multiple wounds he had suffered bore witness to a life spent constantly in battle. Now that he thought about it, he had the feeling it was a miracle he had survived. For him, that did not mean so much really, since he came from a family with a long military tradition that had been at the forefront of wars against the Turks for as long as he could remember. Not that the Seiradakis family was the only one in Crete with a tradition of war. The whole island has always been imbued with a sense of the importance of freedom and opposition to the retrograde Ottoman occupation has left indelible traces from its history.

After long struggles throughout the nineteenth century, the Turks had finally withdrawn from Crete in 1898. It was unthinkable for the Cretans not to fight against any would-be conqueror who would deprive them of their freedom again.

Fugitive in Madares

This had recently been confirmed in the Battle of Crete against the German invaders. But now, in May 1943, the whole of Greece was under foreign occupation. The long-suffering island of Crete was again under foreign yoke and the German occupation had proved to be particularly brutal.

For the last two years Seiradakis had had to move constantly as a fugitive from village to village in the mountains of Western Crete above Madares. He had entrusted his family for greater security to his relatives Seiradakis, who lived permanently in Livadas. He knew that he was in constant danger and that the Germans were looking for him as he had participated in the Battle of Crete; he knew people and situations and was in constant contact with the resistance and the Middle East. The exiled Greek Government with Prime Minister Emmanuel Tsouderos had moved there.[3] Seiradakis was helping to

2 Bois-le-Prêtre is a series of wooded hills near the town of Pont-à-Mousson on the Franco-German border in the province of Lorraine.

3 Emmanuel Tsouderos (1882–1956) came from Rethymno, Crete, and distinguished himself as a politician and economist. He was the first Governor of the Bank of Greece from 1928 to

maintain a network of radios installed in the mountain villages of Moni, Livadas and Koustogerako in the province of Selino to stay in contact with Cairo. Although it posed a danger to the villages if it came to the notice of the Germans, it had proved to be a lifesaver for many of the thousand or more British, New Zealand and Australian soldiers who were wandering fugitives in the mountains of Western Crete looking for a way to escape to the Middle East. Now Seiradakis was in the same position. He was travelling with them in the direction of Tobruk, close to where the historic battles of El Alamein had taken place a year ago.

Over 40 ANZAC soldiers had boarded the ship.[4] They had finally managed to get in touch with the General Headquarters of the Middle East, with orders to assemble before midnight on 8 May 1943 on the beach where the gorge of Tripiti ends, between Sougia and Agia Roumeli, in Southern Crete. The only way to get there was by a rough path through the gorge, one of the many that cross the Cretan White Mountains and end up at the sea. They would surely have lost their way if they had not been guided through the cliffs by George Frantzeskakis, a Cretan Seliniot who knew the area.

Along the way he told the foreign soldiers of the latest developments in German-occupied Crete. They had information that the German *General* Bräuer was to replace Alexander Andrae in command of the German Army occupying Crete. The prospects for the Cretans were bleak.

After a five-hour march, the exhausted soldiers had reached the small beach where the gorge of Tripiti ends. Charalampos Seiradakis had already reached the same place but by a different path. He had also contacted the Greek General Headquarters in the Middle East and received an order to board the same ship with the officers Stelios Papaderos and Manolis Papagrigorakis. Their mission was to reinforce the Greek troops in the Middle East and to support the Allied combat operations against the Axis. The Battles at El Alamein had ended a year earlier with the defeat of the *General* Erwin Rommel and the new British commander-in-chief, Bernard Montgomery, was already planning the landing of the Allied Army in Sicily.

Among the Australian warriors who had gathered on the beach of Tripiti, Seiradakis recognised the young Jim McDevitt.[5] They had met a few days before in the village of Livadas, the place of origin of the Seiradakis family. Jim and two other soldiers were hiding from village to village, trying to escape from the German troops who sought to capture them. They were not the only ones. Several British, Australian and New Zealand soldiers were targeted by the Germans. Many had been captured or were in hiding with the help of Cretan villagers who felt it was their duty, regardless of the harsh reprisals already being taken by the German authorities.

1941. He became Minister of Transport in the government of El. Venizelos and Minister of Finance in the government of Th. Sofoulis. He was prime minister of the Greek Government-in-exile after the Germans entered Athens during most of the Occupation until 1944.

4 ANZAC: acronym of Australian and New Zealand Army Corps.

5 J. McDevitt, *My Escape from Crete* (Auckland, New Zealand: privately published, 2002).

Escape at Night

Aboard *Hedgehog*, the soldiers felt relief. Fortunately, there was plenty of room on board, so no one was left behind. Having completed the boarding in complete silence, the ship had picked up speed and was moving away as fast as its engines would allow. It had to pass the island of Gavdos south of Crete and get out of range of the German planes patrolling the Aegean quickly. Although the *Luftwaffe* had been weakened since some aircraft had been sent to other fronts, it was still feared over the Greek seas. But the calm sea and the starless night helped to get them safely away from the danger zone.

At dawn on 9 May, the ship sailed into the port of Tobruk, on the Libyan coast. The joy of the young Australians and New Zealanders was great when they recognised SOE officer Arthur Reade,[6] whom they had known since the Battle of Crete, on the quay. Despite all the difficulties that they knew they would face in the Middle East, they felt relieved to be spared from captivity and from the hardships in the mountains of Crete. Without a moment's hesitation they boarded the waiting trucks and left for their units. Soon they would take part in the landing of the Allied Army in South Italy.

Along with other cars, a jeep with a Greek driver had stopped at the pier. He immediately recognised the Greek officers and, after welcoming them to their new homeland in exile, they left for Cairo. They had to hurry to cross the desert to Alexandria before the African heat caught up with them. From there they would carry on to the headquarters of the Greek Government and the headquarters of the Greek Army in exile.

6 McDevitt, *Escape*. Special Operations Executive (SOE): an active special service of the British intelligence service.

2

Crete Until the Nineteenth Century

From Mythology to History

Crete is a relatively isolated island. It is in the middle of the Eastern Mediterranean and is about the same distance from Athens as it is from Benghazi in Libya, while Cyprus to the east and Malta to the west are even further away. But the geography of Crete is also special. The island is elongated, 260 kilometres long and 40 kilometres wide on average, with a continuous mountain range of over 2,000 metres that runs like a spine along the southern part of the island and falls steeply into the sea, cut through in many places by deep gorges. In contrast, the northern part of Crete is flatter with plains and sandy beaches open to the sea.

So much singularity and variety in a relatively small space makes the climate changeable. The weather changes abruptly from serene heat to wild storms, while the sun shines in winter and the mountains are still snow-covered until summer. The forests are full of olive trees and when the orange and lemon trees blossom, their fragrance is intoxicating. The seas around the island are exposed and the weather catches them, especially in the passage between Kythira and Gramvousa where strong winds blow eastwards from the whole Western Mediterranean. Storms are intense, with violent winds, and shipwrecks have often occurred since ancient times. Even until the nineteenth century, travel to Crete was a risky business. Sailboats took days to reach the open ports of Heraklion, Chania and Rethymnon in the north, while in the south the ports are few and far between and not at all protected. Crete used to be hard to get to, and those who came had a tough time leaving.

On the other hand, Crete is an island that seduces with its beauty and intensifies the senses – and also the passions. It is through these and a long history that the island's inhabitants and their character have been shaped. The legends reach so deep into the past that the mind often loses the thread. Zeus, the King of Gods, was himself born in the highest cave of Psiloritis mountain and, when he grew up and lusted after Princess Europa in Lebanon, he brought her like a raging bull to the love nest of the Idaeon Andron and then gave her name to the civilised world. And thus the name of Europa/ Europe remained immortal.

In the palace of the wise King Minos, amid royal scandals, Ariadne unravelled her thread to save Theseus, the courageous young man of Athens who had fallen madly in

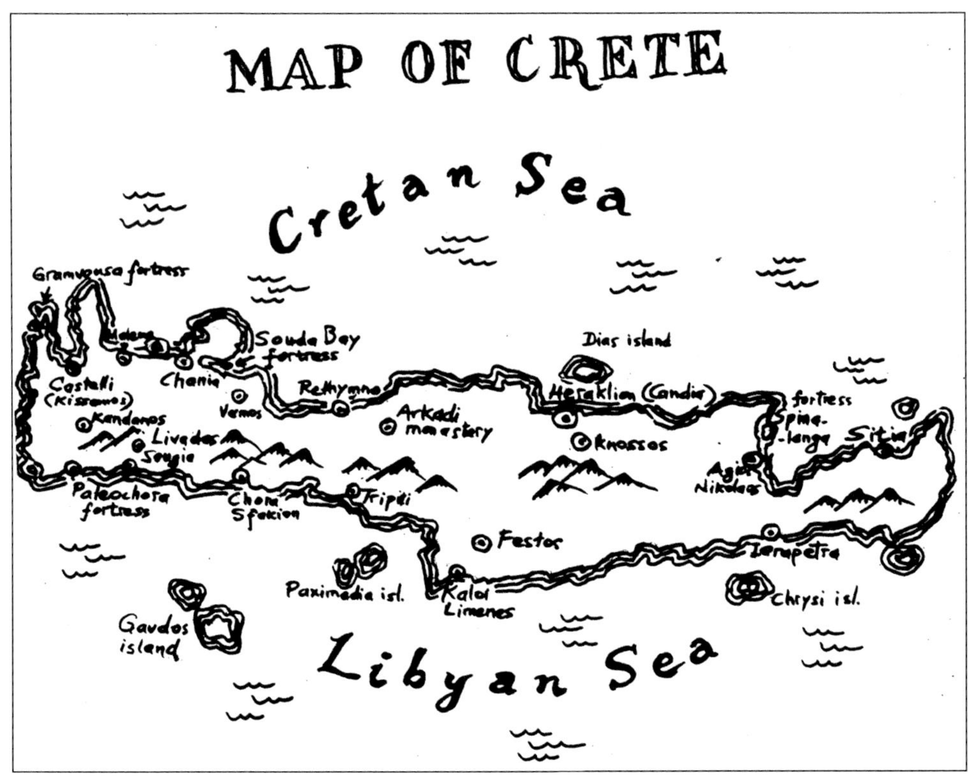

Map of Crete.

love with her. And he, having killed the Minotaur, took her with him and fled. Even when the Mycenaeans took advantage of the destruction of Crete after the deadly tsunami caused by the volcano of Thera,[1] and conquered the 'hundred-city Crete',[2] the island did not stop on its course. The Linear B tablets in Kydonia[3] and Knossos testify that the island's people spoke and wrote Greek from the depths of time. While the Athenians were defeating the Persians at Marathon and Salamis in the first half of the fifth century BCE, the laws of Gortys were written in the Greek alphabet and regulated the relations between the inhabitants of Crete.

1 According to recent theories, the eruption of the volcano of Thera (Santorini) around 1450 BCE caused a 20-metre-high tsunami that destroyed the Minoan civilisation. This weakness was exploited by the inhabitants of mainland Greece who gradually conquered Crete. Cf. J. A. MacGillivray, *Minotaur, Sir Arthur Evans and the Archaeology of the Minoan Myth*, (London: Jonathan Cape, 2000).

2 Homer states: 'The wondrous spearman Idomeneus was the leader of the Cretans / the men of Knossos, of Gortys with its walls … the cities to dwell in Crete, the Ekatobolis; (having 100 cities).

3 Kydonia was the ancient name of the city of Chania. The Linear B tablets (although Linear A tablets were also found) are like those of Pylos and Mycenae.

The Cretans became Christians when bad weather stopped the ship carrying the Apostle Paul to Rome, on the coast of Southern Crete.[4] Since then the Christian faith has remained deeply rooted and has not been diluted despite the efforts to change it by all those who temporarily conquered the island. Islam's first invasion of Crete was by the Arabs of Andalusia in *c.* 824.[5]

For the Eastern Roman Empire of Constantinople, the loss of Crete for over a century was an insult, and in 961 the general – and later Emperor – Nikiforos Phokas organised the largest military campaign of his time to regain it. Crete became Byzantine again and shared its fate with the Empire. After the reconquest, it is said that the descendants of 12 prominent Byzantine families came to Crete and settled in various parts of the island. The legend of the 12 archons remains alive in the minds of the people of Crete ever since.[6]

In Western Europe, the turn of the first millennium created Frankish Kingdoms with ambitious feudal lords who dreamed of dominating the then known world. This ambition was given religious support in 1095 by Pope Urban II at Clermont-Ferrand in France, where he invited Christians to liberate the Holy Land. Thus began the First Crusade which, contrary to predictions, established a Catholic Christian Kingdom in Jerusalem for some 200 years. Other crusades followed, with less success. But the one that had a catalytic effect on Crete and the entire Byzantine Empire was the Fourth Crusade, organised by the Venetians and Franks in 1201.

Cretan Renaissance (*Creta Veneziana*)

Although the Fourth Crusade was originally aimed at Jerusalem, it ended up sacking Constantinople in 1204. It was an incalculable disaster for the city and the Greek world in general, which the Franks divided into several kingdoms and principalities. The fate of Crete was linked to the Venetians, who dominated the island for the next four centuries (1211–1669).

Crete was important for the Most Serene Republic of St Mark. It is in the middle of the maritime trade route from Venice to the Middle East, which was followed by galleys carrying goods to the east and west. The Cretan ports on the northern coast[7] were safe havens for the storage and repair of ships in winter when they were not sailing.

4 'Acts of the Apostles,' 27, 7–8: 'And in due days ... the wind not blowing against us, we sailed over Crete ... to a place called Kaloi Limenes.'

5 V. Christidis, *The Conquest of Crete by the Arabs: (ca. 824): A Turning Point in the Struggle between Byzantium and Islam*, (Athens: Academy of Athens, 1984).

6 The legend of the 12 *archontopouloi* (noble families) is linked to a *chrysovoulon* of the Byzantine Emperor Alexios II Komnenos (1180–1183) who is said to have sent a group of nobles to strengthen the ties between Crete and Constantinople. The nobles were: I. Fokas (later the family took the name Kallergis), M. Skordylis (from whom descend the Kantanoleoi), F. Gavalas, Th. Archoleos, E. Hortatzis, L. Mousouros, K. Varouchas, A. Melissinos, L. Lithinos, N. Argyropoulos (later Agiostefanitis), D. Vlastos and M. Kalafatis (from whom descend the Psaromiligoi). However, there is a question about any historical basis for the 'legend of the 12 archons'.

7 The Venetian galleys from the Adriatic first reached Corfu, Methoni, Kythera, Gramvousa, Chania, Rethymno, Megalokastro (Candia, today's Heraklion), Spinalonga. They then continued to Cyprus and the Middle East (Beirut or Alexandria).

The Venetians fortified Crete with strong castles according to the latest defensive technology[8] and divided it into 'castellanies' where Venetian lords settled. However, relations between the new colonists and the local population were not harmonious. Although they did not impose Catholic Christianity on the Orthodox Cretans,[9] the Venetians harsh behaviour led to constant revolts. In 1299, after 17 years of struggle, the local ruler Alexios Kallergis finally made peace with the Venetians in exchange for important privileges and in the hope of peaceful coexistence.[10]

However, the Byzantine Empire had meanwhile been reconstituted in 1261 by Emperor Michael VIII Palaeologus and the Cretans felt more attached to the Orthodox Christian Byzantium than to the Catholic Venetians. It is characteristic that the loyalty and identification of the Cretans with the descendants of the 12 archons who were of Cretan nobility[11] was constant in the consciousness of the local society throughout time. At the same time, however, there was a progressive osmosis with the Venetian colonists, who in time became integrated and influenced Cretan culture. Although there was no shortage of conflicts with the unruly Cretans,[12] the last century of Venetian rule was a glorious one.

From the beginning of the fourteenth century the Ottoman presence in the East had intensified. When in May 1453 the last Emperor of Byzantium, Constantine XI Palaeologus, was challenged by Sultan Mohammed II, the Cretan archers were among the first to respond to the Emperor's call. But Constantinople lost. *Εάλω η Πόλις!* The fall of the capital of Eastern Christendom marked the end of an era not only for Hellenism but for the West in general.

The Cretan warriors were the last to leave with their weapons from the Tower of Chrysoporta, with the permission of the Sultan who acknowledged their heroism.[13] Along with them, the last Byzantine ships departed for Crete, carrying refugees fleeing the Turkish yoke. Under the common Turkish threat, relations between the inhabitants of Crete and the Venetians improved. Thus, a new era of cultural prosperity gradually developed, which came to be known as the Cretan Renaissance.

8 *Venezia e la difesa del Levante da Lepanto a Candia, 1570–1670*, (Venice, Arsenale, 1986). The fortifications in Crete were designed by the engineer Michele San Michelli between 1550 and 1570.

9 The Venetians were rather irreligious and claimed first to be Venetians and then Christians *(prima Veneziani e poi Cristiani)*.

10 The treaty of 28 April 1299 between the Archon Alexios Kallergis and the Venetian Duke Michel Vitali granted tax, property and religious rights to the Cretans.

11 *Nobilitas cretensis*, Cretan nobility, as opposed to Venetian nobility, *nobilitas venetis*.

12 Spyridon Zampelios, *Kritikoi gamoi. Anekdoton epeisodion tis kritikis istorias epi Veneton (1570)* (Athens: Vretos Valettas, 1883).describes a particularly violent episode between Cretans (Kantanoleoi) and Venetians (Da Molin) at Alikianos around 1560.

13 Ioannis D. Mourellos, *Istoria tis Kritis*, 4 volumes (Heraklion: 'Eleftheri Skepsis', 1931–1934). In vol. 1, p.11, it is said that 42 Cretan archers led by Charcoutsis were the last to leave taking along the last flag of Byzantium.

The fusion of Venetians who had been integrated into Cretan society with Cretans who had studied at Italian universities, mainly in Padua,[14] created a remarkable intellectual and artistic movement. Its most famous representative was the painter Dominikos Theotokopoulos, known as El Greco, from the village of Fodele near Candia, today's Heraklion, who became a leading artist of his time.[15] There were others, however, who distinguished themselves in various art forms.

Frangiskos Leontaritis wrote polyphonic music,[16] Vincentzos Kornaros[17] and Georgios Hortatzis[18] shaped Cretan poetry together with the historical poet Marinos Tzane-Bounialis.[19] In Spain, Dimitrios Ducas was a humanist scholar and printer, Antonios Kalosynas a doctor and writer. Peter of Chandaca was a soldier who followed Francisco Pizarro to the conquest of Peru in 1532. In 1409, the priest Peter Filergos of Heraklion was elected Pope Alexander V in the French city of Avignon. In Germany of the religious reform period, the scholar Jacobus Episcopopulus visited Breslau in 1552 where he wrote the 'Elements of the Christian Faith' printed by Cretan printers. In Switzerland, Frangiskos Portos and his son Emilio, as well as the Cretan Ioannis Kassimatis (Giovanni Greco or Kretense), excelled in Calvinist theology.[20]

At the same time, however, the Ottoman danger to Crete had become real. After the conquest of the Despotate of Mystras in 1456, the last Byzantine stronghold and Greek cultural centre, the Ottomans expanded into the Balkans, and in August 1570 they conquered Cyprus. Although a few months later the destruction of the Ottoman Fleet at

14 In 1463 a Chair of Greek studies was established at the University of Padua, where Marcus Mousouros, Demetrius Chalcocondylis and Alexander Zeno taught. In Venice, there were three printing houses in the Greek language. The first etymological dictionary of the Greek language (*Etymologicum Magnum*) was published in 1486 at the printing house of Zacharias Kallergis, which featured the double-headed eagle on its cover.

15 Dominikos Theotokopoulos, or El Greco, (Heraklion 1541 – Toledo 1614) was trained as a hagiographer in Heraklion and travelled to Venice. In 1577 he settled in Toledo where he lived until the end of his life. His style is considered an expression of the Venetian school and sixteenth century Mannerism. In the twentieth century he was recognised as a precursor of modern art with elements of Eastern and Western traditions.

16 Francis Leontaritis (Heraklion, 1518–1572) was a classic Renaissance composer. He studied music in Venice with the Flemish composer Adriaen Willaert. In 1561 he joined the Munich choir under Orlando di Lasso, the most famous composer of polyphonic music. He returned to Crete in 1568.

17 Vincenzos Kornaros (Sitia, 1553–1614) is considered one of the most important representatives of literature during the Cretan Renaissance. He wrote the narrative poem *Herotokritos* and probably the religious drama *The Sacrifice of Abraham*. He came from a Hellenised Venetian family.

18 Georgios Hortatzis (1550–1610) was a playwright who wrote poetic dramas *Erofili, Katsourbos* and *Panoria*. He studied in Italy but otherwise little is known about his life.

19 Marinos Tzanes Bounialis (1620–1690) was a scion of a Hellenised Venetian family. After the fall of Crete to the Turks in 1669, he recorded the events of the 24-year siege in the rhyming historical poem *O Kritikos Polemos (1645–1669)* (Athens: Stigmi, 1995).

20 Konstantinos I. Giannakopoulos, *Vizantini Anatoli kai Latiniki Dysi* (Athens: Bibliopoleion of Estia, 1966), chapter 5, pp.206–239.

the Battle of Lepanto (or Nafpaktos)[21] demonstrated the Turkish weaknesses, the danger to Crete was becoming increasingly imminent. Having prepared an armada of some 40,000 troops, the Ottomans landed on 23 June 1645 at Moni Gonia in Western Crete and advanced towards Chania. The city was unprepared. The defence of the Venetian and Cretan garrison of Chania was heroic and lasted for a month and a half, but on 12 August the Venetian commander was forced to capitulate. With the fall of Chania and the spread of the Turkish troops in the countryside of Western Crete, some rural inhabitants began to be converted to Islam.

The following year the Ottoman Army captured the Castle of Rethymnon and in 1647 began the siege of Megalo Kastro, or Candia, the strongest Christian castle in the Eastern Mediterranean. The siege was to last for 22 years and involved most of the Christian states sending reinforcements to prevent its fall. Apart from the Venetians, the young French King Louis XIV was the most helpful of all. But despite all the help from the West, the Venetian Francisco Morosini, who was coordinating the defence, was forced to capitulate in October 1669. The Great Castle was left a deserted and ruined city. With its fall, all of Crete was now under the Turkish yoke that would last until November 1898.

The Ottoman conquest immediately wiped out the Cretan Renaissance that had flourished during the last 150 years of Venetian rule, and the island fell into a deep slumber. In Candia, today's Heraklion, where until recently scholars and intellectuals have met at the Academy of the Stravaganti,[22] the largest slave market in the Eastern Mediterranean was now buzzing. In Chania, the Corso Street in the enclosed Kastelli with its Venetian mansions which had given the city its name 'Little Venice' was now a desert. Even Rethymnon, which had been the first spiritual centre, was now also dead. Everywhere there was desolation reminiscent of oriental fatalism. For Crete it was again the end of an era.

National Awakening

The most negative consequence of the Ottoman conquest was the impoverishment brought about over time by mismanagement and corruption.[23] Information from travellers visiting Crete at the time indicated that the population was in a state of decline and the

21 The Battle of Lepanto, 7 October 1571, was fought in the Patraikos Gulf outside Nafpaktos (Lepanto). The Christian fleets of Spain, Venice, Genoa, Savoy, Naples, Sicily and the Papal States, commanded by Don Juan of Austria, Alexander Farnese and Andrea Doria, defeated the Ottoman Fleet commanded by Capudan *Pasha*.

22 The Academia dei Stravaganti was founded in Candia or Megalo Kastro (Heraklion) by Andreas Kornaros, the brother of the poet of Herotokritos, Vincenzos, in 1590. This was preceded by the foundation of a first academy, called Academia dei Vivi, by the scholar Francesco Barozzi in Rethymno in 1560, which had become a nursery for intellectuals and artists. In Chania, the Academia dei Sterili was founded in 1630, completing the triad of humanist centres during the period of the renaissance of Crete.

23 M. Llewellyn-Smith, *Venizelos: The Making of a Greek Statesman, 1864–1914*, (Oxford: Oxford University Press, 2021). In Vol. 1, p.11, Llewellyn-Smith quotes Robert Pashley *Travels in Crete* (London: John Murray, 1837): 'Before the outbreak of the Greek revolution Crete was the worst governed province of the Turkish Empire'.

sanitary conditions were appalling. There was no road from Chania to Rethymnon and Heraklion, and the villages were only connected by steep paths through the mountains.

Although the arable area in Crete was not large because of the island's mountainous terrain, one of the reasons why the valleys were not cultivated was the lawlessness and unequal treatment of Christian Cretans. The inequalities had been exacerbated by the application of Islamic law, which did not tolerate equality among the religious communities of Crete. Over time, the lack of a legal framework contributed to cattle rustling becoming endemic, while the principle of vigilante justice prevailed, and robbery and vendettas became widespread. All cultural movement vanished. At a time when the Enlightenment triumphed in the rest of Europe, in Crete and mainland Greece darkness prevailed.

However, from the end of the eighteenth century, the national awakening of the Greeks had begun. During the Russo-Turkish War of 1768–1774, Tsar Ekaterina II (Catherine the Great) of Russia urged the Greeks to rebel against the Turks. It was the events known as Orlofica, that broke out simultaneously in 1770 in the Peloponnese[24] and in Crete where Ioannis Daskalogiannis[25] stirred up the Sfakiots. But the Turks suppressed the revolt, and he met a tragic end. Half a century passed until the general uprising of 1821.

The Cretans revolted with the other Greeks and for 10 years the battles in the Cretan mountains continued. But the free Greek state created in 1830 did not include Crete. The Ottoman Sultan Mahmoud II had ceded the island to *Pasha* Mehmet Ali of Egypt as a reward for his help in suppressing the Greek revolution. For 10 years Crete came under Egyptian rule, under the command of Mustafa *Pasha*, known as Giritlis, who was to rule it for over 40 years. In 1840 the long-suffering island returned to the sovereignty of the Sultan. Crete had by that time become a matter of contention between the Great Powers in the Eastern Mediterranean.[26]

In this bleak atmosphere, a change took place that was to have decisive consequences for the future of Crete. In 1850 the city of Chania was designated the administrative capital of the island in place of Heraklion. It seems that the Ottomans attempted to give the city a European profile to create a positive impression on the Great Powers of Western Europe, especially Great Britain, France and Austria-Hungary, but also on the emerging Prussia. This became clear after the Crimean War of 1853–1856, in which the British and French had allied themselves with the Ottomans against Tsarist Russia. Russia had lost the war, and the Turks were among the victors, but their European allies impressed on them the need to improve the position of their Christian subjects within the Empire.

24 The Orlov brothers, at the behest of Tsar Catherine, stirred up a revolt in 1770 among the inhabitants of the Peloponnese but fled when the Ottoman Army appeared. Labros Katsonis' participation in the naval battles with the Ottoman Fleet and his inglorious end marked this revolt.

25 Ioannis Daskalogiannis (Sfakia, 1725–1771) was the pioneer of the Cretan revolutions against the Turks. He was a sailor and tradesman in the Mediterranean who put his riches to the cause of freeing Crete from the Turkish yoke. On 25 March 1770 he roused the Sfakiots against the Turks but without success. Although his vision of a free Crete was not realised, he was the first to light the flame of freedom.

26 Miranta Stavrinou, *H Angliki Politiki kai to Kritiko Zitima, 1839–1841* (Athens: Domos, 1986).

Chania, which until then had been neither a populous nor a rich city,[27] gradually began to develop. The presence of administrative services and military authorities increased. A rudimentary business class, mainly merchants, began to take shape. Consuls from European countries gradually appeared, while foreign travellers visited the city more frequently and gave their exotic impressions. Although timidly at first, shops, hotels and entertainment centres began to open. In the general misery of the times, such changes made an impression. The new status of the city had a positive effect on the Greek population, which from the middle of the nineteenth century was experiencing rapid demographic and economic growth. The Christians of Chania wanted to be represented by educated fellow countrymen, and this prompted many young people to study in Athens. The local society began to urbanise, and Chania became a magnet for many young people from the countryside seeking better fortune.

Liberalisation and Revolution

The first liberalisation measure promised by the Ottoman administration was a decree that came to be known as the *Hat-i Humayun*. It was issued after the Crimean War, in February 1856, and referred to the reform of the non-Muslim religions (*millet*) of the Ottoman Empire. Henceforth, all Christian and Jewish subjects were to be treated equally with Muslims. But the expected liberalisation did not materialise in practice. The corruption of the Turkish administration of Crete had become inherent and instead of equality, the oppression of Christians was accelerated. The indignation of the Cretans soon led them to a new uprising – it was the great revolution of 1866 and lasted for three years.

The uprising, culminating in the holocaust of the Arkadi Monastery, ended in 1869 without bringing the desired liberation of Crete. The brutal suppression of the revolt left the countryside in ruins and the Greek population decimated. But the extreme actions of the Turkish Army had raised awareness in public opinion around Western Europe. European governments increased the pressure on the Sultan to implement the liberalisation measures it had promised to appease the Christians on the island.

The Great Vizier Aali Pasha arrived in Crete and promoted a new decree, the 'Organic Law', which promised amnesty and a kind of limited semi-autonomy for Crete. Thus, relative calm prevailed in the desolate countryside over the next decade, 1869–1878.

The calm was partly due to the general commanders appointed by the Ottoman administration in Chania. The best known was Reuf *Pasha*, who served three consecutive terms and carried out significant public works. On his initiative, the main roads outside the city fortifications were laid out, the municipal garden was planted and the mansion that today houses the prefecture and civil courts was built. Chania extended along the coast towards the suburb of Halepa and along the road connecting the town with the port of Souda. But the expectations generated by the 'Organic Law' were soon

27 In 1881 the population of Chania was 14,500. Of these, 10,000 were Muslims, 3,500 Orthodox Christian, 600 Jews and about 400 Catholic Christians and Francophones.

dashed as well. The Ottoman authorities could not control the local Muslim element,[28] which would not tolerate losing its privileges to the benefit of the Christians. Thus, the Turko-Cretans were able to violate the new law with impunity, leading to renewed and even more intense rivalry between the two factions.

Developments in Crete were again influenced by political and military developments in the rest of Europe. In 1877 the new Tsar of Russia, Alexander II, declared war on the Ottoman Empire of Sultan Abdul Hamit I. The Tsar's victory was revenge for the defeat that the Russian army had suffered in the Crimean War.[29] With the defeat of the Sultan's Army and the signing of the Treaty of St Stefano, which created a large Bulgaria from the Danube to the Aegean, it seemed that Russia was close to realising its pan-Slavic plan. But this was contrary to the interests of the other Great Powers, Great Britain, France and Austria-Hungary. The 'Iron Chancellor', Otto von Bismarck, of a united Germany[30] called a conference in Berlin on 13 June 1878, which annulled the decisions of the St Stefano's conference and restored the pre-war balance. The dismantling of the Ottoman Empire had once again been avoided.[31] In return for British help at the Berlin Congress, the Sultan ceded Cyprus to them and promised to implement in Crete the 'Organic Law' which had, in practice, been abolished.

The Halepa Convention

Meanwhile, in 1877, with the declaration of the Russo-Turkish War, Crete was again in turmoil. Revolutionary committees had been founded in Vamos,[32] Chania and Rethymnon, and within a few months new violent conflicts had broken out all over the island. The 'Organic Law' was no longer enough for the Cretan revolutionaries. They had lost their trust in the Ottoman authorities to control the local Turko-Cretans and demanded more guarantees from the Sultan for them to lay down their arms. This time their demand was met.

28 In the nineteenth century the Turko-Cretans had developed into a 'state within a state' in Crete defying central authority. They used all means to maintain superiority over the Christians, often using violence.

29 In the 20 years between 1855 and 1875 the Ottoman Empire had been considerably weakened, with the result that the 'Eastern Question' entered a new phase after its defeat in 1877. Cf Robert Mantran, *Histoire de l'Empire Ottoman*, (Paris: Fayard, 1989), pp.505 et seq.

30 The unification of Germany into the Second Reich under Kaiser Willem I was realised in 1871 by the Prussian Chancellor, Otto von Bismarck, after victorious wars against Denmark (1864), Austria (1866) and France (1870).

31 The doctrine of the integrity of the Ottoman Empire was maintained throughout the nineteenth century but was reversed in the two Balkan Wars (1912–1913) and especially after the First World War (1914–1919).

32 Vamos was the capital of the province of Apokoronas, between Chania and Rethymnon, where a district court and a military garrison were located.

Under pressure from Britain the Sultan agreed to sign the 'Convention of Halepa' in October 1878, which granted semi-autonomous status to Crete. It was a historic turning point for the troubled island.[33]

The new regime contained positive elements and raised hopes that, if properly implemented, it would usher in a new era in Crete. A relative calm prevailed again. The new Governor was a Christian, Kostis Adosides *Pasha*, who pushed through outstanding issues and Chania gave the impression of a tolerant and relatively cosmopolitan capital. Commercial activities increased and political parties were founded with a positive impact on the social life of Crete. The elections of 1888 were won by the Progressive Party of *Xipolitoi* (Barefooters), led by Konstantinos (Kostis) Mitsotakis.[34] But political disputes followed, resulting in the dissolution of the general assembly, and the Christian politicians fleeing to the mountains, again calling on the people to revolt. Terrorism and persecution against Christians increased and the authorities imposed martial law throughout the island.

This new policy of intimidation had been instigated by the local Turko-Cretans who saw the privileged position they had imposed by force in previous years as being at stake. Their anger was often directed at the Ottoman authorities themselves, who were thus unable to enforce order. The most fanatical Turko-Cretans[35] had begun to organise in secret armed groups to prevent by violent means the implementation of the Halepa Treaty. The new rivalry began to bring about changes in the demographic balance of the island. Gradually, many rural Muslims left the villages and gathered in the cities for greater security. But the cities were already suffocating within their enclosed walls and tensions often ended in bloody clashes.

The Ottoman authorities covered up the attacks by their own people with the result that in Chania and especially in Heraklion, where the Muslim majority was more numerous, fear of the Turko-Cretans, and especially the *bashi-bazouks*,[36] became more concerning.

In the mountains of Crete, the customs and traditions of the mountain villagers were always wilder and the rivalries more violent. In the wake of the atrocities in the cities, the Turko-Cretans in the Muslim villages of Western Crete were angry. The inhabitants of Kandanos, Spaniakos and Gerakina were notorious for their brutality and did not miss the opportunity to show it. But in the countryside, the Christian Cretans were the overwhelming majority. For the hardened rebels of the White Mountains, their rage had begun to boil over and there was no doubt that the time of a final showdown was approaching. In Sfakia, Selino, Kissamos and Apokoronas

33 For the first time, the Governor-General of Crete could be Christian, the Muslim representation in the general assembly was reduced (49 Christians against 31 Muslims in proportion to the population), a Cretan *gendarmerie* was established, and literary associations and publication of newspapers were permitted. Greek was established as the official language of the meetings.

34 The other party was the Conservatives, or Karavanades, led by Minos Isichakis.

35 Some Turko-Cretan beys were notorious for their savagery, such as Uzun Hassan, or Uzounis, whose tower on the road to Akrotiri was a centre of terror.

36 The *bashi-bazouks* were a disorderly body from North Africa, who terrorised the Christian element with the acquiescence of the Turkish authorities.

the possession of weapons was widespread, and most Christians were openly armed. Every adult man, and many women, were familiar with the use of weapons which were in plain sight in every house.

But where there was a difference with the Muslims was the Christians' emphasis on education. The village teacher played an important role along with the priest and the chieftains. Young children had to learn to read and write properly as well as the use of a rifle if they wanted to get ahead. The difference with the Turks had to be clear not only in their bravery, but also in their education and culture. Despite all the poverty and oppression that plagued mountainous Crete, the clear priorities for the young generation were bravery and education.

Livadas

The village of Livadas in the southwest of Crete, contrary to what its name would imply, has neither plain nor meadows around it. It is located at an altitude of about 300 metres on the eastern slope of the gorge of Agia Irini as we ascend from the beach of Sougia to the village of Koustogerako, while further up, at 1,000 metres, is the plateau of Omalos. Even higher, at 2,450m, the peaks of the White Mountains are white with snow.

In the summer, Livadas is directly facing the hot sun and in winter the cold gusts of the *maistros*, the northwest wind that comes from the open sea of the Libyan Archipelago. But when the hot wind blows from the south, the heat is unbearable.

Although the soil is not fertile, the area is lush with tall olive trees called *tsounates* that make oil with a special taste. The olive grove of Livadas has always been at the heart of its agricultural wealth. The fields around the village are covered with vines, fruits and vegetables. The best cheeses are made in the apple orchards above Livadas. Everything is of excellent quality but in small quantity. The view from the village is spectacular. On the opposite side of the gorge, you can see Kambanos and other villages of Selino province, while on the left you can just make out the southern Libyan Sea, golden green under the sun. Making your way down the path from Livadas you reach the sea in half an hour. Livadas had its own olive press. But it took two hours to transport olives by mule to the nearby village of Rodovani, and at least five hours to Kandanos, which was the regional centre. This life made people hardy and tough. A tough and frugal life, surrounded by beautiful nature, snow-capped mountains and blue sea.

All the families in the villages of Livadas, Moni and Koustogerako had grown up with weapons and had taken part in the revolutions of the island from grandfather to grandson. It was in this environment that Charalampos Seiradakis was born and bred. From December 1886, when his eldest son was born, his father, Joseph Seiradakis, also known as Kountourossifis, imbued him with the vision of the liberation of Crete from the Turkish yoke and the union with motherland Greece. Young Charalampos and his peers were immersed in this vision and were ready to fight to realise it. At the same time, they had to learn to read and write to keep up with the messages of the new times and to experience the principles of freedom and civilisation that came from the not-so-distant Hesperia.

3

The Youthful Years

The Seirades

The first Seiras, who settled in the village of Livadas around 1630, had come from the village of Agios Ioannis in Sfakia. This is a fact on which those Seiradakis who have investigated the family tree agree. All versions of the origin of Ioannis Seiras are related to the 12 archons of Byzantium. The emotional link with the legend of the 12 archons has to do with the Cretans' search for their Greek roots that were destroyed by the Turkish occupation, and perhaps also with the pride that historical ancestry confers. In any case, this legend continues to permeate the Cretan soul through the centuries like an electric current.

The first version of the story of Ioannis Seiras is that his grandfather was a relative, probably a nephew, of George Kantanoleon[1] who in the mid-1500s, after a family tragedy, turned against the Venetians at Alikianos in Chania. The Venetians violently suppressed the rebellion and persecuted the family of Kantanoleon, who were forced to take refuge in the mountains, changing their name. Two nephews of Kantanoleon escaped to the mountainous Sfakia. One took the name Basias[2] from his eventful stay there, while the other was 'back and forth' between Alikianos and Sfakia and was therefore called Benis. The descendants of Benis were called Seirades because they were of good lineage, *kaloseiroi*. With his new name Ioannis Seiras returned to Selino where he had property and built his house in Livadas, half an hour's drive from Koustogerako.

A vineyard property in the Aochra area of Livadas seems to attest to the origin of Ioannis Seiras from Benis who had fled to Agios Ioannis pursued by the Venetians.[3] In time the Seiras name took the form Seiradakis and the family settled in Livadas. In the mid-nineteenth century, the village had a church, a school and a small olive mill. Many of the 200 families were related to families in the neighbouring villages as well as with each other.

1 Zampelios, *Kritikoi gamoi.*
2 Probably from the phrase 'made his mark', his *έμπα*, in the new residence.
3 'In Livadas existed a vineyard of the Benides at a place called Aochra. It is known that Ioannis Seiras, returning from Sfakia where he fled, succeeded in taking on this property.' Emmanuel Vardis Seiradakis, *Family memoirs*, 23 March 1917, p.2

A second version goes even further back and identifies the founder of the Seirades as Marinos Skordylis, one of the 12 Byzantine noblemen who settled in Crete in the twelfth century.[4] However, the two versions tie together since the Kantanoleon are direct descendants of the Scordylis. Be that as it may, successive generations of Seiradakis participated along with other heroic families in successive revolutions in the nineteenth century against the Turks. The feats of their grandparents became an example to be emulated by their successors with the goal of ending the Turkish occupation, and the unification of Crete with Greece.

Joseph Seiradakis, the so-called Kountourossifis, father of Charalampos, was born in 1820. Son of Charalampos Tzanis Seiradakis, born in 1767, Joseph Seiradakis grew up in the aftermath of the 1821 revolution, which had not brought the longed-for freedom. In 1833, when he was 13, he took part in the Mournies uprising against the Egyptians who then controlled Crete. The suppression of the movement by Mustafa *Pasha*, the so-called Giritlis, was so violent that from that time onwards, Kountourossifis was constantly armed – and he was not the only one. In his thirties he had become a chieftain in Selino and when the revolution by the Chairetis brothers broke out again in 1841 he was in the front line and fought at Vafe,[5] but this uprising too came to nothing.

Over the following decades Crete was in constant turmoil. In the 1858 revolt at Boutsounaria, near Chania, and in the 1866 uprising, which extended to the whole of Crete, all of the armed families of Seirades, Bolieris, Ellinakis, Tsouris, Belivanis, Georgiakakis, Papaderos and others were present. But to no avail. The leader of Selino, Konstantinos Kriaris[6] achieved partial victories,[7] but the holocaust of the Arkadi Monastery in 1869 had left behind scorched earth and the Christian population of the island decimated and disappointed.

The Son of Kountourossifis

The atmosphere that hung over Crete was quiet but depressed when Kountourossifis' first son was born on 17 December 1886. He was named after his grandfather – Charalampos.[8] His mother Eugenia was the daughter of the chieftain and fellow warrior

4 Genealogical manuscripts of General Demetrios Seiradakis (1897–1990), *Archigos Epiteleiou* of the Greek Armed Forces between 1958 and 1959. The document is reproduced in Appendix II. (Personal archive of Charalampos Seiradakis)

5 In February 1841 Chairetis in Western Crete and Vassilogiorgis in Eastern Crete rebelled to prevent Crete from returning to the Ottoman yoke. But in the Battles at Vafe and Vryses in Apokoronas they were defeated and the revolution crushed.

6 Among others of the leaders of the revolution of 1866 led by Constantine Kriaris were, Kountourossifis, Zabiakis, Damilanagnostis and Georgios Georgiakakis.

7 On 14 June 1878 by decision of the Chief of Selino, Konstantinos Kriaris, the honorary rank of *Lochagos* was awarded to Joseph Seiradakis or Kountourossifis: 'Taking into account your patriotism and your devotion to duty as well as the bravery you showed during the revolution of 1866'. (Document is in Appendix II). Personal archive of Charalampos Seiradakis.

8 Joseph and Eugenia Seiradakis had two sons, Charalampos and Ioannis, and three daughters, Amalia, Evaggelia and Styliani.

of Kountourossifis, George Georgiakakis from the neighbouring village Koustogerako. Charalampos' baptism took place just a week after his birth, on Christmas Day, in the church of the village of Agioi Pantes, and was a special event in Livadas. In his memoirs, Charalampos Seiradakis mentions that his godfather Ioannis Korkidis, a battle-scarred captain from the village of Kambanos, 'arrived accompanied by 40 horsemen but with instructions not to sing because of the mourning.'[9] Indeed, after the baptism, no one spoke at the festive table. The signal for the feast to begin was given by the mourning father Kotsifossifis himself, the cousin of Kountourossifis, with a traditional Rizitico song, to end the mourning. Then everyone followed him.

> What is the matter with all of you around me? Why are your hearts so heavy? You do not eat, drink or rejoice. Before the Grim Reaper comes for us and feasts his eyes on the generations. Then chooses those brave men, the heroes who lay siege to castles wherever they find them…

The feast lasted for three days and was a very good omen for the future of the new-born Charalampos. It was a welcome for the new warrior of the Seirades family who was going to make them proud.

Charalampos' early years were spent in the wild countryside of the White Mountains. Climbing with his peers on the grassy slopes of Livadas, hiking down the gorge of Agia Irini, diving in the icy waters on the beach at Sougia, all helped to toughen up the young boy. In the relatively primitive conditions of the time, he learned to milk goats, ride horses and mules, fish in the rock pools, hide in caves and, of course, become familiar with weapons. The Cretan knife and rifle were his companions from an early age, and he became skilled in hitting a target from a great distance.

At the age of six it was time for him to go to school in Livadas.[10] Unlike other children of his age, he seems to have been happy to go. As he noted, 'I was first enrolled in the year 1892 in the Primary School of Livadas, whose teacher was the late John Kosmadakis, still a young man of about 20 years of age, whose calm character and manner of receiving me at school still remain in my memory.'[11] It seems that the combination of growing up in wild natural surroundings and attending his first school lessons with an enthusiastic teacher had the positive effect of forming a well-balanced and ambitious character.

But that year the lessons were constantly interrupted by bloody incidents that increasingly frequently broke out between Muslims and Christians in the villages of Selino. The

9 Seiradakis, *Personal note no. 2*. The first cousin of Kountourossifis, Joseph Kotsifossifis, mourned the untimely death of his son. (Personal archive of Charalampos Seiradakis)

10 Ioannis Androulakis, *I ekpaidefsi stin Kriti* (Chania: privately published, 1990), p.50. In the province of Selino there were eight schools, one of them in Livadas. They were based on the Greek educational system of 1880.

11 Seiradakis, *Personal note no. 2*: 'I never recall my late teacher beating a student, instead he administered our school with advice and encouragement, unlike other teachers of that time. (Personal archive of Charalampos Seiradakis).

clashes were often provoked by Turkish Army units stationed in Kandanos, the regional centre of Selino province, which was inhabited almost exclusively by Turko-Cretans.[12]

The Turkish forces supported garrisons in fortified towers who increasingly raided the Christians in the area, looting and often murdering those who resisted. A climate of terror prevailed in Selino and other provinces of Crete as the Christians in their turn retaliated against the violence. Thus, despite the efforts of the local Ottoman administration to bring calm with the signing of the Treaty of Halepa in October 1878, the situation was deteriorating day by day. The Turkish military commander, Sakir *Pasha*, took this opportunity to impose martial law, effectively abrogating the Halepa Convention. In this atmosphere of terror, the Christians were preparing to rebel again.

After two years the young Charalampos Seiradakis had to leave Livadas to continue his studies. The school was in the village of Kakodiki and Seiradakis had to experience all this cruelty far away from his family. As he noted, 'because of all this, abnormal situations were created and education was neither sufficient nor continuous, and this went on until the revolution of 1896.'[13] In Kakodiki, he found a room where he lived with his younger brother.

Soon the war would come to them. From the beginning of 1895 the magistrate in Vamos, Manousos Koundouros, had tried to restore the liberal provisions of the Convention of Halepa but to no avail, and in November hostilities began again and continued throughout the following year.

During the fighting, the Turkish atrocities were so violent that they provoked a reaction from the Great Powers of Europe. In May 1896, a fleet from Great Britain, France, Russia, Italy, France and Austria-Hungary sailed to Chania, to protect their nationals living in Crete, but also to keep a close eye on the political situation.[14] The 'Cretan Question' had started to become internationalised. Greek officers and volunteers began to arrive on the island to support the Cretan struggle for union with Greece.

Akrotiri and Kandanos

From the beginning of 1897 these developments accelerated. On 23 and 24 January the Turko-Cretans attacked and set fire to the Christian quarter of Chania and proceeded to brutalities. The smoke from the fires could be clearly seen from the warships of the Great Powers patrolling outside the city's harbour. The admirals feared a greater escalation of the Cretan question and declared international occupation of the cities of Chania, Rethymnon and Heraklion.[15]

12 'The Seliniot Turks who were blockaded in Candanos were the most virile of Crete'. Vassilios Tomadakis (ed.), *Ioannou D. Kondylaki Agnosta Apomnimonevmata (1905) apo ti symmerochi tou stin Kritiki Epanastasi tou 1897* (Athens: Kardamitsas, 2002), p.65, quoting reports by the journalist I. Kondylakis from the campaign of *Syntagmatarchis* Timoleon Vassos in Crete in 1897.

13 Seiradakis, *Personal Note No. 2*, p.4. (Personal archive of Charalampos Seiradakis)

14 Georgios Manousakis, *Kritikes epanastaseis 1821–1905* (Chania: Ethniko Idrima Erevnon kai Meleton 'Elefterios Venizelos', 2001), pp.26–28.

15 Manousakis, *Kritikes epanastaseis,* p.29.

In Athens there was intense fanaticism and heavy pressure on the government of Theodore Diligiannis to intervene and support the Cretan insurgents. Thus, in the following days, on 3 February, the Greek Government sent *Syntagmatarchis* Timoleon Vassos to Crete with an expeditionary force of 1,500 men, with orders to occupy Crete in the name of King George I. The Greek detachment landed west of Chania and camped inland in the plain of Alikianos. However, its possibilities for action were limited by the diplomatic pressures of the European fleet, but also because of lack of food and other supplies.

At the same time, while Chania was burning, on the hill of Akrotiri, an incident took place that became a legend. About 100 rebels were gathered to protest to the European admirals and demand the union of Crete with Greece.[16] On 9 February 1897, the revolutionaries in Akrotiri had raised the Greek flag on the hill of Prophet Elias outside Chania in a prominent position that was clearly visible from the town, and by the admirals of the European fleet. This move was considered an insult by the Ottoman authorities in Chania who protested to the European admirals. Although there was no unanimity, the admirals decided to bombard the positions of the rebels on the hill. In the ensuing shelling, a bomb broke the flagpole, knocking it down. Immediately a Cretan, Spyros Kayales, raised the flag again, putting it on his body like a living flagpole. The Cretan warrior's bold act impressed the admirals and the Frenchman in charge of the Allied Fleet, *Amiral* Potier, ordered an immediate ceasefire. The flag incident became a symbol of heroism and passed far and wide by word of mouth. The rebels were inspired with new vigour to continue the fight.

But even more effective for the cause of the struggle was the message of freedom that lawyer and politician Eleftherios Venizelos sent on behalf of the revolutionaries to the admirals of the Great Powers. The young Venizelos was one of the first to go up to Akrotiri and was a member of the revolutionary committee. In his memorandum to the Great Powers, written in Greek and French, he explained the cause of the Cretan struggle and made clear the determination of the Cretans to free themselves from the Ottoman yoke. The era of Eleftherios Venizelos had begun. With his political genius he foresaw the end of the Turkish occupation and that the union of Crete with Greece was approaching.

Soon the revolution had spread throughout the island and the Seliniots joined the struggle. As soon as they were informed of the massacres in Chania, they besieged the Muslim villages in Selino and especially Sarakina where 180 Turko-Cretans lived. After skirmishes that lasted several days, an agreement was reached to evacuate the village but 'on the way there was a fight during which all the Turks and some of the rebels were killed.'[17] Now the main objective of the Seliniots was the capture of the small town of Kandanos, which had caused the most problems in the area. Kandanos was well fortified behind a perimeter wall in the middle of a lush valley enclosed on all sides by high

16 The rebels had crossed over to the peninsula of Akrotiri from Souda bay and had fortified themselves on the top of Prophet Elias Hill that dominates the city and the bay of Chania.

17 Tomadakis (ed.), *Ioannou D. Kondylaki,* p.145.

hills. About 1,000 Turko-Cretans were within the walls, of whom 300 were armed.[18] The entrance to the valley leading to Kandanos was controlled by the fortified tower of Stavros (Cross), where a Turkish garrison was stationed.

Soon chieftains began to flock from the surrounding areas[19] led by *Tagmatarchis* Manousoyannakis of the Greek Army and a troop equipped with three mountain guns. *Tagmatarchis* Manousoyannakis first neutralised the Stavros tower with the guns and then turned them towards Kandanos where panic began to prevail. Indeed, the Turko-Cretans feared reprisals after the massacres recently committed by their compatriots in Chania.

Faced with the risk of a humanitarian disaster, the European powers decided to intervene. The negotiations were undertaken by the British Consul, Sir Arthur Biliotti, who arrived in the village of Kakodiki on 24 February 1897 accompanied by an British captain and a French *capitaine*.[20] He asked the Greek chieftains to lift the siege with the guarantee that he would personally see to the disarmament and withdrawal of the Turko-Cretans from the port of Paleochora, where European ships were to sail to take them to Chania. While the negotiations were going on, an informal truce had been reached, and hostilities had ceased.

The negotiations were successful. Two days after the agreement, the Great Powers arrived at Kandanos with a total force of 600 men.[21] At dawn the next day, the Turko-Cretans began to leave under the protection of European units and continued to do so until late in the evening. Despite all the tension and the accumulated hatred, everything went smoothly, although there was no lack of isolated incidents. The Muslim Prefect of Selino[22] was lauded by the Seliniot chieftains and this contributed to the peaceful disarmament of the armed *nizamis*[23] while the women and children were clearly relieved to be spared the worst. Despite the reactions of the more ardent Cretans who sought revenge, a tragedy that could have had negative consequences for the liberation struggle had been avoided.

18 Kondylakis, p.107, mentions that an old man from Selino had told him, 'strange things about the Turks of Selino. They were all descendants of renegades, and many of them still had Greek surnames' (p. 149). Further down he adds: 'These descendants of the renegades were the bad fate of Crete.'

19 Tomadakis (ed.), *Ioannou D. Kondylaki,* p.117. A. Kriaris and C. Daskalogiannis were at the head of the Sfakiots, old Mantakas of the Kydonians and A. Kriaris of the Seliniots, with Kriaris was Kountourossifis, father of Charalampos Seiradakis.

20 Sir Arthur Biliotti (1833–1915), played a key role in the events of 1896–1897. He was an experienced British diplomat and being of Franko-Levantine origin was aware of the turbulent situation in Crete at that time.

21 'First came the Austrians, then the French, the Germans, the Russians, the English and last the Italians. 600 in all, that is, 100 from each Power… The Cretans looked at the others coldly or glumly, but towards the French and the Italians they showed a certain amount of courtesy,' Tomadakis (ed.), *Ioannou D. Kondylaki,* p.147.

22 The Muslim prefect was Hussein Efendi Yiannitsarakis. From his expression he seemed to imply 'it was written that it would be that way.' The Christians respected him as a generous and responsible man and the Seliniot chieftains would not allow anyone to disturb him,' Tomadakis (ed.), *Ioannou D. Kondylaki,* p.165.

23 *Nizam*: Turkish regular army. *Redif*: reservist army.

With the departure of the Muslims of Kandanos, the Christians of Selino felt relief. A regional Ottoman centre that had perpetuated terrorism for decades and caused untold suffering in the country had finally disappeared. Greek local authorities soon took control of the town of Kandanos with the aim of restoring calm and basic hygiene and of establishing a school.[24] Soon families from the surrounding villages settled there. Among the first to benefit from the new situation were the young students who were to attend the new school in Kandanos. With them was the young Charalampos Seiradakis who soon moved to his new base.

Autonomous Cretan State

Meanwhile, developments in Crete were accelerating and directly affecting the fate of Greece itself. On 6 March 1897 the Great Powers unilaterally declared the autonomy of Crete. Among the Cretan revolutionaries there was a division: many were satisfied with autonomy, which they considered a temporary status, while others would accept only union with their homeland, Greece. However, the European admirals, just in case, proceeded to occupy the island which they divided into zones of influence. The British occupied Heraklion, the Russians Rethymnon, the Italians Chania, the French Sitia, the Germans the area of Souda and the Austrians Kissamos.[25] In the capital, Chania, there were troops from all the occupying forces.[26]

The developments in Crete had stirred up emotions in the Athenian capital. Public opinion was calling for war against the Ottoman Empire even though the country was militarily unprepared and diplomatically isolated. But the battle cries were loud, and the country was finally dragged into war.

Throughout April the Greek Army clashed with superior Turkish troops on the Thessalian border without success. The 'unlucky war' of 1897 proved disastrous for Greece. In addition to war reparations to Turkey, Greece was forced to accept international financial control that burdened the Greek state for decades.[27] The loss of the war of 1897 has since been a matter of national shame, especially for the military.

As far as Crete was concerned, the government of Diligiannis in Athens was obliged to recall *Syntagmatarchis* Timoleon Vassos and his expeditionary force, which had meanwhile been inactive at Alikianos. In July 1898, the Cretan revolutionaries elected a committee which drew up a provisional constitution and accepted autonomous status for the island.[28] Soon the admirals of the Great Powers took over the administration

24 Androulakis, *I ekpaidefsi*, p.102. Article 29 of the Education Law defines the seats of provincial schools. In the province of Selino it was Kandanos.

25 At the beginning of 1899 the Germans and Austrians withdrew from Crete.

26 Manousakis, *Kritikes epanastaseis* p.39.

27 By the Treaty of Constantinople of 22 November 1897 Greece was obliged to pay war reparations of 4,000,000 Turkish lire to the Ottoman Empire.

28 The committee was named 'Executive'. John Sfakianakis became the chairman and the members were: El. Zacharakis, Dimitrios Zafarakis, Antonios Hatzidakis and Nikolaos Yamalakis.

abandoned by the Turko-Cretans. But the following month, dramatic events in Heraklion caused a further escalation of events. All this time the Turko-Cretans in the big cities were looking for excuses to riot to prove to the European powers that the autonomy project had no chance in Crete.

A tragic incident took place in Heraklion on 25 August 1898. A British Army unit was ordered to replace Muslim tax officials with Christians. But this was met with violent opposition, and the Muslims began shooting at the British soldiers while at the same time Ottoman miscreants known as *bashi-bazouks* poured into the city looting Christian homes.[29] It was the proverbial 'last straw that broke the camel's back' and convinced the Great Powers, especially the British, who had hitherto been reluctant, to take drastic measures. The British Admiral Emil Noel occupied the city of Heraklion and organised a military court, which imposed severe sentences on the perpetrators of the incidents. Seventeen Turko-Cretans were hanged, and many others were given long jail sentences. Most importantly, in a joint decision with the other admirals, they forced the Turkish Army to withdraw from Crete.

On 2 November 1898 the Turkish Army evacuated Crete. British sailors cleared out the 'bag and baggage' of the Turks who boarded the ships and sailed from the ports of the island. Along with them, a number of Turko-Cretans left too, realising that times had changed irreversibly for them. For the Turks it was the end of an era. A full 253 years had passed since the Ottoman Fleet had appeared outside Kissamos in July 1645 to conquer Crete. The Ottoman period in Crete was over, but it had taken over a century of struggle and sacrifice to make it happen. A new era was beginning on the long-suffering island, now full of optimism and hope for a better future.

The efforts of the Great Powers turned to the selection of a new ruler for Crete. Prince George, second son of King George I of Greece, was chosen as the most suitable, and was favoured by all. 9 December 1898 was a historic day for Crete. The admirals of the unified fleet of the Protecting Forces received the new High Commissioner George at the port of Souda, and began the 15-year period during which Chania would be the capital not of an Ottoman province, but of an autonomous Cretan state. The experience of the previous decades had properly prepared the city of Chania for its new role.

There was much work to be done. Upon his arrival, High Commissioner George called for elections and on 8 February 1899 the Cretan Assembly met and voted for the first Constitution of the Cretan State.[30] The first ministers, or 'advisers', were notable politicians, and significant progress was swiftly made on long-standing issues.[31] In the judiciary system, the first courts were established. In banking the Bank of Crete was inaugurated, which minted Cretan currency of the same value as that of the Greek state. The establishment of schools and hospitals was accelerated, and a *gendarmerie* was

29 Manousakis, *Kritikes epanastaseis*, p.43. The British Consul was Lysimachus Kalokairinos.

30 The elections took place on 24 January 1899. 137 Christians and 50 Muslim members were elected in proportion to the population of Crete.

31 Eleftherios Venizelos was appointed Councillor of Justice, Manousos Koundouros of the Interior, Konstantinos Foumis of Finance, Nikolaos Yamalakis of Public Education and Hassan Skylianakis of Public Security. Manousakis, *Kritikes epanastaseis*, p.45.

organised with Italian officers. Gradually Chania began to develop outside its walls and building activity multiplied.[32]

New businesses expanded into new markets.[33] The first roads were opened and the infrastructure improved. Crete was entering into modernity.

First Battle Experience

When the British Consul, Sir Arthur Biliotti, was negotiating the surrender of Kandanos with the Seliniot captains in Kakodiki, the young Charalampos Seiradakis was there too. More mature than his 11 years indicated, he had lived alone for some time as he often changed schools. The schoolhouse was in the district of Kallithea where on 24 February 1897 the negotiations between Sir Arthur and the rebels had taken place. A student who had come to the Cretan struggle from Athens served as a volunteer translator.[34] However, Biliotti seems to have been hard of hearing and so the discussions were held in the open air and the loud voices were heard by all – a total of 17 chieftains, their first officers and many curious villagers.[35] Most curious of all were the young students of the schoolhouse with their teacher – the young Charalampos amongst them.

The negotiation with the British Consul had aroused the young boy's curiosity. How could he be absent when such important things were going on in Kandanos? And what about his father, who was also fighting there? Suddenly he made the decision to walk the few hours to Kandanos and find his father Kountourossifis, who, along with his uncle, George Georgiakakis, was fighting with the Greek Army. He told his teacher that he would be back soon and the teacher let him go – what else could he do? He understood the spirited boy's desire to experience the excitement of war first-hand and listen to the soldiers as they waited for Kandanos to fall. The next morning, after four hours on the road, the young boy had arrived at the barracks and asked around to find out where the Livadians were assembled. Soon he embraced his father and uncle who were very surprised to see him. Kountourossifis was wild with pride and delight at his son's daring act, and he realised he had the spirit of a warrior in him.

Early the next day Livadians received orders to go out on patrol and Kountourossifis proposed to his son that he go with them. There was nothing young Charalampos wanted more! They had already approached the wall of Kandanos when the Turkish garrison spotted them and began to shoot at them from the battlements. Kountourossifis saw in

32 Young engineers and architects, such as Michael Savvakis, were active in Chania. Their work contributed to giving a neoclassical character to the new town outside the city walls.

33 A typical case was the oil and soap factory ABEA (Industrial Co. 'Anatoli' S.A.) which was founded outside Chania in 1889 by the French businessman Jules Deiss. It continues to operate, albeit in new premises, to this day (2025).

34 The student translator was called E. Dendrinos and he was a member of the 'University Phalanx in Crete' led by another student of the University of Athens, T. Economopoulos. Tomadakis (ed.), *Ioannou D. Kondylaki,* pp.130–136.

35 'The speech was loud because of the consul's deafness, and all those who were nearby heard what was said.' Tomadakis (ed.), *Ioannou D. Kondylaki,* p.138.

his son's eyes the desire to shoot back and gave him his rifle saying: 'You shoot them too!'

Charalampos had shot a rifle many times before, but this was different. He was facing the enemy himself. He aimed and fired three times. It was his first taste of war. The exchange of shots did not last long. After completing their patrol, they returned to the camp where they were informed that Kandanos was to be evacuated. When at dusk they sat down for their evening meal, the father smiled at his son and said: 'You have done well, my Charalampos, but your time has not yet come to fight. Your education comes first. Go back to your school but remember that today you fought the Turk here.'[36]

Charalampos obeyed his father. The next morning at dawn he took the road back to Kakodiki and returned to his school. But he had already tasted battle. He had fired his first rifle shots and was convinced that this was his life.

Three months later, when the Turko-Cretans had evacuated Kandanos, young Charalampos settled there for the classes that were to begin in the new school. It seemed to him that he had known this place forever. An air of freedom had settled on Selino and despite the scattered hostilities that took place here and there, classes at the new schoolhouse in Kandanos were going on as usual. The company of the Livadians had grown and now consisted of Charalampos, his younger brother, and two of their cousins. Over the next few years as the children became teenagers, they acquired new knowledge and skills. They devoured the news coming from Chania and had the feeling that they were participating in the new world that was taking shape, but political developments from Athens interested them more. The High Commissioner George was for them the embodiment of a free Crete. With the withdrawal of the Turkish Army and the establishment of the Autonomous Cretan State, there was a sense that all their struggles had been worthwhile.

On a visit to Livadas, the 17-year-old Charalampos took an initiative that would go down in the family's history. He invited a photographer he knew from Chania to capture the image of the warriors of the Seirades family. In the historic photograph, taken in May 1902 at the village of Livadas beside the water fountain, 19 Seirades of all ages can be seen, most of them armed and wearing traditional Cretan clothing. Only the teacher is dressed in Western European clothes, giving his message from the world of letters to a family of warriors. It is a photograph that captures the pride of a mountainous Crete that has finally managed to free itself from the Turkish yoke.

36 Oral testimony of Charalampos Seiradakis.

4

Adult

Fugitive in Therisso

Despite the recent significant changes brought about in the new Autonomous Cretan State, developments in the countryside were moving hopelessly slowly. The long-term isolation and abandonment of the villages delayed their modernisation. In addition, the character of the short-tempered Cretans created tensions and personal disputes that often ended in feuds.

In 1904 Charalampos Seiradakis was 18 years old and was finishing school. But an unexpected event was about to happen. Under the new Cretan constitution, the government organised elections in the larger villages for the election of mayors. Such elections were unprecedented, and all villagers rushed enthusiastically and with great fanaticism to support their own candidate.

Seiradakis, together with his cousin Manolis Sifalakis from the nearby village of Moni and some friends, had gone to the elections in Kampanos, the head village on the opposite slope of the gorge of Agia Irini. A detachment of Italian *gendarmes* of the Cretan State had come to maintain order. It seems that at some point a misunderstanding arose between hot-blooded supporters of the mayoral candidates which resulted in a scuffle. Some of them came to blows and became aggressive. The Italian *gendarmes* feared an escalation and reacted violently with gunfire, which soon became generalised as almost everyone there was armed. In the turmoil, a bullet struck Charalampos' cousin and killed him. It is not clear to what extent Seiradakis himself was involved in the melee but as he noted, 'defending myself against the attack of the Italian detachment that killed my cousin Emmanuel Sifalakis, I escaped and was hiding for more than two years.'[1]

So, at the age of 18, Seiradakis found himself on the run in the mountains of Selino. It was an unpleasant situation, and also a dangerous one, since he was wanted and had to hide in the mountains. It was the spring of 1905 and political developments in Crete had taken a different turn. Prince George had lost the glamour he had acquired as High Commissioner of Crete and had come into conflict with his own government, especially with Eleftherios Venizelos, his Counsellor of Justice. In reaction, Venizelos had taken

1 Charalampos Seiradakis, *Personal Note No. 3*, p.3. (Personal archive of Charalampos Seiradakis)

refuge in the mountain village of Therisso with over 2,000 supporters who were unhappy with the high commissioner and demanded his replacement. The village of Therisso is located on a plateau in the mountains of Western Crete at the end of a steep yet beautiful gorge. The view from above is magnificent and especially strategic, as one can easily see as far as Heraklion. The fugitive Seiradakis and a friend hastened to join the ranks of the Venizelist movement. It was a move that was to influence the rest of his life.

What had caused the uprising in Therisso? The first three years of George's tenure had gone smoothly. But the renewal of his three-year term in office brought to the surface his long-standing disagreement with Eleftherios Venizelos over the tactics for union with Greece, and the authoritative way in which George exercised his administration. Many accused the high commissioner of having overlooked the economy, and saw in the democratic Venizelos, the politician of the future who represented the modern ideas of Europe. As Commissioner George was not open to any dialogue, the situation inevitably led to a rupture. Thus, on 10 March 1905, Eleftherios Venizelos, Konstantinos Manos and Konstantinos Foumis had taken refuge in Therisso with their followers and had declared, 'the political union of Crete with the Kingdom of Greece in an indivisible, free constitutional state.'[2]

For the patriots of Crete who were eager to see the union with Greece, Eleftherios Venizelos had acquired a political glamour beyond the ordinary. His personality combined at once the reformist and the responsible leader. The revolution in Therisso soon spread throughout Crete and important personalities sided with Venizelos' 'Provisional Government of Crete'. His tactic was to seek diplomatic solutions before engaging in hostilities and this resonated with the European admirals. The memorandum submitted by the revolution in Therisso on 22 May 1905 had a positive impact.[3]

Thus, in the talks Venizelos had with the European admirals in Mournies, near Chania, to end the uprising in Therisso he achieved one of his two objectives: the withdrawal of High Commissioner George from power in Crete. The second goal, which was the union of the island with Greece, had to wait.

In Therisso, Seiradakis met with many relatives and friends. He also met a close friend of his father and uncle, Ioannis Papagiannakis from the village of Perivolakia in Kissamos, president of the revolutionary assembly and head of the military encampment. Most of all, however, the 19-year-old Charalampos was fascinated by the personality of the politician Venizelos. Observing him, he learned a life lesson after the recklessness he had shown in Kampanos which had made him a fugitive in his own country. He understood that weapons alone were not enough to achieve political goals. He needed political ability and only a few had it. Venizelos became an idol to Seiradakis, and his esteem for him was to last a lifetime and lead him to an adventurous as well as successful military career both within and beyond the borders of Greece.

2 Manousakis, *Kritikes epanastaseis*, p.51.
3 The Therisso Memorandum is reproduced in Appendix II.

At the Customs Office

For the High Commissioner of Crete, Prince George, September 1906 was a disappointing month. He remembered the enthusiastic reception he had received from the Cretan people in December 1898 in Souda, when they had just thrown off the Ottoman yoke and looked forward to a better life. In his memoirs the Prince seems to blame Venizelos for his misfortune, but the reasons were deeper.[4] He had not provided solutions to the island's accumulated problems, and the liberal and irascible character of the Cretans was incompatible with the Prince's absolutism. Successive wrong decisions had undermined his position until he lost the confidence of the Great Powers of Europe. Venizelos' uprising in Therisso was the inevitable outcome. However, George truly loved Crete and bitterness over the unfortunate outcome of his term of office was to follow him throughout his life.

The new High Commissioner of Crete was the experienced Greek politician Alexandros Zaimis who followed a reasoned policy which further strengthened the ties of the Autonomous Cretan State with the Greek state.[5] A new liberal constitution replaced the old one and the political situation on the island was normalised by the granting of amnesty. This was of particular importance for Charalampos Seiradakis who was a fugitive no longer and was finally able to return to his family in Livadas. It was good timing, because his father Kountourossifis had fallen ill, and his mother needed the help of her eldest son for the needs of the family. His younger brother Ioannis was still in school and one of his sisters was soon to be married in Chania.

Kountourossifis had olive trees that needed care and so Charalampos entered agricultural life. But the income from olive oil was not enough, so Charalampos accepted the offer made by a relative from nearby Moni village to take a second job: customs officer in the seaside village of Sougia. Sougia was a small port for fishing trawlers with no special requirements and so it did not seem to put much strain on Charalampos' other occupations. On the contrary, the half-hour walks down the mountain to the beach gave him a break from the rural life of Livadas and, when he finished his business at the customs office, a chance to dive into the blue waters of Southern Crete. But his interaction with colleagues at the small customs office in Sougia had another positive effect; it brought him into contact with Chania customs officers, and from conversations with them he learned about the life and interests of the town. Charalampos listened to everything with great interest.

Soon his father recovered, and one of his sisters married and moved to Chania. Charalampos felt the need to spread his wings and was looking for an opportunity to leave Livadas. The opportunity quickly presented itself when, in 1909, a post of customs

4 Prince George of Greece, *Anamniseis ek Kritis 1898–1906* (Athens, G. Rodis, 1959).

5 Alexandros Zaimis was High Commissioner of Crete in the period 1906–1908. He was the only Greek politician to hold many offices in modern Greece: six times prime minister, twice president of the House of Representatives, twice President of the Senate and one time as President of the Hellenic Republic.

officer opened at the Chania customs office. At the age of 21 Charalampos was starting a new life.

Chania, 1900

Since 1850, when it became the capital of Crete, the city of Chania had experienced impressive growth, and the efforts of the Ottoman administration to give the city a more European profile had been successful. Although Chania was not particularly populous or wealthy, it was nevertheless a charming and well-built city by the sea, an *euktimenon ptoliethron*.[6] The Turks had not noticeably altered the appearance of the houses except for wooden balconies which they had added everywhere.[7] The most impressive palaces and Venetian mansions, where the Ottoman administration had until recently been based, were enclosed within the inner walls of Kastelli, a castle within a castle that was the old Byzantine and Venetian citadel.[8]

As early as 1896, when the fleets of the Great Powers were sailing out of the port of Chania, the city was filled with European officers and military convoys. The sailors of the ships with their colourful uniforms had given a new air to the devastated city where reminders of the violent events of January 1897 were still visible. There were no significant buildings outside of the Venetian walls until the latter part of the nineteenth century except for a few fortified towers on the way to Akrotiri and the *metochia*, which were mostly inhabited by wealthy Muslim families.[9] But the city was suffocating within the Venetian walls and needed to expand. The first urbanisation outside the walls begun in the 1870s. A large urban triangle was created outside the walls that ended at the impressive prefecture building, while new roads led to the port of Souda and to Halepa, the suburb of the city that was constantly expanding. The Autonomous Cretan State accelerated this development. The Venetian fortifications were opened in several places, and commercial activity began to move outside the walls, but nevertheless, most of the population continued to live in the old town.

When the High Commissioner George arrived in 1898, he initially settled in a Venetian building in the old Kastelli where the old Venetian citadel was located, although he soon moved to a neoclassical building in Halepa, which he affectionately called 'his little house'. Halepa thus became a political and administrative centre, as most of the public services and consulates of the European countries were concentrated around the residence of the high commissioner. Diplomatic intrigues were frequent and foreign diplomats battled for more influence in the new state. At the same time, the intense and

6 The poet Homer describes Athens as '*ευκτίμενον πτολίεθρον*', meaning a well-built city: '*Οι δ'αρ Αθήνας είχον ευκτίμενον πτολίεθρον δήμον Ερεχθήος μεγαλήτορος*' (*Iliad*, v. 546).

7 Called *hagiatia* or *sahnisia*. They were the wattle-and-daub covered balconies with windows that gave an oriental tone to the Ottoman cities of the Balkans and the Middle East.

8 Charis Xirouchakis, *ABEA 1889–2019: Chania kai ABEA – Mia koini poreia,* (Chania: Bank of Chania, 2019), p.37.

9 Most of the *metochia* were fortified land estates outside the city walls owned by Muslim landowners, although some were Christian.

slightly libertine private life of the European admirals and their officers had added to the European air and the social life of the city. The *Belle Époque* of Europe had now moved to Chania and the era of *Madame* Ortance and her amorous services had begun.[10] The urbanisation of the city was proceeding apace, and the presence of new businesses and industrial units was creating a burgeoning bourgeoisie.

Charalampos Seiradakis was soon introduced and took over as stationmaster at the Chania customs office. This was an historic Venetian building under the citadel of Kastelli in the centre of the harbour by the sea.[11] From this position he enthusiastically experienced his new life in the capital of the Autonomous Cretan State. He soon found a room in Topanas, which was the Christian quarter in the western part of the city, while the eastern part of Splantzia, which was the more populous, was mainly inhabited by Muslims. Between the two was Ovriaki, which was the Jewish quarter of the city, with two synagogues built in the Venetian era. He was immediately struck by the diversity of the people coming from all over. Peasants in local costumes, merchants in European clothes, Jewish shopkeepers and rabbis, black Benghazi *halikoutes*,[12] European officers and soldiers in colourful uniforms, Orthodox priests and monks, Catholic monks with rosaries, Muslim mullahs, Turks with red fezzes. A true medley of people.

It was not long before Seiradakis connected with friends and colleagues who had also sought their fortune in Chania. Soon he began to get involved in the cultural life of the place and attended lectures at the literary society 'Chrysostomos', which had been founded 11 years before on the initiative of Eleftherios Venizelos. But he was more interested in meeting those who had military experience or were interested in joining the Greek Army. And there were many of them. The desire of the Cretans to liberate the Greek people in Macedonia, Thrace, the islands of the Aegean and everywhere where Greeks lived, pushed them to enlist and fight for Greece. Charalampos Seiradakis was one of these and was waiting for the right opportunity to do so.

However, he did not fail to fulfil his father's request to call on his uncle Emmanuel Seiradakis, who was then Mayor of Chania.[13] He was surprised to learn that his uncle did not like Venizelos at all. Young Charalampos expected that after Venizelos' success in Therisso, most, if not all, would have a positive opinion of him. But he realised that Venizelos' strong personality caused mixed feelings and there were more than a few who disliked him. The elements of his character that many adored, such as his enthusiasm and personal charm, together with his modernising policies, were precisely what made

10 The notorious French *Madame* Ortance had accompanied the French *Amiral* Potier when he arrived in Chania in 1896. She was immortalised in the historical film *Alexis Zorbas* (1965) based on a book by Nikos Kazantzakis.

11 This historic building, which had a relief of the Lion of Saint Mark at the entrance, no longer exists. It was demolished along with many other Venetian monuments a few years later.

12 They had been brought by the Ottoman authorities from Benghazi, Libya, mainly for manual labour.

13 Emmanuel Seiradakis was the first elected Mayor of Chania and was in office between 1906 and 1910. Among other things, he accelerated the construction of the municipal market which was inaugurated by Mayor N. Skoulas in 1913, and is still the focal point of the city.

him a red rag to others who hated him. In any case, Seiradakis himself remained fascinated by the rising Chaniot politician.

In the Greek Army

Political developments in recent years had been tumultuous. Although the struggle waged on the country's northern border between Greek patriots and Bulgarian *comitadjis* had faded since 1908, the danger for the Greek populations of Macedonia continued to exist. The Greek state had successfully reacted to the terror exercised by the Bulgarian *comitadjis* against the Greek populations of Macedonia to integrate into a greater Bulgaria.[14]

Greek volunteer fighters had organised units in the mountains of Pindos to protect the Greek villages there. The death of Pavlos Melas in October 1904 had moved the nation and had given many Greeks the courage to join the Macedonian struggle. Many of these were Cretans, such as Georgios Katehakis, Tsontos Vardas, Konstantinos Mazarakis and many others. One was Pavlis Gyparis from the village of Asi Gonia in Western Crete, and whom Seiradakis would soon get to know. Their collaboration was to last for a lifetime.

At the same time, Greece was trying to overcome the agony of the 'luckless' Greek-Turkish War of 1897. The government of Georgios Theotokis in 1904 had proposed several measures to upgrade the Greek Army, but many of the army's officers, especially low-ranking ones, did not consider them sufficient. The political climate had also been poisoned by the appointment of the young heir to the throne, Constantine, as head of the army, but who was considered by many to be responsible for the defeat of 1897. Developments were accelerated by a series of events in 1908, chiefly by the Young Turk movement and the absorption of Bosnia by Austria-Hungary. On 15 August 1909, a group of mainly low-ranking military officers, headed by *Syntagmatarchis* Nikolaos Zorbas, gathered in Goudi, near Athens, with a series of demands for the government aimed at modernising the country and strengthening the army. The coup became known as the Goudi Movement.

All the demands of the Goudi officers and their 'Military League' were accepted by the political leaders and by King George I. But the one that was to have the greatest impact was to invite the rather unknown politician, Eleftherios Venizelos from Crete, to lead the country. In November 1910 Venizelos arrived in Athens and called for early elections, which he then won by an overwhelming majority and became prime minister. He also assumed the office of the ministry of defence, thus confirming the absolute priority he gave to strengthening Greece's defence capabilities – both by land and by sea.

Developments in Greece had a catalytic effect on the now 25-year-old customs officer, Seiradakis. The old voices inside him were stirring up his feelings. How could he remain at the customs office when his country needed him? At a time when Venizelos, his

14 The Bulgarians envisioned the 'Greater Bulgaria' of the 1878 Treaty of St Stephano, a country that would have extended from the Danube to the Aegean and from the Albanian territories to the Black Sea.

political idol, had taken over the fate of the country? In Chania, the new Cretan militia was recruiting volunteers.

He did not think twice about it. In February 1911 he resigned his position at the customs office in Chania and volunteered to join the first infantry battalion of the Cretan militia. After the basic training he immediately passed exams and was promoted to *dekaneas*. His military career started from the bottom.

Meanwhile in Greece, things were moving quickly. At the beginning of 1912, rumours were rife that the Balkan War that everyone expected was on the verge of breaking out. Seiradakis' battalion was among the first to be asked to be ready to take part in the coming battles. Thus, in September 1912, the *Anexartito Syntagma Kriton* (Independent Regiment of Cretans) boarded the steamship *Nikolaos* of the Katrakis Shipping Company, bound for Piraeus. From that first trip they realised that nothing would be easy. The great powers' fleet was patrolling the Aegean Sea with orders to prevent Cretan units from joining the Greek Army. The Autonomous Cretan State was not at war with the Ottoman Empire and the Great Powers that were patrolling the seas wanted to prevent any complications. A warship stopped the *Nikolaos* midway and forced it to return to Chania – but not for long. The men were given new instructions to provide themselves with civilian clothes and set sail again the very next day for Piraeus. This time the great powers' ships turned a blind eye, and the ship arrived at its destination without a hitch.

Seiradakis' battalion was one of three battalions that made up the First Independent Cretan Regiment of the Greek Army under the command of *Syntagmatarchis* Lambros Synaniotis. It was not long before the orders arrived for the regiment's departure for the Epirus Front. The military life that Charalampos Seiradakis had dreamed of since he was a boy was finally becoming a reality.

5

First Balkan War, 1912–1913

The Balkans in the Nineteenth Century

'The Balkans produce more history than they can consume.'[1] In their long history, the Balkan peoples have certainly made sure that Winston Churchill's words about the instability that has always characterised the southern end of Europe is true.

During the long period of Ottoman rule, the Balkans remained isolated and regressive, as if in slumber. Despite the apparent calm, however, rivalries developed which took on new dimensions in the mid-nineteenth century. Many factors contributed to this, the most important being the rise of nationalist tendencies and movements throughout Europe. The liberal uprisings of 1848 led to the creation of new nation states that served as a model for the Balkan peoples. At the same time, the Ottoman Empire was in decline. The Great Powers were quick to become actively involved in the 'Eastern Question' with a view to increasing their influence in the Balkan provinces of the 'big invalid'. The irredentist tendencies in the Balkans were strong and were waiting for the opportunity to manifest themselves.

In the nineteenth century the European Great Powers had established their presence worldwide. The economic prosperity of Great Britain and France was on the rise and Germany was rapidly following suit. The political unification of Italy and Germany after 1870 elevated their role on the European and international stage. The techniques of warfare acquired new destructive power and armaments increased rapidly. Political upheavals led to new alliances that shifted the balance in Europe. Tsarist Russia and France signed the *Double Entente*, with France and Great Britain soon after agreeing the *Entente Cordiale*. The opposing pole was the Central Powers of Germany, Austria-Hungary and Italy,[2] to which the Ottoman Empire and Bulgaria were later added.

1 'The peoples of the Balkans produce more history than they can consume, and the weight of their past lies oppressively on their present.' Winston S. Churchill (https://quotepark.com/quotes/1944356-winston-s-churchill). Although the quote is attributed to the British politician, there are doubts about its actual origins.

2 Italy did not enter the First World War as a part of the Central Powers but in 1916 joined the Allies.

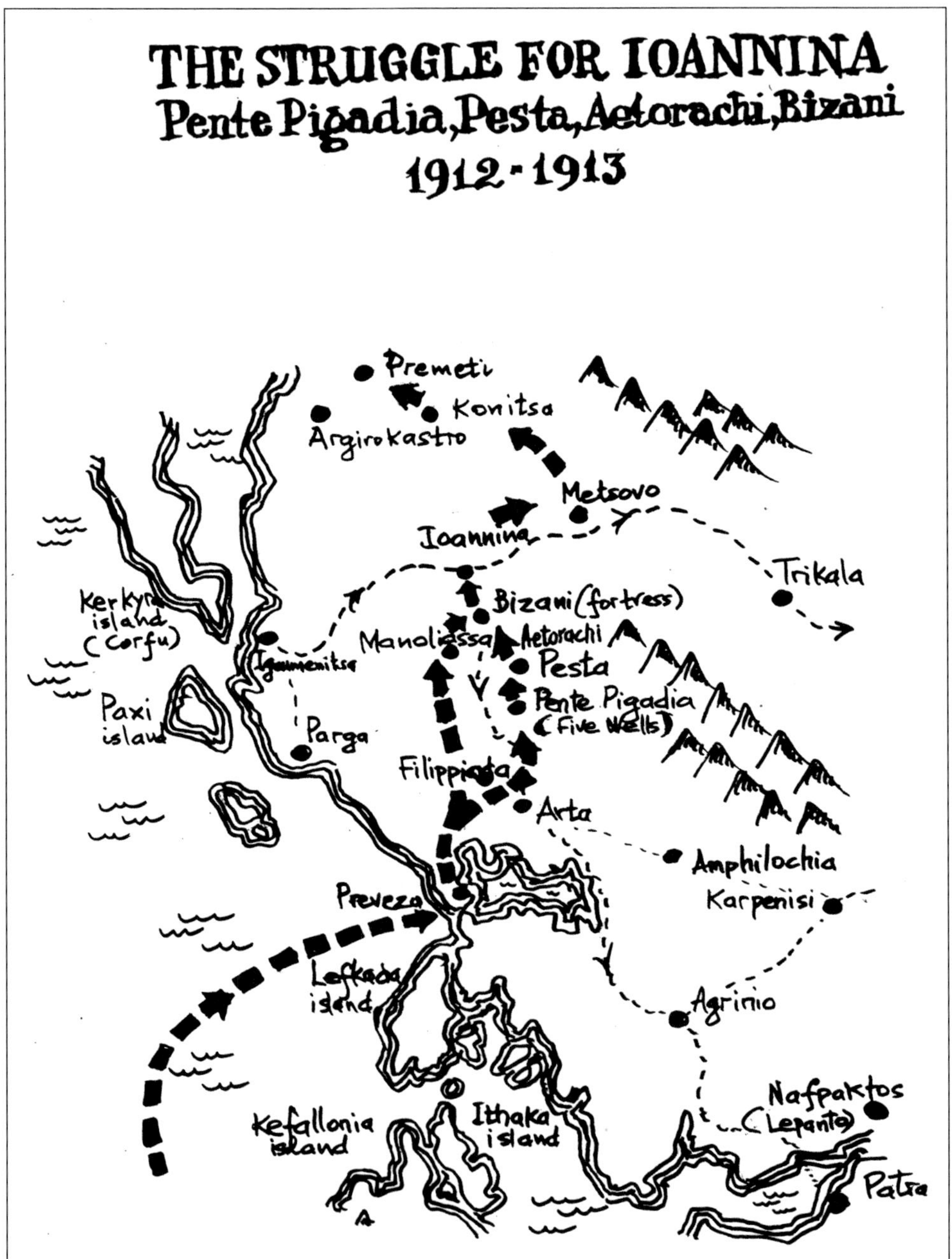

The Struggle for Ioannina, 1912–1913.

However, at the beginning of the twentieth century Western Europe was still living in the rhythm of the *Belle Epoque*. A growing part of society was enjoying the pleasures offered by the new wealth. The arts were flourishing and new trends were emerging in painting, music, theatre and literature. Paris was a centre of international intellectuals. London was a financial paradise. It seemed a carefree time and most people did not imagine that all this would soon disappear in the whirlwind of war.

In the Balkans, everyone was eager to be free of the Ottoman yoke. Greece had been the first to revolt in 1821 and had gained independence in 1830, although the narrow boundaries imposed on her did not include Crete or other areas of Hellenism. Since then and throughout the nineteenth century, Greece lived with the vision of the 'Great Idea' – the unification of all Greek populations into a single large state. The other Balkan peoples, mainly the Bulgarians and partly the Serbs and Montenegrins, saw their own dreams realised with the Russo-Turkish War of 1877–1878, which was disastrous for the Ottoman Empire. But the Treaty of St Stephano, which had created a great Bulgaria, had been annulled by the Berlin Congress of July 1878 that laid the foundations for a new balance in Eastern Europe.[3] It limited the borders of the newly created Bulgaria by creating the province of Eastern Rumelia, it created an autonomous – but smaller – Serbia, made Romania and Montenegro independent, ceded Bosnia-Herzegovina and Novi Pazar to Austria-Hungary, and Bessarabia to Russia. Greece also benefited, having annexed Thessaly and the region of Arta in 1881. Despite all the losses, the Ottoman Empire had managed to retain a significant part of its European territories.

But the Balkans were simmering cauldrons. Nationalist organisations were active in many European Ottoman provinces. The first overturning of the Berlin Treaty was made by Bulgaria, which annexed Eastern Rumelia in 1885. It was a move that provoked strong reactions in Greece as the region was home to a solid Greek population. Bulgaria did not stop there, however, and soon formed guerrilla groups that aimed to 'Bulgarianise' the populations of Macedonia.[4] Greece reacted, and after the death of national fighter Pavlos Melas in October 1904, which galvanised the nation, formed groups of volunteers to enter the Macedonian territories to counter the Bulgarian *comitadjis*. The fierce 'Macedonian struggle' prevented the de-Hellenisation of the Macedonian territories.

But in July 1908 an important development took place in the Ottoman Empire: to reverse the downwards trend of their country, Turkish nationalists organised the Neo-Turkish movement which had a liberal character.[5] The fighting stopped and by the end of 1908 the situation seemed to have calmed down.

But that was not the case. Although the Young Turks had appeared as a progressive movement, it was not long before its extreme nationalist character became clear. Soon measures were taken to convert the Christian populations in the Ottoman territories to

3 The Treaty of Berlin of July 1878 remained in force until the Balkan Wars of 1912–1913.

4 The Bulgarian Central Macedonian Committee was organised in Sofia in 1893.

5 The term 'Neo-Turks' (Turkish: *Jön Türkler* and *Genç Türkler*) was used to describe the Turkish nationalist party 'Union and Progress' founded in Ottoman-occupied Thessaloniki in July 1908 with the aim of overthrowing the autocracy of Sultan Abdul Hamit II and modernising the state.

Islam, either by persuasion or – more often – by force. A new situation was evolving in the Balkans and the status quo created by the Berlin Treaty for over three decades was changing under the pressure of events. The newly established Balkan states began making contacts to forge alliances in preparation for a coming conflict with the Ottoman Empire. But it was not only the Balkan states that were involved in the conflict. Austria-Hungary and Russia were particularly interested and had a direct influence on the Balkan nations, each for their own reasons. Russian diplomacy supported the agreement between Serbia and Bulgaria, which signed a bilateral defence alliance in February 1912 based on the partition of the Macedonian territories in the event of a victorious war against the Turks.[6]

Greece soon became a member of the Balkan coalition. There was no problem with Serbia, as the two countries had always maintained friendly relations. However, relations with Bulgaria had to be normalised after the tensions caused by the Macedonian struggle. Thus, after a first contact in 1910, the government of Eleftherios Venizelos accelerated the negotiations and in May 1912 the two countries signed a bilateral defence alliance in Sofia.[7]

With the accession of Montenegro the alliance covered all the Balkan countries.[8] The understanding between the Balkan states had been accelerated by the Italo-Turkish War in Cyrenaica in Libya the previous year, which had ended in the defeat of the Ottoman Empire.[9] The Allies were presented with an opportunity that they had to seize immediately.

War Preparations

As the Greek-Turkish War of 1897 had demonstrated, the Greek Army at the end of the nineteenth century was not ready for war and had significant shortcomings both in terms of organisation and in the strength of its armed forces.[10] Its modernisation had begun under the Theotokis government in 1904 and had been accelerated and completed by the

6 Richard Hall, *The Balkan Wars 1912–1913: Prelude to First World War* (New York: Routledge, 2000), p.11. In addition to mutual defence assistance, they recognised Bulgarian claims in Thrace, Serbian claims in Kosovo and Albania, and a settlement of the 'disputed territories' of Macedonia where they accepted the mediation of the Russian Tsar.

7 Spyridon Ploumidis, *I 'Sidira' Dekaetia. Oi ethnikoi polemoi tis Ellados (1912–1922)* (Athens: Minoas, 2022), pp.39 et seq.; Hall, *Balkan Wars*, p.12. The Greek-Bulgarian defence agreement of Sofia (16/29 May 1912) strengthened cooperation between the two parties but did not touch upon the partition of Ottoman territories which were left to be settled after the end of the war. Greece was mainly to contribute at sea to prevent Turkish reinforcements on the European front

8 Serbia and Montenegro signed a treaty of defence cooperation in Lucerne on 27 September 1912.

9 The Italo-Turkish War of 1911 ended with the signing of the Treaty of Ouchy at Lausanne on 15 October 1912.

10 Dimitris Malessis, *Itta, Thriamvos, Katastrophi. O Stratos sto Elliniko Kratos apo to 1898 eos to 1922* (Athens: Ekdoseis To Vima, 2022), p.39. There were 25,180 men in service, with a possibility of adding a further 11,000.

government of Eleftherios Venizelos after the Goudi Movement in 1909. The priority Venizelos gave to war preparations is apparent in the fact that he had personally taken over the Ministry of Military Affairs. The army in 1912 had grown to 110,000 men, and had been supplied with modern artillery[11] and its training had been improved by inviting a group of French military consultants under *Général* Eydoux.[12]

However, despite the increase in its potential, the Greek Army was significantly inferior to the Allies. The Bulgarian Army was the largest in the Balkans with 350,000 men, and the Serbian army numbered about 220,000. Similarly, the Ottoman Army in the European territories of the Empire numbered about 340,000 men, but with the possibility of transporting significant reinforcements from Syria.[13]

The Turkish forces in the Balkans had also been modernised by the end of the nineteenth century by German officers who had built defensive lines according to the latest military techniques. Two main forts were considered impregnable. The first was the infamous Bizani which protected the city of Ioannina, and the second was the fortifications of Chatalza which protected the Ottoman capital Constantinople.

Under these circumstances, the Greek Navy, which had the mission of preventing the transfer of Turkish reinforcements to the European fronts, acquired strategic importance. This was one of the main reasons that Bulgaria and Serbia wanted Greek participation in the Balkan alliance, as the navy had contributed significantly to the Italian victory in the Italo-Turkish War. The Greek Navy had recently been strengthened and was able to successfully carry out this mission. Already at the end of the nineteenth century it had acquired three French-built warships, but its superiority was based on the battleship *Averof*,[14] which had joined the Greek Navy after diplomatic manipulations by Prime Minister Venizelos and was the naval head of the fleet.[15]

The Venizelos Government had recruited the British Admiral Tafnell to assist in the modernisation and training of the navy.[16] The importance of the navy in the Balkan Wars was soon to be seen as, with the occupation of the islands of the Eastern Aegean, it acquired anchorages near the Dardanelles, mainly at the port of Moudros in Lemnos,

11 Malessis, *Itta, Thriamvos, Katastrophi.*, p.56. A French made Schneider-Creuzot mountain gun that proved effective in the Balkan Wars. The type used in Greece was named after *Stratigos* Panagiotis Danglis.

12 *Général* Eydoux, with *Major* Bosquier as Chief of Staff. The French delegation arrived in Greece in early 1911 and undertook the formation of three infantry divisions. The Greek Army had four divisions (each with a mountain artillery regiment) and six battalions of *Evzones* (εύζωνες).

13 Ploumidis, *The 'Iron' Decade*, p.40. The Turkish 8th Army was 400,000 strong and was based in Syria.

14 John C. Carr, *Thorikto Averof – Keravnos sto Aigaio* (Athens: Psychogios, 2015).

15 Thanos Veremis, *Oi epemvaseis tou stratou stin elliniki politiki, 1916–1936* (Athens: Alexandria Publications, 2018), p.40. Apart from the battleship *Averof*, the Greek Fleet possessed the warships *Hydra, Spetses* and *Psara*, 14 destroyers, 8 torpedo boats, 1 submarine and several smaller ships.

16 Malessis, *Itta, Thriamvos, Katastrophi.*, p.98. Admiral Lionel Grand Tufnell arrived in Greece in May 1911 and took command of the fleet. He contributed significantly to its reorganisation and to the improvement of training at the Naval Cadet School.

from where it was able to control the movements of the Turkish Fleet. But perhaps the most important advantage of the Greek Navy was its seamanship, the great familiarity of its manpower with the sea, which was to be an important advantage in the naval battles in the Aegean over the Turkish Fleet.

Prime Minister Venizelos realised that, along with its strengthening, the Greek Army needed an improvement of morale through national unity. He was aware that the disagreements that had led to the Goudi Movement had not subsided.

There was opposition both on the part of Crown Prince Constantine, who had been deprived of his leadership role, and from the body of officers who felt they had no prospects of advancement in the army. Constantine was a special case: unlike his father, King George I, who had shown moderation in political matters, he was interested in becoming dynamically involved in the country's government, and particularly in the army.[17]

This tendency was accentuated after his visit to Berlin, where he was influenced by Prussian absolutism. This mentality was represented in Germany by the rather rigid style of Kaiser Wilhelm II, whose militarism was rejected by his European crowned relatives. But not by Constantine, who tightened his ties with him even more, as he soon met and married the Kaiser's sister Sophia. From then on, Constantine's policies were fully aligned with those of Germany. Additionally, his military advisers, such as Ioannis Metaxas, Victor Dousmanis and Xenophon Stratigos, most of whom had studied in Germany, actively encouraged this political line.

However, on the eve of the war, King George I had decidedly supported Venizelos' pro-Western policy, with which he himself agreed. The modernisation of the army and navy was soon successfully completed, and the decision taken by Prime Minister Venizelos was to have a decisive effect on its fighting morale. To ensure unanimity within the army, Venizelos decided to restore the heir Constantine to the position of commander-in-chief. This pleased him, although it did not please many officers of the Military League, especially *Syntagmatarchis* Nikolaos Zorbas.[18] But Venizelos was aware that what was needed at this juncture was national unity so that there would be no conflicts in the face of the coming storm. For the moment this unity had been secured.

Towards the Front

In September 1912 the political intrigues of the looming war were largely unknown to Charalampos Seiradakis, who was seeking to join the Greek Army. Along with him, thousands of Cretan volunteers had rushed to do the same, especially as soon as it became known that Prime Minister Venizelos had announced that Crete would be

17 In 1898, Crown Prince Constantine attended the Berlin War Academy. See Veremis, *Oi epemvaseis.*

18 *Syntagmatarchis* Nikolaos Zorbas was at the head of the Movement of Goudi in 1909. It is reported he had told Prime Minister Venizelos: "I exhort you, Mr. President, not to persist in the question of the Prince and the Staff … you will heat up in your bosom a snake which, once revived, will first bite you, their life-giver and benefactor, … but also the most vital interests of this country'. Quoted in Malessis, *Itta, Thriamvos, Katastrophi.*, p.92.

actively present in the coming war. The young people in Chania, as throughout Crete, rushed to the aid of their local leader.

This was preceded by general mobilisation in the European provinces of the Ottoman Empire on 11 September 1912. A week later, on 17 September, Greece and the allied countries of Serbia, Bulgaria and Montenegro declared a general mobilisation too. The following day, Crete was also mobilised. Those who rushed to report to the Cretan militia in Chania were not only civilians who had left jobs, like Seiradakis, but also many students and graduates of the Chania Gymnasium – and even their teachers.[19]

So many turned out that a question arose between officers and captains how best to organise the combat units. Eventually they all gathered at the Pedion Areos field, an open space in the centre of Chania, and decided to form two separate volunteer corps, one under chieftains command[20] and one under the militia.[21] The Cretan students were organised into a special company with a total strength of 240 men and 27 officers, which received the name 'Holy Company of Cretan Students' – *Dragatsanion.*

29 September 1912, was a moving day in Chania. The whole town, together with the volunteers who were to form part of the Greek Army, gathered at the metropolis of Chania for a solemn mass.

The next day everyone was at the port to bid a cheering farewell to the young men who were leaving for Piraeus on the steamer *Nikolaos.* With them were numerous volunteers who had come from Heraklion, Rethymnon and Lassithi. Charalampos' parents had also come from Livadas to say goodbye to their son. Kountourossifis was proud but worried because he knew how daring his son was and that his enthusiasm could cost him dearly, but he had no doubt that his son would pursue a military career in the future. His mother Eugenia and his siblings were moved to see Charalampos waving to them as the ship pulled away. Would they see him again? The next day they would return to the village, and they had a long way to go to Selino province. It was getting close to time to pick the olives so they could not be late.

The first group of volunteers consisted of a fighting corps with about 3,500 men commanded by veterans of the Macedonian struggle.[22] The second group was equivalent in size and included those who had joined the Cretan militia – a total of 16 companies with 3,500 men. When the militia reached Piraeus, it was formed into four battalions divided into two sections. Three battalions were assigned to the Army of Epirus and

19 Graduates of the Gymnasium of Chania had also volunteered in the Macedonian struggle.

20 Sotiris Kamenopoulos, '*21 Fevrouariou 1913: I symvoli ton Kriton stin apeleftherosi ton Ioannino*' (published in daily *Chaniotika Nea*, 23 February 2016). It is stated that: 'the Cretan volunteers raised 77 companies totalling 3,500 men, led by Gyparis, Ipitis, Kyriakos Mitsotakis, Deligiannakis, Makris, Skoulas, Manos and others'.

21 G. Karkanis, *The Formation and Actions of the Cretan Student 'Holy Company'* (*'Ιερός Λόχος'*) *during the Wars of 1912–1913*, citing Leonidas F. Kallivretakis as a source, 'They received a letter from the students informing them that the enlistment of volunteers was allowed by decree. www.eriande.elemedu.upatras.gr/eriande/synedria/synedrio4/practika1/karkanis.htm

22 I. S. Alexakis, *O protos stratos tis Kritis: I kritiki politofylaki,* (Athens: privately published, 1969),

formed the First Independent Cretan Regiment commanded by *Antisyntagmatachis* Lambros Synaniotis.[23] *Dekaneas* Seiradakis was assigned to the seventh company and thus found himself close to friends and acquaintances that he had known for a long time.[24] Military training in Piraeus was fast paced as war was imminent. In any case, the Cretans were familiar with weapons and had a greater need for discipline and modern techniques. On 14 October, Prime Minister Venizelos himself had come to the camp and presented the Colours of the First Independent Cretan Regiment in a moving ceremony. The young soldiers' chests were puffed out with pride at the honour they had been given.

The fourth battalion of the militia formed the Independent Cretan Battalion which was incorporated into the Thessalian Army under the command of *Syntagmatarchis* Georgios Kolokotronis.[25] It wrote its own heroic march in the Balkan Wars – it was the first to enter the liberated Thessaloniki on 26 October 1912 as the vanguard of its division.

War!

The First Balkan War was officially declared on 4 October 1912, and hostilities began the following day. In fact, the first of the Allies to attack the Ottoman Army on 25 September were the hardy Montenegrins. A few days later the fighting had spread to the fronts of Thrace, Macedonia and Thessaly. On the Thrace front, the Bulgarian Army in two decisive battles forced the Ottoman Army to retreat to the fortified Chatalja.[26] There the front was stabilised and in less than a month the Bulgarians had become masters of Thrace. The Serbs, for their part, reinforced by a Bulgarian division, advanced southwards and defeated the Ottomans at the Battle of Kumanovo (10–11 October 1912). They then headed towards Monastiri (Bitola) where the Turkish Army was retreating. Soon the Serbs were in control of the 'disputed' Macedonian territories under the Serbo-Bulgarian Treaty. They already had an advantage based on the 'law of the holder'.[27]

The strategy of the Greek Army was to advance on two fronts. The first and most important was the Thessaly front, where the bulk of the Greek Army was concentrated with 100,000 men, headed by the heir Constantine with the rank of commander-in-chief. His

23 Lambros Synaniotis came from Epirus in northern Greece. Charalampos Seiradakis was in the first battalion (commanded by *Tagmatarchis* Tsolakopoulos), seventh company (*Lochagos* Fysintzidis). (Personal archive of Ch. Seiradakis).

24 The companies of Cretan students and teachers were incorporated into the first battalion of the same regiment, commanded by *Lochagos* Stavros Rigas.

25 Georgios Kolokotronis (1866–1913) was the grandson of the 'Old Man of Moria', hero of the Greek War of Independence of 1821. He was killed in the fighting of the Battle of Ano Tsoumagia on 12 July 1913.

26 Richard Hall, *The Balkan Wars 1912–1913*, pp.26–38. These were the Battles of Lozegrad (Forty Churches) at the beginning of October, and of Lule Burgas – Bouni Hissar, 9 to 18 October 1912.

27 Principle of *uti possedetis*, see Ploumidis, *I 'Sidira' Dekaetia*. p.52.

aim was to advance through the Sarantaporo Straits and proceed towards Thessaloniki. The second was the Epirus Front with considerably fewer forces – initially not more than 20,000 – headed by *Antistratigos* Konstantinos Sapountzakis. His mission was to provide cover to the Thessalian Army from the west and advance north of Arta towards Ioannina, which was protected by the strong fortifications of Bizani.

Operations in Thessaly began immediately after the declaration of war. On 5 October the Greek Army crossed the border of Melouna and after forcing the Straits of Elassona[28] attacked the Turkish fortifications of Sarantaporo. By 10 October they had triumphed. It was a difficult victory because the fortifications were commanded by German officers and, like Bizani, were considered impregnable.[29] The victory at Sarantaporo was proof of how drastically the Greek Army had improved, something that had not been realised by either the Ottoman Army or the Balkan allied staffs.[30] On 13 October Constantine was heading for Monastiri to 'destroy the Turkish Army'. However, the course the Greek Army was to take was critical as Prime Minister Venizelos had information that the Bulgarian Army was on its way to Thessaloniki, and it was now a race to see who would enter the historic city first. The decisive pressure that Venizelos exerted on Constantine at that moment proved to be a lifesaver. Fortunately, at the crucial moment, King George I supported Prime Minister Venizelos' view and 'annulled his son's insistence on pursuing a military rather than political agenda.'[31]

The road to Thessaloniki, however, passed through Giannitsa, which was defended by powerful units of the Turkish Army. After a fierce battle the Turkish units retreated, and the Greek Army accelerated its march. The entry into Thessaloniki took place at dawn on 26 October 1912, the feast day of St Demetrius, the patron saint of the city. It was a historic moment when the Turkish commander-in-chief, Hassan Tahchin *Pasha*, handed over the city to Constantine, the heir to the Greek Crown. Indeed, Venizelos' concerns were not long in coming true.

Not even 24 hours had passed after the entry of the Greek Army when the first Bulgarian troops, led by the two sons of the Bulgarian King Ferdinand, entered the northern suburbs of Thessaloniki. When they demanded that the Turkish commander surrender the city to them, his response was historic: 'I have only one Thessaloniki and I have already surrendered it' – to the Greeks.[32] The Greek occupation of Thessaloniki was formalised on 29 October when King George I triumphantly entered a Thessaloniki flooded with blue and white flags. [33]

28 The fortified Straits of Elassona were defended by the Eighth Corps of the Ottoman Army with a force of 40,000 men under the command of Hassan Tahchin Pasha.

29 Hall, *Balkan Wars*, p.60.

30 'The Bulgarians had little faith in the military abilities of the Greeks and were confident that their larger and stronger army could seize the territories in Macedonia they sought before the Greeks could arrive. This arrogant attitude would have important consequences.' Hall, *Balkan Wars*, p.12; see also Malessis, *Itta, Thriamvos, Katastrophi.*, p.39.

31 Hall, *Balkan Wars*, p.60.

32 Hall, *Balkan Wars*, p.62.

33 King George I arrived in Thessaloniki and remained there until his assassination on 5 March 1913. This atrocious act was to have far reaching consequences for Greece over time.

No one knows what the fate of the city and the whole of Macedonia would have been if the Bulgarians had managed to enter first. For the time being, an uneasy coexistence prevailed in Thessaloniki. 25,000 Greek soldiers had the barrels of their guns pointed at 15,000 Bulgarians who were waiting for the right opportunity to establish their own control over the city. After the triumphant entry into Thessaloniki, the Greek Army continued its advance north. The fifth division, after an initial failure, captured Florina on 7 November and continued to Korytsa which it entered victoriously a month later, on 7 December. The Greek victories had now entered the sphere of interest of the Great Powers, especially Italy and Austria-Hungary, who were interested in the establishment of an independent Albania that would act as a check to a large Serbia.

Victories at Sea

The role of the Greek Fleet in the Balkan Wars proved to be decisive. As the Bulgarian General Ivanov told *Navarchos* Kountouriotis on the bow of the battleship *Averof* in May 1913, 'the action of the Greek Fleet and above all of the *Averof* itself was the main factor in the success of the Allies.'[34] Indeed, the dominance of the Greek Fleet in the Aegean, with the blockade of Turkish ports, prevented the transfer of the Asian Ottoman Army to the European war fronts. On the contrary, it facilitated the coordination of the Allied forces by transferring at critical moments reinforcements that were needed on other fronts.

The domination of the sea had already begun at the beginning of October 1912 with the capture of the islands of Tenedos and Lemnos, thus blockading the Turkish Fleet in the Dardanelles. The islands of Imbros, Samothrace and Thassos followed, while in December Chios, Lesbos and Psara were liberated. Only on Lesbos and Chios did the Greek Fleet meet resistance from the local Ottoman garrisons, but it did not take long to overcome it. The Turkish Fleet reacted in December. At dawn on 4 December the main body of the Turkish Fleet attempted to break the Greek blockade off the Dardanelles. Although no ships were sunk in the ensuing naval battle, *Averof*'s fire-power and the manoeuvres of the Greek warships forced the Turkish Fleet to return to its base. This first success in the Dardanelles was soon complemented by a second naval battle that took place a few weeks later off Lemnos. The Greek Fleet for the second time confirmed its superiority and effectively blocked the Turkish Fleet in its base throughout the Balkan Wars.

At the same time, the fleet continued its activities in the Ionian Sea and the Adriatic Sea. Its support for the capture of Preveza by sinking two Turkish warships was decisive. From December 1912 until February 1913, the Greek Fleet blockaded the ports of Avlona (Vlore) and Dyrrachium (Durres) in Albania to put pressure on the provisional Albanian Government. The Greek Fleet had accomplished its mission successfully.

34 Hall, *Balkan Wars*, p.65.

The Role of the Great Powers

While the Army of Epirus was besieging Bizani, the ambassadors of the six Great Powers who had signed the Treaty of Berlin were meeting in London. They correctly foresaw that the Balkan War was in danger of spiralling into a wider European conflict – as it did two years later in 1914. The heads of state were also concerned about the future of Albania. The disagreements were not so much about its southern borders, where they accepted the Greek occupation of Ioannina, as about the northern ones, which were disputed by Serbia and Montenegro. Austria-Hungary and Italy wanted a larger Albania to control Serbia, while the Russians preferred a smaller Albania. In the meantime, an Albanian assembly had been set up and was soon recognised by the Great Powers. In March 1913, the Powers decided that Scodra (Scudder) would be part of the new Albanian state regardless of the outcome of the ongoing siege by Serbs and Montenegrins.

In the meantime, however, other disagreements had arisen between the Balkan allies. The Second Balkan War was about to break out.

6

Bizanomachos

Preveza, Pente Pigadia, Pesta, Aetorachi, Bizani

The mission of the Epirus Army was difficult. First, it had to advance through the rugged peaks of Pindos under miserable weather conditions. It also had to face a powerful Ottoman force of over 35,000 men with strong artillery under the command of Esat *Pasha*, one of the most competent Turkish officers. As Balkan War historian Richard Hall notes, Esat *Pasha* forced the Greeks to 'fight for every step they took on Epirus.'[1] A third reason was the hostile attitude of many Albanians who often sabotaged the Greek Army.

At the beginning of October 1912, the Army of Epirus was assembled via Lefkada Island at the port of Aliki in the Amvrakikos Gulf. The regular infantry forces[2] were reinforced by the First Independent Cretan Regiment, the volunteer corps of Greek redshirts known as the Garibaldines led by the Italian Rizziotti Garibaldi,[3] and 70 Corfiot volunteers led by the MP and poet Lorenzos Mavilis. Moreover 223 expatriate volunteers from America had also arrived, bringing with them four mountain guns. They became known as the Holy Company of Philadelphia or the American Company. Mention should also be made of the presence of the American, Brigadier General Hutchison, who participated as a volunteer in the battles of Epirus.[4] Together they did not exceed 23,000 men.

The first objective of the Epirus Army was the capture of Preveza. For this purpose, the superiority of the Greek Fleet was called upon. Two Greek anti-torpedo boats quietly entered the bay of Preveza and neutralised two Turkish warships protecting the

1 'Djavid *Pasha* and Esat *Pasha*, the defender of Jannina, were the two most intrepid Ottoman commanders of the First Balkan War,' Hall, *Balkan Wars*, p.85.

2 15th Infantry Regiment (Arta garrison) commanded by *Antisyntagmatarchi* Polymenakos and Third *Evzones* Battalion commanded by *Antisyntagmatarchi* Al. Kontoulis.

3 Ricciotti Garibaldi was the son of Giuseppe Garibaldi, the Italian general who pioneered the reunification of Italy and participated in the Greek-Turkish War of 1897.

4 The American officer Thomas Setzer Hutchison volunteered in Epirus after he met some Greek patriots in New York who were leaving for the front. After returning to America in 1913, he wrote, *An American Soldier under the Greek Flag at Bezanie: A Thrilling Story of the Siege of Bezanie by the Greek Army, in Epirus, during the War in the Balkans*, (Nashville, TN: Greek-American Publishing, 1913).

port. The first clashes with Turkish garrisons followed at the end of October near the ruins of the ancient city of Nikopolis[5] and Grimbovo. After fierce fighting, the Greek units forced the Turks to retreat, thus isolating the garrison of Preveza, which was forced to capitulate. The port of the city was a key point for the operations in Epirus because it was a supply base throughout the campaign. The capture of Preveza was the first success of the Epirus Army.

The Greek Army advanced in two columns. The first was directed towards Arta and then towards Filippiada, which was the headquarters of the Greek Army. The second column advanced north of Arta and crossed the River Arachthos towards the mountain pass of Pente Pigadia (Five Wells) opposite the Pesta Hill. There a strong Turkish force was entrenched, commanded by the governor of Ioannina in person, Esat *Pasha*. The Five Wells Hill was of strategic importance as it was the first of the forts that formed the Bizani-Ioannina defence line. The battle for the fortress of the Five Wells was fierce and lasted four days, from 24 to 28 October. It was a baptism of fire for the First Cretan Battalion, which together with the Third *Evzones* Battalion fought hard until they overwhelmed the more numerous Turkish contingent.[6] The victory of the *Evzones* and of the Cretan volunteers, according to one account, made it easier for the oncoming units because 'it pushed the soldiers towards the end of the hill ... and so as a reserve we were spared from the hardships of the front line.'[7]

A severe winter had already set in in Pindos and the weather conditions were miserable. After a short rest and resupply, the Greek units were ordered to advance on the Pesta Hill. The Pesta Fortress was located at the top of a rugged area of Makrivouni, 26km south of Ioannina, where a strong Turkish garrison had gathered. In the meantime, the company of Cretan students, who were to be thrown into the fray for the first time in this battle, had arrived at Pesta.

The Battles of Pesta were particularly fierce and lasted for two days – 29 and 30 October. In the final assault there was hand-to-hand fighting with many casualties on both sides. Eventually the Turks were forced to retreat. It was a hard-won battle.

The next day, under torrential rain, the Greek divisions entered Pesta – the first to march with honour was the Cretan students' company led by *Lochagos* Stavros Rigas, followed by the First Cretan Battalion and the Third *Evzones* Battalion.[8] Seiradakis had already taken part in two fierce battles in the rugged mountains of Epirus, but the Battle of Pesta was decisive for the Epirus campaign and the liberation of Ioannina. The name 'Pesta' has since been engraved on the metope of the Monument to the Unknown Soldier in Syntagma Square in Athens in memory of the battle and its victims.

5 In Nicopolis the first military airfield in Epirus was organised which carried out reconnaissance flights and bombing missions at Bizani during the Epirus campaign.

6 Charalampos Seiradakis was wounded twice in the Battles of Five Wells (Pente Pigadia) and Aetorachi. In his military archive it is mentioned that he was 'distinguished' in the battles in Epirus and especially at Bizani.

7 L. Kallivretakis, 'Campaign Diary 1912–1913. Marching and war notes from Epirus, Macedonia, Thrace of volunteer K. Kapidakis' in *Istor* 2, 1990, p.60.

8 In the battle of Pesta, *Lochagos* Rigas was wounded in the face, fortunately not fatally. See Karkanis, *Cretan Holy Company*.

This was preceded by two decisive battles near Ioannina. The first took place at Drisko on 28 October 1912. In it, a battalion of red and white Garibaldines led by Alexandros Romas fought together with a tactical army unit. It was an important victory, but it was overshadowed by the tragic death of the deputy and poet Lorenzos Mavilis.[9] Three days later Metsovo was liberated. On 31 October an infantry unit under *Antisyntagmatachis* Stamatios Mitsas, together with Metsovian partisans and Cretan volunteers, had reached Metsovo by crossing the steep Katara Pass. They immediately attacked the Turkish forces who soon surrendered. The next day, the Greek flag was flown from the church of Agia Paraskevi. But the Turks had not said their last word. On 8 November, a strong Turkish detachment returned to attempt to retake Metsovo. The final battle took place on 10 November at Plaka, where the church of Prophet Elias is located. At dusk, the Cretan *Lochagos* Kleidis, defying the Turks who were ensconced in the church, rushed in with the cry 'Go get them, brothers!' He was killed fighting heroically. His comrades-in-arms followed him and soon avenged his loss. The Turkish forces retreated and never returned.[10] The historic Metsovo was free.

Meanwhile, the First Cretan Battalion, together with the American Reserve Company and sections of *Evzones* were slowly advancing up the steep Xirovouni. But they were delayed by wild weather that did not let up and it was already late November. Their orders were to guard the crossing between Aetorachi (literally 'eagle spine') and Pesta and to advance towards Ioannina. A strong Turkish garrison was barricaded in the fortress of Aetorachi, which was part of the defensive line between Bizani and Ioannina. It was reinforced with units from Monastiri and had mountain artillery – which the Greeks did not have. Nevertheless, the first skirmishes went favourably for the Greek units that advanced to the surrounding highlands. But when they were confronted with the Turkish artillery any movement was impossible. The deadly artillery fire caused many casualties and 'destroyed the morale of the units which made it difficult for them to hold their positions.'[11]

Taking advantage of their superiority, the Turkish units attempted a counter-attack. The losses of the First Cretan Battalion were numerous and it was forced to retreat to Mandres Hill. If the Turks occupied it, there was a danger that the entire Greek defensive line would be broken. A fierce hand-to-hand battle ensued. The soldiers of the battalion and especially the company of Cretan students put up a heroic resistance and after repulsing four consecutive Turkish attacks, they attempted a counter-attack 'by the spear'. It was then that the war cry *Αέρα* (*Aera*, Air) was heard for the first time.[12]

9 *Lochagos* Lorenzos Mavilis led 70 Kerkyran (Corfiot) volunteers along with Greek *Erythrochitones* (known as Garibaldines). Mavilis's last words when he was dying at Drisko in Ioannina have become historic: 'I had not hoped for such an honour, to give my life for Greece'. See, among other sources, Kamenopoulos, *I symvoli ton Kriton*.

10 Michael Tritos, *I apeleftherosi tou Metsovou (31 Oktovriou 1912)* (Ioannina: privately published, 2012). The Cretan corps were commanded by Klidis, Balantinos, Kriaris, Birakis, Bolanis and Voloudakis. The Epirus corps were commanded by Karagiorgis, and Papanikos.

11 Kallivrettakis, *Campaign Diary*, p.62. Description by reservist K. L. Konstantinidis: 'There are Turks lying dead, but also your best friends are close to you bleeding. What a horror!'

12 There are many accounts confirming that the war cry '*Aera*' was first heard by the First Cretan Regiment of Synaniotis. For example, Kamenopoulos, *I symvoli ton Kriton*.

The impetuous counter-attack forced the Turks to retreat. The commander of the Cretan student company, Rigas, praised the victors of the Battle of Aetorachi with the words: 'You have brought honour to our army, you have saved Epirus.'[13]

But the losses were appalling. About half of the men of the First Cretan Battalion were dead: 'Of the 1,400 men of the battalion to which the student company had been attached, 567 were left alive. The remaining 833 had fallen on the battlefield and the battalion was reorganised into a divisional battalion.'[14]

Another casualty at Aetorachi was the fatal wounding of Petros Saltampasis, second in command of the Cretan student company. But Seiradakis himself was also seriously wounded in the battle with a stabbing in the ribs in hand-to-hand combat. The wound was almost fatal, and he was to suffer from it for the rest of his life. The morale of the whole unit had been adversely affected by the casualties, the constant bombardment and the miserable conditions that prevailed in the frozen mountains of Aetorachi.

'The men throughout this time did not move from their battle positions. Each one ate, drank and slept behind a stone – that is to say he did none of those things – with his finger on the trigger... The situation obviously exhausted both bodies and nerves... Every day there were 100 wounded and as many dead.'[15] *Dioikitis* Synaniotis asked for reinforcements 'due to the excessive fatigue' of his men and a company of *Evzones* came to support the decimated battalion.

Bizani

It was early December 1912 when the Third Battalion of *Evzones*, the First Regiment of Cretans and the Company of American Volunteers arrived at Bizani where they joined the rest of the Epirus Army. Already the main body of the army had advanced from Philippiada to the outskirts of Ioannina and gazed in awe at the fortifications – they seemed impregnable. Bizani was a series of steep hills fortified with reinforced concrete defences. It was protected by 32 large Krupp guns, machine guns, three rows of barbed wire and deep trenches.[16] At the head of the Turkish garrison was Esat *Pasha*, who had about 40,000 men under his command after the reinforcements from Monastiri and from the forts abandoned by the Turks (Five Wells, Pesta, Aetorachi, Manoliasa and Drisko).

Already, on 29 November, the Greek Army of Epirus had attempted a first attack at Bizani but had retreated with heavy losses. The only success was the capture of the

13 Karkanis, *Cretan 'Holy Company'*.

14 Kamenopoulos, *I symvoli ton Kriton*. Testimony of Kostis Kapidakis, a Cretan law student volunteer in the 'Holy Company' and later head of the Secretariat of the Court of Appeal.

15 Kamenopoulos, *I symvoli ton Kriton*.

16 They were recently built (1909–1912) by German engineers according to the latest defence techniques. At the head of the German expedition was *General* von Goltz (Colmar Freiherr von der Goltz). The fortifications at Bizani covered about 30km around and were invisible to the attackers. There were 32 large guns and other smaller ones – 112 in total. The Greek soldiers had given the artillery batteries the fearsome names Skylla and Mavrobaroutis. See among others Kalivretakis, *Campaign Diary 1912–1913*, p.63.

fortress of Manoliasa by the Cretan volunteer unit of the chieftain Konstantinos Manos.[17] Bizani represented a new kind of defensive warfare with impregnable fortifications that did not allow for a direct attack. The battles that were just beginning were to prove particularly deadly and would put the Greek Army in great difficulty. It was then that the term *Bizanomachoi*, literally Bizani fighters, was put forward for soldiers who suffered from hardships and were stuck in martial inactivity.

The Greek Army was not prepared for such an operation in frost, snow and mud, and cases of frostbite and sickness increased alarmingly. Food and ammunition were in short supply and sanitary conditions were substandard. At the same time, the incessant shelling had a negative effect on the psychology of men. Death lurked everywhere. The soldiers could not move safely nor sleep. It was a new kind of industrial warfare, a forerunner of what would follow on a more massive scale a few years later with the outbreak of the First World War.

But in early December the leaders of the Army of Epirus had in mind the victorious attack in Sarantaporo two months earlier. Thus, *Antistratigos* Sapountzakis had ordered a general attack on the Turkish lines at Bizani on 3 December. The fighting was fierce and particularly deadly with many casualties. The Turks managed to repulse the attack and then counter-attacked with the aim of recapturing the fortress of Manoliasa. In the meantime, the First Cretan Regiment arrived from Xerovouni and immediately took part in the fierce fighting. The Cretan student company, although decimated, emerged 'once again as the protagonist of the battle'[18] and the Greek units were able to hold the fortress of Manoliasa. However, by the end of December the situation at Bizani had reached a stalemate. The heavy bombardment by Turkish artillery had brought the Greeks to a standstill and it was clear that a frontal attack under the present circumstances was doomed to failure.

At Christmas 1912, the Cretan volunteers met together again in the mountains of Epirus.[19] The conditions were not ideal, with the hammering of the continuous bombardment by the Turks and the worst winter weather of the century. But the joy was great for the soldiers of the First Independent Regiment, the students and teachers' company, and the numerous volunteers under the command of Cretan chieftains.[20] Three months had passed since the meeting on the Pedion Areos field in Chania, where everyone had declared their participation in the nation's liberation struggle. Most old comrades-in-arms exchanged news about relatives and friends, developments in Crete and information about previous battles. The chieftains had already been informed about the victories at Pente Pigadia, Pesta and Aetorachi where the war cry *Αέρα* had resounded from the men of Synaniotis for the first time. They laughed and said that soon this cry would echo in the mountains of all Epirus and Macedonia. Little did they imagine then that for some

17 Fellow warrior and close friend of Eleftherios Venizelos. Konstantinos Manos, together with Nikolaos Foumis, had led the uprising in Therisso in 1905.

18 Malessis, *Itta, Thriamvos, Katastrophi.*, p.68.

19 I. S. Alexakis, *O protos*, p.645. The winter of 1912 was one of the harshest that Epirus had known, 'and the warriors, who were unused to this cold climate, suffered greatly, especially the Cretans.'

20 Kamenopoulos, *I symvoli ton Kriton.*

younger people it would still echo 28 years later – in the Greek Italian war of October 1940.

Charalampos Seiradakis had found the opportunity to have his wounds treated in an open-air military hospital. The sanitary conditions in the frozen tents under the rain were not ideal but fortunately his wound was healing.[21] Next to him among the gasping wounded he recognised an old classmate from the school of Kandanos. He was badly wounded but it looked as if he would probably survive. He belonged to the group of the chieftain Konstantinos Manos who had followed the main body of the Epirus Army. In the deadly attack of 29 November under Bizani, Manos's Cretans had fought at Manoliasa.[22] Seiradakis had met his young classmate again at Therisso. Seven years had passed since they had succeeded in 1906, with Venizelos as their leader, in ousting the High Commissioner George. The two wounded Cretans did not refrain from commenting on the current situation.[23]

> "How fast time passes, it is already seven years since Therisso, when we chased away the Prince George..."
>
> "And to think that he was the younger brother of the heir to the throne Constantine."
>
> "Did you hear that he's coming here in Bizani, with all the other princes? But by God, to do what?"
>
> "Well, I have heard that Venizelos himself will soon be here as well. As if he'd leave them alone. He knows better!"

Venizelos, the idol of the young Cretans was now Prime Minister of Greece. Their prime minister! Surely, he was about to bring about the union of Crete with the motherland. After all, had he not himself invited the Cretan deputies to the Greek Parliament a few days before the declaration of war? His enemies had therefore wrongly accused him earlier of having put off inviting them. He knew better. He would find a way to liberate Macedonia, Epirus, Thrace. And the Aegean islands. All Hellenism. Venizelos' brilliance now went beyond the borders of Crete. The Greeks could hope.

In Ioannina

But the situation in Bizani had stalled. So, when at the end of the year the Ottoman Empire, having suffered continuous defeats, asked the Great Powers to mediate a peace,

21 He was wounded with a spear at the Battle of Aetorachi but also suffered a minor wound at the Battle Pesta. In the following years he would be wounded again several times.

22 The following narrative is from Seiradakis himself in the year 1965. The name of the young man from Kandanos has been forgotten over time.

23 Quoted from a private conversation at which the author was present.

Greece refused. It did not want to negotiate before the fall of Bizani and accelerated its efforts to launch a final offensive.

The situation of the army had deteriorated, as Crown Prince Constantine found out when he arrived at Bizani on 10 January.[24] This was due to the extreme weather conditions with constant snowfalls and, above all, the epidemics that plagued the troops. The *Bizanomachoi* suffered the worst. So, the war council decided to make drastic changes. First, Constantine himself took over command of the Epirus Army. There was also a complete replenishment of ammunition and artillery, and the conditions of food, living and medical care were greatly improved. At the same time the regular army was reorganised and most of the volunteer corps were demobilised on the grounds that they had increased casualties – but also had symptoms of indiscipline. Only the Cretan volunteers remained and continued to form an organic part of the First Independent Cretan Regiment, to which the battalion of Charalampos Seiradakis belonged, along with the student company.

The presence of the heir to the throne Constantine as commander-in-chief in the camp had boosted the army's morale. His recent victories had won him title of *stratilatis*, or soldier-hero, and his ease in sharing the hardships of war with ordinary soldiers had made the future monarch the idol of the army. Constantine himself would soon take advantage of this adoration of the troops for him when the conflict with Prime Minister Venizelos would erupt in the coming national division.

The soldiers had regained their enthusiasm for the final offensive at Bizani, and with the new reinforcements the total strength of the Greek Army on the eve of the attack had increased to about 40,000 men, making it equal to the Ottoman Army.[25] On 15 January Constantine moved his headquarters to the Emin Aga Inn, south of Ioannina.[26] He sent a personal letter to the head of the Turkish forces, Esat *Pasha*. He asked him to surrender the city to avoid unnecessary bloodshed as the Ottoman Empire at the London Conference had relinquished the territories between the Adriatic and Thrace. Also, his army would be free to go to a safe neutral place with their weapons. Esat *Pasha*'s reply was given two days later and was negative. The reason was that despite the blockade the Turkish forts were still able to be resupplied, they had a sufficient supply of ammunition, and the fortifications were not seriously damaged.

Thus, by early February 1913 the army leadership was focused on the final offensive. Everyone was waiting for the arrival of Prime Minister Eleftherios Venizelos, who arrived at the front on 6 February together with *Archigos Epiteleiou*, *Stratigos*

24 Malessis, *Itta, Thriamvos, Katastrophi.*, p.9, where he mentions that 'in January 1913 a general feeling of resignation prevailed in the Greek Army'. He quotes V. Dousmanis, a Staff Officer close to Crown Prince Constantine, that 'the bitter cold, the lack of sufficient food and the poor sanitary situation had reduced the Greek Army to a wreck.'

25 Malessis, *Itta, Thriamvos, Katastrophi.*, p.76. The Army of Epirus was reinforced with the IV Division (about 10,000 men) from Thessaloniki, the VI Division from Korytsa (7,500 men) and other units. It was also almost equivalent to the Turkish Army in artillery firepower: 93 Greek guns against 113 Turkish guns.

26 The Emin Agha Inn is located 15km from Ioannina. The building that housed the Greek headquarters is nowadays the Museum of the Balkan Wars 1912–1913.

Panagiotis Danglis. At the meeting with Commander-in-Chief Constantine they decided on a new strategy: instead of a frontal attack, the Greek Army would attempt to overrun the eastern fortifications of Bizani and attack from the west. It was a risky operation and required careful coordination. The attack was set for 20 February 1913. Esat *Pasha* had anticipated the Greek attack and had prepared as best he could to repel it. He too was ready for the final confrontation.

20 February dawned a rainy day with thick fog.[27] At dawn the Greek artillery began a merciless bombardment of the Turkish fortifications in the eastern part of the city with a parallel attack by infantry units. These were diversionary moves as the largest part of the army had gathered in secret opposite the Manoliasa-Tsouka sector on the western side of the fortifications and launched a ferocious surprise attack. The attack was led by the *Evzones* of the first regiment and the infantry of the ninth battalion under *Tagmatarchis* Ioannis Velissariou. The Turkish units were not expecting an attack from the west and taken by surprise by the rush attack of the *Evzones* were forced to retreat. By midday the *Evzones* had occupied a series of hills flanking Bizani from the west and soon moved heavy mountain guns up the hills. Surprised, the defending Turks in Bizani realised that they were being fired on from all sides, even from the western hills, which until a few hours ago had been occupied by their own units.

That same afternoon, *Tagmatarchis* Velissariou and *Tagmatarchis* Iatridis had realised that there were no significant Turkish divisions before the next village, Agios Ioannis Bonilas in the direction of Ioannina. Together with two units of *Evzones* and under the cover of the fog, they advanced to the village and cut off the communication of Bizani with the central command in Ioannina. It was a daring move, but it proved to be decisive. Esat *Pasha* had no communication with the headquarters and thought that the Greek forces in the western hills had advanced towards Ioannina. He considered that he was in danger of being surrounded because he was unaware that in Bizani and the eastern sector the Turkish forces were actually still holding their positions. That same evening, he notified the Commander-in-Chief Constantine of his decision to capitulate. It was night when, for the first time in months, the guns of Bizani were silenced. The impregnable Bizani was no longer a barrier to the Greek forces. The road to Ioannina was open.

While *Tagmatarchis* Velissariou was performing the daring move to the west, the VIII division, in the front line of the fortifications of Bizani, was fighting all day, and the Independent Cretan Regiment had been incorporated into it.[28]

The first and second battalions, to which the Cretan student company also belonged, had taken up positions in the outposts. When the Turkish guns fell silent just before midnight, all the soldiers felt relief and a wild joy. Their struggles and sacrifices for so long had not been wasted. They had finally won at Bizani! At dawn, everyone waited

27 Kallivrettakis, *Campaign Diary*, p.64, n. 31. Ion Dragoumis (also mentioned in Chapter 11) notes in his Memoirs: 'Continuous rain. Worst of all are the nights. In the front line there was almost no sleep… In the morning the Turks started the cannonade at 9 o'clock, unless we had a surprise.'

28 After the reorganisation, the First Cretan Regiment was subordinated to the VIII division. Kallivrettakis, *Campaign Diary*, p.64.

anxiously for developments. At 5:30 a.m. the first white flags appeared and at around 7:00 a.m. a Turkish officer appeared in the outpost of the first battalion waving the Bizani surrender document. It was the Cretan students who oversaw carrying the historic document to the Greek headquarters of Emin Aga.[29] They handed it over with their chests swollen with pride.

The protocol for the surrender of Ioannina was signed at the Greek General Headquarters on the afternoon of 21 February.[30] The entire Turkish garrison, headed by Esat *Pasha* and his officers, numbering over 30,000 men, surrendered to the Greek Army. The Turkish garrison had shown unparalleled courage during the months-long siege and the treatment of the Greek military authorities was impeccable.[31] But the Ottoman central command also recognised the heroism shown by Esat *Pasha* and the Bizani garrison during the long siege and honoured him with the title of *Pasha* and chief of staff.[32]

But first, it was Greece's time. Following the entry of the Greek Army into Thessaloniki, the time had now come for the liberation of Ioannina. The entry of the Greek Army was celebrated ecstatically by the people who had poured out into the streets to celebrate the end of Ottoman rule. The enthusiasm of Hellenism from all quarters was unbridled and was combined with patriotic messages, speeches and joyous events. The people in Athens were enthusiastic. Thessaloniki and Ioannina, capitals of Macedonia and Epirus, two regions with solid Greek populations, now belonged to Greece.

The news went round the world and caused a sensation in the European capitals. The fortress of Bizani was considered impregnable and its capture by the Greek Army was considered a significant military feat. Greece was now a key player in the Balkans and could not be underestimated. The song of the fall of Ioannina echoed throughout Greece:

> We took Ioannina
> Many lips say it, many eyes see it,
> Among laugh and cry

Charalampos Seiradakis was also one of the heroic *Bizanomachoi*; the image of warriors who left their mark on Greek military history for their fighting spirit and heroism, despite brutal fights, hardships, injuries and epidemics they had suffered for months. Fifty years after the victory at Bizani, in February 1963, the Greek state was celebrating the jubilee of the liberation of Ioannina. King Pavlos I and the authorities of the country had invited all the veteran *Bizanomachoi* to Ioannina to pay tribute to those who gave their lives for

29 Kamenopoulos, *I symvoli ton Kriton*. K. Kapidakis, wrote of the Cretan 'Holy Company': 'February 21, the day of surrender of Bizani, found the enemies facing each other at only 200 metres. But the document of the surrender of Ioannina was placed in our hands.' This is also mentioned in E. Mavrogonatos, *The Cretans in the Balkan Wars*.

30 It was signed by the Turkish commander of Bizani Fortress, *Yarbay* (Lieutenant Colonel) Vehip Bey, and the Greek Staff officers Ioannis Metaxas and Xenophon Stratigos.

31 Turkish officers were allowed to move around Ioannina with their swords.

32 Esat *Pasha* later played an important role during the Allies' Gallipoli Campaign in 1915 during World War I.

the liberation of the historic capital of Epirus. The veteran Charalampos Seiradakis was one of the guests of honour.

Indicative of the emotional atmosphere that prevailed in those days was the letter of *Lochagos* Vassilis Mountakis of the Ioannina garrison, who on 26 March 1963 had replied to a letter of thanks from Seiradakis with the following:

> But nothing I have done, and what I may do in the future, will equal the boulders that all of you, both as a generation and as individuals, have placed in our great national edifice, the architect of which was the esteemed man of Akrotiri [meaning Prime Minister Eleftherios Venizelos] and on the other hand you, who were the pioneers of our fellow Cretans.[33]

33 Letter from *Lochagos* Vasileios Mountakis to Charalampos Seiradakis, Ioannina 26 March 1963. (Personal archive of Ch. Seiradakis) The document is shown in Appendix II

7

From War to War, 1913–1914

Northern Epirus

The victory at Bizani and the liberation of Ioannina are milestones in many ways. It was an all-out campaign in which fighters from all parts and all political factions of Greece had participated. There was also a synergy of political leaders – with Prime Minister Venizelos leading the way – and military leaders, especially the Commander-in-Chief Constantine (then heir to the throne) and his staff. Even though rivalries endured, there were no antagonisms or pettiness which not infrequently arise in similar circumstances. Patriotism was the dominant message. Also, the *Bizanomachoi* soldiers maintained an exemplary attitude by enduring unprecedented hardships, while the officer corps presented a united front. This national solidarity had a crucial effect: first the liberation of Thessaloniki and now the liberation of Ioannina. It was a striking proof of what Greeks, when united, could achieve.

Soon, however, problems appeared. Not two weeks had passed since the triumphant entry of the Greek Army into Ioannina, when the world froze with the news of the violent death of King George I. He had been murdered in Thessaloniki by an alleged psychopath.[1] It was a devastating development that was to have a catalytic effect on the course of the country. During the general mourning, the army in Ioannina proclaimed as new King of Greece, Constantine, the favourite of the troops, who had now acquired the prestige of 'soldier-hero' of the Balkan Wars. A new page was being turned in Greek political life as the young King made no secret of his intention to become directly involved in the shaping of the country's political life.

But for now there was no room for complacency as the war was still continuing. The Greek Army had to secure the borders it had conquered in the Balkan Wars.[2] The mission had been undertaken by III and VIII divisions – to the latter of which had been attached the Independent Cretan Regiment after the restructuring of the units.

1 Malessis, *Itta, Thriamvos, Katastrophi.*, p.114 and n. 213. The assassin of King George I was described as a 'psychopath' although the circumstances of the murder were never fully clarified.

2 The London Ambassadorial Conference of 7 December 1912 referred only to the loss of territories of the Ottoman Empire and not to the distribution of territories among the victors.

The fighting at Bizani had not yet ended when on 24 February the VIII division was assembled in Ioannina with orders to advance rapidly towards Argyrokastro. It was a race against time. Two battalions and the Cretan volunteers, within four days, 'battered and panting', crossed Kalpaki and advanced towards Dervitsani. There they met tough resistance from Ottoman units reinforced by Albanian irregulars. The Turkish resistance was broken after a fierce battle and the Greek troops entered Argyrokastro, where they received a triumphant welcome, on 3 March 1913. There were hopes that the day of liberation had arrived for the Greeks of Northern Epirus. The two battalions continued their advance and two days later, on 5 March 1913, they overthrew the Turkish garrison outside Tepelenni after tough fighting. In the meantime, another unit of Cretan volunteers led by *Syntagmatarchis* Ipitis liberated the port of Agioi Saranda, which Greek units entered after a victorious battle at Delvino and Kleisoura. In less than a month the Greek Army had completed the occupation of Northern Epirus from Himarra to Korytsa.

The Greek units continued their march towards Premeti. The description of the march in the mountains of Northern Epirus shows the difficulties encountered: 'We climbed the steep mountain slopes through snow, pushing and slipping, like drunken men staggering on the icy surface; after three hours we arrived tired and hungry at the village of Eleousa at the foot of the mountain near Premeti, and we descended to the outskirts of the village.'[3] In Premeti they were to stay, on and off, for about two months, until June 1913. The danger of attacks by Albanian irregulars was great and strong division guards were posted in the surrounding villages for greater protection. Indeed, Albanian nationalists were lurking to attack the Greek villages encouraged by the London Conference which had decided to establish an Albanian state.[4] But for the Greek units stationed there it was a pleasant period as the inhabitants of the long-suffering villages did their best to make them feel at ease.

In a symbolic gesture addressed to the Great Powers, the new King Constantine visited Konitsa on 5 May 1913. The Independent Cretan Regiment headed by the first and second battalions and the company of Cretan students had already gone there to welcome the warrior-king.

At the celebration organised by the Greek villages, Cretan troops marched in an emotionally charged atmosphere. But despite all the efforts of the Greek Army to consolidate its occupation of the Greek northern lands, the Great Powers had decided otherwise. The Treaty of Florence of 17 December 1913 had definitively assigned areas with solid Greek populations – Korytsa, Argyrokastro and Himarra – to the newly established Albanian state.

In return, Greece would receive the islands of the Eastern Aegean. It was a difficult diplomatic struggle, and the Venizelos Government continued to negotiate with the Great

3 Kallivrettakis, *Campaign Diary*, p.65.

4 On 13 November 1912 an Assembly in Vlora composed of representatives of all Albanian parties, had declared the independence of Albania with a provisional government recognised by the Ambassadorial Conference in London on 7 December 1912. An international commission was to determine the borders of the new Albanian state.

Powers. This had been preceded by the London Peace Treaty of 17 May 1913, which determined the Ottoman losses and had finally awarded Crete to Greece. However, of greater consequence were the disputes that had arisen between the Balkan allies.

Disagreements of the Balkan Allies

The uneasy cohabitation of Greek military units with Bulgarian units in Thessaloniki did not bode well. Despite all the efforts of the two sides to downplay the skirmishes that broke out every now and then in the streets of the city between the two armies, it was obvious that there was tension. The Bulgarians had underestimated the capabilities of the Greek Army, which had moved faster and occupied areas in Macedonia that they themselves coveted. As there had been no territorial settlement between the two countries, the Bulgarians were faced with the consequences of a situation that had gone wrong for them. The pro-war Bulgarian faction seemed determined to reclaim the Macedonian territories from the Greeks by means of a new war.

However, Bulgaria did not only have a problem with the Greeks. Having focused its attention on Thrace, it had allowed the Serbs to occupy large 'disputed' Macedonian territories which the Bulgarians considered theirs. Thus, they found themselves excluded from all the Macedonian territories which Greeks and Serbs seemed to share between them. Nor could the Bulgarians have relied on the mediation of the Russian Tsar, who was in a difficult position, having to choose between the two Slavic countries. The Bulgarians seemed to have no other way out than to take them by force. As if all this was not enough, they had to face the Romanians who were demanding from Bulgaria the territory of Dobruja in the Danube Delta. And not to be outdone, the Turks took advantage of the situation and attacked Adrianople.

The Bulgarians were diplomatically isolated and faced the risk of invasion from all their neighbours. Moreover, at this crucial moment the country was divided between the appeasing policies of Prime Minister Gessov and the pro-war line of the Russophile Stoyan Danev.[5]

Conflict seemed inevitable. Since April 1913, Bulgaria had begun to strengthen its military forces and to take steps that indicated its non-acceptance of the status quo. In response, Greece and Serbia agreed a treaty of mutual assistance for a period of 10 years, which was signed in Thessaloniki on 19 May. At the same time they contacted both Romania and Turkey and, although they did not sign agreements, it was clear that their interests were in alignment.[6] All the Balkan countries were strengthening their forces.[7]

5 Hall, *Balkan Wars*, p.101. The Bulgarian Prime Minister Geshov had tried to negotiate with Eleftherios Venizelos, but his efforts were torpedoed by the opposition. In June 1913 the hard-liner Stoyan Danev took over as prime minister.

6 Hall, *Balkan Wars,* p.102.

7 Greece had transferred three additional divisions to Macedonia (I, VI and VII) with a total strength of 110,000 men, while the Greek Fleet patrolled at sea in the Northern Aegean and off the Chalkidiki Peninsula.

The War Continues

Hostilities began on 16 May 1913. A Bulgarian Army attacked the Greek forces and another the Serbs with the aim of cutting them off from each other. At first the surprise attacks seemed to succeed, but the Greeks and Serbs immediately launched counter-attacks.[8] On 20 and 21 May the Greek forces attacked the main body of the Bulgarian Army at Kilkis-Lachana. The battle was one of the bloodiest as the Bulgarian positions were well fortified, but the rush of Greek units overthrew the defence and forced them to retreat. It was the most important battle on the Macedonian Front and essentially decided the Greek-Bulgarian conflict.[9] A little earlier in Thessaloniki, the Cretan *gendarmerie* had cleared the city of the Bulgarian units that had remained there, putting an end to the uneasy 'cohabitation' that had created many anomalies. For their part, the Serbs defeated the Bulgarian Army on 23 May in another decisive battle.[10]

However, the Bulgarian Army remained strong. The Greeks continued the pursuit and achieved two more decisive victories in the battles of Doirani and of Beles. On 26 June the Greek Army had entered Sidirocastro and Serres in victory.

The victorious march continued towards Meleniko and Nevrokopi and on 11 July they crossed into Bulgarian territory through the mountainous Kresna Gorge. There their march was halted as the soldiers were exhausted, and there were problems with supplies. But Bulgaria had also reached its limits as the nightmare scenario of simultaneous invasion from all neighbouring countries had become a reality. Having suffered continuous defeats from four Balkan countries, the Bulgarians called for an armistice on 10 July 1913.

Prime Minister Venizelos was ready for negotiations, understanding Greece's advantageous position and the international situation. But at the crucial moment King Constantine disagreed. He insisted on pursuing the opposing army until Bulgaria relinquished all the territory it had lost in the fighting. Ignoring Venizelos' exhortations, the depletion of the army, which was plagued by sickness and a shortage of artillery, Constantine pushed the army into the Kresna Gorge and Upper Tzumagia. It was a daring venture. The prime minister himself visited the young King to try to persuade him to accept the truce, but to no avail. On 17 July, the Bulgarians counter-attacked with superior forces and looked like surrounding the Greek Army. Faced with the prospect of defeat, Constantine sent a telegram to Venizelos agreeing to the armistice – which had meanwhile been accepted by all the attacking forces in Bucharest.[11]

8 Hall, *Balkan Wars,* pp.105 et seq. The Bulgarian Prime Minister Danev tried unsuccessfully to argue that Bulgaria had 'peaceful intentions'. But Greece and Serbia did not miss the opportunity to take advantage of the Bulgarian attack in the negotiations that followed the war.

9 Hall, *Balkan Wars*, p.113. 'The defeat of the second Bulgarian Army by the Greeks was the most important military disaster suffered by the Bulgarians in the Second Balkan War and the greater Greek success of both Balkan Wars.' However, about 9,000 Greek soldiers fell on the battlefield.

10 At the Battle of the Bregalnitsa River, near Krivolak, 23 May 1913.

11 Hall, *Balkan Wars,* p.122. Constantine's telegram was: 'My army is physically and morally exhausted. I can no longer refuse the armistice or suspension of hostilities.'

It was an indication of the new King's stubbornness that could have devastating consequences. Although the Commander-in-Chief, Constantine had been a model warrior-king in the Balkan Wars, but in several cases, such as in Thessaloniki and Kresna, he had misjudged the situation. Venizelos undertook diplomatic approaches in the Romanian capital, and had assumed the role of a 'mediating' country in the Balkans. On 28 July 1913, the Treaty of Bucharest was signed, recognising the recent Greek victories. It was a glorious Greek success.

The Second Balkan War had lasted a total of 33 days. At the end of the hostilities, Greece had doubled its territory and population.[12] Apart from the major cities of Thessaloniki, Ioannina, Serres and Kavala,[13] it now occupied more than half of the territory of Macedonia and Epirus, Crete and the islands of the Eastern Aegean Sea.[14] The Greek successes were significant even though the Greek Army had to withdraw from Western Thrace, which was eventually ceded to Bulgaria, and from Northern Epirus, which was ceded to the newly created Albania. Greece's territories were confirmed by the Greek-Turkish treaty signed in Athens on 1 November 1913. Similar treaties with Turkey were signed by Bulgaria on 17 September 1913, and by Serbia on 1 March 1914. They were to seal the two Balkan Wars that transformed the map of the Balkans in less than a year.

First Independent Cretan Regiment

Meanwhile the VIII division, which was in the village of Premeti, had received an order on 22 June to sail to Thrace to reinforce the Greek forces. The first battalion, to which the student company belonged, was assembled in Premeti for the march to the port of Agioi Saranda, opposite the island of Kerkyra (Corfu), where a Greek warship was waiting for them, to take them to Kavala. The Cretans had spent two months with the northern Epirotes of Premeti and relations had become so friendly that separation was difficult. In such uncertain times no one knew what was to follow. 'On 28 June 1913 a prayer was made by the inhabitants of Premeti in favour of the Greek armed forces. Muslims were also present. The mixed schoolboys and schoolgirls sang various national songs ... The departure was very moving, the women and men cried.'[15]

From 29 June to 5 July the VIII division was constantly on the march, one day in the rain and the next under burning sun. They reached the port of Agioi Saranda on the Adriatic coast and from there they boarded a Greek warship.

12 Ploumidis, *I 'Sidira' Dekaetia.* p.108. Total territory: from 63,211 sq.km. in 1897, to 121,794 sq.km. in 1913. Population: from 2,631,95 to 4,832,167 in 1913.

13 Hall, *Balkan Wars*, p.124 and Ploumidis, *I 'Sidira' Dekaetia.* p.105. The city of Kavala was ceded to Greece after personal intervention by Kaiser William II, who, in this case, supported his son-in-law, King Constantine.

14 Although Turkey at that time had not agreed to the cession of the Eastern Aegean islands, it did so by the Greece-Turkey Treaty of 1 November 1913.

15 Kallivrettakis, *Campaign Diary*, p.66.

The journey by sea to Kavala around the coast of Greece took two days. Sailing along Thassos island they were impressed by the imposing presence of the Greek Fleet, especially the flagship *Averof*, which, with *Navarchos* Kountouriotis at its head, had just liberated the city of Kavala. In the castle of the harbour the Greek national flag, blue with white cross, was flying high. From Kavala the Cretan Regiment advanced eastwards and on 22 July it was assembled in the city of Drama.

The war experiences of the Cretan volunteer regiment, after a year or so on the front line, were soon to come to an end. On 24 August news came that a unit was to be discharged and would soon be returning home. Three days later, the first part of the unit took the train to Thessaloniki and from there, via Piraeus, sailed on 7 September to Chania.

They were the first volunteers to return to the Greek capital in Crete with the glory of victory. The crowd gave them all a hero's welcome on their arrival in Chania. But the main part of the First Cretan Regiment, to which the first and second battalions belonged, had to wait a little longer. It had been given a mission to return to Korytsa in Northern Epirus to protect the Greek inhabitants from any attacks until their incorporation into the newly established Albanian state. They took the train to Thessaloniki and from there began the exhausting march to return to Korytsa. The presence of the Cretan detachment in the villages of Northern Epirus was the last glimmer of hope for the disillusioned northern Epirotes who saw the union with Greece receding once again. Indeed, at the end of October the detachment received orders to return to Ioannina. At the beginning of 1914 they were notified of the dismissal of the remaining volunteer detachments, and on 8 January they sailed for Chania where again the Chaniots gave them a warm welcome.

* * *

During the two years that Charalampos Seiradakis had been in the army, he was continuously on the front line. He had taken part in many battles and had been wounded twice – once seriously. His superiors had quickly identified him as a true military man. He had something fearless about him in the face of danger and his heroism had often been an example to his unit. They were impressed by his discipline and devotion to duty. He had high expectations of himself and others. Additionally, his comparative old age – in 1913 he was 27 years old – inspired respect in his younger comrades-in-arms.

At the same time, however, he was reckless and could easily be drawn into risky acts – his Cretan blood ran red when he got excited or when he saw injustice. In May 1913 he became a *lochias*. He had seen it as the natural next step in his military advancement.

On 22 October 1913, the *anthypaspistis* of the first battalion, D. Konstantinidis, had written to Kountourossifis with news of his son from Florina.

> The purpose of this letter is to congratulate you for the bravery and self-sacrifice that your dear son has shown in all the battles, honouring his country and his parents

> and winning the admiration ... that so richly deserves and to recommend that your honourable son be awarded the medal of valour for his excellence service...
>
> Yours sincerely,
>
> D. Konstantinidis, *Anthypaspistis*
>
> P.S. Tomorrow we depart for Korytsa, your son is getting well.[16]

The last phrase was of course intended to reassure the worried father who knew that his son had been badly injured a few months before.

In the Epirus campaign, Seiradakis made friendships and trusting relationships with many of his fellow soldiers. With some of them he was to fight again soon outside Greece, in war-torn France. When the battles receded, he pondered on the situation in Greece. He understood the reasons that had led to the Goudi Movement, he was aware of the conflicting interests in Greek society, of who represented which faction, he grasped the international alliances, the military cliques, the politics in Greece. Although the national split had not yet manifested itself, Charalampos Seiradakis sensed that an underground war against Venizelos was underway, directed mainly by the palace and the military staff.

Chania, 1 December 1913

It was one of the few times in life that Charalampos Seiradakis had felt envy. His comrades-in-arms had returned to Chania in October 1913 and thus had the opportunity to attend the ceremony of the union of Crete with Greece. The raising of the Greek flag at Firkas Fortress, in the harbour of Chania on 1 December 1913 was attended by Prime Minister Eleftherios Venizelos, King Constantine, former Prime Minister Zaimis, who had served as a commissioner of autonomous Crete, Stefanos Dragoumis, the local authorities, religious leaders, teachers and many citizens. The whole town had descended on the harbour.

And of course, all the chieftains and fighters who had fought for decades for the longed-for union were present, including *Kapetanios* Anagnostis Mandakas, who was now 98 years old and had taken part in all liberation campaigns. He had raised the Greek flag, glowing with the honour of having lived to see this historic day. Aristides Kriaris had come from Livadas and Koustogerako with Koundourossifis and many other chieftains, fellow countrymen and relatives. From Kissamos, Selino, Apokoronas and Sfakia, all of Venizelos' old comrades-in-arms had come from Therisso, friends and acquaintances, patriots from all over Crete, lots of people. All deeply moved. Union Day! A dream and a vision for many decades. Even though many Turko-Cretans had come to attend the ceremony of raising the Greek flag, they were certainly reminiscing about the past days when they were in charge of the fate of the island.

16 This letter is preserved in the personal archive of Ch. Seiradakis. In a handwritten note dated 8 December 1968, Seiradakis adds that: 'The late Demitrios Konstantinidis was killed fighting heroically in 1921 in Asia Minor campaign as a *Tagmatarchis*.' The document is reproduced in Appendix II.

But the battalion of Seiradakis had not returned to Chania in time to witness the ceremony. In the deep of winter in Albania everything had gone slowly, and Christmas was spent in Ioannina. It was not until 10 January 1914 that they boarded the same steamer they had sailed on two years earlier, the *Nikolaos*, to return to Chania. It was a grey winter day, and the port of Chania is open to the north and with the strong wind they almost drowned until the boats from a ship that had stopped at the quay pulled them out onto the pier as the waves covered the jetty. But the strong wind caused the Greek flag to flap wildly on the mast of the Firkas Fortress, opposite the historic lighthouse of the harbour, as if to shout to everyone, 'Here I am, look at me!' Wreaths from the hoisting of the flag a month ago were still left on the pedestal and the sense of celebration was still strong. Although the soldiers of the first battalion of the former Independent Cretan Regiment were not present when Venizelos delivered his solemn speech, the mere sight of the Greek flag on Firkas gave the young men shivers of emotion.

As 11 January dawned, the harbour pier was full of Chaniots waiting to welcome their children from the front. They were all soaked from the rain, so the welcome did not last long. Soon Charalampos met his sister, who was now married in Chania and was quickly taken to her house in Kastelli, in the heart of the old town. His young nephews were waiting for him to tell them stories from the war. Uncle Charalampos became the mentor of the family, both adviser and protector. He would stay with them for a few days to see friends and acquaintances again, and then he would go Livadas to meet his parents, brothers and sisters, relatives, all his fellow countrymen.

The next day Seiradakis went out early into the streets of the city. The first impression was that the rivalry and hatred that separated the two elements of the island, Christians and Muslims, had receded. His brother-in-law had told him that during the Balkan Wars many Turko-Cretans had left the island and those who remained had changed their behaviour. Their old arrogance had subsided and most of them were trying to find themselves a place in the new situation; however, mutual suspicion had not disappeared, nor had they forgotten the violence of the previous years. It did not take long for Seiradakis to realise how much Chania had changed. He remembered that before he left, they had begun to tear down the Venetian walls next to the old castle gate, Kastroporta,[17] so that the city could emerge from the walls that surrounded it.[18]

Now the walls in Katolas were no longer there. The moat in front of them had been filled in and where the fortress of Piattaforma had been before, a new central marketplace now stood.[19] As Mayor, Charalampos' uncle Emmanuel Seiradakis had contributed to its construction. It was a beautiful cross-shaped building of neoclassical style that brought together all the retail shops that had previously crowded haphazardly outside

17 The Venetians called the gate Porta Rettimiota because it led to Rethymnon. The Turks called it Kale Kapisi, or 'Gate of the Castle'.

18 It was felt that the old fortifications were suffocating the city.

19 Piattaforma Fortress was the central bastion of the Venetian walls facing south. It was demolished between 1910 and 1913 to allow Chania to expand outwards and to enable the building of the new central market.

the walls and blocked all traffic. It had been opened a few months before, and as a result the streets were finally cleared of dirt and rubbish. The old town was beginning to come together with new shops being built outside and along the old walls. People had certainly been relieved at the opening of the market, although the violent demolition had destroyed important architectural monuments that had for centuries given the city its special medieval character.

Chania was rapidly expanding around the axes that had been opened at the end of the nineteenth century, towards Halepa, the port of Souda to the east, and towards Kissamos to the west. People were gathering in their new haunts, the first cars had made their appearance, and although it was no longer the capital of the Cretan autonomous state, society was still evolving continuously as it had since the days when European admirals set the tone. On the other hand, the city remained the same in many ways.

The same smells, the same crowds of people wearing such a variety of coloured clothes, and the chimney of the ABEA soap factory smoking more than ever, filling the city with its characteristic smell. The road out of the market led Seiradakis to the beach in the district of Koum Kapi that ended at the second largest castle gate. There everything was unchanged. The beach was still crowded with the huts of the *chalicutes*, the labourers from Benghazi in Libya who had been brought by the Turks some years ago to do the heavy manual jobs in the city. Although their presence was picturesque, with their dances and songs, it was not in harmony with the new surroundings. Charalampos Seiradakis entered the old town through the gate of Koum Kapi and went to meet his old comrade-in-arms Andreas Gyparakis.

Seiradakis' old haunt in the harbour had not changed at all. Sailors and fishermen, shopkeepers and merchants, idlers and soldiers, all sipped their coffee and chatted animatedly. Andreas Gyparakis was waiting for him there, a *Bizanomachos* too, a few years younger than Charalampos, originally from Asi Gonia in Apokoronas. They had met a few times in the mountains of Pindos and had said they would meet again in Chania as soon as the war was over. Andreas introduced him to Kostas Giannakakis, a sturdy young man who had also taken part in the Epirus campaign with Pavlis Gyparis' group of volunteers. Andreas was a nephew of Gyparis who had gained a reputation as a Macedonian fighter but also as a tough military man and a confidant of Venizelos. Together the three friends found themselves discussing their military adventures, political developments, and of course the conflict between King Constantine and their prime minister, Eleftherios Venizelos.

Polarisation

In January 1914 Greece was living in the aftermath of the triumph of the Balkan Wars and everything in the atmosphere was optimistic. Crete was part of Greece, as were Epirus, Macedonia, Thrace and the islands of the Eastern Aegean. Nevertheless, there were worrying signs. Amid the national enthusiasm lurked the threat of polarisation that would not be long in coming.

It began with antagonism to see who contributed the most to the war successes. Publications in the Athenian royal press, especially by *Scrip*, downplayed the role of the prime minister while glorifying King Constantine, whom they portrayed as a kind of demigod with the aura of a Byzantine Emperor.

After all, the press had not forgiven Venizelos for the eviction of Prince George from Crete eight years earlier. But Constantine's complacency had reached a fever pitch with the adulation he received at the events that followed his visit to Berlin, where his wife's brother Kaiser Wilhelm II had honoured him with the title of *Feldmarschall*. For the conservative inhabitants of the old Greece, the old political parties, military men who were dependent on the palace, it was King Constantine, the 'soldier-king', who led the way to victory. He embodied the 'Great Idea' of the nation.

Such excesses did not seem serious to the progressive people of Greece, where people wanted to modernise the country; to at last get rid of the old partisanship that had short-circuited Greece and kept it backward and stagnant. For the progressive section of society, the rising bourgeoisie, the young officers and above all the Greeks in the newly liberated regions, the 'New Lands', Prime Minister Eleftherios Venizelos was the main factor in the victory. He had already proven himself as a capable reformer. In his very first term of office, he modernised the constitution and made social reforms. He had reequipped the army and fleet, led two victorious wars and successfully negotiated international treaties that doubled the size of the country and its population. Greece now enjoyed an international prestige it had never enjoyed before.

In a people prone to fanaticism, it only needed a spark to ignite and turn polarisation into division. This was understood by the three young Cretans who felt their concerns were well founded. They agreed that all patriots ought to protect the new Greece in every way possible. They would stay in touch and alert each other to anything that might happen. Charalampos greeted his friends and prepared to leave for Livadas, where he would remain for only a few days as he had to return to his unit in the northern town of Serres. In Livadas everything was charged with emotion. The tears of joy of his parents, the hugs from brothers and sisters and all the family, the drinks with friends in the village café. The next day he went to Koustogerako where he saw the Georgiakakis, the cousins from his mother's side of the family, and other fellow villagers. He walked to Sougia and smelled the saltiness of the Libyan Sea. The memories of his childhood came back to life.

After a few days he returned to Chania and immediately sailed to Piraeus. From there he took a train to Thessaloniki and then to Serres. He was already back in his unit by the end of February when he learned that he had become an *epilochias*.

Seiradakis enjoyed military life, and he especially missed the action on the battlefield that he had experienced in the previous two years. For the time being he lived in the camp and watched the developments like everyone else. Things had calmed down in Greece but developments in the Balkans and all over Europe were leading again to the smell of gunpowder.

First World War

The other country that had emerged victorious from the Balkan Wars was Serbia, which enjoyed the confidence – and support – of Russia on the European chessboard. This, of course, was a red flag for Austria-Hungary, which was concerned about Serbia's growing interest in Bosnia-Herzegovina and Northern Albania. As for the losers of the Balkan Wars, Bulgaria and especially Turkey, they were quietly arming themselves and waiting for the right moment to strike and claim what they had failed to win in the previous war. In other words, the Balkan powder keg was smouldering and waiting for the right spark to light it again.

The other Great Powers watched the developments anxiously. The two rival coalitions were the *Entente Cordiale*, consisting of Great Britain and France which was in turn allied to Russia (hereafter usually referred to as the Allies), and the Central Powers, consisting of Germany, Austria-Hungary and Italy. The danger in these alliances was that through chain reactions they could drag each other into a general conflict – this was not long in coming. On 24 June 1914 the heir to the Habsburg throne, Franz Ferdinand, was assassinated by a Serbian nationalist during a visit to Sarajevo in Bosnia. The shock in Austria-Hungary was great, and Vienna's reaction quickly got out of the control of the elderly monarch Franz-Joseph. The terms demanded by the Austro-Hungarian government from Belgrade were so outrageous that they made war inevitable. In July, Austria-Hungary attacked Serbia. Since the two countries were at war the situation had the knock-on effect of a game of dominoes. Russia jumped in to defend its protégé Serbia and this drew Germany into the war, which was also quick to rush to the aid of its ally Austria-Hungary.[20] Russia's two great allies, France and, a little later, Great Britain, followed suit, and by the end of August 1914 the conflict had become widespread. The Great War had begun.

For the Balkan countries, of course, the war had not stopped for a moment, as the conflicts continued despite the signing of the peace treaties. This time, however, the military map was changing, not only in Europe but almost all over the world, as the colonies of the European states on other continents – Asia, Africa and Oceania – joined the war. Greece was watching these developments with anxiety and was right to be concerned. The effects of the war would soon descend on the country like an avalanche.

Hellenocretan Legion

In September 1914 Charalampos Seiradakis received an unexpected message in his unit. It was from Andreas Gyparakis inviting him to meet in person. The meeting – which probably took place in Thessaloniki – was quite interesting for Seiradakis. Andreas announced to him that his uncle, *Lochagos* Pavlis Gyparis, was in consultation with Prime Minister Venizelos about how Greece could support the French war effort against

20 Italy, despite being the third party of the Central Alliance did not enter the war until 1916, and then on the side of the Allies not of Germany and Austria-Hungary.

Germany on the front in Lorraine where things were difficult for the French. Since Greece's official policy was neutrality – a policy that would create endless problems for Greece in the future – Greek assistance had to be voluntary and not on a national basis.

Gyparis had already recruited about 300 men and needed loyal and expert lieutenants to join him in leading the legion. Seiradakis would be his first aide-de-camp and Kostas Giannakakis his second. Was Charalambos willing to fight with the French on the distant Lorraine Front in France? His absence from his unit could be arranged by the ministry and so it was not a problem. Seiradakis did not need to hear the invitation for a second time – he accepted without hesitation. The two friends agreed to meet in a month or so in Athens to prepare for their departure for France. A new adventure would soon begin for the now 29-year-old Charalampos Seiradakis.

Thus, at Christmas 1914 he was in a training centre somewhere outside Athens preparing, in complete secrecy and with other volunteers, for the campaign in distant France. There he met Kostas Giannakakis again, and also Andreas Gyparakis, where they felt united not only by a common goal but also by a bond of friendship. At the head of the whole effort was *Lochagos* Pavlis Gyparis. He was omnipresent, although he was often absent for consultations on the difficult mission he was undertaking. After several attempts, in February 1915 they boarded a French warship that took them from Piraeus to Marseilles.

8

At The Lorraine Front, 1915

The Guns of August[1]

The French warship anchored in the port of Marseilles at dawn on 26 February 1915. It was a rainy day with fog and mist in the south of France. The atmosphere was gloomy with the shouting of the captain giving orders to drop anchor and tie up as quickly as possible. The ship had to land the Greek expeditionary force that had been brought over from the port of Piraeus without delay and set sail at once. The Western Mediterranean was dangerous, with German U-boats lurking off the southern coast of France. The country was at war. French warships and units of the British Fleet had been ordered to ensure that war-torn France was supplied with soldiers, food and ammunition by every means possible.

France was in dire need of them, as the war that had broken out six months earlier was critical. The first German attack against France had been launched on 4 August on the northern front, having violated the neutrality of Belgium. After four weeks of vicious fighting, the French Army was finally able to halt the German advance. But the front was dangerously close to Paris, only 50 kilometres away, and it extended 250 kilometres along France's northern border to Verdun, in the province of Lorraine. The two opposing armies had taken up defensive positions with fortifications, setting the tone for the war that was to follow. It was a war of trenches.

The Germans did not expect such a development. The Schlieffen Plan drawn up by their staff foresaw a 'blitzkrieg' with a rapid advance to Paris. But the plan had failed. Five weeks after the declaration of war, on 14 September 1914, a new commander-in-chief, von Falkenstein took over and moved the main front from Belgium to the western border with France.[2]

His name was thus associated with the bloody battles of Verdun. Indeed, in the same month a German Army prepared to invade from Metz in the Lorraine fields and attack

1 The title is that of Barbara W. Tuchman's book, *The Guns of August*, (Ballantine Books, New York, 1994). A fascinating account of August 1914, the first month of World War I.

2 *Generalmajor* Helmuth von Moltke was replaced by Erich von Falkenstein, Minister of War in the Government of Kaiser Wilhelm II.

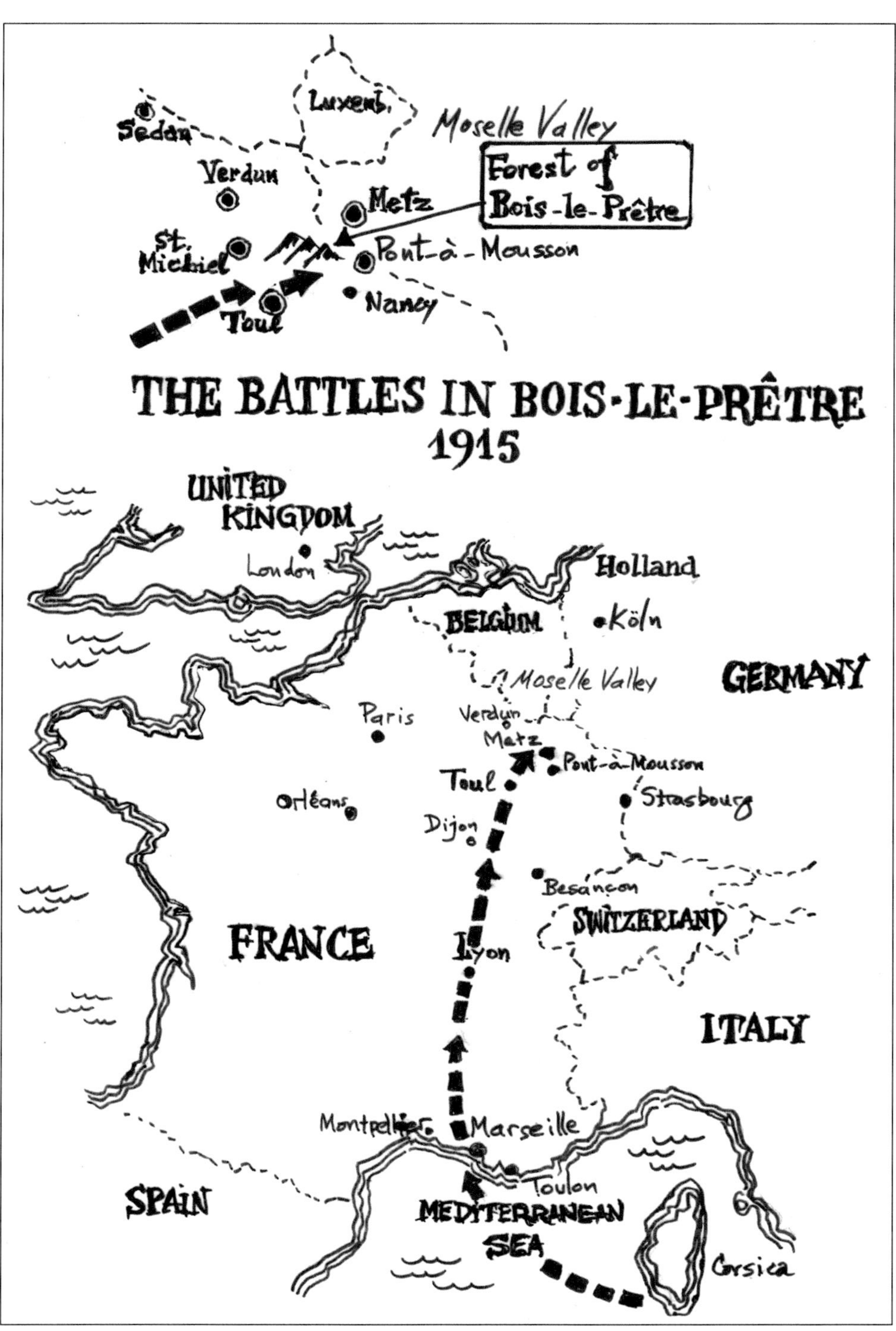

The Battles in Bois-Le-Prêtre.

the Verdun heights.[3] These were well fortified by *Général* Séré de Rivières, who had already realised their strategic importance in the event of a German attack.[4]

In preparation for the main attack on Verdun, the German Army advanced on 24 September to the fortified town of Saint-Mihiel, south of the fortifications, to cut the French supply lines. The battles of Saint-Mihiel resulted in thousands of casualties and soon spread to the dense forests between Apremont and Bois-le-Prêtre. These forests lie in a line 50km long that leads to the town of Pont-à-Mousson on the banks of the Moselle River.[5] The town had recently been taken by the Germans who had fortified themselves in the hills, although the French had taken care to concentrate a strong military force in the woods of the neighbouring village of Monthauville behind the German fortifications. Their orders were to repel the Germans and to secure a link with the strong town of Toul, 85km to the south, where the French Army's supply base was located.[6] Verdun's fate depended on these supplies. It was in the town of Toul that the Greek expeditionary force which had just arrived in Marseilles was to prepare for the Great War, and from where it was to head for the forests of Bois-le-Prêtre where vicious hand-to-hand fighting was already taking place. The French were in desperate need of reinforcements.

Beginnings of Division

Prime Minister Eleftherios Venizelos had made no secret of his intention from the outset that Greece should enter the Great War on the side of the Allies. For Venizelos, the British and the French, who dominated the sea, were Greece's historical friends and the alliance with them was dictated by the country's geographical position.

As has been correctly stated, 'the geopolitics of its territory left Greece no room to remain neutral. Its policy of neutrality *did not even ensure neutrality*, i.e. the inviolability of Greek territory... Greece was compelled to agree with the maritime powers of the Mediterranean.'[7] Indeed, Greek neutrality did not prevent the Allied forces from controlling Greek territory whenever their war effort demanded it.

Additionally, the Ottoman Empire and Bulgaria, the two countries traditionally hostile to Greece, had been armed by Germany and it was only a matter of time before they took a position in support of the Central Powers. Despite all the Kaiser's assurances to King Constantine that Germany would defend Greek interests, it was clear that in the event of victory, priority would be given to the peoples who fought on their side – the Turks and Bulgarians.

3 The German III Army Corps (Bavaria) was under the command of *General der Infanterie* Hermann von Strantz.
4 Nicolas Czubak, *Les batailles du saillant de Saint-Mihiel 1914–1918* (Hellecourt: l'Est Républicain, 2017), pp.3–9.
5 The River Moselle is a tributary of the Rhine. It originates in the Vosges Mountains and crosses France, Luxembourg and Germany.
6 Toul was the headquarters of the 501e French Logistics-Transport Division.
7 Ploumidis, *I 'Sidira' Dekaetia*, pp.123–124. Author's emphasis.

Greece was therefore in danger of finding itself without allies and friends, whatever the outcome of the war. As for the war potential of the belligerents, Venizelos foresaw that, despite all the readiness and apparent superiority of the German Army, it was by no means certain that it would be able to overpower the Allied forces of France, Great Britain and Russia. In addition to their superiority at sea, the Allies were able to draw on reserves from colonies in Africa and Asia, as well as from Australia, New Zealand, and Canada. And although America remained neutral at the beginning of the war, when it was forced by circumstances to take a stand, its preference for the Allies was a given.

From the very beginning of the war, Prime Minister Venizelos had proposed to King Constantine that Greece enter the war on the side of the Allies. The King had refused, and Venizelos had submitted his resignation which had not been accepted. At the beginning of the twentieth century, it was not uncommon in Europe for the palace to determine foreign policy. But in Greece, King George I was not directly involved in politics. His son, the young King Constantine, tried to change this by taking a position in favour of neutrality in the war, a seemingly prudent policy which, however, favoured Germany. Constantine was obviously influenced by the Kaiser Wilhelm II, who, as a European monarch, was a rather special case. The Kaiser's pro-war stance and general behaviour had caused consternation at the European royal courts, although not to Constantine, who apparently held him up as a role model. The pressure he was under from his family and his military staff, and above all the unbearable pressure from Berlin, consolidated his pro-German stance.

In February 1915 the crown council had been convened twice to decide the position that Greece would take in the war. Although all the previous prime ministers who participated in the council 'were in favour of the policy of Venizelos', Constantine refused to accept their decision.[8] The Venizelos Government resigned again, and new elections were called for May. At the same time there was the question of constitutional legitimacy since King Constantine's intervention had violated Greece's constitution.

In the *Légion Étrangère*

From the beginning of his premiership Venizelos was in contact with the ambassadors of the Great Powers in Athens. He had built up a relationship of trust with them and was considered a reliable interlocutor in the European capitals. Contacts with the French and British ambassadors were necessarily closer, as their military missions were responsible for modernising the country's armed forces. When war was declared, the head of the French military mission in Greece, *Général* Villaret, returned home with the wish that in the future the Greeks 'would remember their old associates.'[9] The active French

8 Ploumidis, *I 'Sidira' Dekaetia*, p.125. The Crown Council met on 18 and 20 February 1915. The meeting was attended by the former Prime Ministers Stephanos Dragoumis, Kyriakoulis Mavromichalis and Dimitrios Rallis. Their position in favour of Venizelos' policies is significant as they were all avowed pro-royalists.

9 Malessis, *Itta, Thriamvos, Katastrophi.*, p.135.

ambassador in Athens, Charles Jonnart, was also present at the ceremony. Venizelos conveyed to him Greece's intention to join, even if only symbolically, the French war effort. France's response came quickly. Although Greek military assistance was not possible because of Greek neutrality, an expeditionary force composed of volunteers would be welcome.

Venizelos knew who to turn to. He had contacted his acquaintance Pavlis Gyparis who had accepted with enthusiasm. Soon and in utmost secrecy he had begun to recruit old comrades-in-arms, veterans from the Macedonian struggle and *Bizanomachoi*, while at the same time he had instructed his nephew Andreas Gyparakis to scout out friends and acquaintances from Crete. Thus, Giparakis had contacted his friend Charalampos and had suggested that he and Kostas Giannakakis take on the duties of adjutants of the team. In December 1914, an expeditionary corps of volunteers had been formed under the name of the Hellenocretan Legion.

It is not certain exactly how many people were involved in the French campaign. Greek sources give the number of volunteers of about 600, 300 from Crete and 300 from the rest of Greece.[10] However, French sources state that the *Clan Crétois* (Cretan Corps) which was registered in the *1er Régiment de Marche de la Légion Étrangère* in Marseilles on 26 February 1915, consisted of 158 men:[11] the commander, Pavlis Gyparis, a French reservist named Avezou who spoke Greek, two *ypaspistes*, four *lochies*, eight *dekaneis*, a *dekaneas aggelioforos* and 141 *Stratioti*. Not all the names of the soldiers in the unit have survived. But the two adjutants are mentioned: Charalampos Seiradakis and Kostas Giannakakis, as well as an assistant doctor named Stavroulakis, the only Greek who knew a little French.[12]

For most of the volunteers it was the first time they had travelled outside Greece. As soon as they arrived at the port of Marseille, the impressions of the young Greeks were particularly vivid. First, the city itself and especially its port gave off a Greek aura. The history of the city is inextricably linked to ancient Greece, since it was built in the sixth century BCE by colonists from the city of Phocaea in Asia Minor. Ancient monuments scattered everywhere spoke of this history. When the Greek volunteers landed in the harbour, there was intense unrest which reflected the warlike atmosphere. But amid the turmoil, everything went smoothly and discipline and order prevailed. This made a particular impression on Seiradakis who, before joining the Greek Army, had served as a customs officer of the Cretan State and could see the difference that a disciplined administration made.

Charalampos Seiradakis appreciated the French. In the year he had come to Chania in 1909, six years before, the Protecting Powers were about to leave, having secured the stability of the new Autonomous Cretan State. They had come to Crete during the last

10 Andreas Gyparakis, *Anamniseis apo ti genia mou,* (Athens: privately published, 1978), pp.70 et seq.

11 *1er Régiment de Marche de la Légion Étrangère – RMLE.* The *Légion Étrangère* was raised in 1841 and was based in Aubagne, Bouches du Rhone, South France. It was the only unit of the *Légion Étrangère* to fight on French soil in the First World War. It had a strength of 510 men, all volunteers. Its motto was and is *Honneur et Fidelité.*

12 JMO 346 RI (*Journal des Marches et Operations, 346e Régiment d'Infanterie*), 1915.

stand against the Turks where he had taken up the rifle, and their intervention had led to the expulsion of the Turkish Army. During the 11 years that they remained there, the most obvious presence was that of the French, and especially of *Amiral* Potier.

Their whole attitude had left a positive impression and had brought a new breath of life to the culture-hungry Chania after the long Turkish occupation. There was already a small but active European community of military and businessmen in Chania. The most important of these was the Frenchman Alfred Zerain, president of the olive oil and soap company ABEA, which had been founded just outside Chania 26 years earlier by another Frenchman, the industrialist Julius Deiss.[13]

As the Greek expeditionary force was moving in formation through the centre of Marseilles, the building of the city's central market attracted the attention of Seiradakis. He thought again of the market building that had been inaugurated two years earlier, in 1913, in Chania. The Mediterranean character of the city, its Greek past, the physiognomy of the people, all reminded Seiradakis of Crete. But he could see that things there were better organised and more disciplined. This was needed in his home town. In Seiradakis' vision of Greece after the war, Marseilles played a large part.

The Greek corps marched to the headquarters of the *1er Régiment de Marche de la Légion Étrangère* on the outskirts of Marseilles. There the first registration of Cretan group was made, which took the name of *Detachément* or *Clan Crétois* (Cretan Detachment), and they were provided with lodgings until they left by train for the city of Lyon. The only problem the French registrars faced was how to render the names of their new colleagues more correctly in French. Indeed, transcription was not an easy task. Seiradakis, for example, appears under the number 29438 as 'Siradaquis Haralambe' although in a later list he is listed as 'Sidaraquis'.[14] Other comrades-in-arms had similar problems. The first days went smoothly in the *Légion Étrangère* camp. What most intrigued the Greek volunteers was the plethora of communities that had gathered there for basic training before being sent to the battlefields of Northern France. The *73e Division d'Infanterie* was based in Lyon. The Greek Legion was to be an autonomous unit of the *346e Régiment d'Infanterie de Réserve* and was soon supplied with makeshift military uniforms and light weapons.[15]

The armament was known to the Greek volunteers as most of the weapons of the Greek Army were French made. Other weaponry, however, was more sophisticated and adapted to the conditions of a new type of warfare – defence and trench warfare. Seiradakis and many of his fellow *Bizanomachoi* would soon discover similar situations to those they had experienced in the mountains of Pindos outside Ioannina.

On 1 March the train left Marseilles station and headed north along the Rhone River. As they travelled the 315km that separated them from Lyon, the weather deteriorated.

13 Jules Alphonse Deiss (Alsace, 1842–1901) was a French entrepreneur and inventor. He invested in 'Marseilles-type' soap in Salon-de-Provence in Southern France and in Tunisia. In 1889 he founded the ABEA factory in Chania, which is still in operation today. Deiss was decorated by the French state for his services with the *Légion d'Honneur* on 14 July 1884.

14 *Dépôt des 2e et 3e Régiments de Marche du 1er Étranger*, Marseille, 26 February 1915. The registration transcript is reprinted in Appendix II.

15 *Historique du 346e Régiment d'Infanterie.*

To their right, the snow-covered French Alps were misty and the whole valley was flooded by the overflowing river. In the afternoon they arrived. From the railway station in Lyon, they walked to the camp of the *346e Régiment* outside the town and there they encountered a different situation. Everything spoke of war. Military units were moving towards the battlefields. Heavily loaded trucks and horse-drawn wagons carried guns, ammunition and food to the fighting units. Units of cavalry crossed the muddy roads. Hospital cars carried the wounded to the nearby hospital. The only sounds were sharp orders.

The next day they were given uniforms. In March 1915, the French infantry was still using the traditional uniforms which had as their main characteristic the '*capote Poiret*', with red trousers and cap, all made of stiff cloth. But because they had recently understood that bright colours made soldiers easy targets for enemy fire, the French uniform was undergoing a radical change. The Greek volunteers did not get to wear the new horizon-blue uniform with the metal helmet which was introduced in early 1916, by when they had already left France. The basic armament of the French soldier was a long rifle with bayonet, a short sword and hand grenades. Each unit had a few Saint Etienne machine guns and mortars. The equipment included blankets and full expeditionary supplies weighing about 30 kilos.

The German infantry was similarly equipped. However, the uniform and the cap, also made of stiff cloth, were *feldgrau* (field grey) in colour, which made it easier to hide in the forests of Northern France. Nor had the German Army yet introduced the metal helmet that later became the hallmark of the German soldier. The rifle and bayonet used by the infantry were relatively short and this made them easier to use in the narrow trenches. The German soldier's whole fighting kit was similar and was of around the same weight as that of the Frenchman. However, the infantry units were equipped with more and new types of machine guns, grenades and mortars, to which were added flame-throwers.

The differences in weaponry were of enormous importance. Victory and, above all, the survival of the soldiers in the new conditions of war depended on it. In the following years, war technology evolved in the two armies with new, even more destructive, forms of warfare. But in mid-1915 the new techniques had not yet evolved and often the trench battles were fought hand-to-hand. These were the conditions that the volunteers of the Hellenocretan Legion would soon face on the battlefield.

The next two months were spent in hard training, getting used to new weapons and working with instructors who did not speak the same language. The role of the French reserve interpreter Avezou was crucial. The three *ypaspistes* – Seiradakis, Gyparakis and Giannakakis – who were to form the officer team, received more in-depth military training. Along with field exercises, they attended a comprehensive programme in new tactics of war, maps and logistics. They were also to learn some French that would later be valuable to them. For Seiradakis, learning the new language was, as he later said, one of the most positive experiences of his life because it allowed him to better understand the country and its people.

Within two months the unit was ready to fight. The commander, Pavlis Gyparis, the ranking officers Seiradakis, Giannakakis and Gyparakis as well as the whole Cretan team, the *Clan Crétois*, were preparing for a new military expedition.

The Wolves of Bois-le-Prêtre

At the beginning of May 1915, the legion received orders to move from Lyon to the supply-transport division in the town of Toul, in Lorraine. This was the main supply unit of the entire North-Eastern Front commanded by *Général* Riberspray. The camp had been in a state of war for eight months. Clashes were raging all along the front, particularly at Bois-le-Prêtre, just 30km from Toul, where the fighting was particularly bloody. At the start of hostilities in September 1914, a German Army[16] had occupied the hills around the only building in the forest, which was known as Maison Forestière du Père Hilarion (the Forest House of Father Hilarion).[17] French units had received orders to take it and by the end of October were preparing to attack.[18] The distance between the two opponents was less than 50 metres.

At 8 o'clock on the morning of 7 December 1914, a terrible explosion shook the forest. The French had blown up underground tunnels under the barbed wire and created gaps in it. The attack was fierce with many casualties, but they managed to push the Germans back into the forest.[19] The Maison Forestière was captured and remained in French hands until the end of the war. However, the ferocity with which the French of the *73e Division* attacked impressed the Germans, who gave them the name *Loups* (Wolves). The *73e Division* became known by the name *Loups* (*Loups du Bois-le-Prêtre*) in the history of the First World War.

The fighting did not stop there. By attacking continuously, the *Loups* managed to occupy an area 4km long and 1km deep in the forest, where the new front line was consolidated. Each side was fortified with trenches that were enclosed by double and triple rows of barbed wire. The living conditions in the frozen forest were miserable for both opponents. To sleep and protect themselves from the rain and enemy fire, the soldiers dug underground tunnels up to six metres deep in the wet earth. Four to six soldiers could sleep in each shelter. The worst problems came from the cold and the damp. To avoid frostbite, the soldiers had to be replaced every four days by rested soldiers from the rear.

Not that the miserable conditions prevented the fighting from continuing. Attacks and counter-attacks went on almost daily. In one month the French repulsed nine German attacks and made as many more counter-attacks. The bombardments were constant from and on both sides. No one was safe to go out of his shelter. After Christmas 1914 and throughout January and February 1915 the forest was covered in snow. Fighting continued sporadically and the two enemies prepared their next attack for the spring when they expected the weather to improve. But in April, the winter was as cold as in January.

16 German Fifth Army was commanded by *General der Infanterie* Hermann von Strantz.

17 It was built in the eighteenth century by Carmelite monks. Its strategic location was due to being the only source of drinking water. Cf B. Rouyer, *Avoir 20 ans au Bois-le-Prêtre*, (Haroué: Gerard Louis Editeur, 2015), pp.57 et seq.

18 This was the French *73e Division* and the mixed brigade of Toul under *Général* Lebock, of three infantry regiments Nos 167, 168, 169.

19 The attack was carried out by seven French battalions under the command of *Lieutenant Colonel* Pourel with heavy artillery cover.

In April 1915 the Greek corps completed its combat training at the camp of Toul. It was immediately ordered to move to the front line and reinforce the French forces of the *73e Division* at Bois-le-Prêtre. The arrival of the rested Cretans, eager to show their worth on the battlefield, encouraged the battle-hardened *Loups.* Soon, and as quietly as they could, as any noise could bring death, they too dug the sloughs in which they would rest at night. Directly opposite them were the German trenches, which in many places were no more than 15 to 20 metres away. They were separated by only two rows of barbed wire. They were so close that when he was on guard duty, Seiradakis could hear the guards across the way urinating.

Already, from the first day, the *Clan Crétois* began to take part in the fighting that continued non-stop under miserable conditions throughout May. The shelling was constant. On 27 May the Greek detachment took part in the attack of the French battalion which occupied a hill to the north-west of the hill where they had dug their bunkers. It was one of the places stubbornly claimed by both opponents. The fighting was hand-to-hand with many dead and wounded. But the Cretan fighters defended their positions well. They had begun to gain the respect of the battle-ravaged *Loups.* Indicative of the opponents' stubbornness was the battle to block the road leading to the neighbouring village. The French took it one day and the next day the Germans retook it. The fighting continued through June and July with the same tenacity.[20]

In discussions with the *Ypaspistes* Seiradakis and Giannakakis, *Dioikitis* Gyparis admitted that the Germans were tough warriors, and their superior weaponry gave them a significant advantage. However, the French were brave men and perhaps a symbolic victory could boost their morale. An act of sabotage, perhaps? It was something they would have to discuss with the French commander. Next day the three of them went to find the commander, *Major* Rozier. They met him in his muddy shelter under pouring rain and every now and then a bomb would go off next to them.

Le Croix des Carmes[21]

Behind the German lines was a wooden cross that the Germans had taken with them from Maison Forestière du Père Hilarion when they had retreated six months before. The cross was about three metres high and, as it was 350 metres away from the French lines, it was clearly visible because there were no longer any trees in the woods! Indeed, any trees that the soldiers had not cut down for warmth had been destroyed by the shelling. The symbolic value of the cross for both the French and the Germans was high. It was a sacred relic from the time when the Carmelite monks used the Maison Forestière du Père Hilarion as a monastery and its recovery by the *Loups* would be a symbolic victory and a boost to their morale.[22]

20 Czubak, *Les Batailles,* p.36.

21 'The Cross of the Carmelite Monks', this was a religious relic with symbolic value for both French and Germans.

22 The Carmelite monks lived in the Maison Forestière de Saint-Hilarion until 1840. Afterwards, the building was a retreat and a forest shelter.

After discussion with the Greek officers and with the help of the unit's translator, the French commander Rozier agreed to the idea of an act of sabotage. Why not recapture the cross? They agreed to stage an attack in the next few days with the aim of taking back the cross. However, in the preparation for the attack, a sudden obstacle appeared; the French observers had spotted in the no man's land separating them from the cross an outpost secretly built by the Germans. It was probably intended to be a machine gun post. Although it was not certain what level of completion it was at, it was clear that a machine gun post there would have hampered the whole project.

Gyparis proposed to *Major* Rozier a daring solution to overcome the obstacle of the machine gun post. On the evening before the assault, he and some Cretans would carry out a raid on the enemy lines to ascertain the exact position and how near completion it was. They would try to destroy it, but if that was not possible, they could at least give precise instructions so that the artillery could neutralise it the next day. But to cross the German lines with three rows of wire was a foolhardy action, and those who undertook such missions rarely returned alive. Although a risky venture, Gyparis and his men were ready to take it on.

On the night of 7/8 June 1915, at two o'clock in the morning, Gyparis' group, consisting of himself, the *Ypaspistes* Seiradakis, Giannakakis and Gyparakis and 20 other brave Cretans, proceeded to crawl towards the German lines.[23] Three who were in the lead quietly cut the wire entanglements. Others crawled through German lines to the outpost under construction while the others covered them. They saw that the work on the outpost had progressed and that the machine guns were ready for action. They were about to set the explosives when a German patrol spotted them and raised the alarm. A barrage of gunfire followed, and the men had to withdraw immediately. They crawled back with difficulty to the barbed wire, trying to escape in the darkness. Two Cretans fell, hit by German bullets.[24] The rest of them picked the wounded men up by their feet and crawled back to their lines in the darkness under French covering fire. The reconnaissance operation of the Cretan volunteers had achieved its main objective, but to succeed in recapturing the Carmelite cross, the machine gun had to be neutralised immediately.

At dawn on 8 June the operation began. At 6:00 a.m. the whole area was shaken by a terrifying explosion. The French had blown up seven underground mines which they had dug over the previous days under the German trenches. There were breaks in the barbed wire. At the same time, the battalion's artillery began to bombard the German positions according to the precise instructions given by the Cretan patrol. The bombardment lasted for about an hour, targeting the German machine gun and destroying it. The road was now clear. At 7:30 a.m. four battalions of *les Loups* under Major Rozier and Gyparis' group charged the German lines with bayonets fixed. They passed through the gaps in the three rows of barbed wire and crossed the 350 metres separating them

23 See JMO 346 RI, 8 juin 1915: *2 heures. Une patrouille du groupe Crétois sous les ordres du Lt Ghyparis va reconnaître un petit poste Allemand en construction en avant de l'ouvrage 2 de Viley. Il parvient jusqu'au réseau de fil de fer qu'il coupe mais il est obligé de se retirer sous le feu de l'infanterie et des grenades. Deux blessés: Thomadakis et Xirakis Emmanuel.*

24 Czubak, *Les Batailles,* p.37.

from the Carmelite cross, firing continuously. The Germans put up a resistance, but it was not enough to hold back the onrushing *Loups* and Cretans. The French wasted no time and with an axe cut down the cross and retreating to their lines, took it with them. The Germans immediately called for reinforcements from the flanking battalion, which soon appeared and counter-attacked with a barrage of fire. But it was too late, the French had acted with lightning speed and were already returning to their lines having taken their booty, 15 machine guns and 12 mortars.[25] The daring operation had succeeded. *Les Loups* had confirmed their reputation. Such was the shock of the French attack that in the following days there was relative calm at the front.

The next day, 9 June 1915, *Major* Rozier marshalled his men and congratulated them on their heroism in battle. He made special mention of the heroic Cretans who had so worthily stood by the French.[26] He and a detachment of soldiers then carried the Carmelite cross to the military cemetery at Petang, 4km to the rear and where the forest begins, and erected it there. It was a moving moment for the French soldiers who had been fighting continuously for nine months. They felt vindicated that the historic cross was returned to its old location, where it still stands today, on the spot where *les Loups* erected it on 9 June 1915. Buried in the Petang cemetery are 6,000 French soldiers who died heroically in the deadly battles of Bois-le-Prêtre.

At the point where the battle for the recapture of the cross was fought, at the top of the hill where the daring Cretans raided the German gun installation, there is today a monument to fallen soldiers. There are inscribed the names of the dead, as well as those of other Allied units that fought alongside the Wolves of the 73rd infantry division. Among these names one can easily discern the honorary dedication to the detachment of Cretan volunteers:

> *'DETACHEMENT DES VOLONTAIRES CRETOIS'*[27]

After the Battle

At the same time on the other fronts of the war, developments were not positive for the French. In the neighbouring heights between Saint-Michel and Pont-à-Mousson the Germans had managed to break through the French lines. The French losses were enormous: in just five weeks, from 26 March to 30 April 1915, 64,000 French soldiers were casualties. This meant that reinforcements were needed immediately, so military units had to leave Bois-le-Prêtre to reinforce other fronts. When the men of the *73e Division* were informed of the news, they realised that weakening their lines at such a critical moment could be disastrous.

25 Czubak, *Les Batailles,* p.38.

26 See document in Appendix II: *L'Adjudant Seiradakis Charalampos a servi à la Légion Étrangère du 26 février au 15 aout 1915. Il a pris part aux combats en Lorraine avec le 346e Régiment d'Infanterie. Il a reçu de ses chefs les meilleurs éloges.* [Signed] Le *Chef de Bataillon* I. Romieu, Tenedos le 15 aout 1915.

27 See photo: The monument is a war memorial and every year an official ceremony is held by the local authorities. It is visited by thousands of civilians annually.

As if that was not enough, there was more bad news. Their colleagues, the men of the *Clan Crétois* who had fought alongside them and with whom they had endured so many hardships together, also had to leave the front. Indeed, at the end of June *Lochagos* Gyparis announced to his men that he had received orders for them to leave the front and return to Marseilles immediately. There a British warship was waiting to take them back to Greece, to the island of Tenedos. The Hellenocretan Legion was undertaking a new mission on the Gallipoli peninsula, where the Allies were trying to penetrate the Dardanelles, which were defended by Turkish troops and had been fortified by German officers. The Allied forces were facing difficulties there and suffering heavy losses.

By the end of June, the Greek units had left Marseilles. On the Bois-le-Prêtre front everything was soon to change. While large parts of the *73e Division* had left by the end of June for other fronts, the Germans, for their part, reinforced their lines. It had not escaped their notice that the French forces had been weakened. From 1 July German artillery did not stop shelling the French lines for four days.

The trenches and barbed wire had been dug so deep that they had become one with the earth. On 4 July, the Germans launched a general attack. The balance of power was now so changed that in just one day they had broken through the French lines and forced them into a retreat. The Germans recaptured almost all the territory they had lost in the previous eight months and by the end of July they had reached Maison Forestière du Père Hilarion, but there the French were able to stop them. A new front line was formed around the hilltop from which *les Loups* had begun their attack last December.

Thus, everything went back to the previous situation, but at least the Maison Forestière du Père Hilarion and the source of drinking water remained in the possession of the French. So did the Carmelite cross that had been placed a month earlier in the forest cemetery after its heroic recapture. Three months later, on 15 November 1915, French Prime Minister Poincaré visited the martyred site to encourage the defenders. Indeed, *les Loups* had already become a legend among French soldiers. Their successes, though temporary, had boosted the morale of the French Army. As French victories on the Western Front in 1915 were few and far between, the heroism of the *73e Division* was an example.

At the end of June, the Hellenocretan Legion was back to the *1er Régiment de la Légion Étrangère* in Marseilles, ready to sail for the island of Tenedos. Their war experience on the Lorraine Front had taught them much. The shape of war was changing and their experience against the Germans would prove valuable in the battles ahead. This would be especially true for Charalampos Seiradakis who was to face the German Army again in the future. A year later he would fight them on the Macedonian Front and again 26 years later at the Battle of Crete. But now he was heading for the Dardanelles, the Gallipoli campaign, where the French, British, New Zealanders and Australians were fighting to break the Turkish defences.

He had already been promoted to *lieutenant* in the French Army and had been decorated for his heroism on the Lorraine Front. After the war, Seiradakis was invited every year by the French Embassy in Athens for the national day of 14 July. The French knew how to honour those who participated in their wars.

The Legend of *les Loups*

Three years later, in 1917, the United States of America had also entered the war on the side of the Allies. The course of the war was as the Greek Prime Minister Eleftherios Venizelos had accurately predicted from the outset, and the balance of power had begun to tip in the direction of the Allies. On the Bois-le-Prêtre front, a division of American troops arrived at the end of 1917 to reinforce the overworked *Loups*. When the Americans advanced into the German lines they met no resistance. The Germans had retreated a few days before from the trenches they had occupied in the woods for four years.

The account of the battles at Bois-le-Prêtre would not be complete without reference to a legend that has since become famous. It is said that in the intervals between the battles, French and German soldiers called a truce and allowed each other to drink water from the only spring in the area, which was located outside of the Maison Forestière du Père Hilarion.[28] To the extent that this fact corresponds to reality, it must have been done against the orders of the officers on both sides. There was therefore no official confirmation of such solidarity by soldiers, since anyone who admitted to it was in danger. But it seems very likely that in the horrors of war the soldiers made a secret agreement with each other to avoid suffering from thirst at a time when no one was sure whether they would be alive the next day. The legend shows the human side of a battle in which thousands of young men from all over Europe breathed their last – and with them many Cretan volunteers from the legendary *Clan Crétois*.

28 Rouyer, *Avoir 20 ans à Bois-le-Prêtre*, p.61.

The Seiradakis family in Livadas, Crete, in 1902. Charalampos Seiradakis is standing second from the right. (collection of Ch. Seiradakis)

The port of Chania as viewed from the sea, late nineteenth century. (collection of K. Naxakis)

End of the Ottoman occupation of Crete. The Turkish Army evacuates Crete, 2 November 1898, (collection of K. Naxakis)

The High Commissioner of Crete, Prince George of Greece (middle) with the admirals of the Great Powers, from the left: Noel, Potier, Canevaro, Skrydlov. Souda Bay, December 1898, (collection of K. Naxakis)

Left: Crete, Therisso uprising, April 1905. Charalampos Seiradakis is standing left with two comrades-in-arms, Chania, (collection of Ch. Seiradakis)

Below: Memorandum submitted by the Revolutionary Assembly of Therisso to the admirals of the Great Powers, 22 May 1905, (collection of Charis Xirouchakis)

ΤΥΠΟΓΡΑΦΕΙΟΝ ΠΑΠΑΔΑΚΗ

ΤΟ ΥΠΟΜΝΗΜΑ

ΤΗΣ ΕΠΑΝΑΣΤΑΤΙΚΗΣ ΣΥΝΕΛΕΥΣΕΩΣ

Θέρισσον 22 Μαΐου 1905

Ἀριθ. 213

ΚΥΡΙΕ Γ. ΠΡΟΞΕΝΕ

[illegible]

THERISSO Le 22 MAI / 4 JUIN 1905

MONSIEUR LE CONSUL GENERAL

Nous avons pris connaissance de la proclamation en date du 29 Avril / 12 Mai 1905 adressée aux Crétois par les représentants des Grandes Puissances protectrices à la Canée et publiée dans le journal officiel.

Nous nous excusons de n' avoir pu répondre plus tôt, comme il était de notre devoir, à l' invitation contenue dans cette proclamation. Mais nous espérons que cette lenteur sera justifiée lorsqu 'on voudra prendre en considération d' une part les difficultés de l' arrivée des représentants des provinces éloignées de l' île, d' autre part la nécessité dans laquelle nous nous trouvions de ne pas faire une démarche aussi sérieuse sans l' autorisation de tous les représentants.

La décision catégorique des Puissances Protectrices de ne pas permettre dans les conjonctures actuelles l' annexion de l' île au royaume de Grèce remplit de douleur le coeur de tous les Crétois.

N' ayant jamais songé à porter nos armes contre les Puissances protectrices, de la bienveillance desquelles nous avons toujours fait dépendre l' accomplissement définitif de nos voeux nationaux, nous sommes obligés de nous incliner encore devant leur nouvelle décision.

Mais jusqu' au jour où les Puissances protectrices auront décidé de donner leur sanction à cette solution de la question Crétoise qui est la seule naturelle, juste et définitive, le peuple Crétois est convaincu qu' elles daigneront lui créer des conditions de vie plus conformes aux exigences de la civilisation.

Comme nous l' avons déjà expliqué dans notre mémorandum en date du 12/25 Mais 1905, la proclamation de l' union a été provoquée en premier lieu par l' impatience du peuple Crétois contre la proclamation du régime politique hybride qu' il n' avait accepté que comme provisoire.

Cette impatience, naturelle d' ailleurs, a été accrue par la gêne financière contre laquelle devait lutter un pays aussi petit et aussi pauvre, devant suffir aux dépenses d' une vie politique à part, et se trouvant dans l' impossibilité de pourvoir à l' exécution de travaux publics, ou à d' autres dépenses nécessaires pour le développement économique du pays.

Les entraves financières en outre, auxquelles la Turquie est soumise grâce aux capitulations, restreignant la liberté de l' état quant au reglement de l' imposition et des droits de douane, empêchent non seulement l' augmentation des revenus publics, mais rendent impossible la protection et par conséquent le développement de l' industrie et de l' agriculture du pays.

La situation politique, d' ailleurs provisoire et incertaine, dans laquelle se trouve l' île, ne contribue guère à attirer les capitaux étrangers qui lui font défaut et dont ce pays a pourtant absolument besoin.

Un défaut encore plus capital du régime provisoire actuel, est la séparation douanière de l' île de tout autre organisme politique. La Crète, déjà séparée de l' Empire ottoman et pas encore annexée à la Grèce, voit ses produits se heurter à leur importation, soit en Grèce, soit en Turquie à des droits de douane, aux-

Above: First World War. Rare photo of the Hellenocretan Legion in Lorraine, May 1915. Back row, from left: E. Mourgianakis, Mamalakis, Ch. Seiradakis, K. Giannakakis. Front row, from left: P. Antonakis, P. Gyparis, S. Gavgiotakis, Stavroulakis. (collection of Ch. Seiradakis)

Right: First World War, Lorraine Front. The *Maison Forestière du Père Hilarion* where the battles of the French '*Loups*' and the Hellenocretan legion took place in 1915. (collection of Charis Xirouchakis)

First World War, Lorraine Front. Fountain at the *Maison Forestière du Père Hilarion*, the only source of drinking water during the battles of Bois-le-Prêtre. (collection of Charis Xirouchakis)

First World War, Lorraine front. Memorial reference to the *détachement des volontaires crétois* ('detachment of Cretan volunteers'). (collection of Ch. Xirouchakis)

First World War, Lorraine front. War memorial on the hill of Bois-le-Prêtre where the fight for *Le Croix des Carmes* (the Cross of the Carmelite monks) took place on 8 June 1915. (collection of Charis Xirouchakis)

First World War, Lorraine front. French soldiers next to *Le Croix des Carmes* (the Cross of the Carmelite monks) after the attack on 8 June 1915. (collection of Charis Xirouchakis)

First World War, Lorraine front. One of the underground shelters where soldiers slept during the battles of Bois-le-Prêtre. (collection of Ch. Xirouchakis)

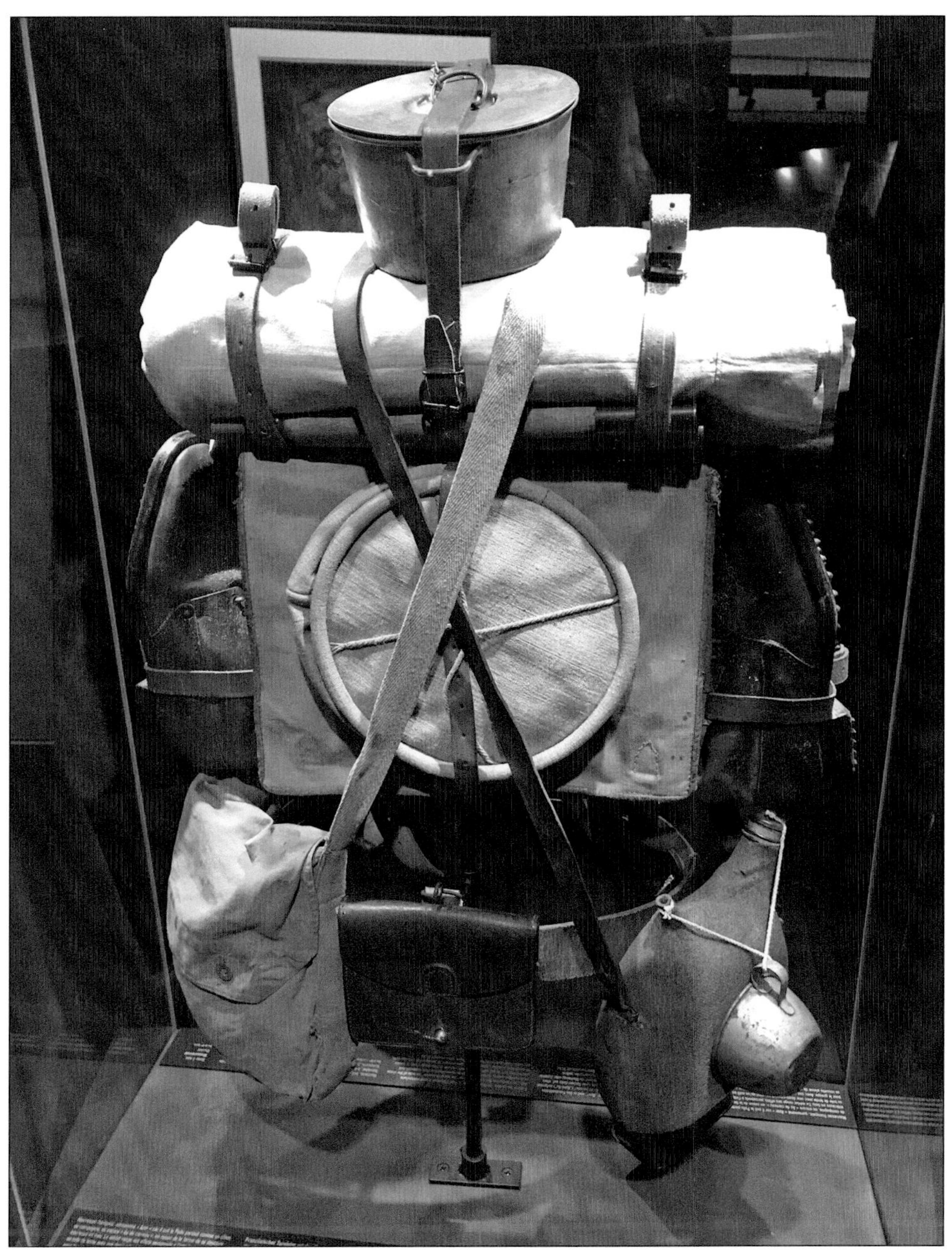

Field pack of a French soldier during the First World War. (courtesy of Verdun War Museum)

Field pack of a German soldier during the First World War. (courtesy of Verdun War Museum)

Left: First World War, Macedonian front. Charalampos Seiradakis (left) and Andreas Gyparakis, *Ypolochagoi* of the Greek Army with the Venizelist National Defence, Thessaloniki ,1917 (collection of Ch. Seiradakis)

Below: First World War, Thessaloniki. The 'triumvirate', Greek government of National Defence, 1916. From left: *Stratarchis* N. Danglis, Prime Minister El. Venizelos, and *Navarchos* P. Kountouriotis. (collection of K. Naxakis)

First World War, Macedonian Front. Franco-Serbian camp at Banitsa, Serbia, 1916 on a contemporary postcard (collection of Ch. Xirouchakis)

First World War, Macedonian front. Italian units that have come to reinforce the Army of the East on parade, Thessaloniki, 16 August 1916 on a postcard of the period. (collection of Ch. Xirouchakis)

First World War, Macedonian Front. Infantry unit on the march, Zeitinlik, Thessaloniki, 1915 from a contemporary postcard. (collection of Ch. Xirouchakis)

First World War, Macedonian Front. French biplanes in Thessaloniki, 1916. Contemporary postcard. (collection of Ch. Xirouchakis)

First World War, Macedonian Front. The commander-in-chief of the Allies, Général Emmanuel Sarail on horseback with officers. Thessaloniki, 1916. Contemporary postcard. (collection of Ch. Xirouchakis)

First World War, Macedonian Front. British military camp in Zeitinlik, Thessaloniki, 1917. Contemporary postcard. (collection of Ch. Xirouchakis)

First World War. Rare photograph of officers of the Hellenocretan Legion. Seated from left: Pavlos Antonakis, Pavlos Gyparis, Leonidas Mamalakis. Standing from left: Andreas Gyparakis, Kostas Giannakakis, Charalambos Seiradakis. (collection of Ch. Seiradakis)

Major Charalampos Seiradakis (in military uniform) with, from left, C. Alavanos, President of Greek Parliament, well-known sculptor Giannoulis Chalepas, F. Zaimis Prefect of Cyclades, and T. Alavanos, Mayor of Cyclades. Island of Tinos, March 1917. (collection of Ch. Seiradakis)

The Seiradakis family in a rare photograph, Thessaloniki, April 1934. *Tagmatarchis* Ch. Seiradakis with wife Fani, née Louka, mother-in-law Helen and four daughters. (collection of Ch. Seiradakis)

Second World War, Battle of Crete, 20 May 1941. *Fallschirmjäger* dropping from Junker Ju 52 transport airplanes at Maleme airport. (collection of K. Naxakis)

« ΝΕΡΟΣΠΗΛΙΟΣ »
ΠΡΟΣΩΡΙΝΟ ΔΙΟΙΚΗΤΗΡΙΟ ΤΩΝ ΣΕΛΙΝΙΩΤΩΝ
ΠΟΥ ΣΤΙΣ 24 - 25 ΜΑΪΟΥ ΤΟΥ 1941
ΣΤΗ ΜΑΧΗ ΤΟΥ ΦΑΡΑΓΓΙΟΥ ΠΟΛΕΜΗΣΑΝ ΗΡΩΙΚ
ΤΑ ΓΕΡΜΑΝΙΚΑ ΣΤΡΑΤΕΥΜΑΤΑ.
24 - 5 - 2008
ΚΙΝΗΣΗ ΠΟΛΙΤΩΝ - ΠΡΩΤΟΒΟΥΛΙΑ ΚΑΝΤΑΝΟΥ

Above: Second World War, Battle of Crete, 20 May 1941. Inscription in the Gorge of Kandanos at the location 'Nerospilios' where the battles of 24 and 25 May 1941 took place. (collection of Ch. Xirouchakis)

Left: Second World War, Middle East. Charalampos Seiradakis commander of the fifth battalion of the second brigade, Cairo, Egypt, June 1943. (collection of Ch. Seiradakis)

Second World War, Middle East. Charalampos Seiradakis commander of the Recruitment and Screening Centre, Ismailia Desert, Egypt, 1944. (collection of Ch. Seiradakis)

Charalampos Seiradakis, prefect of Chania (right), with general commander of Crete, Christos Tzifakis, outside the prefecture building, Chania, March 1947. (collection of Ch. Seiradakis)

Prefect of Chania Charalampos Seiradakis invited by Rear Admiral Lancelot on board the French warship *Gustave Zédé*, Souda Bay, 1947. (collection of Ch. Seiradakis)

50-year anniversary celebration of the Greek victory at Bizani, Ioannina. The *Bizanomachoi* below the fortifications of Bizani Fortress, 1963. (collection of Ch. Seiradakis)

The political administration of Crete during the turbulent year 1947. Seated from right: Ch. Seiradakis, prefect of Chania, Chr. Tzifakis, general commander of Crete. Standing from right: G. Markopoulos, prefect of Lassithi, A. Nathenas, prefect of Heraklion, Ch. Xylouris prefect of Rethymnon. (collection of Ch. Seiradakis)

Political leader Sophocles Venizelos at a Liberal party event in Chania. Standing on his right is the prefect of Chania Ch. Seiradakis, April 1947. (collection of Ch. Seiradakis)

50-year anniversary celebration of the Greek victory at Bizani, Ioannina, in the presence of King Pavlos I. Behind Queen Frederica stands Ch. Seiradakis. Ioannina, 1963. (collection of Ch. Seiradakis)

50-year anniversary celebration of the the 'National Defence' in Thessaloniki (1916). Remembrance of 'Amynites' officers assembled in Syntagma Square, Athens, 1966. Ch. Seiradakis stands in front row, fourth from the left. (collection of Ch. Seiradakis)

20-year anniversary of the Battle of Kandanos during World War II. Charalampos Seiradakis laying a wreath to the victims of the martyred town, 1961. (collection of Ch. Seiradakis)

20-year anniversary of the Battle of Kandanos during World War II. Charalampos Seiradakis delivers a speech in the presence of Bishop Irenaeus, Kandanos, 1961. (collection of Ch. Seiradakis)

Charalampos Seiradakis with his grandson, Charis Xirouchakis, on the island of Lemnos, August 1964. (collection of Ch. Xirouchakis)

9

Gallipoli, 1915

The Dardanelles Campaign

In November 1914 the Ottoman Empire had allied itself with the Central Powers against the Allies. This was not surprising as Germany had overseen the reorganisation of the Turkish Army since 1880. But the Turkish decision to fight the Allies had been accelerated by the Ottoman Fleet's attacks on Russian targets in the Black Sea with two German warships, which Germany had recently donated to the Turkish Navy.[1] Russia, already under pressure on the Eastern Front, felt the threat on its southern border and called for support from its Allies.[2]

The British First Sea Lord at the time was Winston Churchill, who had conceived a bold plan: entering the Dardanelles and capturing Constantinople.[3] If successful, the Allied forces would neutralise the Ottoman threat and help the Russians. Although ambitious, the plan was relatively simple and, if successful, could have had a positive impact on the course of the war. However, a prerequisite was surprise and coordinated action by the Allies, which was difficult with so many fronts open. But the plan received the approval of the Allied war staff, and by December 1914 preparations had begun. A fleet of 20 or so British and French warships was to force an entry into the Dardanelles, and at the same time an expeditionary force of 450,000 soldiers under the British General Sir Ian Hamilton, consisting of British, Australians, New Zealanders, Indians and French troops, was to land on the shores of Gallipoli.[4]

The Allies' campaign in the Dardanelles had heightened concern in Greece. Prime Minister Venizelos believed that the policy of neutrality was a transitional phase and when the conditions allowed it, Greece should fight alongside the Allies. The Gallipoli

1 The Battleships *Goeben* and *Breslau* which were renamed *Yavuz Sultan Selim* and *Mydilli* had joined the Turkish Fleet. They were commanded by German *Vizeadmiral* Wilhelm Anton Souchon.

2 After the defeat by Germany at Tannenberg on 30 August 1914, Russia was on the defensive on the Eastern Front.

3 Winston Churchill held the title First Lord of the Admiralty, the senior *political* post in charge of the British Fleet. Admiral of the Fleet John Fisher was the actual commander of the British fleet, although he was under the direction of the government through the First Sea Lord.

4 *'The Dardanelles campaign'*, https://www.sansimera.gr/articles/921.

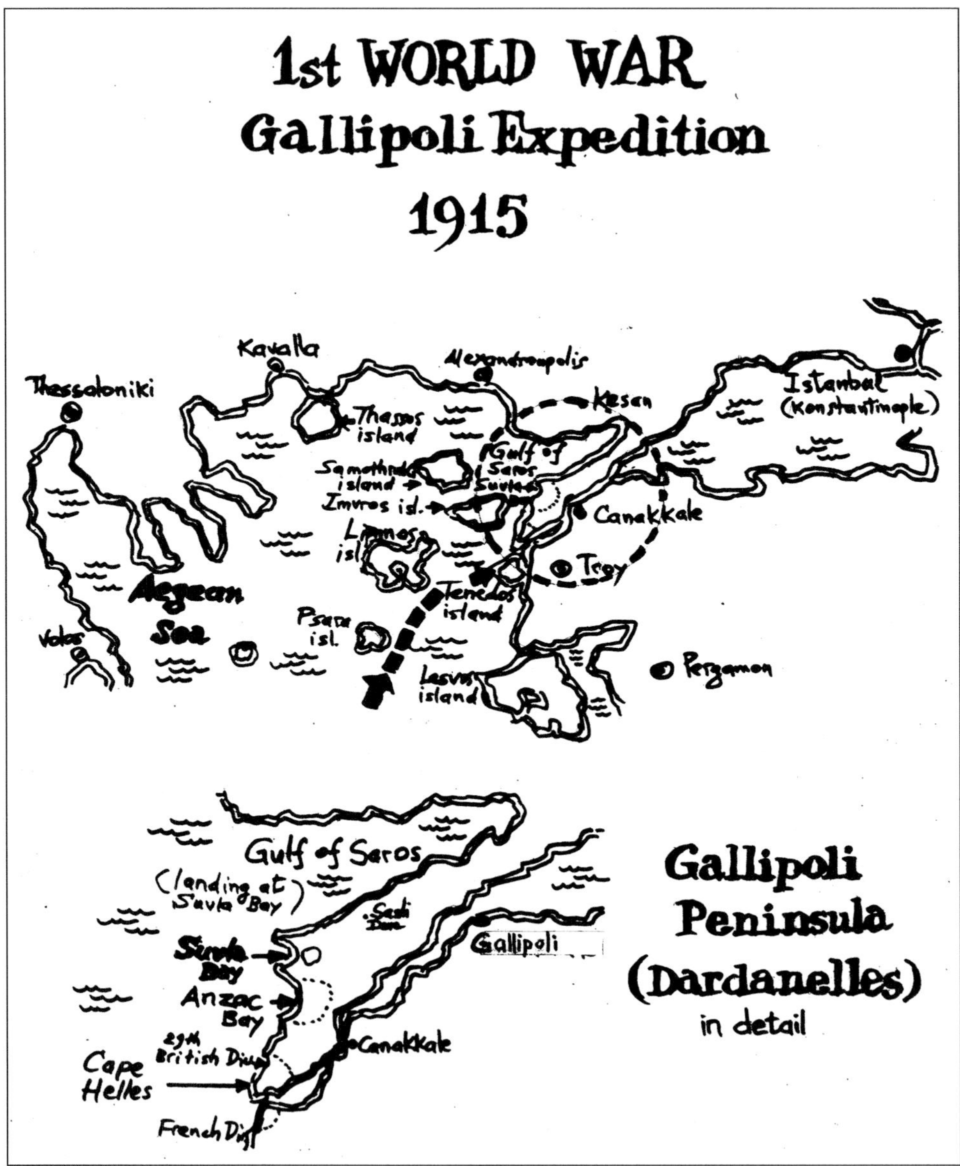

First World War, Gallipoli Expedition, 1915.

campaign offered a suitable opportunity and Venizelos felt that Greece should take advantage of it – the Allies' request was accompanied by the offer of significant territorial rewards. Thus, in January 1915 Venizelos had submitted a memorandum to King Constantine with the reasons for Greece's participation in the Gallipoli campaign with 40,000 troops.

Venizelos' proposal had been discussed at two crown councils in February 1915, where all the political leaders had agreed – but King Constantine was opposed. In a counter-memorandum chief military adviser Ioannis Metaxas argued that Greece should not participate in the Gallipoli campaign on the side of the Allies on the grounds that the Germans would eventually win the war. Nor should Greece claim Western Asia Minor as territorial gain. Metaxas's position against any intervention in Asia Minor had always remained firm. Venizelos had no alternative but to resign and call new elections. He won the election by a large majority. Despite the popular verdict, which was again favourable to Venizelos and the Allies, King Constantine did not change his mind.

Thus, the Allies had started the Dardanelles campaign without the participation of Greece. Unfortunately for them, nothing went according to plan. The plan was known to the Germans, who had instructed *General* von Sanders[5] to fortify the Dardanelles Straits with machine guns, coastal guns and sea mines. When the Allies finally decided to attack the Dardanelles, they had lost the element of surprise and met strong resistance. The Anglo-French fleet had entered on 19 February 1915 but had been repulsed with heavy losses.[6] The Allies therefore decided on a mixed operation. On 25 April, an Allied force of seven British, French, Australian and New Zealand (ANZAC) divisions under British command landed at Gallipoli with a parallel naval offensive. But again, they failed as they met fierce resistance from six Turkish divisions.[7] The indecisiveness of the military leadership exacerbated the situation. The Allies had pinned their hopes on a new assault in early August.

In Tenedos

The new landing of the Allies would be at the bay of Xeros, or Saros, on the beach of Gallipoli. It was a difficult operation as the soldiers would be exposed to the enemy machine guns on the surrounding hills that dominated the coast. It was obvious that to have any chance of success they had to neutralise the enemy machine guns first. This implied that a group of commandos would have to penetrate the enemy lines to destroy them. But there was no such group in the Allies' forces on Gallipoli.

5 The German *General* Otto Liman von Sanders oversaw the Turkish fortifications on the Gallipoli Peninsula.

6 From February to March 1915 the Anglo-French fleet with 18 warships constantly failed to penetrate the Dardanelles. Three warships were sunk, and three others were seriously damaged.

7 As well as the well-known Esat *Pasha*, the Turkish officer Mustafa Kemal, the later Atatürk, had also participated in the battles on Gallipoli.

Venizelos was in constant contact with the ambassadors of France, Charles Zonart, and Great Britain, Sir Francis Elliot. Zonart confided to Venizelos that a major problem during the landing at Xeros Bay was attacks by irregular Turks and he was concerned about how to deal with them. Soon Venizelos had visited the islands of Lemnos and Tenedos and took the opportunity to suggest to the Admirals of the Allies that the Gyparis group could help. The admirals agreed and the French asked the War Ministry for the immediate dispatch of the Gyparis force from Lorraine to the Dardanelles. It was to be accompanied by the French *Major* Romieu and the interpreter *Anthypaspistis* Avezou who had stood by his side all this time.[8] The Hellenocretan Legion was ready to undertake a new, and daring, operation, this time closer to home.

Thus, at the end of June 1915, a British warship had picked up the Hellenocretan Legion from Marseilles and was heading for the Aegean. Before they left, *Général* Riberspray of the Toul Army had decorated them for their heroism in the battles of Bois-le-Prêtre. The Cretan troops, le *Clan Crétois*, had proved their worth as equals to *les Loups*, and they now shared the same legendary status. Soon they landed without incident in Tenedos.

An Air Raid

In Tenedos, the legion found itself on its native soil. The group was reinforced with new volunteers, about 300 armed men, most of them from Crete. The group was still commanded by *Lochagos* Pavlis Gyparis and his trusted officers Charalampos Seiradakis, Kostas Giannakakis and Andreas Gyparakis. French *Major* Romieu was the liaison with headquarters and *Anthypaspistis* Avezou assisted in translation.[9]

Islands Lemnos and Tenedos were the bases of the Allied Army throughout the Dardanelles campaign. Thousands of soldiers were camped on the two islands where naval and air activity had increased significantly. The Allied command was headquartered in the port of Moudros on Lemnos where the Allied fleet was based. In the interior of the island, open-air hospital care units had been organised for the thousands of wounded. In Lemnos, a military airfield had also been built with mainly British aircraft that were often active. This was necessary as they were facing the powerful *Die Fliegertruppen des Deutschen Kaiserreiches*[10] which used the nearby Kavala airfield

8 See https://www.greatwarforum.org/topic/234339-greek-infantry-at-gallipoli/ 'This irregular force was commanded by the Greek *Anthypaspistis* [Pavlos] Gyparis, and accompanied by two French officers, *Chef de Bataillon* Romieu and *Sous Lieutenant* Avezou'.

9 There is little information about the following events. The presence of a Greek military force in the Gallipoli Campaign was unknown until recently. On history websites, many scholars express surprise when they are informed that, apart from ANZAC, Greek forces also participated in the bloody landing at Xeros Bay in August 1915. Seiradakis himself often referred to the Gallipoli Campaign, but his written accounts have not survived. Only Andreas Gyparakis mentions some incidents. What attests to the heroic, albeit brief, action of the Hellenocretan Legion in the Dardanelles are the medals of honour awarded to them by the Allied command at the end of the war.

10 The German Air Force of WW1, from 1916 it became *Der Deutsche Luftstreitkräfte*.

as a base. Air battles were frequent as were bombings, though still in primitive form. Convoys loaded with soldiers, ammunition and supplies crossed the Aegean every day. From the beginning of 1915 a warlike frenzy had been going on in the Greek islands near to the Dardanelles.

At first the battle-worn soldiers of the legion had remained inactive. Although they had been warned to prepare for a landing, they had not heard any more for over a month. The reason was the delays and postponements that had plagued the Gallipoli campaign from the start. However, the legion officers were in constant contact with headquarters in Lemnos where they travelled regularly for briefings. From Tenedos the journey by steamer to Moudros took only a few hours. On one of these trips to Moudros, Seiradakis had an interesting experience.

Major Romieu had introduced Seiradakis to a British pilot who flew tactical reconnaissance flights over the Dardanelles. His plane was a two-seater Vickers FB5 known as the 'Gunbus'. As the second pilot who was to accompany him fell ill, Seiradakis offered to fly with him and, to his joy, the British pilot accepted, and soon Seiradakis took his first flight. Not just a flight, but his first bomb run as well. Indeed, the second pilot in the Vickers was equipped with a machine gun (a Lewis gun) and with bombs placed in special baskets. Soon the FB5, with Seiradakis sitting behind the British pilot, flew low over Hellespont to locate the Turkish fortifications. Over a Turkish machine gun and through heavy fire, the British pilot nodded to Seiradakis 'now!' and he let – literally – the bomb baskets fall on the enemy outpost. As the plane was gaining altitude, they saw the outpost going up in flames. The plane had soon returned and landed in Lemnos where Romieu and their friends welcomed Seiradakis as a hero. When they returned to Tenedos, Seiradakis was recounting the flying experience to his friends. He always liked to tell it – and he had every right to do so.

In the Bay of Xeros

Finally, in mid-July, a signal came to the legion to prepare. Thousands of Australians and New Zealanders were ready to board warships and land in makeshift boats in Xeros (Dry) Bay. One of the destinations was the beaches beneath the fortifications of Suvla. The fortifications were built on a steep hill overlooking the entire beach. It was defended by a relatively small garrison as the Turks did not expect an invasion there, but now they hurried to reinforce it with a whole division. On the evening of August 6, the legion boarded two British warships, the *Minerva* and the *Jed.* The landing at Xeros Bay took place at dawn on 7 August 1915 in an orderly manner and in complete silence. But as soon as the legion came ashore, they were greeted by enemy fire from the surrounding hills. The Greek soldiers were alerted and found that the fire was coming from a group of Turkish irregulars. They quickly managed to surround them and force them to withdraw to the hilltop fortifications. Fortunately, there were no casualties from the firing. After dawn, they advanced to the ridge near the fortifications. From there they could see the whole beach and the surrounding area.

They quickly organised their defences in case of an enemy attack. Their orders were to create a diversion by acts of sabotage to facilitate the main Allied landing on the nearby beaches.

The legion was to control the road to Keshani and blow up a bridge near the village of Grabounar.[11] It split into groups and advanced inland. The first village encountered was Sasli Dereh where they captured the police station and destroyed the telephone lines. But suddenly, as they advanced, they were met with heavy artillery fire. They soon realised that it was not from irregulars but from a Turkish division that was rushing to reinforce the Suvla defences. The Greek groups were forced to retreat towards the ridge from which they had started.[12] Soon the legion was under concentrated fire from the Turks who were reinforced with cavalry and artillery. It was very hard to hold the ridge; the legion was in a vulnerable position and it had no choice but to retreat to the beach. The problem was that they had no contact with the British warships, which had sailed away behind a rocky islet to avoid Turkish artillery fire. Fortunately, a British steamer saw the signals from the shore and approached to pick up the wounded. However, the British warships were being dragged back away from Xeros island and did not return Turkish fire.

Gyparis' men were in a difficult position. They had to find a way to delay the Turkish attack on them so that they could get down to the beach and have the ships pick them up. Halfway between them and the Turkish Army in the hills of Sasli Dereh there was a pine forest. Gyparis gave orders to set it on fire and soon the place was filled with smoke which provided them with some cover. Now they had to hurry as the Turks were trying to outflank them. Suddenly a Turkish shell struck the British steamer that was on the beach to pick up the wounded. At last, the British captain realised the urgency of the situation and at his request the two warships came out of hiding and fired on the Turkish positions. Soon the Turkish guns were silenced, and the legion soldiers were able to descend to the beach in greater safety. It was already beginning to get dark as the British steamer transferred the entire Greek contingent to the British warships.

The Greeks were exhausted by the fight and had several dead and wounded.[13] They were not facing Turkish irregulars, as they had expected, but an organised all-arms division of the Turkish Army with artillery.

11 www.greatwarforum.org/topic/234339-greek-infantry-at-gallipoli. 'Split into several groups and operate against the Kechan-Kavak road, to blow the bridges at Grabounar … in short, to draw the enemy's attention towards that region'.

12 www.greatwarforum.org/topic/234339-greek-infantry-at-gallipoli. 'The partisans eliminate the outposts and occupy the village of Sasli Dere, where they … destroy the telegraph apparatus and damage the lines. Pushing beyond the village, the detachment runs into a prepared position, 4km from the coast, with machine guns and two pieces of artillery. It is forced to retire'. www.greatwarforum.org/topic/234339-greek-infantry-at-gallipoli. 'The detachment saved itself by retreating towards the shore, burnt the forest on both sides of Sazli Dere pouring petrol and gasoline as they were retreating'. Cf Gyparakis, *Anamniseis*, pp.6 et seq.

13 www.greatwarforum.org/topic/234339-greek-infantry-at-gallipoli. 'During this confrontation the Greeks took 28 casualties and left 3 POW behind. The Turkish casualty toll was 8 dead and 12 wounded '.

On board the ship, Gyparis realised that three of his men were missing.[14] Some of them had been seen left behind, stranded on rocks from where the British steamer could not pick them up. Gyparis would not leave his men helpless. He demanded that the captain give him a boat to search for them in the dark. Unwillingly in view of the tough situation, the British captain gave him a boat but warned that the two British warships would have to leave immediately for Tenedos. In the end Gyparis, however much he searched the rocks, could not locate his missing men. Before dawn, with a heavy heart he was forced to go back out to sea as the Turks began to descend towards the beach. All the next day, the boat was adrift and at the mercy of the waves. Fortunately for Gyparis and his companions, a French ship which had been in nearby waters saw them and picked them up. They had been at sea for over 12 hours.

The Army of Thessaloniki

The Hellenocretan Legion stayed in Tenedos for another month. Its participation in the Gallipoli campaign had lasted a total of three months, one of which was spent on the battlefield. As they learned afterwards, the Australian and New Zealand withdrawal had been devastating. All hopes of the Allied campaign at Gallipoli had vanished. By September, it was clear that the campaign had failed and the Allies abandoned all further attempts. Inadequate preparation, delays due to poor coordination, strong fortifications that the Germans had built in anticipation and sickness had all contributed to the failure of the campaign. But the idea of organising an eastern front was beginning to gain ground in Allied strategic thought. So, the Allied forces that had been concentrated at Gallipoli had to move to other places to continue the war. Some units left for Egypt but most of them began to gather in Thessaloniki, which was the best place to establish a new front in the war. It was a focal point from which the Allied forces could support their allies the Serbs and attack both the Ottoman and Bulgarian forces. The new front where the multinational Army of Thessaloniki had gathered would have a significant impact in the war, but also on the political and military developments in Greece. The national division, which had already begun, would lead the country to deep schism with consequences that would last for decades.

14 Gyparakis, *Anamniseis*, p.77.

10

Macedonian Front, 1917–1918

National Division

In October 1915, the Allied forces retreated from Gallipoli; a multinational army of British, French, Australians, New Zealanders, Africans and Indians, was heading towards Thessaloniki. Their aim was to create a new front that would act as a diversion from the west and the east where the war was being fought.

At the same time, Charalampos Seiradakis had returned to his unit in the 18th Regiment of the Serres Division. In the time that had elapsed since he left with the legion for France and Gallipoli, the internal situation in Greece had deteriorated. This was clearly visible in society. There was no uniform perception by the people of the events and their significance. Everyone interpreted them according to where they belonged, to the 'Venizelist' or the 'royal' faction. Prime Minister Eleftherios Venizelos had tried to maintain a conciliatory attitude towards King Constantine, but to no avail. After the King's refusal to sign the crown council's decision to enter the war on the Allied side, the Venizelos government had resigned in February 1915 and new elections were called for 31 May. In these elections Venizelos' Liberal Party had again obtained a clear majority, approving his policy.[1]

And yet, King Constantine refused again to implement the policy of the new Venizelos Government, who thus had to resign for a second time on 22 September. New elections were called for December. One of the reasons for the fall of the government was the military conscription that had taken place in September, in reaction to Bulgaria's entry into the war alongside the Central Powers. The conscription in Greece had not gone smoothly. Apart from organisational shortcomings, the main problem was that each faction had a different view of why it had been carried out. The government saw it as the first step before going to war, while the royal opposition saw it as having been done to protect the neutrality of the country.

After the resignation of the Venizelos Government, King Constantine instructed politician Alexandros Zaimis to form a caretaker government until the new elections.

This time Venizelos considered that the King had exceeded the limits imposed by the constitution and changed his tactics. In a message on 8 November 1915 he declared

1 The Liberal Party won 189 seats out of a total of 316.

First World War, Macedonian Front, 1916–1918.

that his party would abstain from the December elections and accused Constantine of violating popular sovereignty by wanting to impose a 'monarchical constitution like the Prussian one, where the monarch is the sovereign organ of the state.'[2] Most people agreed with these accusations against a King who did not want to accept the verdict of the people after two elections. In the 'new lands' in particular, this position had general resonance. But many in 'old Greece' considered it offensive to a King who had won laurels on the battlefield and had the prestige of a warrior-king. Venizelos' proclamation deepened the rift between the two factions, which was now developing into mutual hatred. The royal press, especially the *Scrip*, began to demonise Venizelos, while Constantine was portrayed as a minion of the German Kaiser by the Venizelist press, especially the newspaper *Patris*. This factionalism would hold the Greek people and their politicians hostage for decades to come. Greek society had been poisoned.

2 Ploumidis, *I 'Sidira' Dekaetia*, p.126.

The Thessaloniki Front

Under the pressure of the war, the policy of neutrality advocated by King Constantine was having negative implications for Greece. As Venizelos had correctly assessed, the Allied forces were able to intervene in Greek territory without neutrality being an obstacle. During the Gallipoli campaign of 1915, British and French forces had occupied many islands in the Aegean and Ionian Seas and in October they imposed a naval blockade on Greece which caused serious food shortages.[3]

The most important military development on the Balkan Front was the coordinated invasion of Serbia by the Central Powers in September 1915. Germany and Austria-Hungary had attacked from the north and four days later Bulgaria from the east, so that Serbia was fighting on two fronts. It was obvious that it could not survive this double invasion.

The only way for the Allies to defend its ally Serbia was to organise a new line of defence in the southern Macedonian territories. So, the Allies ordered the French *Général* Sarrail,[4] who had recently withdrawn from Gallipoli, to establish himself in Thessaloniki to cover the south of Serbia from there. It was the first centre of the so-called Army of the East, which was to play a decisive role in the Great War over the next two years.

The Greek Army in Macedonia and Thrace was experiencing painful war developments. It was doomed to inaction at a time when the Bulgarians had attacked Serbia and were making regular raids on Greek targets. Greek officers had frequent reports of Bulgarian raids in the surrounding villages but because of their position of neutrality they could not react. Many were resentful and as early as December 1915 had begun to organise groups of officers who were determined not to let the situation deteriorate.[5] This was also helped by the fact that the balance of the warring factions had changed. After Bulgaria's alliance with the Central Powers, the Allies had again asked the Greek Government of Venizelos on 6 September 1915 for its participation in the war in return for substantial territorial compensation.[6] For the British and the French, the Balkan Front was in immediate need of 110,000 experienced Greek troops. Venizelos had accepted the proposal, but King Constantine's refusal resulted in the resignation of the government.

Constantine remained steadfast in his neutrality. Many have wondered about the reasons that led him to take this negative stance when national interests were at stake. He certainly harboured undivided admiration for German militarism and believed that

3 The Anglo-French Fleet had initially occupied Lemnos and then the islands of Syros and Milos, the port of Souda in Crete and all of the Ionian Islands.

4 The French *Général* Maurice Paul Emmanuel Sarrail was the first of the three French generals to head the Armée d'Orient (Army of the East). He was replaced in 1917 by *Général* Marie Louis Adolphe Guillaumat who was in turn also replaced shortly afterwards by François Franchet d'Espèrey.

5 Thanos Veremis, *Oi epemvaseis tou stratou stin elliniki politiki, 1916–1936,* p.49. P. Argyropoulos, former *Nomarch* of Thessaloniki, had information that the Allies would hand over the administration of the city to the Serbs effectively evicting the Greek authorities.

6 Ploumidis, *I 'Sidira' Dekaetia*, p.145. The Allies offered Greece the part of Thrace occupied by Bulgaria – the coastline up to Alexandroupolis and Cyprus.

the Germans would eventually win the war. The historian Spyridon Ploumidis refers to a revealing letter from the German Ambassador in Athens stating, 'Constantine expressly ordered Greece to remain neutral under any circumstances.'[7]

At the same time, there were vital interests for the royal family which, in Constantine's case, were of paramount importance. In any case, his obstinacy was to deprive him of the throne after two years, and with it the chance of a prominent place in Greek history. Indeed, Constantine, more than any other King of Greece, had the opportunity to fulfil with national distinction his role as a soldier-king in the Balkan Wars. In this he failed badly.

However, Greece's refusal to join the Army of Thessaloniki did not prevent the Allies from strengthening it considerably. By the end of October 1915, the army numbered more than 150,000 men and was still growing. In the meantime, the Bulgarians had taken revenge on the Serbs for their defeat in the Balkan War and had soon occupied all Serbian territory in Macedonia. *Général* Sarrail had attempted a counter-attack from the south but was forced to retreat to Thessaloniki. In April 1916 the defeated Serbian army with 115,000 men fled to Kerkyra (Corfu) to reorganise. Soon it was able to reinforce the Macedonian Front, which now numbered over 300,000 men. It was a multi-ethnic force with a great mixture of peoples from all over the world. The problem was general inertia which allowed the Bulgarian forces time to organise strong defensive lines. By early 1916 the Bulgarians had been reinforced by German units.[8] Everything was preparing the Eastern Front for the battles that were to follow.

The concerns of the Greek officers had increased with the advance of the Bulgarian Army and the collapse of Serbia. Initially the Bulgarians were under orders from the German staff not to breach the Greek border and their forces were in defensive positions. This was because the German Kaiser appeared to agree with King Constantine that he would respect the integrity of Greece. So when, in January 1916, the Bulgarians asked the Germans for permission to attack the Allies in Thessaloniki, they were not allowed to do so. Gradually, however, Bulgarian pressure for 'small-scale' interventions within Greek territory worked and the Germans gave in despite their reservations. Horrified, the Greek garrisons in Serres, Kavala and Drama watched as Bulgarian units occupied positions on the Greek-Bulgarian border. The worst thing was that the Greek Government did not seem to object.[9]

The development of the front in Macedonia meant that the war had now reached Greece. The policy of neutrality had evaporated as both factions put pressure on Athens to make concessions. The culmination of the pressure was the episode at Rupel, one of the fortresses protecting the Greek-Bulgarian border. On 3 May 1916, a Bulgarian Army attacked the Greek fort. But while the garrison was on the defensive, on 13 May

7 Ploumidis, *I 'Sidira' Dekaetia*, p.133. In German: '*Griechenland musse neutral bleiben unter allen Umstaenden'*.

8 It was the German 11th Army of the Mackensen Group, based in Skopje.

9 The Bulgarians occupied places where they had been defeated two years before, such as Doirani, Beles, Gevgeli and the banks of the Strimonas River. The Greek Government that did not react to the Bulgarian attack had as prime minister Stefanos Skouloudis who was appointed by King Constantine.

the Greek Government gave an order to the commander, *Tagmatarchis* I. Mavroudis, to surrender the fort to the German and Bulgarian forces without fighting![10] The surrender of Rupel caused a storm throughout Greece. The Venizelist press denounced it as an act of national treason. The fact was that it opened the passage to the River Strimonas (Struma) and soon the Bulgarian forces were masters of Eastern Macedonia. It was also a major blow to the Allied forces who found themselves surrounded to the east. After the surrender of Rupel, the British and French Governments decided to no longer tolerate the policies of King Constantine and his governments.

National Defence

The greatest shame of the surrender of Rupel without a fight was felt by the Greek officers and soldiers serving in Northern Greece. For the Greek Venizelist officers who had been active there since December 1915, the surrender of Rupel was the straw that broke the camel's back. Thus, on 17 August 1916, the military National Defence Movement was born.[11] Its first armed nucleus was from 400 men of the Cretan *gendarmerie*.[12] Many from the divisions of the Fourth Army Corps in Kavala that had fled to Thassos when the Bulgarians attacked, also joined the movement. After consultation with the French Général Sarrail, the units that had joined the National Defence Force (Amynites) were carried by British ships to Thessaloniki to join the Army of the East. Among them were 3,500 men late of the Fort Rupel garrison headed by the Amynitis *Syntagmatarchis* Nikolaos Christodoulou, who had escaped from German captivity.

The Amynites' core members also included many junior officers and non-commissioned officers who had joined the National Defence Force. Among them was Charalampos Seiradakis who had just been promoted to *anthypolochagos* in September 1916. Being one of the pioneers, albeit a less prominent one of the movement, he was happy that he was now able to fight under Greek colours for the Allies. Especially after his recent experience in France and at Gallipoli, he considered it a duty and an obvious next step in his military career. As an officer of the Army of the East he would make every effort to restore the confidence of the Anglo-French command in the Greek forces. It was no easy task after the hostile movements of Athens towards the Allies, but his experience

10 Much has been written about the surrender of Rupel to the Bulgarians on 13 May 1916. A large part of the garrison, 6,000 men under *Tagmatarchis* Hatzopoulos, surrendered to the German Army and was sent to the town of Gerlisch, in Germany, where it remained throughout the war.

11 Dimitris Malessis, *Itta, Thriamvos, Katastrophi. O Stratos sto Elliniko Kratos apo to 1898 eos to 1922* (Athens: Ekdoseis To Vima, 2022), pp.162–163, and Ploumidis, *I 'Sidira' Dekaetia*, p.169. The chairman of the National Defence Committee was *Syntagmatarchis* Ep. (Pamikos) Zymvrakakis and its members were Al. Zannas, Per. Argyropoulos, N. Pallis, P. Graikos and Th. Koutoupis. Among the pioneers were N. Gregoriadis, K. Angelakis, D. Digas, N. Manos, D. Paizis et.al.

12 The head of the Cretan *Gendarmerie* was *Syntagmatarchis* Ep. (Pamikos) Zymvrakakis. Its officers were Nikolaos Christodoulou, Konstantinos Mazarakis, Georgios Kondylis, Theodoros Pangalos and Dimitrios Kokkalas.

and partial knowledge of French were now invaluable assets. He soon took on the duties of liaison officer between the Greek National Defence staff and the Army of the East.

The key for the decision-makers of National Defence was to ensure that Eleftherios Venizelos was prepared to head the movement. Indeed, initially Venizelos was not convinced of its feasibility. Even at the last minute he was trying to change Greece's position in the war by political means. But the political confrontation had now developed into hatred. The monarchists held Venizelos responsible for any insult to the country, including the formation of the Army of the East.[13] The Venizelist press responded that Venizelos' policy served national interests, in contrast to the royalists' handing over of Fort Rupel to Greece's enemies without a fight. The mutual accusations added fuel to the fire and exacerbated the division.

But what made Venizelos change his mind and put himself at the head of National Defence was the capture of Kavala and the advance of the Bulgarians in Eastern Macedonia. Thus, on 14 August 1916 he had organised a massive rally in Athens where he blamed the palace for its destructive policy. Three days later he left for Chania, where he announced that he was forming a revolutionary government, the Government of the Triumvirate. It included two of Greece's most distinguished military men, *Navarchos* Pavlos Kountouriotis and *Stratigos* Panagiotis Danglis. The Minister of Foreign Affairs was Nikolaos Politis, and the Minister of Military Affairs was Emmanuel Zymvrakakis. On the same day, 17 August, Venizelos addressed a revolutionary declaration to the Greek people, stressing that the new government's aim was to save the nation and called on them to take up arms to expel the Bulgarians from the Macedonian territories.

From Chania the new government sailed directly to Thessaloniki, which was to be its base. Its primary concern was the organisation of a strong army to assist the Allies in an effective way. It was not an easy task, however, as many Greek officers were pro-royal or felt bound by their oath to the King. The core of the army of the National Defence Force consisted of the Serres Division – in which *Anthypolochagos* Seiradakis was serving – which was already in Thessaloniki. To these were soon added another 6,000 Cretan volunteers who formed the basis of the Cretan Division. The ranks of the Amynites were mainly swelled by refugees from the 'new lands' as thousands had fled to Thessaloniki from Asia Minor, persecuted by the Turks. Volunteers also came from Macedonia, Thrace and the Aegean and Ionian islands. But there was no corresponding enthusiasm from the regions of 'old Greece'. First, the Third Army Corps of Thessaloniki, headed by *Syntagmatarchis* Trikoupis, not only refused to participate in the movement, but reacted violently to the attempt to recruit them.[14] There were also several bloody incidents in Chalkidiki and Katerini when Amynites officers tried to recruit new reservists.[15]

13 The Army of the East was a strategic decision made jointly by Chiefs of Staff of Britain and France, following the failed Gallipoli Campaign. Cf Ploumidis, *I 'Sidira' Dekaetia*, p.144.

14 The mediation of the *Général* Sarrail prevented the bloodshed and consolidated the position of the Amynites. Most of the Third Army Corps returned to Athens.

15 Ploumidis, *I 'Sidira' Dekaetia*, p.172 and Malessis, *Itta, Thriamvos, Katastrophi.* p.176. It is reported that in September 1916 the Amynite officers Georgios Kondylis and Pavlis Gyparis used extreme violence to recruit new reservists for the National Defence Force.

Athens did everything it could to make it difficult to recruit new Amynites. One of the measures it took in September 1916 was to recall the reservists it had recruited a few months earlier. Although the decision to demobilise was intended to merely hinder their work, it ended up having another, much more unfortunate consequence. The 'retirees', or *epistratoi*, and those demobilised came together and regrouped into associations that formed the most vocal anti-Venizelist group, leading to an extremist movement against the Venizelists. They were responsible for attacks and beatings that intensified the atmosphere of 'gloom and terror' that had already prevailed in Athens for some time. It is no coincidence that the main instigator of the *epistratoi* was Ioannis Metaxas, one of King Constantine's most trusted, and hard-line, advisers.

Nevertheless, in a relatively short period of time and despite the difficulties, a quite remarkable military corps had been established in Thessaloniki. In less than seven months, in the spring of 1917, the army of the National Defence Force numbered about 60,000 men, of whom about 1,500 were officers. They were organised into three divisions, Serres, Archipelagos and Crete.

As most of the soldiers were new recruits, they were not called upon immediately to take part in the spring offensive of the Army of the East against German and Bulgarian positions. But the opportunity to participate in the fighting did not take long to present itself. On 1 May 1917, the Greek headquarters in Thessaloniki received an order to occupy the strategic hill of Raviné.[16] It would be a baptism of fire for the new Greek Army. On the evening before, Eleftherios Venizelos had visited, in the gorge of the Bergerie, the Serres Division that was to undertake the attack.[17] The testimony still exists of a fellow soldier and friend of Charalampos Seiradakis from the Battle of Raviné in which the two Cretans had taken part and had fought with passion. In a publication several years later, he mentions that on the eve of the attack Venizelos visited the camp and had encouraged the soldiers with warm patriotic words. 'My children, this is the most critical moment of the Greek nation and to you belongs the honour of saving the Fatherland.'[18] The Serres Division fought with heroism and after two assaults with bayonets drove the Bulgarians from the hill. The new army of the National Defence had proved themselves worthy in battle.

'Noemvriana' and the Overthrow of King Constantine

In November 1916 the conflict between the government of Athens and the National Defence in Thessaloniki had reached its heights. Two 'distinct' states were gradually taking shape, Athens and Thessaloniki. The French tried to intervene but King

16 Raviné Hill is located west of the Axios River, near Skra di Leggen, where the Greek Army would soon attempt their most important attack on the Macedonian Front.

17 The Serres Division was commanded by *Syntagmatarchis* N. Zafiriou and included the later well-known officers G. Kondylis and V. Dertilis, as well as Ch. Seiradakis.

18 From an open letter by *Stratiotis* Constantine Poratsakis, who participated with Charalampos Seiradakis in the Battle of Raviné, addressed to Sophocles Venizelos, then Prime Minister of Greece (1951). (Personal archive of Ch. Seiradakis)

Constantine's insistence on neutrality was now causing serious problems for the Allies. In mid-November the French *Amiral* Fournet asked Athens to align its policy with that of the Allies, otherwise they would impose their terms by force. Fournet carried out his threat on 18 November when an Allied force of 3,000 men landed at Piraeus and advanced towards Athens. The Greek First Corps put up resistance and fighting broke out in the city with hundreds of casualties on both sides, as well as among civilians. King Constantine, not expecting such a development, asked the Greek troops for an immediate ceasefire. But the situation had deteriorated, and the worst was yet to come.

What followed was one of the darkest days in the history of Athens. A mixed mob of armed pro-royalists surged against Venizelos' supporters. In an orgy of terror, led by the *epistratoi* group, they arrested and beat up those they considered Venizelists, accusing them of being responsible for the Allied attack on Athens and the naval blockade of the Allies.[19] Dozens of houses were looted. Hundreds of civilians were victims of this atrocity, which became known as the Noemvriana episode. *Amiral* Fournet then proceeded with a naval blockade of Athens, which exacerbated the city's food shortage and intensified the hatred of the royalists. The pogrom not only did not stop but reached its climax two weeks later.

Until then the riots were tolerated by the police and the army. But now the church was also called in, although it was also deeply divided. The metropolitans of 'old Greece' under the Archimandrite Theokletos of Athens had sided with King Constantine, while the metropolitans of 'new Greece' had sided with Venizelos. Thus, with the encouragement of the palace and the tacit support of the authorities, Archimandrite Theokletos organised an 'anathema' against, or official rejection of, Venizelos on 12 December 1916.[20] The day before, an invitation to a demonstration had been published in the press to 'all Greek people' to come to the Areos Field in the centre of Athens 'to anathematise the thrice-cursed traitor Venizelos.'[21] The participation of the people was significant and each demonstrator 'threw a stone' while at the same time pronouncing 'anathema' against Venizelos. It was a purely symbolic act, but it reflected the fanaticism and the intensity of the passions of the time.

The Government of Thessaloniki indignantly condemned the Athens pogrom. It accused the 'bloodthirsty' King Constantine, whom it now considered deposed from the throne, of being the perpetrator of the incidents. But the leaders of the National Defence began to be seriously troubled by the hatred of the royalists, which no longer directed its attacks against political opponents alone, but also against ordinary citizens who were considered Venizelists.

19 The slogan circulated by the conscripts during the attacks against the Venizelists is indicative: 'He who kills a Venizelist does not kill a man'.

20 See 'The Venizelos 'Anathema'' at https://www.sansimera.gr/articles/3. The commission that later took over investigating the complaints of the victims of the violence confirmed 35 murders, 922 illegal imprisonments, 503 cases of looting and 31 suspensions of newspapers.

21 More than 100,000 Athenians participated in the demonstration. The anathema reported among others: 'Against Eleftherios Venizelos, who imprisoned high priests and usurped the kingdom and the country, damn him'. https://www.sansimera.gr.

Measures should certainly have been taken to protect them from any further attacks by the *epistratoi* who had the protection, if not the active support, of the authorities. In particular, the involvement of the church was considered unacceptable and reminiscent of past dark times. The solutions provided by the National Defence to the problem of pro-royalist terrorism would have a direct impact on the military career of Charalampos Seiradakis, as he would soon find himself at the centre of repressive measures.

But the countdown to King Constantine's departure from Greece had begun. Five months later, in May 1917, the French ambassador in Athens delivered an ultimatum to Alexandros Zaimis (who had once again assumed the prime ministry) urgently demanding that Greece align itself with the policy of the Allies. Constantine felt that he could no longer remain on the throne, and so, on 1 June 1917, he left Greece, accompanied by the entire royal family, and went to Switzerland. The only one who remained in Athens, as the new occupier of the throne, was his youngest son Alexander, who now exercised the royal functions. Alexander preferred to follow the prudent policy of his grandfather, King George I, exercising his duties discreetly instead of following the interventionist policy of his father. His reign was to be short but would leave a positive impression.[22]

Eleven days after Constantine's departure, Eleftherios Venizelos returned to Athens as prime minister of the now united Greece. The country was in a state of war and his priority was to form a strong government and prevent any action that would jeopardise the war effort. It was Greece's last chance to assist the final Allied attack on the Macedonian Front. The first measures taken by Venizelos were to declare the country under siege and to reinstate the Parliament that had emerged from the elections of 31 May 1915 – the one that has since become known as the 'Parliament of Lazarus'.[23] The following month, on 2 July 1917, the military units of Athens and Thessaloniki were united, officially ending the policy of Greek neutrality by declaring war against the Central Powers.

It was inevitable after all that had preceded that there would be purges of members of the pro-royalist faction. In the following days many of Venizelos' political opponents were exiled, deported or placed under surveillance, while state officials were dismissed or suspended.[24] In the military sector in particular, the purges were drastic.[25] Although there was bound to be a desire for revenge on the part of the Venizelists, the persecutions were perhaps excessive. This was partly because some key posts in the ministries were taken over by hard-liner Venizelists who were taking uncontrolled initiatives,[26] but also partly because royal officials who remained in their posts continued to put obstacles in the way of the government's work. The war was entering a critical phase and Venizelos had to ensure that there were no undermining actions on the home front. Indeed, the home front was a boiling pot.

22 King Alexander publicly condemned those who had collaborated with the enemies of Greece and thus gradually broke away from Constantine's paternal influence.

23 Veremis, *Oi epemvaseis*. Venizelos had declared from the outset that the dissolution of the Parliament resulting from the elections of 31 May 1915 was unconstitutional.

24 Dimitrios Gounaris, Ion Dragoumis, Georgios Pezmazoglou, Konstantinos Eslin, Victor Dousmanis and Ioannis Metaxas were exiled to Corsica.

25 Although it is not known exactly how many officers were persecuted, the number must have exceeded 2,500, and the number of officers of the *gendarmerie* was similar.

26 Mainly *Syntagmatarchis* Theodoros Pangalos, who had taken over as Chief of Staff at the Ministry of Defence and had undertaken a radical reclassification of military personnel.

'The Epic of the Army of the East'[27]

Meanwhile the Allies' Army of the East, thanks to constant reinforcements, had grown to a strength of almost a million men, a surprisingly high number by the standards of the Macedonian Front. In April 1917, Commander-in-Chief *Général* Sarail had undertaken a new series of attacks in which Greek forces participated, but without significant gains. The Macedonian Front had turned into a quagmire, as had the Western Front on the Franco-German border. To reinvigorate the Army of the East, the Allied leadership replaced Sarail with *Général* Guillaumat as Commander-in-Chief;[28] Guillaumat remained in post until May 1918 and brought about significant improvements in the multi-ethnic Army of the East. In contrast, the Bulgarian troops, numbering some 700,000 men, a huge number for a relatively small state, were becoming depleted in strength and were facing problems of food and supplies.

After the new conscription carried out by the Venizelos Government in January 1918, the Greek Army in Thessaloniki increased in size significantly. In April it numbered a total of around 200,000 men grouped into 12 divisions, constituting the largest part of the Army of the East.[29] In May the new head of the Allied forces, *Général* Guillaumat, ordered the Greek forces to attack the fortress of Skra di Leggen in the prefecture of Kilkis, a fortified site near the Raviné hill which they had recently occupied.

It was a difficult operation as the Bulgarians had fortified the rugged mountainous area with machine guns, barbed wire and underground tunnels that made it nearly impregnable. The operation was undertaken by the Army Corps of National Defence, and on the eve of the battle, Prime Minister Venizelos had visited the Greek units from the Archipelagos, Serres and Crete Divisions to encourage them.[30] The Greek soldiers were ready for action.

27 English translation of the title of the book by the last commander-in-chief of the Army of the East, François Franchet d'Espèrey, *L'épopée de l'Armée d'Orient* (Paris: privately published, 1965). In this short work the French general refers to the battles that gave victory on the Macedonian Front in 1917–1918. On page 27 of the book is a photograph of *Ypolochagos* Charalampos Seiradakis.

28 Antonios Satrazanis, *Oi treis Galloi archistratigoi tis 'Stratias tis Anatolis' sti Thessaloniki: Maurice Paul Emmanuel Sarrail, Marie Louis Adolphe Guillaumat kai Louis Felix Marie Francois Franchet d'Esperey* (Thessaloniki: University Studio Press, 2015). Guillaumat had an organisational mind. Apart from reorganising the Army of the East, he improved the railway network and infrastructure in Thessaloniki. He supported the Greek element, especially the young children and refugees from Asia Minor, for whom he founded schools and organised free distribution of food.

29 To the three corps of the Greek Army (A, B and National Defence) with seven divisions, were added five more to make 12 in total. In the Army of the East there were also eight French divisions, six Serbian, four British and one Italian. See Malessis, *Itta, Thriamvos, Katastrophi.* p.155 and Ploumidis, *I 'Sidira' Dekaetia*, p.91.

30 The main burden was borne by the Archipelagos division with the support of the Crete and Serres divisions and French reserve divisions. *Ypolochagos* Charalampos Seiradakis and *Ypolochagos* Andreas Gyparakis served in the Serres and Crete divisions respectively. See Andreas Gyparakis, *Anamniseis apo ti Genia mou*, (Athens: privately published, 1978), p.83.

They proved it with the aggressive attacks that started on 16 May 1918.[31] The Bulgarian fortifications extended over 12km in length and between 1km and 2km in depth, and the Bulgarian fifth division put up a strong defence. However, the attacks of the Greek Army with bayonets under artillery cover were so impetuous that with successive attacks over three days they managed to overwhelm the Bulgarian defence and occupy the hill. They then repulsed the Bulgarian counter-attacks and consolidated their positions in Skra Hill. It was the most important Greek victory on the Macedonian Front – other Allied forces had failed in the same task a year earlier – and it demonstrated the strength of the Greek Army, with *Général* Guillaumat describing it as 'infantry of unparalleled bravery and impressive bravado.'[32]

The most important result of the battle was an increase in the Allies' confidence in the capabilities of the Greek Army. Politically, it was a validation of Eleftherios Venizelos' insistence on assisting the Allied forces, even at the last moment.[33] For the Greek armed forces, it was a tremendous boost to their morale and self-confidence.

In June 1918, French *Général* François Franchet d'Espèrey[34] replaced *Général* Guillaumat as the new commander-in-chief of the Army of the East. His orders were to break through the enemy defences and advance north towards Bucharest. Although the Allied forces had been reinforced with Greek and Serbian divisions, the mission was not easy as they had to face impregnable fortifications constructed during the previous years by German engineers.

On 5 September the divisions of Serres and Crete and two British Army corps launched an attack on the Bulgarian fortifications at Lake Doirani. The fighting was particularly bloody as the Bulgarian defences had large numbers of machine guns and dense lines of barbed wire. Both the Greeks and the British suffered heavy losses and were forced to retreat to defensive positions.[35] Over the same days, French and Serbian troops attacked the Bulgarian lines at Dobro Pole.[36] The fighting was tough, especially in Kaimaktsalan Hills, but the Allies overthrew the defences with a series of sudden, violent attacks and forced the Bulgarians to retreat to Skopje. In a final battle, the Crete Division together with British units managed to drive the Bulgarian forces from the Belles Heights. It was the final victories that sealed the fate of the Macedonian Front.

31 In total 14,546 Greek infantry with 287 guns took part in the attack. These included five infantry regiments, two of the Archipelagos Division under *Ypostratigos* D. Ioannou, two of the Crete Division under *Ypostratigos* P. Spiliadis and one of the Serres Division under *Ypostratigos* Ep. (Pamikos) Zymbrakakis. In the last was *Ypolochagos* Charalampos Seiradakis.

32 Ploumidis, *I 'Sidira' Dekaetia*, p.176. Casualties were 300 dead, and over 1,800 wounded.

33 The Greek victory in Skra was highly appreciated by the Allied command. *The Times* called it 'Greek Success' and 'Greek Troops' fine performance'. Ploumidis, *I 'Sidira' Dekaetia*, p.176.

34 D'Espèrey had been planning an attack on Germany from the Balkan Front since 1914. Four years later he was called upon to carry out his plan and did so successfully.

35 The Serres and Crete Divisions of the Greek Army and the 12th and 2nd Army Corps of the British Army each had around 3,000 dead – 6,000 in all.

36 Dopro Pole (literally: flat valley) is located on the northern border of Greece, on the road to Skopje.

The new French *Général*, d'Espèrey, had achieved a decisive victory, and the Bulgarian defeat was total and soon a rebellion overthrew King Ferdinand and the new government that took power called for an armistice. The policy that Eleftherios Venizelos had proposed from the outset of forming an alliance with the Allies had proved to be correct. Greece's participation in the final victory secured the country's northern borders and ensured it a place at the table of the victors.

11

Internal Front

'In a Security Battalion'[1]

As a young officer who had supported Eleftherios Venizelos from the time of the Cretan struggles, Charalampos Seiradakis had sided with the National Defence from the very first moment. The policy of neutrality in the Great War seemed incomprehensible to him. From a purely military point of view, he saw no overwhelming advantage in favour of one side or the other. Those who had had the experience of fighting in Lorraine, like himself, had witnessed that the French and Germans were roughly equal and that the much-vaunted German fighting ability was only comparable to that of the French. Proof of this was the stagnation on the Western Front.

On the other hand, he saw that there were important reasons for Greece to join forces with the Allies. The French officers who had reorganised the Greek Army had succeeded in their task, as had the British with the Greek Navy. Besides, Greece's enemies, the Turks and the Bulgarians, were fighting alongside the Germans who gave them free rein to attack the northern Greek border despite Greece's neutrality. Indeed, neutrality had proved to be a dead letter in practice, when Fort Rupel had surrendered without a fight, and the Bulgarians had occupied Kavala in May 1916. Seiradakis, and many others, held King Constantine and his entourage solely responsible for these events. Taking advantage of the mindless adoration of the common people and the loyalty of his officers, he had dragged Greece along a dangerous path, a path that had also brought national discord. The division that had erupted with the declaration of the Great War was flaring up day by day. In Athens, anyone claiming to be a Venizelist was in danger. Hundreds had suffered in the pogrom of November. Something had to be done immediately, but what?

The entire leadership of the National Defence was concerned with this issue while the war dragged on. The problem became more acute with the departure of King Constantine in June 1917 and the formation of Venizelos' Government of National Unity. The internal front had to be protected from extremist elements such as the *epistratoi* who were looking for an opportunity to cause trouble. Not a day went by without the pro-royalist

1 This is the indication given in the personnel file of Charalampos Seiradakis in the Greek Army archives for 1918.

press publishing libels against Prime Minister Venizelos. A new form of policing was needed. The *gendarmerie* was not a solution as it had declared itself to be pro-monarch and it would take time for that to change, if it changed at all. In the extreme conditions in Athens in 1917 a dynamic solution was needed. Some kind of militia that would enforce order. But who was willing to take on the idea?

When, after the Battle of Skra, Charalampos Seiradakis met with his old friend and comrade-in-arms Andreas Gyparakis in Thessaloniki, it was like a meeting from the old days. After their common experience at Lorraine and Gallipoli, they had fought together again at Skra and Doirani. But now the topic of conversation was different. Gyparakis was bringing him a new message from his uncle, *Lochagos* Pavlis Gyparis. He had received orders to form a militia corps with the mission to protect Athens from extremist elements and to enforce order while the war lasted. The state of siege declared by the new government of national unity would help to create a calmer atmosphere and in time settle things down. The removal into exile of the more fanatical pro-royalists was another factor which would logically help to bring about peace. Seiradakis was undecided. On the one hand, he understood the need to ease the tension in Athens and facilitate the prime minister's work. On the other hand, he was not prepared to abandon the Macedonian Front where he was still active. But the war was coming to an end, and he understood that it was important to maintain calm in Athens while the peace negotiations in Paris were going on. Seiradakis could not refuse.

By the end of 1918 he had been transferred to the seventh regiment of Athens and from there, early in the new year, he was transferred to the newly created 'security battalion', or independent company Gyparis, where he assumed the duties of adjutant.[2] His service in it was to last almost two years, until the elections of 1 November 1920 and it proved to be a difficult and often painful experience.

Internal Conflicts

The first thing that Seiradakis realised in Athens was that the domestic front was much more difficult than the foreign front. When the country is attacked from outside, the enemy is clear – and the soldier must fight. Things are not so clear inside the country: when citizens have different opinions, to what extent can the state resort to violence?

The response of the Gyparis security battalion was reasonable enough in the light of how the *epistratoi* had faced the Venizelists in the '*Noemvriana*' and afterwards. Although understandable, this approach was one of the reasons why the use of violence became the norm in maintaining order in Athens.

But there were other reasons as well. One was the continuing pro-royalist propaganda. Venizelist officers often had to resort to violent means to counter it. The officer

2 In March 1918, while the war was still going on, the Greek Parliament had passed a law for the establishment of a Security Battalion. Its purpose was to enforce order, preserve internal security and oppose the enemies of the nation. Initially one company was formed, then a second company was added. It belonged to the Athens Military Administration.

Alexandros Mazarakis mentions instances of distribution of pro-royalist pamphlets to the troops which spoke of the foreign policy of Venizelos as 'traitorous'. Some of them went so far as to state that 'behind the Bulgarians are our friends the Germans and our beloved King Constantine.'[3] The usually measured General Danglis confirms that there was systematic propaganda by pro-royalist officers, resulting in a proliferation of mutinies in the army. In February 1919 the Lamia garrison experienced a mutiny which was suppressed by a battalion of Cretans. Soon mutinies at the garrisons of Thebes, Atalanti and Kalavryta were also suppressed. Perhaps the most serious mutiny was in the third division where many of the *Evzones* deserted.

The Venizelists' way of dealing with all these incidents proved to be harsh. Similarly, aggressive measures had been taken in Chalkidiki by some hard-line 'Amynites' officers[4] against *epistratoi*, whom they considered responsible for violent incidents. The situations that had arisen in Katerini, in Naxos in the village of Apeiranthos, and even in Heraklion, Crete, where the anti-Venizelist Antonis Michelidakis had taken the lead, were bloody. In many cases the use of violence was excessive and with an obvious desire for revenge.

Many moderate Venizelists were uncomfortable about these incidents. The historian Dimitris Malessis quotes some remarks by writer Penelope Delta and politician Konstantinos Zavitsianos. The former had already noted two years earlier:

> Tuesday 4 July 1917 ... There were atrocities and vandalism then, now there are arbitrary acts and injustices. The monstrosities of November did not bother me as much, even though they touched me as closely as the present ones. Because today's events are upsetting my liberal feelings, whereas back then I knew them to be vandals and influenced by the German systems of persecution. And I want my people to be kinder.[5]

Additionally, Constantine Zavitsianos observed: 'And the unfortunate thing was that this miserable internal administration was invented by the Liberal Party, which for the most part had been praised for the internal administration that it practised from 1910 to 1915.'[6] The most critical comments against the security battalion came from Cretans. Particularly scathing against Gyparis and Seiradakis himself was the pro-royalist officer Tsontos Vardas, a Cretan, who had fled as soon as Venizelos became prime minister. The historian Thanos Veremis quotes from Tsontos' archives a characteristic text:

3 Malessis, *Itta, Thriamvos, Katastrophi,* p.197, referring to Mazarakis' 'Memoirs' (pp.234–236).

4 In this case it is the well-known *Lochagos* Georgios Kondylis. The measures provided that 'their houses would be demolished, their property confiscated, and their families deported'. But *Tagmatarchis* Pavlis Gyparis had also frequently used violence during the recruitment process of 'Amynites'. See Malessis, *Itta, Thriamvos, Katastrophi.* p.174.

5 Malessis, *Itta, Thriamvos, Katastrophi.* p.190, where he refers to Penelope Delta (p. 38), and immediately afterwards, to Konstantinos Zavitsianos.

6 Malessis, *Itta, Thriamvos, Katastrophi.* p.190, where he refers to Penelope Delta (p. 38), and immediately afterwards, to Konstantinos Zavitsianos.

'especially the Cretans [of the security battalion] are thugs and butchers, avoiding their military service, headed by Gyparis and a *anthypolochago* who followed him to France, Seiradakis (from Selino).'[7] Although Veremis has serious reservations about the objectivity of the accusation, this choleric attack confirms that the deep enmity that divided the royals and the Venizelists was intense even in Crete.

Thus, Seiradakis' service in the security battalion of Gyparis had begun badly. On the other hand, the security battalion was to provide some solution to the immediate problem of restoring order, at least for as long as the war and the Versailles Conference in Paris lasted. Indeed, the next two years saw relative calm in Athens. This was necessary as, from January 1919, Prime Minister Venizelos had been absent for long periods at Versailles, where the peace negotiations of the First World War were under way. But the calm that prevailed was only superficial. Not only had the division not subsided but, on the contrary, it had settled deep in the psyche of the Greeks.

Little is known about the individual activities of the Gyparis security battalion during these two years. Reports vary according to the political position of each one in the divided society of the time. Certainly, there were more critics because of the nature of the battalion's mission, and the personality of the tough-minded *Lochagos* Pavlis Gyparis who did not incline him to hesitate to impose strict measures. However, neither Seiradakis nor anyone else in the battalion hesitated to fulfil the mission. In Athens, no one any longer dared to commit violence with impunity.

From Versailles to Sèvres

The eleventh hour of 11 November 1918 marked the effective end of the First World War. The bloodshed in Europe and the whole world for four long years had finally come to an end. The dead in the war-torn countries numbered in the millions, and even more were left disabled. Hundreds of thousands had been displaced from their homes. The political balance in Europe had completely changed. Old monarchies had disappeared forever – the Hohenzollerns in Germany, the Habsburgs in Austria-Hungary, the Romanovs in Russia, and with them many dynasties in smaller countries. The material damage to infrastructure, agricultural and industrial production and livestock was incalculable. The human suffering of the millions of victims was tragic. All this had deepened the desire of the victors for revenge. Revanchism was pervasive in Versailles outside Paris when the representatives of 30 Allied countries gathered in early 1919 to decide on the terms to be imposed on the defeated countries. Among the victors, France, Great Britain, the United States and, to a lesser extent, Italy would play a leading role.

On the other hand, there were no representatives of the defeated countries of Germany, Austria-Hungary, the Ottoman Empire and Bulgaria, nor of Russia where the Bolsheviks had succeeded the Romanovs in power. Greece was represented at the conference by Prime Minister Eleftherios Venizelos, with the prestige of a political leader who had sided with the Allies from the outset and had been vindicated. His talent as a skilled

7 Veremis, *Oi epemvaseis*, pp.71–72.

mediator shone through in the negotiations, which lasted over six months. The persuasive skills he gradually acquired with the leaders of the Great Powers were decisive for the Greek claims in the unredeemable areas. Greece claimed Northern Epirus, Western and Eastern Thrace, the Dodecanese Islands with Kastellorizo, the islands of Imvros and Tenedos, and in Asia Minor a zone from the Propontis to Makri. The negotiations were going to be difficult for Greece. It would have to face not only the President of the United States with his '14 points' for self-determination and the creation of the League of Nations, but above all Italy, which had conflicting interests in Asia Minor and the Dodecanese, especially the island of Rhodes.[8]

At the very beginning of the negotiations a new issue arose. France and England requested the help of the Greek Army for a campaign against the Bolsheviks in Ukraine. Venizelos agreed with a view to strengthening his negotiating position at the conference. Indeed, two Greek divisions soon departed with 70,000 Allied troops for the Crimean Peninsula[9] and from there to the Donbass regions of South-Eastern Ukraine. The campaign lasted about five months but, in the ensuing fighting, the Allied troops had no luck. The Bolsheviks outnumbered them, and the Ukrainian winter decimated the Allied Army. Greece was probably harmed by its participation in the campaign as the victorious Bolsheviks turned against the Greek populations in southern Ukraine and Crimea. The Greek troops retreated to Romania where they regrouped before returning to Thessaloniki in April. From there they would depart on 27 April 1919 for the historic landing in Smyrna. The campaign in Asia Minor was about to begin.

Meanwhile, negotiations at Versailles continued. The first significant Greek success was the signing of the Treaty of Neuilly by which Bulgaria accepted the annexation of Western Thrace to Greece with a parallel exchange of populations.[10] Bulgaria had once again failed to gain an outlet in the Aegean Sea. Venizelos' next diplomatic success was the agreement with the Italian foreign minister on the Albanian issue.[11] Greece recognised Italy's sovereign role in the newly created Albanian state, while Italy recognised the rights of the Greeks in Northern Epirus and Western Thrace. Of greater importance, however, was the agreement on Asia Minor. On 22 April Greece had been authorised by the Allies to land troops in Smyrna to impose order and protect the Greek populations.[12] The 'Ionian Vision' seemed to be becoming a reality.[13]

8 One of American President Wilson's '14 Points' was opposition to the dismemberment of the Ottoman Empire.

9 The Greek force consisted of the First Army Corps with two divisions and a total strength of 23,500 men under the command of *Strategos* Constantine Nider and Alexander Othonaios as chief of staff. See also F. Dracontaidis (ed.) *Konstantinos X. Nider – Ekstrateia stin Oukrania, Ianouarios-Maios 1919* (Athens: Kedros, 2015).

10 Treaty of Neuilly-sur-Seine, 27 November 1919. It was beneficial to Greece as it validated the gains that Greece had made during the war. For Bulgaria, on the contrary, it was disastrous.

11 The Venizelos-Tittoni Pact of July 1919.

12 It was the First (the 'Iron') Division under *Syntagmatarchis* N. Zafiriou. Venizelos' message giving the green light for the campaign ended with the exclamation 'Long live the nation!'

13 The Greek campaign in Asia Minor is analysed in depth by Sir Michael Llewellyn-Smith in *The Ionian Vision: Greece in Asia Minor 1919–1922* (London, Hurst & Co, 1998.)

On 2 May, the first Greek troops set foot on the soil of Asia Minor amidst the general excitement of the Greeks in the region. Soon the two divisions that had campaigned in Ukraine came to reinforce the Greek forces. The lawyer Aristides Stergiadis was appointed high commissioner in Smyrna.

At the same time, two political trials were beginning in Athens, which were destined to exacerbate tempers even further. The first began on 14 May 1919 and concerned the 'Noemvriana' of 1916. The accused were the *epistratoi* who had armed the people and induced them to attack Venizelists in Athens, leading to the well-known bloody outcome.[14]

The second began on 14 October and concerned the surrender of Fort Rupel to the Bulgarian and German units in May 1916. The accused were the officers who had been on King Constantine's military staff.[15] As expected, the fanaticism during the trials had reached extreme proportions. Publications in the press added fuel to the fire and daily demonstrations in the centre of Athens threatened to get out of control. The security battalion was increasingly obliged to intervene with repressive measures, some of them too severe. Arrests and imprisonment in the battalion's detention centres in Pefkakia, in the Neapolis quarter,[16] became so frequent that the centre became a feared place for the monarchists.[17] The only positive thing was that with Gyparis's measures no other major incidents occurred and individual incidents were limited in scale.

The Vision of Ionia

From May 1919 and for the next three years the whole of the Hellenic world watched with anxiety the developments on the Asia Minor front. Although the campaign had begun with relatively good prospects, as time went by more difficulties arose. The timing of the Greek landing had been accelerated to catch up with the Italian troops that had landed in Antalya in Asia Minor over the same days. Italy had, from the start, disagreed with the Greek expansion into Smyrna and was fostering Turkish nationalism. In a devastated Turkey, a new leader had emerged who rejected the Ottoman Sultan and recruited groups of irregulars to resist the Greek expedition. Mustafa Kemal Atatürk was no stranger to the Greek Army. He was an officer in the Ottoman Army and had fought successfully

14 The defendants were: Konstantinos Eslin, Spyridon Mercouris, Georgios Pezmazoglou, Ioannis Sayas, K. Konstantopoulos, Anastasios Papoulas and I. Inglessis. The sentences imposed were, one death sentence (which was not carried out), imprisonment and one acquittal (Papoulas).

15 They were the well-known officers Victor Dousmanis, Ioannis Metaxas, Xenophon Stratigos and Athanasios Exadaktylos. Metaxas was sentenced to death (but had escaped to Italy) and Dousmanis to life imprisonment. The other two were acquitted.

16 The militiamen of the battalion were stationed at the Thon mansion in Ambelokipi.

17 'I asked some citizens who they were … and a venerable gentleman explained to me. 'These, my son, belong to the Gyparis battalion … he hangs and unhangs with just one word, he is a henchman of Venizelos.' Philippos D. Drakontaeidis (ed.), *Christos Karagiannis, I istoria enos stratioti: Mia synglonistiki maryria gia tis ellinikes ekstrateies (1918–1922)* (Athens, Kedros, 2013), p.164.

against the Allies at the battles on Gallipoli in 1915. He was a formidable opponent. Faced with the new danger, the Greek staff further reinforced its forces in Asia Minor, which by the end of 1919 had reached about 90,000 men. In February 1920, *Ypostratigos* Leonidas Paraskevopoulos took command of the Asia Minor Army.

However, the Greek Army was not allowed to take offensive actions without the approval of the Allies. Thus, it was forced into a standstill which allowed Atatürk to gradually reinforce his troops. Soon the Turkish persecution of the Greeks in Asia Minor was intensified, resulting in a constant flow of new refugees from inland to Smyrna. They were all in a desperate state and full of fear. But the persecutions resulted in the Great Powers finally giving the Greek Army approval for deep operations to limit Atatürk's attacks. Greek units with a successive series of victories had soon advanced into the Asia Minor hinterland as far as Prusa. But they had spread over a wide area and the supply lines began to show shortcomings.

In August 1920 the negotiations at Versailles were nearing their end. With the agreement of French Prime Minister Georges Clemenceau, British Prime Minister Lloyd-George and American President Woodrow Wilson, who was now in agreement with Venizelos, a treaty with the same name was signed in Sèvres outside Paris.[18] It was an impressive success for the Greek prime minister Venizelos and a complete vindication of his policy.

The Greek territory gained included Eastern Thrace as far as Chatalja, all the islands of the Eastern Aegean including Imbros and Tenedos and confirmed the occupation of the Greek Army of the greater Smyrna area for five years until its fate could be decided by a referendum. Similar concessions were made to France and Great Britain in the Middle Eastern territories, and to Italy in Antalya. It was the end of the Ottoman Empire, signed by Sultan Mehmet VI, although he was to be the last Sultan. Mustafa Kemal Atatürk from the depths of Asia Minor repudiated the treaty and the Sultan himself. He was now the new leader of the Turks and would fight for the independence of Turkey. The Greek uprising was now facing Turkish nationalism and a determined leader.

The Elections of 1 November 1920

After the success of Sèvres, which brought Greece closer to 'the five seas and two continents', Eleftherios Venizelos felt that the time had come to renew the popular mandate. It is not clear why he took this decision. Perhaps the fact that the Parliament, the so-called 'Parliament of Lazarus', had completed its mission, perhaps with the impending difficulties in Asia Minor a new mandate was needed, perhaps it was an opportunity to quell the passions of the long-standing national division, or perhaps it was something else. The fact is that his associates were alarmed. The Venizelists understood that the people were tired of the constant wars of the last eight years and that the opposition would go into the elections with the slogan 'enough wars'. The hatred of the monarchists against them

18 The Treaty of Sèvres was signed on 10 August 1920 between the victors of the War and representatives of Sultan Mehmet VI of the Ottoman Empire.

was limitless and manifested itself at every opportunity. The violence of the extreme Venizelists had contributed to this. It was by no means obvious that Venizelos would win the elections. After all, the campaign in Asia Minor was in dire need of the prime minister who had envisioned and implemented it. The Great Powers trusted him. No one else. It was not the time for electoral experiments.

But Eleftherios Venizelos thought differently. He had confidence in the democratic and patriotic instincts of the Greek people. For him, Greek society could not ignore the fact that the Treaty of Sèvres was the vindication of the struggles and sacrifices of the previous years. National issues were above political factions. Besides, the elections would also involve the populations of the 'New Lands', who were clearly in favour of Venizelos. The elections were set to take place on 25 October 1920.

In the end, the road to the elections proved to be anything but smooth. Just two days after the signing of the Treaty of Sèvres, and as Venizelos was preparing to board the train for his return to Greece at Lyon train station in Paris, an assassination attempt was made on him. Two pro-royalist officers were in hot pursuit and shot him, but fortunately he was only slightly wounded.[19] The outrage of the Venizelist world at the heinous attempt in Paris against their leader was fierce. How was it possible to shoot the prime minister now that he had achieved the greatest triumph in the country's history? And by Greek *officers*? None of the Venizelists, even moderates such as business magnate Emmanuel Benakis, were prepared to let such a challenge go unanswered.

On the other side the monarchists seemed delighted. Hatred, but above all envy of the success of their sworn enemy had so blinded Venizelos' opponents that they would rather see him dead than triumphant in Athens. This infuriated the Venizelists still more. Thus, one can easily imagine the atmosphere that prevailed at the headquarters of the security battalion of Gyparis. If they had overseen the protection of the prime minister in France, no one would have dared to attack him. They had to make sure that when Venizelos arrived in Athens there would be no excesses. So from the next day they increased their patrols and controlled all the roads with roadblocks waiting for the arrival of the prime minister. In the heat of the electoral campaign and with the precedent of the assassination attempt, an atmosphere of terror had begun to prevail in Athens. No one was allowed to move around without a permit and those who dared to do so risked their lives. The monarchists and especially those well-known names in government were the primary targets.

One of them, Ion Dragoumis, was a particular type of aristocratic intellectual.[20] He had had a brilliant education and a successful diplomatic career abroad in cities with

19 The attempted assassination of Venizelos in Paris was carried out by two pro-royalist officers, *Anthypaspistis* Georgios Kyriakis and *Anthypaspistis* Apostolos Tserepis. Both were dismissed from the army.

20 Born into a family of politicians, Ion Dragoumis (1878–1920) studied law, served as a diplomat and fought in the Macedonian struggle. After the Young Turk movement in 1908 he supported the idea of a Balkan confederation, an untimely view in an era of nationalism. Initially he collaborated with El. Venizelos but soon turned against him. After the 1920 elections that Venizelos lost, and Venizelos' murder attempt, Dragoumis was arrested and executed by the security battalion. A marble column was erected in his memory at Ilisia in central Athens.

Greek communities. He had proven his patriotism during the Macedonian struggle. However, his views on the future of Hellenism echoed romantic ideas that were at odds with the aggressive nationalism of the twentieth century.

His support for King Constantine was a red rag to the Venizelists. Two days after the attempt against Venizelos, Dragoumis decided to move from Kifissia to the centre of Athens. On the way he was stopped by the security battalion blockades near the centre of Athens. No one there knew what to do with him. The instructions they asked for and received were vague. Some sought revenge and others told them to let him go. In such tense situations, extremists usually prevail. And so it was in the tragic case of Ion Dragoumis. He was taken to the side of the street and summarily executed. It was a cold-blooded murder.[21]

Violence breeds more violence. The gruesome murder of Ion Dragoumis caused a wave of emotion in Greece. It also became a symbol of the monarchist forces in the upcoming elections, who exploited it to portray the Venizelists as a barbaric faction. No other single event had done as much damage to the Venizelist camp as this one. More than any other event it destroyed the reputation of the 'Gyparians' who had by then undertaken the difficult task of maintaining order in a highly divided society. Their role had been indelibly tarnished. Ironically, the battalion was about to be disbanded at that time and, had it not been for Dragoumis' death, the reputation it left behind would have been different.

But these two extreme incidents – the murderous attempt on Venizelos and the execution of Dragoumis – would not be the last tragic acts before the elections. In the last three years the young King Alexander, who had replaced his father on the throne, had shown rare political maturity. At a turbulent time when divided Greek society was on the move in Asia Minor while crucial negotiations were taking place in Paris, he had remained sober and kept out of party infighting. But what endeared him to the people, apart from his youthful appearance, was his love affair with the young Aspasia Manou, whom he intended to marry. Although his planned marriage to the beautiful Greek girl, who came from a simpler background than Alexander, had the government's approval, it had nevertheless caused the disgust of his father Constantine, who believed that Alexander had fallen victim to the machinations of Greek politics. If Constantine had intended to return to the throne, he was right to be concerned as he had information that his young son was comfortable in the exercise of his royal duties and intended to continue them. Although he was constantly sending his son instructions from Switzerland, it seems that Alexander had decided to follow his own line. His determination was evident when on 14 September 1920 he attended the *Epinikeia* with Prime Minister Venizelos. It was a magnificent event commemorating the national wars at the Panathenaic Stadium in Athens in the aftermath of the Treaty of Sèvres. But it was also the King's swan song.

21 The responsibility of *Lochagos* Pavlis Gyparis in the murder of Dragoumis was never clarified. Gyparakis, *Anamniseis*, p.346, says that Gyparis could not have given the order for the execution because of the personal bond that had developed between all Macedonian fighters above political ideologies.

An unexpected and tragic event was about to overturn all that. In an attempt to prevent his beloved dog from attacking a monkey in the royal garden of Tatoi, the frightened animal bit King Alexander and his wound became infected.[22] Alexander had a strong constitution and endured for many days. Eventually, however, he succumbed to the wound and died of septicaemia on 12 October 1920. It was two weeks before the election. Alexander's death was to have disastrous consequences for the country.[23] *Navarchos* Pavlos Kountouriotis was appointed regent, and the elections were postponed for two weeks. They were finally set for 1 November 1920. The assassination attempt against Venizelos, the killing of Ion Dragoumis and the unexpected death of the young King Alexander, all would play a decisive role in the outcome.

In the elections the Venizelist party was defeated. The royalist party United Opposition, led by Dimitrios Gounaris, although it received fewer votes overall, won a large majority in the new Parliament.[24] Venizelos himself, who a few months earlier had been proclaimed by the Parliament 'a worthy benefactor of Greece and saviour of the country', was not even elected as a Member of Parliament and, disappointed, he fled into self-exile in Paris. Dimitrios Rallis became the new prime minister. It was no surprise that the first decision of the new government was to hold a referendum on the return of King Constantine. As expected, the result was in favour of royal restoration, and Constantine returned in triumph on 8 December 1920. It was the end of an era.

In The Wake of the Political Upheaval

A picture of Athens a few days before the elections of 1 November 1920, is available from an unexpected source. The soldier Christos Karagiannis was one of the heroic warriors who had taken part in the fierce battles of Asia Minor and had miraculously survived. His diary has been preserved and offers us valuable information. In August 1920 his unit had fallen into a Turkish ambush, and he was the only one to survive.

The headquarters sent him back with orders to report to the Gyparis security battalion. The description of the uncompromising Karagiannis is indicative of the tense atmosphere in the battalion and the fanaticism of the people on the eve of the elections. Although Karagiannis had escaped the hardships of the war, the situation he faced in the battalion caused him an unprecedented level of stress.

The same charged atmosphere must have been felt by everyone around him. The war of nerves became increasingly intense until the election results were announced. When the defeat of the Liberal Party became known, it was as if the Gyparis security battalion no longer existed. As Karagiannis notes: 'a large crowd with flags in their hands and with

22 There are many versions of King Alexander's tragic accident with the two animals that led to his death. Seiradakis, who witnessed the events up close at the time, was of the opinion that it was not the monkey, and the unfortunate King had been poisoned.

23 As was the death of his grandfather, King George I, eight years earlier.

24 The United Opposition received 368,678 votes (49.36 percent) with 251 seats, while the Liberal Party received 375,803 votes (50.31 percent) with only 118 seats. The disproportion of votes and seats was a result of the peculiar electoral system.

images of the King [Constantine] and of Gounaris cut off our march. Athens had become a front line – from all over the place we could hear gunshots.'[25]

In this atmosphere those who served in the battalion were obliged to leave immediately. In November 1920, Charalampos Seiradakis, who had in the meantime been promoted to *ypolochagos*, left for the 20th regiment in Comotini, Northern Greece. From this time, he disappeared without a trace for about two years. The march sheet states that he was 'placed on leave for political reasons'. He must have continued further east to find military units in Thrace or Propontis, on the way to the Asia Minor front.[26] He was probably in contact with Venizelist officers he knew who had fled to Constantinople in an attempt to re-establish the 'National Defence'.[27] But he failed to reach the Greek Army. It seems that he had been arrested and ended up as a prisoner for political reasons. For how long is also unknown. He must have been going through a bad phase in his life. As the last choices he had made had cost him dearly, Seiradakis had decided to change many things in his life. But for this he would have to wait until the end of the campaign in Asia Minor, which proved disastrous for Greece. In 1922 Seiradakis was already 36 years old.

* * *

The return of King Constantine to Greece did not bode well for the country. Abroad, the balance of power was changing rapidly. For the victors of the First World War, the British and French, Constantine was the Germanophile King who had caused them a myriad of difficulties until they forced him to give up the throne.

The French in particular could not forget the dozens of dead during the 1916 attack on Athens that ended in the bloody 'Noemvriana'. Although they had made it clear to the politicians of the royal camp that with Constantine as King, they should not expect support for the implementation of the Treaty of Sèvres, those politicians had preferred to ignore them.[28] Now the new Prime Minister Rallis's priority was no longer the 'small but honourable Greece' that would end the campaign in Asia Minor, but the implementation of the Great Greece of the Treaty of Sèvres that his predecessor Eleftherios Venizelos had achieved. But the balance had changed, and Greek interests no longer had the same appeal to the Allies. In one view, 'the new political leadership gave the three Allied powers the pretext they were looking for to abandon Greece diplomatically.'[29] The Italians had objected to the Greek campaign from the outset, and now the French

25 Drakontaeidis, *Christos Karagiannis*, pp.163–171.

26 At that time *Syntagmatarchis* Al. Mazarakis Ainian, known to Seiradakis, had undertaken operations in Raidestos in Eastern Thrace, against Adrianople and in the Evros Valley.

27 At the head of the group of about 150 Venizelist officers in Constantinople was *Strategos* Ioannou. See Malessis, *Itta, Thriamvos, Katastrophi.*, p.82.

28 Giorgos Mavrogordatos, *1915, O Ethnikos Dichasmos* (Athens, Patakis, 2015), p.141. 'In the eyes of the Allies (France, Great Britain, Italy), the restoration of Constantine to the throne would cause a deterioration of their relations with Greece and release them from any commitment'.

29 Ploumidis, *I 'Sidira' Dekaetia*, p.289.

had also begun to change their policy.[30] The British, although they continued to support Greece, clearly did not trust the new Greek Government. Soviet Russia was also now actively supporting Kemal Atatürk's army.

Inside, the situation was mixed. On the one hand, the new Rallis government began radical purges in the public administration and those who had been favoured by the previous regime soon lost their positions. Conversely, those who had been discharged from the army soon returned, resulting in a rush to military ranks. On the other hand, the needs of the campaign in Asia Minor prevented the retirement of most of the Venizelist officers who remained in their posts at the front. An exception was made for some senior Venizelist officers.[31] In command of the Asia Minor Army, *Ypostratigos* Anastasios Papoulas replaced Leonidas Paraskevopoulos. In 1921 the Greek Army in Asia Minor numbered more than 200,000 men and was the most numerous the Greek state had ever assembled. The fighting in the Asia Minor hinterland continued and the Greek Army pursued Kemal Atatürk's Turkish Army into increasingly remote locations. In this sense, both space and time were working against him.

30 Ploumidis, *I 'Sidira' Dekaetia*, p.202. 'Greece did not live up to the confidence of the Powers. It disowned Venizelos, a 'great political leader' and restored to the throne Constantine, the brother of the wife of [Kaiser] William II ... who was considered a traitor and an enemy.' Ploumidis cites René Pinot, *L'avenir de l'entente Franco-Britannique,* as his source.

31 Veremis, *Oi epemvaseis*, p.82. The first to resign were *Strategoi* Othonaios, Hadjimichalis, Al. Mazarakis and A. Nider. Also out of the army were *Strategoi* Ioannou, the brothers Zymvrakakis and Mazarakis, Cheroulis, Pangalos and Colonels Kondylis, Zafeiriou and Sakellaropoulos.

12

After The 'Disaster'

The End of Ionia

In September 1922 the remnants of the Greek Army from Asia Minor were returning to Athens. Along with it, hundreds of thousands of refugees who had managed to escape the Turkish atrocities against the Greeks, were arriving. It was the end of the Greek campaign in Ionia, which had begun some three years earlier after the triumph of the Treaty of Sèvres and ended with the uprooting of Asia Minor Hellenism from its ancestral homes.

The Greek Army had fought heroically in the Asia Minor campaign and had emerged victorious in almost all battles with Kemal Atatürk's forces. In the months following the landing in Smyrna on 2 May 1919, it had gained significant victories, such as the Battle of Tumlu Bunar on 28–31 March 1921, and had advanced into the Asia Minor hinterland. On 29 May 1921, King Constantine had arrived in Smyrna with members of the government and his staff to encourage the Greek forces. But Constantine was now a shadow of his former self. His final decision was to advance the troops towards Kutachia with the aim of destroying the Turkish Army. On 4 July the Greek detachments, after fierce fighting, had captured Kutachia and had entered Eski Shehir. But the Turkish Army had retreated even further east, and they had to continue their pursuit. Thus began in August 1921 the campaign towards Ankara, which presented enormous difficulties. The distance from Smyrna to Ankara is about 600km and the Greek units had to cross the River Sangarios and especially the Salt desert which offered no cover. The supply of food and ammunition was problematic as the Turks controlled the only railway line. Nevertheless, the Greek Army crossed the desert and, in the decisive battle of Kale Grotto, again defeated Kemal Atatürk's army, which in the meantime had been reinforced and put up stiff resistance. But heavy losses, inadequate supplies and telecommunications, and fierce Turkish resistance had pushed the Greek Army to the limits of its capabilities.

The Greek Army stopped its advance in September 1921 at Afion Karahisar, Eastern Anatolia. It was to remain there, stuck in a state of complete inactivity, 300km away from Ankara, for almost a whole year as the military personnel had no clear idea how to continue the campaign. It was a disastrous wait in the depths of inhospitable Anatolia that shattered the morale of the Greek Army. At the same time, Kemal Atatürk was receiving significant reinforcements and preparing his counter-attack.[1] This manifested itself on 13 August 1922 with an attack on all fronts. The Greek forces had been deployed over too wide an area and the Turks managed to break through their defences. The army was forced to retreat. The constant battles, fighting and retreating, allowed thousands of Greeks from the hinterland to take refuge in Smyrna and temporarily escape the vengeful fury of the Turks. Several army units managed to reach the sea in a coordinated manner and were transferred to the Aegean islands. Others, however, made a disorderly retreat and some were even surrounded and forced to surrender.[2] By 3 September the fighting had ended with the defeat of the Greek Army. A few days earlier, on 27 August, the Turkish Army had entered Smyrna, where an orgy of terror against the Greek parts of town had begun, culminating in the burning of the city.

It was a disaster with incalculable consequences. However, as historian Spyridon Ploumidis notes, 'the campaign was not doomed to failure from the outset, as in May 1919 Turkey was defeated and by the spring of 1920 the Turks of Asia Minor were disarmed and disorganised. It was certainly not a reckless military campaign but a political necessity of the highest national importance.'[3] The defeat of the Greek Army was accelerated by a series of mistakes and above all by the disastrous consequences of the national division that isolated the country diplomatically and economically.

Revolution and Revenge

The defeat had provoked the indignation of the entire Greek world. The army's anger was directed mainly against the government, which they held primarily responsible for the defeat. The officers who had taken refuge in Chios[4] and the head of the army, Stylianos Gonatas, in Mytilene, organised a revolutionary movement and demanded the resignation of King Constantine, the formation of a new government and the reinforcement of the Thracian army.

On September 14, 1922, for the second time, King Constantine was forced to leave the country.[5] But the most immediate concern was the reinforcement of the Thracian front to strengthen the Greek position in the negotiations that were to follow. It was also a hopeless attempt to keep Eastern Thrace as Greek territory, although the Great Powers had forewarned the Greek delegation that this was extremely difficult. The armistice

1 Malessis, *Itta, Thriamvos, Katastrophi.* p.259. On 16 March 1921 Kemal Atatürk had signed a Treaty of Friendship and Cooperation with the Soviet Union which offered him access to considerable technical and economic assistance. He signed similar agreements in October, with France (the Franklin Bouillon Pact) and with Italy.

2 Such as the divisions under the command of *Ypostratigos* Nikolaos Trikoupis, near Ushak.

3 Ploumidis, *I 'Sidira' Dekaetia*, p.267.

4 The 'triumvirate' of the 1922 revolution were *Syntagmatarches* Nikolaos Plastiras and Stylianos Gonatas, and *Yponavarchos* Dimitrios Fokas.

5 This time his departure was final as he died soon afterwards, on 11 January 1923, of a heart attack, in Palermo, Sicily, at the age of 55. He was replaced on the throne by his son King George II.

signed at Moudania on 29 September 2022 marked the end of the three-year Asia Minor campaign. It also defined the borders of the two countries that would eventually cede Eastern Thrace to the Turks. As Venizelos telegraphed from Paris, 'it was a disaster beyond repair'.[6]

At the same time another tragedy was unfolding. Hundreds of thousands of refugees from Asia Minor were fleeing to Greece by whatever means they could find, trying to build a new life, having lost everything in their ancestral homes. Thus, in addition to the political and economic crisis that followed the military defeat, came the titanic task of housing and rehabilitating hundreds of thousands of refugees. By 1928 it is estimated that more than a million refugees had settled in Greece.[7] Most of them went to Thessaloniki and the wider region of Macedonia (550,000) and to Central Greece and Evia (280,000). One positive consequence of this internal migration on a massive scale was that the Greek population was now predominant in regions that had suffered in the recent past from persecution by Turks and Bulgarian nationalists.

But what mainly concerned the revolutionary government was the question of punishing those guilty of bringing about the Asia Minor catastrophe. Once again, opinions were divided between extremists and moderates.[8] In the end, the hard line prevailed as the extremist Theodoros Pangalos took charge of the investigative process.[9] The accused were eight politicians and military officers who had run the country for the past three years.[10] The charge was 'high treason' in the sense that they 'deliberately and intentionally ceded Greek territories to the enemy.'[11] Although the accused bear heavy responsibility, the trial served mainly political purposes. The military wanted to silence popular anger by blaming the politicians for the defeat. The trial was short. The summoning as a witness for the prosecution of *Archistratigos* Anastasios Papoulas, who had been commander-in-chief of the Greek Army in Asia Minor for a year and a half, while his successor, the accused *Archistratigos* Hatzanestis, had only been there for two and a half months, was about appearance and moral order. The sentences imposed by the military court were six death sentences and two life sentences. The execution of the 'six' took place in Goudi on 15 November 1922.[12] Greek society froze at the news of the executions. The national division was responsible for more loss of blood, with the result that the rift between the two factions deepened. The monarchist faction never forgot this and hungered to take revenge.

6 Malessis, *Itta, Thriamvos, Katastrophi.*, p.284.

7 In the 1928 census 1,069,957 refugees were registered, representing 17.2 percent of the country's population of 6,205,000 inhabitants.

8 Among the moderate Venizelists was *Strategos* Panagiotis Danglis (then leader of the Liberal Party), while among the intransigent ones were *Syntagmatarchis* Theodoros Pangalos and *Syntagmatarchis* Georgios Kondylis.

9 *Syntagmatarchis* Alexandros Othonaios was appointed as president of the military court.

10 Dimitrios Gounaris, Petros Protopapadakis, Georgios Baltatzis, Nikolaos Theotokis, Nikolaos Stratos, Georgios Hatzanestis, Michael Goudas and Xenophon Stratigos.

11 Veremis, *Oi epemvaseis*, p.121. Veremis adds that the accusation of deceit was not believed by any cool-headed observer.

12 For a detailed account of the trial see Thanasis Diamantopoulos, *I diki ton 'Exi'. Ethnikos dichasmos kai i korifosi tou. Exilasmos i dikastikos fonos*? (Athens, Patakis, 2022).

Back to the Troops

On 4 September the last units of the Third Army Corps had passed from Artaki in Asia Minor to Raidestos on the coast of the Sea of Marmara.[13] There they merged with other units to form the Evros Army which reinforced the Thracian front. It soon became a significant force with nine divisions commanded by experienced senior Venizelist officers.

Along with them, many junior officers were recalled to duty. Among them was Charalampos Seiradakis, who in October 1922 rejoined the army and was assigned to the *44o Sýntagma Pezikoú* in Thessaloniki, where he was to serve for the next three years.[14] Although he remained a staunch supporter of Venizelos, he had taken the decision not to get involved in military movements with political aspirations or in battalions of a repressive nature. He had found that many Venizelist officers were taking advantage of this troubled period to satisfy personal ambitions. The best known of these was *Syntagmatarchis* Theodoros Pangalos, who had begun to create a clique of loyal officers, distancing himself from the Venizelist faction. Some had also approached Seiradakis to participate in voluntary 'democratic battalions',[15] but his experience in the Gyparis battalion dissuaded him from getting involved again. Seiradakis believed that only Venizelos' return to the prime ministry could ensure a smooth parliamentary solution. For the time being, however, Venizelos was negotiating in Lausanne the new treaty that would determine Greece's future relations with Turkey. The restored government had asked him to save what he could from the catastrophe.

The Lausanne negotiations lasted over seven months. The final document signed on 24 July 1923 was the definitive settlement of relations between Greece and Turkey allowing both countries to concentrate on their internal problems.[16] Indeed, Greece was facing several challenges and their solution required political stability. Instead, the inter-war period was marked by the greatest number of military interventions ever. The first occurred three months after the signing of the Treaty of Lausanne by *Stratigos* Leonardopoulos and *Stratigos* Gargalides. It was a disparate movement of disaffected

13 The Third Army Corps with three divisions, the independent, the seventh and the tenth (formerly Archipelagos and Crete respectively) had retreated from Asia Minor in a coordinated manner under *Ypostratigos* Georgios Leonardopoulos.

14 Seiradakis notes: 'Recalled by the revolution of 1922 of N. Plastiras as soon as it was established, and from October 1922 assigned to the *44o Sýntagma Pezikoú* [44th Infantry Regiment].' (Charalampos Seiradakis Military Archive)

15 Ioannis V. Daskarolis, *Dimokratika Tagmata. Oi 'praitorianoi' tis B' Ellinikis Dimokratias, 1923–1926* (Athens, Ekdoseis Papazisi, 2019).

16 Turkey renounced all claims to the old territories of the Ottoman Empire and guaranteed the rights of minorities in Turkey. A compulsory population exchange was agreed (1,650,000 Christian Ottoman subjects were moved from Asia Minor and Eastern Thrace to Greece, and 670,000 Muslim Greek subjects from Greece to Turkey – the criterion was simply religion). Turkey recovered Eastern Thrace and the islands of Imbros and Tenedos. Although it agreed not to establish a naval base on the Aegean islands (Lemnos, Samothrace, Samos, Chios, Lesvos, Ikaria), Greece acquired the right to militarise the islands of Lemnos and Samothrace by the Treaty of Montreux in 1926, and Turkey the right to militarise the Straits and the islands of Imbros and Tenedos. (https://el.wikipedia.org/wiki)

pro-royalist officers, and it was easily suppressed by the strongmen in the government, resulting in the removal of many monarchists from the army.[17] The most extreme opponents of the monarchy considered King George II to be complicit in the movement and forced him to leave Greece. Admiral Paul Kountouriotis was again appointed regent. Thus, the regime issue once again became central in the elections that were called for 16 December 1923.

The elections were won by the Liberal Party and in January 1924 Eleftherios Venizelos returned to form a government. However, the counter-concerns about the regime issue poisoned his relations with his own party and Venizelos left in bitterness within a month. Finally, Alexandros Papanastasiou, a left-leaning Venizelist, formed a government and on 13 April 1924 he called a referendum on the regime question. The result was clearly against the monarchy which was immediately declared deposed. Greece was proclaimed a Republic.

Although the National Assembly was called upon to draw up the country's new charter, political instability continued.[18] Within two months, the Papanastasiou government resigned as his left-wing ideas caused heated debate among the moderate Venizelists. The military was even more strongly opposed to Papanastasiou as they could not forget the disruptive effect of 'communist ideas' on the army during the Asia Minor campaign. There followed a brief change of governments until Pangalos' coup finally came about.

Throughout this period a peculiar rivalry prevailed among the Venizelist army officers. Those who were not adherents of any faction or who wished to remain neutral were in a difficult position. The tension was exacerbated by the actions of the democratic republican battalions, which were constantly creating incidents. Although most of these were taking place in Athens, the military officers serving in Thessaloniki and other cities in Northern Greece were also affected by such activities.

* * *

In October 1923 Charalampos Seiradakis was promoted to *lochagos*. He had gained increased prestige and esteem in the highest military hierarchy; his promotion was accelerated by the gaps left in the officer corps by the last movement. Seiradakis had impressive combat experience to his credit and had demonstrated skills in managing people both on the Macedonian Front and during his recent service in Thessaloniki.[19] Thus, by June 1923 he had been assigned company command. The year 1924 had begun with good omens for him. But what was soon to change his life forever was Fani.

17 About 1,200 pro-royalist officers were removed from the army. Ioannis Metaxas, who had supported the Leonardopoulos-Gargalides movement, was forced to leave Greece.

18 The new constitution of the Greek republic came into force in 1927.

19 Evaluation document of 30 December 1923: 'Of general education, but of major professional value. He is qualified for battalion staff duties. Capable of campaigning ... performs company command duties effectively'. Signed by the Commander of the 44th Regiment, Emmanuel Tzanakakis. (Military archive of Charalampos Seiradakis)

Fani

Among the Chaniots living in Thessaloniki at the time was a cousin of *Lochagos* Seiradakis, whose name was Yannis Daountakis. He was married to Elisabeth Louka and lived in a large two-storey house in the centre of the town, on the parallel road of Tsimiski Street, next to the church of Acheropoiitos. Daountakis, his wife and their son lived on the ground floor and Elizabeth's mother, Helen, lived upstairs with her younger daughter Fani and the even younger son Kleon. Eleni still wore black because her husband had been killed by the Turks in an ambush during the Macedonian struggle. The three children had been orphaned from an early age. Regularly on Sundays, Seiradakis would go to see his cousin and catch up. On a rainy Sunday afternoon in March 1924, Seiradakis was on his way from Eptapyrgion Fortress uphill to the church to visit his cousin. It was blowing a strong wind that froze the bones as he went through the Upper Town. It was a picturesque neighbourhood down the hill that had been spared from the fire that had destroyed Thessaloniki in 1917 during the Great War. Seiradakis had been there and remembered the fire that burned for many days. Seven years later, Thessaloniki had changed significantly. The sea front had begun to be filled with impressive buildings and many of the projects proposed by French engineers to regenerate the city were underway. But Thessaloniki's most urgent need at that time was to provide shelter for the hundreds of thousands of refugees who had found refuge there, after being driven out of Asia Minor and the Pontus near the Black Sea. Everywhere you could see roughly constructed houses that had been built to house entire families.

That Sunday, Elizabeth's mother Helen had gone downstairs to have coffee with her daughter and son-in-law and to finally meet his cousin about whom she had heard so much. She did not see people very often and the young officer could tell them about the news from Athens since he was in the thick of things. After they had talked for a while, Helen excused herself to go to the kitchen to prepare coffee and offer it to them along with some tasty local pastries – mini baklava.

She had not realised that her other daughter, Fani, and little Kleon were peeking through the crack in the door. So as soon as Helen entered the living room with the coffees, the mischievous Kleon gave a shove to Fani who suddenly found herself in the middle of the living room, blushing with embarrassment. Their mother politely scolded the naughty Kleon and asked the two children to sit with them. The children obeyed, and they all started talking together.

Fani was a beautiful girl of 16 with pale skin and blue-green eyes. At the sight of her, Seiradakis felt as if he had been struck by lightning. At 38 years of age, he was not inexperienced with women, but Fani's beauty and bright glow impressed him. He tried not to look at her constantly while Daountakis told him news from Chania, but when he looked at her their eyes met. The young girl was certainly impressed by the sturdy young man's gentle manners. When they parted later their mutual attraction was clear for all to see.

For the next few days Seiradakis could not get Fani out of his mind. He tried to convince himself that 22 years' difference in age was too much, that she was too young for him. In vain. He felt that all the wars, the battle fronts, political rivalries and movements, everything else mattered less than his fascination for Fani. Suddenly he made up his mind. Fani was the woman of his life, and he was going to ask her to marry him. In a few days he visited his cousin's house again. He confessed to him his feelings for Fani, which of course Yiannis had already perceived, and he felt elated to hear that young Fani had felt the same way about him. She had taken a liking to the young officer who stood so straight and tall. So did her mother who felt that this man could be the protector of the family.

The next Sunday Charalampos Seiradakis went with flowers to the house of Helen Louka. His cousin Yiannis and his wife Elizabeth were present when he asked Mrs Helen for the hand of her daughter Fani. He loved her and wanted her permission to ask Fani to be his wife. Mrs Helen had no objection, but there was the question of age. At 16 Fani was still a minor and as she no longer had a father, she was under the protection of the Bishop of Thessaloniki who would have to give his approval for the marriage.[20] The bishop was a venerable old man with great influence in the city. *Lochagos* Seiradakis lost no time and the very next day he went, wearing his uniform, to the Despotate of Thessaloniki. The Bishop of Thessaloniki had been through a lot in his life. He had experienced persecutions, atrocities, constant wars.

He was known for his charitable works and had taken under his wing many orphans and underage girls, many of whom he had undertaken to endow. Seiradakis politely asked for his approval to marry the underage girl, Fani Louka. The bishop listened to him attentively. He tried to explain to the young *lochagos* that military obligations would keep him away from his family, and that Fani was still too young to bear such a burden. Besides, the difference of 22 years was too great. Would it not be better to wait until Fani was of age and think about it again when she was 18?

Seiradakis did not want to hear any of this. He had found the woman of his life and was in no mood for postponements and sermons. Nor could he wait another two years. When the bishop repeated his reservations, Seiradakis could not take it. He put his hand discreetly but clearly on the revolver he had cocked, and without any hesitation said to him:

> "Bishop, please listen to me. I love Fani and I want to take her as my wife."
>
> "But, my son, why don't you wait until she's grown up first?"
>
> "Your Grace, let me be quite clear [gently putting his hand on the gun] I ask you to marry us right now, otherwise there could be trouble..."

The Bishop of Thessaloniki could not refuse such a convincing argument. He had experience of military men, and the appearance of the battle-hardened officer before him showed that he meant what he said. He had no way to convince him to back down. So he agreed, telling him:

20 The incident with the Bishop of Thessaloniki was told to the writer by Seiradakis' younger daughter, Helen-Ellas (Lilly), who knew the story from Fani's brother, Kleon Loukas

"Let me tell you something, *Lochagos* Seiradakis. If you love her, you can marry her. I will marry you myself. But I want you to give me your word of military honour that you will respect and protect her and her family."

"You have it, Bishop! Fani is the woman of my life. Her family is now mine. As long as I live, no one will harm them."

Lochagos Charalampos Seiradakis kept his word to the bishop. His marriage to Fani Louka was a happy one and their love lasted until old age. Charalampos was madly in love with his wife and Fani with him. The wedding took place on April 19, 1924, in the church of Acheropoiitos, near the house where Fani lived. They were married by the bishop himself. The couple's best man was his cousin Yannis Daountakis and the wedding ceremony was attended by the commander, Emmanuel Tzanakakis, and many fellow officers. Although Seiradakis' parents were elderly and could not come to Thessaloniki, his brother Yiannis and three beloved cousins arrived with wedding gifts from Livadas and Koustogerako.

The couple soon moved to a comfortable house near Fani's family. Suddenly Charalampos Seiradakis' life had taken a new turn. Despite their age difference, the couple's chemistry was good, and their life was going well. It was not long before they had their first daughter who took the name of Charalampos' mother – Eugenia. She was born on 17 October 1925 in Athens as Seiradakis had taken over the duties of liaison between the garrisons of Thessaloniki and Athens during that restless period. In early 1926 Fani was pregnant again. The couple had returned to Thessaloniki where their second daughter, Maria, was born in November 1926. It would be another six years before their third daughter, Elizabeth, came into the world in 1932, and another two years before the fourth, Helen-Ellas, was born. Seiradakis may not have had the son he most likely desired, but he was triumphantly happy with his daughters and especially his wife Fani. Their life would be a constant adventure, but the couple's love would last a lifetime.

13

Movement of 1935

Pangalos Dictatorship

Three years after the Asia Minor catastrophe, political instability continued as the members of the Venizelist Liberal Party were unable to find common ground. At the same time, in the army, some officers made no secret of their ambition to play a leading role in political developments.[1] After the referendum of 13 April 1924, which established the Republic, governments were short-lived and proved unable to impose themselves on the military.[2] The situation was exploited by *Syntagmatarchis* Theodoros Pangalos, who seized power in a coup d'état on 25 June 1925. It was first manifested in the Third Army Corps with the support of the democratic battalion of Thessaloniki,[3] extended to the navy and prevailed in Athens, mainly because of the reluctance of the political leaders to react. Subsequently, and in general confusion, the Parliament gave him a vote of confidence and thus his government gained legitimacy. However, it did not take long for Pangalos to show his true intentions when, at the beginning of the new year, he gave himself total power and became President of the Republic.

The worst thing was that all these conspiracies had eroded the mentality of the officer corps. It was now common for many to change sides when circumstances changed. So it was with the Pangalos case. Many officers who had supported him to occupy the outpost led by the republican battalions, turned against him and supported his rival *Syntagmatarchis* Georgios Kondylis. With the complicity, or at least the acquiescence, of the politicians of the democratic faction, Kondylis arrested Pangalos on 22 August 1926 and handed over power to the politicians. Although Kondylis concealed his ambitions for

1 Mainly *Syntagmatarchis* Theodoros Pangalos who controlled the democratic battalions in Athens and Thessaloniki, and *Syntagmatarchis* Georgios Kondylis who had organised groups in the countryside under the name of *Oi 'Kynigoi'* ('Hunters').

2 Between 1924 and 1925 four separate governments had been formed under Venizelist politicians Kafantaris, Papanastasiou, Sofoulis and Michalakopoulos.

3 The officers Bakirtzis and Karakoufas of the democratic battalions took advantage of the absence of the commander of the Third Army Corps, *Antistratigos* Al. Othonaios (Daskarolis, *Dimokratika Tagmata*). The commander of the 44th regiment, *Strategos* Emm. Tzanakakis and the officers under his command, such as *Lochagos* Charalampos Seiradakis, were not involved in the Pangalos movement.

power for a while, he secretly intended to claim it at a more favourable juncture. For the time being, new elections were called for 7 November.

Concerning the professional consciousness of the military of that period, the historian Thanos Veremis makes an interesting observation.[4] The first change in the ethos of the military was linked to the Goudi Movement. Before 1909, officers came from the elite of the ruling class and, together with strict dedication to their duties, had close ties to the palace. After Goudi several 'politicised petty-bourgeois officers from the reserves' had swollen the ranks of the army. A typical case of the new category was *Lochagos* Seiradakis, who joined the army during the Balkan Wars and after participating in the campaigns of Lorraine and Gallipoli was made permanent in the army as a 'permanent ex-reserve'. Most of this new generation of officers – let alone Cretans like Seiradakis – supported Eleftherios Venizelos and, as 'Amynites' fought with the Allies on the Macedonian front. They had strict professional conscientiousness and Venizelos' success gave them prestige. But after 1922 a difference in the behaviour of many of them appeared. The more ambitious of those who had been side-lined in the years 1920–1922 formed a mentality of 'nineteenth century mobsters'[5] which, combined with guild interests, sought to control power. Conspiracies and intrigues in the army became endemic. The politicians of the Venizelist party were not without responsibility for this development as they tolerated, and not infrequently encouraged, the interventions of the army, expecting the military to take difficult decisions that they themselves were unable to make. All of this this added to political instability with frequent coup attempts and deportations.

Return of Venizelos

The result of the elections of 7 November 1926 was promising for the political life of the country. The new party affiliations allowed the formation of a universal government with the evergreen Alexandros Zaimis as prime minister and ministers from all parties.[6] It would have been able to accomplish important work if it had not been hindered by the thorny issue of balance in the army. The Popular Party, representing the monarchists, had called for the reinstatement of many royalist officers, who had been dismissed in the 1923 coup.[7] The liberals did not want to upset the existing balance that was favourable to them and argued that officers should be judged based on participation or not in insurrectionary movements. Thus, despite the government's efforts to find an interim solution, the issue of restitution was the beginning of new antagonisms.

4 Veremis, *Oi epemvaseis*, p.179.

5 Veremis, *Oi epemvaseis*, p.180.

6 Ministers: Interior: P. Tsaldaris, Foreign Affairs: G. Michalakopoulos, Finance: G. Kafantaris, Defence: Al. Mazarakis, Transport: I. Metaxas, Agriculture: Al. Papanastasiou.

7 It was the failed movement of *Stratigos* Leonardopoulos and *Stratigos* Gargalides that had resulted in the dismissal of many officers, most of them monarchists.

The Third Army Corps in Thessaloniki had often found itself in the vortex of inter-party conflicts. The commander, Alexander Othonaios, was one of the key Venizelist cadre and many senior officers, such as Emmanuel Tzanakakis, to whom Seiradakis reported, were old 'Amynites'. The democratic battalion of Thessaloniki had taken part in the Pangalos coup in June 1925 with officers loyal to him, although without the participation of Othonaios and Tzanakakis. Seiradakis was at that time serving in the Thessaloniki garrison and his mission to the Athens garrison in the second half of 1925 may have been aimed at averting the coup – but without success.[8] In any case, the military hierarchy must have appreciated his management and intelligence skills to entrust him with the organisation of the Thessaloniki garrison at a troubled time. As the 1927 evaluation states, 'despite the scarce means available to the service, he built it up to provide valuable assistance to the work of the garrison.'[9] At the same time, he was assigned to teach technical subjects at the Infantry Application School. He combined rigour with a sense of courtesy that was well received by the young officers. The commander of the School reported that his performance 'contributed greatly to the moral education of the students and generally cultivated the military spirit in them.'[10] Perhaps Seiradakis' greatest asset was the combat experience he had gained on the battlefield. On the other hand, his weak point was his lack of tactical training in a military school, which he was constantly improving through training programmes. Although Seiradakis belonged to the Venizelist officer group, he avoided being exposed at the present juncture to intra-Venizelist quarrels. His experience 10 years before had taught him much; thus, he concentrated on his military duties, and as a result was soon promoted to the rank of *Tagmatarchis*.[11] Seiradakis was now a distinguished officer of the Greek Army. He had come a long way since he had left Livadas to fight in the Balkan Wars.

After the fall of Pangalos and the elections of 7 November 1926, the collusion and conspiracies between officers continued unabated. Especially the question of the reinstatement of monarchical officers had made working in the military corps like walking on quicksand. The victims of the controversy were not long in coming to light, and among the first was *Antistratigos* Othonaios who was quickly removed from command of the

8 For the second half of 1925 the evaluation document of Seiradakis states: 'Responded well to the posts Adjutant of the Guard as well as Information Officer'. Signed: *Frourarchos* K. Tzavellas, Thessaloniki, 18 February 1926. (Personal file of Ch. Seiradakis from the Greek Army Archives)

9 Evaluation document 30 July 1927, *Frourarchos* Emmanuel Tzanakakis. (Personal file of Ch. Seiradakis from the Greek Army Archives)

10 Report from the military school of Thessaloniki, 31 December 1930, Signed: *Syntagmatarchis* C. Poulos. (Personal file of Ch. Seiradakis from the Greek Army Archives)

11 Proposal for promotion to *Tagmatarchis*, 28 February 1932: Soldier by family tradition took part in the Allied war ... He is of sound and positive judgement and develops very good initiative. He is exceptionally genius in the duties of an intelligence officer, used very successfully by the Third Army Corps in matters of extreme delicacy and confidentiality. I therefore recommend him to be promoted to the higher grade by election. Signed: Thessaloniki, Commander C. Poulos. (Personnel file of Ch. Seiradakis in the Greek Army Archives)

Third Army Corps in Thessaloniki.[12] The coalition government was trying to maintain its authority along with balance in the army. Both proved particularly difficult in practice.

The confrontations in the committees that examined the reinstatement of officers continued when Eleftherios Venizelos returned to Greece on 20 April 1926. His return after three years of absence gave a new impetus to the Venizelist camp to overcome their differences. From Chania, Venizelos began intensive contacts with his colleagues in the Liberal Party and in the army. Although he had reservations about the effectiveness of the coalition government, he soon found himself wavering on the issue of reinstatement of army officers. Alexander Othonaios and Nikolaos Plastiras, both devoted Venizelists, disagreed radically on this issue and it was not the first time they competed for influence in the army, but also within the Liberal Party. In any case, in June 1927 the reintroduction of many royalist officers to the army was approved. It was to prove fatal for the future of the Venizelist camp. On the one hand, it brought back many experienced officers who had participated in political coups. On the other hand, it strengthened the royalist faction with officers who 'would in future constitute a core of pro-monarchism and anti-Venizelism within the army.'[13]

The return of Eleftherios Venizelos to political life led to new elections on 19 August 1928. The result was an overwhelming victory for his Liberal Party, which won 223 seats out of the total of 250. The electorate showed that people trusted Venizelos to end political instability and military interventions in the country. In this they were right. Venizelos' four-year term, 1928–1932, was the longest government of the inter-war period and at the same time the most productive in terms of modernisation of the country.

The decisions taken during these four years in almost all areas of administration proved decisive for the following decades.[14] However, towards the end of the four years, problems had begun to accumulate, mainly due to the international economic crash which soon affected the already meagre finances of the Greek state.

At home, at the end of 1932, there was again a sudden revival of the regime question. Venizelos himself was not blameless in this. He had thought that by drawing attention to the danger of a possible return of King George II he could rally the democratic world.

Plastiras Coup

Within the Venizelist camp oppositions with personal motives risked damaging the republicans. The elections of 25 September 1932 showed that rivalries within the Liberal

12 *Antistratigos* Alexander Othonaios was under suspicion and surveillance by the royals as he was the president of the military tribunal that sentenced the 'six' to death in 1922. His successor in the Third Army Corps was *Stratigos* Th. Manetas.

13 Veremis, *Oi epemvaseis*, p.190.

14 An example was the purchase of buildings in central locations in several capitals to use as the embassies and consulates of Greece. As a result, the country's diplomatic presence was upgraded. Large-scale infrastructure projects were carried out, hundreds of new schools opened, and the banking sector strengthened with the establishment of the Central Bank of Greece and the Agricultural Bank.

Party had deprived it of a self-reliant majority. Although it had gained two more seats than the royalist Popular Party of Panagis Tsaldaris, the decision of Venizelist politicians Georgios Kafantaris (15 seats) and Alexandros Papanastasiou (8 seats) to present splinter parties prevented the Liberal Party from forming a government. Thus, Tsaldaris' Popular Party formed a minority government after declaring that it accepted the republican regime. But his government only lasted two months before the country was forced to hold the new elections of 5 March 1933. The result for the Venizelists was a repeat of the disastrous election of 1 November 1920. Although the votes for two major parties were roughly tied, the electoral system gave a significant majority of seats to Tsaldaris' royalists. The Venizelist camp had been defeated.

All Venizelists were upset, but those who were most worried were the military. The new factor influencing the army was the conversion of Georgios Kondylis. He had now openly expressed his leadership ambitions, had renounced Venizelos and taken position in favour of Tsaldaris' Popular Party. The prospect that as Minister of Military affairs he intended to alter the composition of the army in favour of the monarchists was grim for the Venizelist officers. The one who reacted first was Nikolaos Plastiras. Despite the reservations of many fellow Venizelists, on 6 March 1933 he organised a coup against the Tsaldaris Government. In the morning of that day, it appeared that the coup would prevail, but as most Venizelist military officers did not support him, by evening he had abandoned the attempts.

The worst thing for him was that he handed over power to his implacable internal enemy Alexander Othonaios, who had temporarily taken over the government of the country. It was an unfortunate moment for the 'Black Rider' of the Asia Minor campaign who was forced to flee abroad. Although Venizelos had not approved of Plastiras's coup, he had intervened to ensure that a government of generals under Othonaios temporarily took power until the situation was clarified.

But with the Plastiras coup, the political situation had become more critical. Plastiras' fears that the return of the monarchical officers would change the balance in the army proved well founded. The officers who returned were fanatical royalists who pushed the situation to the extreme. In the tense atmosphere, a new assassination attempt was made against Venizelos. It was the evening of 6 June 1933 when he was returning with his wife Elena to Athens after a visit to the writer Penelope Delta in Kifissia, in the suburb of Maroussi, when a car with its lights off blocked Venizelos' car and began to chase them, shooting continuously. The escort car was immobilised, and a bodyguard was killed. The would-be assassins then continued the chase for at least half an hour. Fortunately, the skill of his driver, Ioannis Nikolaou, who managed to escape from the pursuers spared the lives of the Venizelos couple. Elena had been wounded by a bullet, fortunately only slightly, while Venizelos himself escaped with only minor injuries.[15]

The new dastardly attempt to assassinate Venizelos caused general revulsion. While memories of the assassination attempt in Paris 13 years earlier and the 'Noemvriana' were brought back to the Venizelists minds, many monarchists seemed to rejoice, as

15 'The second assassination attempt against Eleftherios Venizelos' https://www.sansimera.gr/articles/149

manifested in publications of the pro-royalist press.[16] The interrogations in the following days led to the arrest of the police chief, Ioannis Polychronopoulos, and two other policemen. The notorious bandit Karathanasis was also involved but remained at large. Although Prime Minister Panagis Tsaldaris had condemned the attempt from the beginning, moral involvement was established for two members of the Popular Party.[17]

Karathanasis was finally arrested on 25 October 1934 by Venizelist officers, all 'Amynites' members,[18] and handed over to the police, but again the trial was hopelessly delayed. When it began, two years later, important revelations were made, such as the fact that 2,000,000 drachmas had been allocated for the attempt by an unknown financier. However, the trial never ended. It was postponed indefinitely when the Venizelist coup of 1 March 1935 broke out. Eventually all the accused were acquitted.

Preparations for a New Coup

On 17 June 1933 Charalampos Seiradakis was transferred to the 41st Xanthi regiment.[19] He was now 47 years old and the previous decade in Thessaloniki had been the happiest and most successful in his life. Not that the political uncertainties and upheavals had disappeared, but he had an established position in the military hierarchy and the esteem of his superiors. His personal life was going happily. He had always been in love with Fani, their two daughters were grown and were now in primary school, and they had just had a third daughter. Seiradakis' transfer to Xanthi was politically motivated. It was a consequence of the electoral victory of the Popular Party which as soon as it formed a government began to change the balance of the army by removing from key positions the Venizelist officers. Seiradakis was one of the 800 or so who were transferred to secondary commands.[20] He had already reconsidered his original position of not participating in movements and was in close contact with other Venizelist officers about the coup that was being prepared.

The transfers were the work of the Minister of Military affairs of the Popular Party Georgios Kondylis and it was only the beginning of what was being prepared against the Venizelists. The transformation of Kondylis was complete and from a Venizelos supporter he had evolved into a pro-royalist and ruthless persecutor of Venizelists. He

16 On 8 June the newspaper *Elliniki,* an organ of Ioannis Metaxas, wrote in an editorial: The heroes of Kifissia Street, those whose names will be honoured by national history with golden letters, let us all imitate them, since the highest interests of the Fatherland demand it. To the threats of Venizelism, anti-Venizelism must respond with deeds of the wildest aggression … Giants of the anti-Venizelist people, rise and attack! And in your momentum let there be neither pity nor mercy for the crushing and annihilation of your opponents. https://www.sansimera.gr/articles/149.

17 Minister of the Interior Ioannis Rallis and the MP Petros Mavromichalis.

18 Among the officers who arrested him was Andreas Gyparakis (cf Gyparakis, *Anamniseis*, p.122).

19 March document 70309/6-5-1933 (Military Archive of Charalampos Seiradakis).

20 Veremis, *Oi epemvaseis*, p.206. Approximately 800 officers out of a total of about 5,000 were moved to secondary commands. Along with Seiradakis also moved to the 41st Xanthi regiment was *Syntagmatarchis* K. Ventiris, a prominent Venizelist.

had been informed that a Venizelist coup was in the making and was lying in wait for when it would manifest itself to decide what to do.

For its part the Venizelist camp was heating up, impatient to organise the coup, but as there was no coordination between them several conspiracies began to form at the same time. The first was the 'Democratic Defence', by senior officers who wanted to return to the army and were eager to act.[21] Their head was *Stratigos* Anastasios Papoulas.[22] At the same time, a second group of low-ranking Venizelist officers under the name 'Greek Military Organisation', had been conspiring since 1932.[23] In an attempt to coordinate these groups, on 3 July 1933 the Liberal Party appointed a three-member committee to head the organisation as guarantor of democracy.[24] However, all these Venizelist fractions had significant differences among themselves, and their coordination was minimal.

At the time Parliament was preoccupied with two issues. The first was another amendment of the military yearbook to further alter the balance in the army in favour of the royalists. The second was a new electoral law put forward by the Tsaldaris Government. The law was finally agreed to by a compromise between Venizelos and Tsaldaris. The leaders of the two major parties sensed that there was a risk of dictatorship and did their best to come to a compromise. But there was no agreement on the army issue. It was blocked by Kondylis and Metaxas who, despite their mutual hatred, prevented Tsaldaris from coming to terms with Venizelos as both aspired to a dictatorship. Metaxas had repeatedly attacked the parliamentary system in public.[25] As a result the army question remained an unresolved Gordian knot for the two major parties and society at large. Tsaldaris was thus under pressure from extreme elements in his party to reduce the influence of the Venizelists in the army. After the 1922 Asia Minor campaign Venizelist officers constituted the majority in the army and held important command posts.

In 1934, however, as prospects were turning against them, they were determined not to allow any further change in the status quo. The problem was that relations between various Venizelist groups were far from harmonious. Things got worse after the failed Plastiras' coup in 1933, which created antipathies among the Venizelist camp.[26] Notwithstanding these differences, the time to move was approaching. The final decisions for the Venizelist coup were taken on 26 February 1935.[27] The general command of

21 Veremis, *Oi epemvaseis*, p.208. The officers Zervas, Kolialexis, Spais, Diamesis and Koimisis are also mentioned. All were in contact with N. Plastiras who was outside of Greece

22 *Stratigos* Papoulas had renounced his royal beliefs after the Asia Minor Campaign where he served as commander-in-chief of the Greek Army. He now belonged to the Venizelist camp.

23 Veremis, *Oi epemvaseis*, p.216. The originators were officers Yannis Tsigantes, his brother Christodoulos (Lakis) Tsigantes, M. Kladakis, Skanavis, et al. *Synrtagmatarches* S. Sarafis, Sp. Georgoulis, P. Grigorakis, and *Tagmatarches* Sfetsios, Chondros and Psarros joined later.

24 It was composed of Zannas, Sarafis and Kolialexis. Later Gonatas replaced Zannas.

25 Veremis, *Oi epemvaseis*, p.236, n. 14.

26 Among those opposed to N. Plastiras was *Antisyntagmatachis* S. Sarafis who was close to A. Othonaios, an avowed opponent of Plastiras.

27 Veremis, *Oi epemvaseis*. The final meeting was attended by Venizelist officers Sarafis, Vlachos, Kolialexis, Demestichas, Diamesis, Spais, Gravanis, Nikolaou and Papathanasopoulos.

the movement had *Stratigos* Kammenos, head of the Fourth Army Corps in Kavala.[28] In Athens Venizelist officers would organise diversionary movements, while *Antinavarchos* Demestichas would mobilise the fleet and sail to Thessaloniki where he would join *Stratigos* Kammenos with the Fourth Army Corps. In Thessaloniki they would then form a provisional government.

1 March 1935

The army officers Sarafis and Spetsios were to depart on 27 February from Athens for Thessaloniki with a message that the coup would break out on 1 March. But Sarafis was prohibited from travelling[29] and Sfetsios was left to act alone. Under pressure he became confused, and a misunderstanding arose between the two officers. Sfetsios wrongly understood that the movement had been postponed and notified the units in Northern Greece accordingly. But on the morning of 1 March the movement was in full swing. Indeed, the fleet had already left Piraeus, although instead of sailing to Thessaloniki it was wrongly heading for Chania, Crete. It was doubtful that it could join Kammenos' units in time. Also, the counter-insurgency movements in Athens were uncoordinated and their suppression was achieved in a matter of hours.

Therefore, the success of the movement depended on the Fourth Army Corps in Kavalla, Northern Greece. But General Kammenos had received the wrong message about the postponement of the coup and so on the evening of 1 March he cancelled the alert, and his units did not move. Neither did the 41st Xanthi Regiment, which *Tagmatarchis* Seiradakis had placed under the command of *Stratigos* Kammenos.

The only unit that did mobilise was the seventh division from the nearby city of Drama, but it could do nothing when informed of the postponement of the coup and the fact that no other unit had moved.[30] The message that the movement was on after all arrived only the next day. Again, however, *Stratigos* Kammenos was delayed and only moved his units and those of Seiradakis in the morning of 3 March, after receiving an ultimatum from Minister of Defence Kondylis to surrender. But it was too late. Kondylis had acted immediately on 1 March and had gathered considerable loyal forces to deal with the mobilisers of the fourth corps in Kavalla.

Stratigos Kammenos had fortified the banks of the River Strymonas (Struma). With him were the officers Bourdaras, Bakirtzis, Seiradakis and others. But they were alone. None of the officers of Thessaloniki, Larissa, Kozani, Serres and Veroia moved in accordance with the plan. So, the skirmishes on the River Strymonas were short. Kondylis soon overthrew Kammenos' defences, and the Fourth Army Corps surrendered – fortunately with few casualties. The instigators had no other solution than self-exile in neighbouring

28 Initially, the leadership was entrusted to *Antistratigos* A. Othonaios but he had refused as he had taken on other tasks within the organisation.

29 He was recognised by the royalist officers and was arrested.

30 Veremis, *Oi epemvaseis*, p.261. *Antisyntagmatachis* Tountas of the seventh division telephoned Kammenos who informed him of the postponement.

Bulgaria. Kammenos together with Bourdaras, Seiradakis, Bakirtzis and other officers headed through the mountains to Bulgaria to Karlovo. They were to remain there until amnesty was granted. It was a grim moment for the corps of Venizelist officers who, from one moment to the next, had lost everything. The Venizelist world had suffered a defeat from which it would never recover.

After the Coup

The most immediate consequence of the 1 March coup was a drastic clearing out. A total of 1,130 politicians and military officers of the Venizelist faction were tried, and 60 of them were sentenced to death, although 55 of these had already fled abroad.[31] The sentences were marked by a strong desire for revenge, although the only high-ranking officers executed on 5 April were *Stratigoi* Anastasios Papoulas and Miltiades Koimisis, both of whom were prosecution witnesses in the trial of the 'six', 13 years before. Papoulas in particular was not forgiven by the monarchists for changing sides and joining the Venizelist camp.

Also executed on 5 April was the officer Stelios Volanis who had put up a resistance on his own in Thessaloniki. Of the rest, 57 were sentenced to life imprisonment and 76 others to shorter sentences. In total 1,500 Venizelist officers, out of a total of 5,000, were dismissed from the army, navy and air force.[32] Thus the 1935 Venizelist coup enabled the monarchists to restore the 'balance' in the army, eliminating practically all Venizelist officers and humiliating many of them by public deposition on 2 April 1935.

But the political consequences of the movement were much more important. In the post-coup elections held on 9 June with the abstention of the Liberals, Tsaldari's Popular Party won a large victory with 65.4 percent of the vote. However, the time had come for the extreme pro-royalists. Four months later, on 10 October, Tsaldaris himself was forced to resign after a coup pioneered by the royalist officers Alexandros Papagos, Georgios Reppas and Dimitrios Economou. The republican constitution of 1927 was abolished, and the Constitution of 1911 was reinstated. Kondylis became dictator – and also regent! Moreover, a new referendum was called to decide again the regime issue. The referendum of 3 November was probably the most corrupt in Greek history. With an unrealistic 97 percent of the vote, King George II returned to Greece on 25 November 1935. In the new elections held on 26 January 1936 by simple majority, no party secured an absolute majority. So, King George II asked Ioannis Metaxas to form a minority government. On 4 August 1936, Metaxas dissolved the Parliament and imposed a dictatorship. It was the end of parliamentary democracy. The regime of 4 August, as it became known, would remain in power for the next four years until the beginning of the Second World War.

31 Among whom were Eleftherios Venizelos, Nikolaos Plastiras (who was already in France), Pericles Argyropoulos.

32 Veremis, *Oi epemvaseis*, p.268. See also the classic work of Grigorios Dafnis, *I Ellas metaxy dyo polemon, 1923–1940* (Athens, Ikaros, 1974).

The year 1936 signalled the end of an era for modern Greek history. Within a few months of that year, the protagonists of the inter-war period, Eleftherios Venizelos, Panagis Tsaldaris, Georgios Kondylis, Alexandros Papanastasiou, Konstantinos Demertzis and Andreas Michalakopoulos, all died. The death of Venizelos in Paris at the age of 72 closed an important chapter in Greek history.[33] A history that covers decades of struggles for the liberation of Crete and the Balkans and world conflicts, and the doubling of the size of Greece with the annexation of Macedonia, Epirus, Thrace, Crete and the islands of the Eastern Aegean.

Despite the myriad problems that followed the Asia Minor catastrophe, during the four years of Venizelos' government from 1928 to 1932 Greece had made a major leap forward in modernisation. However, on the eve of the Second World War, Greece was following the trajectory of other totalitarian regimes in Europe while anxiously listening to the drums of war sounding again.

* * *

After the failed coup of 1935, *Tagmatarchis* Charalampos Seiradakis trod the same path as other Venizelist officers. From March 1935 he remained in exile in Karlovo, Bulgaria, worrying about his family and waiting for news that would grant him amnesty. But the waiting in Karlovo felt eternal. Fortunately, he had maintained correspondence with many friends and comrades-in-arms who kept him informed of developments. On 8 May he received a letter from Nikolaos Plastiras from the French town of Vence, where he too was in exile. What he wrote is indicative of the views of the Venizelist liberals after their failed movement. Plastiras writes to Seiradakis that 'the trials are almost coming to an end. Today we had … the result of the Larissa trial, fortunately none to death. I was very afraid for Mr. Bourdara's head, but fortunately he saved it. And so the unfortunate Volanis, Papoulas and Koimisis paid for everything, the last two of them completely unjustly.'[34]

He then focused on the upcoming elections of 9 June 1935 where he stated, 'it is not impossible that we may have surprising results in favour of the democratic faction, given that Metaxas has broken away and declared a relentless war against the Government.' But Plastiras was wrong in his predictions. The Liberal Party had not taken part in the elections and Metaxas' defection from the Tsaldaris party had not influenced the election result in his favour. On the contrary, he was already planning a dictatorship. Plastiras's remarks to Seiradakis were indicative of the confusion that prevailed in the Venizelist camp at that time.

33 When Venizelos fled to France following the failed coup of 1 March 1935, Andreas Gyparakis went with him, as he was his bodyguard. He was with Venizelos when he died in Paris, on 17 March 1936. Gyparakis, stood by Venizelos until his last breath and gives a moving description of Venizelos' last moments on pages 173 to 181 of his book (on page 181 he even noted that the announcement of Venizelos' death in the French Parliament caused deep consternation). Gyparakis, *Anamniseis*.

34 Personal archive of Charalampos Seiradakis. The document is reproduced in Appendix II.

The crisis of Venizelism was universal. The exiled officers experienced it most painfully. First, they had learned that by a controversial, if doubtful, referendum almost the entire country seemed to approve of the return of a King it hardly knew.[35] Then they mourned Eleftherios Venizelos, who had died on 18 March 1936. As if that were not enough, on 4 August 1936 they were informed that Ioannis Metaxas had imposed a dictatorship with the consent of the new King. However, in the new situation that was taking shape, the Metaxas regime felt safe enough to grant amnesty and so the defecting officers who had taken part in the 1935 coup could return home. But they would have to settle away from the military units in Athens or Thessaloniki.

In November 1936 Seiradakis was reunited with his beloved Fani and his daughters in Thessaloniki. Fortunately, during the year of his exile the family had stayed at Fani's mother's house and the girls attended school normally. But soon they would have to move from Thessaloniki to Chania, and so they prepared for another change in their lives. After a long journey, the family arrived in December 1936 in the ancestral village of Livadas in Western Crete. Charalampos' mother, Eugenia, finally met her daughter-in-law Fani and her four granddaughters – including the eldest who was now 11 years old and was named after her. Charalampos' siblings were thrilled. For a while, they all had to adjust to the different circumstances of rural life in Livadas. But soon the older girls would go to high school. The family should find a home in Chania.

Seiradakis was back in his old town at the age of 50. His military record stated that 'he was discharged on 7/7/1935, when he was dismissed from the force and put on leave.'[36] Was he at the end of his military career? It seemed so, although in three years the situation was to change again. The Second World War was approaching, and Crete would be at the centre of a tumultuous battle. The military life of Charalampos Seiradakis would soon take a new turn.

35 The referendum that became known as 'unlawful' was announced on 10 October 1935 (Government Gazette A 456) and was held on 3 November. It had been organised by the dictatorship government of Georgios Kondylis, who had seized power in a coup d'état and had convened the Fifth National Assembly which abolished the constitution of the Republic.

36 Komotini, 13 November 1935, Infantry Command XII Division, Razis, *Syntagmatarchis*. (Charalampos Seiradakis military archive.)

14

The Battle of Crete, May 1941

Greece Under German Occupation

April 1941 was disastrous for Greece. After the Prime Minister Ioannis Metaxas courageously replied 'No' to Mussolini's impudent attack on 28 October 1940, and the Italian offensive in the mountains of Epirus was repulsed, the Greek Army soon found itself confronted with a new powerful opponent. On 6 April Nazi Germany launched a simultaneous attack against Yugoslavia and Greece. It is unlikely that Hitler would have decided to launch it had it not been preceded by Mussolini's failed attack on Greece. Hitler had given priority to Operation Barbarossa against the Soviet Union, but the Italian failure in Greece, combined with the accession of Bulgaria to the Axis forces on 1 March, had created a new situation. He wanted to protect his rear from a possible attack on the Romanian oil fields at Ploesti.

Another new factor was the prospect of occupying the island of Crete, which presupposed the submission of Greece. Crete holds a strategic position in the Eastern Mediterranean and both Hitler and Churchill attached importance to the role it could play in the development of the war.[1] Thus, at the beginning of April, Hitler activated Operation 'Marita' in the Balkans and soon the German panzer divisions, having overcome Yugoslav resistance, entered Thessaloniki.[2] Despite the resistance put up by the Greek Army in the northern forts with the Allied 'W' force of British, Australian and New Zealand units, the Germans advanced to Athens, which they entered on 27 April 1941.

The Greek territory was under German occupation. Three days earlier an evacuation order had been issued for the capital. The Greek Government under Prime Minister Emmanuel Tsouderos[3] and King George II barely had time to leave for the still free

1 Richter, Heinz A., *H Machi tis Kritis*, (Athens, Govostis, 2011). Original: *Die Eroberung der Insel Kreta im Mai 1941*, (Ruhpolding: Franz Philip Rutzen, 2011). Churchill considered Crete as a naval base (a new Scapa Flow), while Hitler considered it as a base for air attacks on the Middle East and North Africa (p.45).

2 The Yugoslav Army capitulated on 17 April 1941.

3 Ioannis Metaxas died on 29 January 1941. A new prime minister was appointed, Alexandros Koryzis, who committed suicide on 18 April, before the Germans entered Athens. He was succeeded by Emmanuel Tsouderos, Governor of the Bank of Greece, who remained prime minister of the Government-in-exile until April 1944.

The Battle of Crete, Kandanos, May 1941.

Crete. At the same time, allied troops were gathering in Crete with orders to defend the island 'at all costs' from a possible German attack. It was an obligation that Great Britain and Churchill personally had undertaken towards the Greek Government. Indeed, with the departure of the Cretan fifth division to the Albanian front, there was no longer a Greek Army on the island.[4] Soon more than 29,000 British, Australians and New Zealanders sailed into the port of Souda and camped on the road to Chania. Most of them were exhausted and morale was low. They were about to take part in one of the most unorthodox and bloody battles of the Second World War.

Preparations of the Allies

Since mid-April there had been scattered rumours in Crete about an imminent air attack. Crete was not adequately prepared for defence, and the matter was now becoming urgent. The urgency was compounded by secret information from a source unknown to most people at the time. It was a closely guarded secret that in 1941 British intelligence had deciphered the German Army's secret code system.[5] To the extent that the information could be exploited, it neutralised the element of surprise on which the Germans relied. As early as April, messages from the British intelligence services were already pouring in about an imminent German attack on Crete with 'air' forces.

But what exactly did 'air' mean? Although German paratroops had recently undertaken raids in Norway and The Netherlands with impressive results, it was not certain that they would dare attack a large target like Crete. In any case, it was clear that the defences at three airfields had to be reinforced: Maleme, 30km west of Chania, Heraklion and a smaller one at Rethymnon.

An attack from the air could be combined with a sea landing which was also reported in the 'Ultra' messages. Indeed, for many officers in Crete, an attack from the sea was more likely. An attack with exclusively airborne forces was a concept unknown or even unrealistic to veterans of the First World War, such as the New Zealand Lieutenant General Bernard Freyberg, who had arrived in Chania on 29 April to take charge of the island's defence. And yet he was the only one in Crete who, on Churchill's orders, was regularly informed of the 'Ultra' messages – although without knowing their source.

Freyberg wasted no time in organising the defence. The Allied forces in Crete numbered 29,000 British and Commonwealth troops[6] and another 10,000 Greek troops. Soon the division into sectors was made. The most critical zone was the north-western beach

4 Antony Beevor, *Crete, the Battle and the Resistance*, (London: John Murray, 1991). References here are from the Greek translation by Govostis, published in Athens in 2004 (see Bibliography), pp.94 & 95.

5 It was only in 1972 that it became known that the British had deciphered the German Army's encrypted communication system 'Enigma' in early 1941. The decoding operation, codenamed 'Ultra', took place at Bletchley Park, north of London. Among the earliest messages decrypted were those about the attack on Crete.

6 Richter, *H Machi tis Kritis*, p.159. There were 15,000 British, 7,100 New Zealanders and 6,500 Australians.

of Chania from Souda to Maleme airfield. New Zealand forces were deployed there, but without fully covering the mainland as they left a gap from Kissamos to Maleme airfield. It turned out to be a great strategic error. A few Matilda tanks and Bofors anti-aircraft guns covered the landing strip and the surrounding hills.[7] Nevertheless, despite some shortcomings the defence line at Chania seemed strong. In the Heraklion and Rethymnon zone, British, Greek and Australian units were deployed tactically, as well as gendarmerie detachments. Lieutenant General Freyberg had his headquarters on the heights of Akrotiri near Chania. From there he could observe the beaches of Chania and as far east as Rethymno. But he was far away from the battlefields, without good communication with the divisional commanders. Indeed, the poor state of radios and telephones was the weakest point of Creforce.[8]

Preparations of the Greek Government

Prime Minister Tsouderos and the Greek Government, who had taken refuge in Crete, were facing urgent problems. The Greek forces in Crete were not negligible. They included the first class of the Military (Evelpidon) School with about 300 men, eight battalions of recruits from Nafplio and Tripoli, a unit of the fifth division who had managed to make it back, and men of the Gendarmerie School.[9] Although they were under joint Allied command, they had to be commanded by Greek officers.

This was in fact the first decision taken by Prime Minister Tsouderos in Crete. By a decree issued in Chania[10] he reinstated officers who had been dismissed six years earlier because of their participation in the 1935 coup. One of them was Charalampos Seiradakis, who returned to military service. Tsouderos thus proved his democratic credentials, contradicting those who thought he was a supporter of the Metaxas dictatorship. Most importantly, it strengthened the Greek Army with experienced officers. Many of them would play an important role in the Battle of Crete and in the Greek Army in exile in the Middle East.

On 26 April Tsouderos called a meeting in Chania with the senior officers.[11] At this crucial meeting it was decided to establish a militia and to defend 'to the utmost'.[12] As

7 In particular, the adjacent hill which was codenamed 'Hill 107'. It was to be a fateful location that would decide the Battle of Crete.

8 Creforce: short name for the Allied defence forces in Crete (Cretan force).

9 Yannis Kochylakis, *H epopoiia tis Machis tis Kritis kai tis Ethnikis Antistasis* (Athens: Smyrniotakis, 1993), p.30. According to Beevor, *Crete,* p.149, the Greek forces amounted to 9,000 men organised in eight regiments.

10 Tsouderos government decrees A.L. 3013/9-5-1941 'On the reinstatement of Officers and Non-Commissioned Officers of the army for political reasons', and A.L. 3058/27-6-1941 'On the interpretative provisions of articles 1 and 2 of Law 3013/9-5-1941'.

11 The meeting was attended by *Ypostratigos* Gagaras, *Antisyntagmatarches* P. Gyparis and Ch. Seiradakis, and *Tagmatarches* E. Nikoloudis, M. Mandakas, G. Volanis, S. Gerogiannis and I. Manolarakis. The subject was the implementation of order A.P.4 of the Military Command of Chania (see also following footnote below).

12 Information contained in *Polemiki ekthesis apo ti Machi tis Kritis – Machi tis Kandanou,* submitted by *Antisyntagmatachis* Charalambos Seiradakis in Cairo in August 1943 (hereafter

Seiradakis mentions in his war report on the Battle of Crete, they decided 'on the means required for the organisation of the militia … especially the immediate supply of arms and ammunition.' The issue of arms had a history in Crete. During the Greek Italian war, the Metaxas Government had appealed to the Cretan people to surrender their arms for the needs of the regular army. The circular 'resonated with the souls of the Greek people and … they were quick to hand them over. The province of Selinon alone delivered 364 hand weapons.' It was a big sacrifice for the Cretans to surrender their weapons, one which should not be underestimated. Although the government had publicly praised the Cretans' contribution, there was a motive for the praise. The Metaxas regime had not forgotten that Chania had been the site of the only anti-dictatorial movement three years earlier, in 1938. Since then, there had been a reluctance to rearm the Cretans, with the result that there were now no guns, and thus the formation of a militia was delayed.[13]

However, the militia raised additional questions. The most important was that in the event of war the militias ran the risk of not being considered as belligerents covered by the laws of war under the Geneva Convention. There was an imminent risk of being exposed to enemy reprisals. Of course, for the Cretans, defence against any would-be conqueror was self-evident and was not subject to any restrictions. Although the Greek leadership was aware of the Geneva Convention, for the ordinary inhabitants of the countryside it was unknown and this meant that everyone collectively would defend their homeland if their freedom was at stake. After all, the enemy was Nazi Germany, for which there was a clear precedent. Although Eleftherios Venizelos had died five years before, his political legacy in favour of the British and French had general resonance in Crete. There was anger among Cretans at the unjust imminent attack by the Germans to their island and a general will to fight against them. In the end, inaction on the issue of militia had disastrous results. Many would soon face the consequences of this delay. One of them was Seiradakis. Literally at the last moment, on the afternoon of Monday 19 May, he received an order from the government to depart for the province of Selino with instructions to organise a militia and resist the enemy 'to the last'.[14]

Polemiki ekthesis.). A copy of the original exists in his personal archive, but it was also published in a special report in the newspaper *Chaniotika Nea* on Monday 25 May 2009, pp.21–28.

13 The man who had tried to arm the Cretans in November 1940 was the Englishman, John Pendlebury. He had requested 10,000 rifles from the Middle East but only 3,500 had arrived and were delivered to the Cretans on the day of the battle by *Antisyntagmatachis* Pavlis Gyparis, Yannis Kochylakis, *H epopoiia tis Machis tis Kritis kai tis Ethnikis Antistasis*, (Athens: Smyrniotakis 1993), p.53. On Pendlebury's life, see Imogen Grundon *A Rash Adventurer, A Life of John Pendlebury*, (London: Libris, 2007). Pendlebury had special ties to Crete and considered himself the 'Cretan Lawrence of Arabia'. He was killed at Heraklion fighting during the Battle of Crete.

14 Seiradakis, *Polemiki ekthesis*, 'Order for the allocation of officers to the Cretan Military Command to organise a militia: The following officers are placed at the disposal for the organisation of the Militia. 1. *Tagmatarchis* P. Gyparis, 2. *Lochagos* M. Mantakas, 3. *Lochagos* G. Ntigrintis, 4. *Tagmatarchis* Ch. Seiradakis, 5. *Anthypaspistis* P. Koumanakos. Chania, 14 May 1944. Minister E. Tsouderos.'

But luck was not on his side. Not even eight hours had passed since his arrival in Kandanos when the German attack occurred at dawn the next day, Tuesday 20 May. As he had no time to organise a militia, he had to fight as best as he could. As has been rightly pointed out about the Cretan clashes, 'from the first moment of its occurrence the battle had no plan. The leaders did what they could with what they had been able to organise up to that moment. From then on, the battle had its own rhythm.'[15] This was also the case in the fighting in Selino. The lack of a regular Greek Army and the Cretans' impulse to fight the foreign invader meant that the battles were not fully controlled, even though they were conducted by officers of the Greek Army. This does not in the least diminish the heroic effort of the fighters, nor the desperate attempt by Seiradakis to coordinate his units in the battles of Kandanos. Although the Germans eventually prevailed in Kandanos, as they did throughout Crete, the echo of the battle there was of an act of heroism and self-sacrifice.

A final issue that plagued the Greek Government and the Allies was the question of whether the government and the King would remain in Crete. The commander of 'Creforce', Freyberg, pressed for their departure to Egypt, while the British Ambassador, Palairet, believed they ought to stay. The answer was provided by the pressure of events. As soon as the first German paratroops began to land, the Greek Government hastily left for the Middle East. They crossed the Therisso Gorge and the White Mountains on foot and barely managed to escape to Egypt from the southern beach of Aghia Roumeli, avoiding capture.

Preparations of the German Army

Of all the new corps that Hitler had introduced into the German war machine of World War II, the most innovative was that of the *fallschirmjäger* (paratroopers).[16] It was largely the achievement of *Generalleutnant* Kurt Student who had established an elite corps with great potential. The *fallschirmjäger* were young men who had volunteered and had proved their worth in commando operations in Northern Europe. But Student was anxious to prove that the new corps was capable of longer-range operations, and the attack on Greece presented a new opportunity – the capture of Crete and Student had convinced Hitler that it was feasible with exclusively airborne forces. Although Hitler had reservations, on 25 April he finally issued an order giving the green light for operation 'Hermes', or 'Merkur'. The countdown to the occupation of Crete had begun.

One problem was the short deadlines. The operation was originally scheduled for 17 May and preparations had to be accelerated. Soldiers and ammunition began to arrive in secrecy at the airfields around Athens.[17] The force formed an impressive body of

15 Panagiotis Katiforis, *H Elliniki Amyna sti Machi tis Kritis* (Athens: Ariston Books, 2017), p.240.

16 The *fallschirmjägers*' previous operation was in Narvik, Norway, where they had worn winter uniforms. They had not had time to change and fought in these uniforms in Crete, in extreme hot conditions – almost 40o C.

17 Richter, *H Machi tis Kritis*, p.130. The airfields were Ellinikon, Megara, Corinth, Elefsina, Tanagra and Dadis.

15,000 *fallschirmjäger* and 8,500 experienced *gebirgsjäger* (mountain troops). But more formidable was the air fleet of 550 aircraft of all types – bombers, transports, fighters, and a large number of gliders. Each Junkers Ju52 transport plane could carry 12 paratroopers and all together in a single mission the fleet could carry 6,000 men in total. The date of the air attack was finally set for 20 May after some days' delay in the arrival of fuel for the airplanes, with paratroopers dropping on four different targets: Maleme, Chania, Rethymno and Heraklion. The air assault was to be followed by a landing from the sea by infantry units departing in slow boats for the northern coast of Crete.

Despite the impressive preparation, operation 'Hermes' was from the start hampered by two factors. Both were related to intelligence. The first was the disclosure by the 'Ultra' system to the British secret services, which removed any trace of surprise. The second was the misjudgement of the situation in Crete, for which *General* von Kanaris' (Wilhelm von Kanaris) secret services were probably to blame. First, they had not foreseen that the terrain in Crete was rough and rocky and that many paratroopers would be injured on their landing. It is also astonishing that the paratroops were under the impression that they would receive friendly reception in Crete. Even more so that the Cretans would not put up any resistance but would surrender their island without a fight.[18] This misinformation was the cause of misunderstandings which subsequently aggravated the already strained atmosphere during the occupation years.

The Battle Breaks Out

When the sirens sounded at dawn on Tuesday 20 May 1941, a feeling of awe overcame the inhabitants of Chania. They had heard about the Stukas aircraft, but they had not imagined that their city would be bombed from the air. The air raid on Chania was mainly aimed at the headquarters of the fifth division in the citadel of Kastelli, in the old harbour. At the same time military targets were bombed all along the northern beach of Chania to Maleme where the Germans were targeting Allied positions. But despite the density of air attacks, these posts were well hidden and were not seriously damaged. However, the medieval town of Chania with its impressive Venetian monuments was almost destroyed, while ironically the buildings of the fifth division were left unscathed. The damage to the old city was irreparable.

The bombardment had not ended when, from the west, the sound of transport planes approaching in groups of three began to be heard. First the gliders appeared and began circling and landing on the rough and rocky ground. Then the blue spring sky was filled with parachutes slowly descending across the area from Chania to Maleme. Perhaps the only one who was not surprised was the commander of the Allied forces, Freyberg, who in a phlegmatic manner simply commented that 'they are dead on time'.[19]

The mistakes of German intelligence had their first victims. Many gliders were crushed on the rocks during landing, with several casualties. The paratroops were greeted by fire

18 Richter, *H Machi tis Kritis*, p.139.
19 He had been informed by the 'Ultra' system of the exact time of the paratroopers' drop.

from New Zealand soldiers in concealed positions who fired on them unanswered. The Germans were not prepared for this, and their units were decimated. Only those who were lucky enough to fall into places far from outposts managed to take up defensive positions. But there were not many, and few survived from the first waves of paratroops. Among the casualties were many officers and the units were left without command. In the first day alone, more than 2,000 paratroopers had been killed.

But at the crucial moment they were helped by proper preparation, the opponents' mistakes, and luck. Those who had survived contacted each other by radios and began to gather in small groups. Lower ranking officers or even soldiers took the initiative. The turning point was the control of the airport of Maleme. They noticed that there were no New Zealand soldiers west of the airfield on the Tavronitis River. If they could control Hill 107 next to the airfield, they would have a better chance of taking it and moving reinforcements. In this, the New Zealanders themselves had unwittingly helped them. As their communications were inadequate, the head of the Maleme sector, Lieutenant Colonel Andrew, thought he was surrounded, and in the evening asked for and received permission to retreat.[20]

The Germans seized the opportunity. By dawn their units controlled Hill 107 and notified headquarters in Athens to attempt a trial landing at Maleme airfield. Early the next morning a Ju52 plane managed to land in a barrage of fire, pick up some wounded and return to Athens.[21] From that moment on, reinforcements from the experienced mountain troops started arriving at a rapid pace.[22] Although the Germans had virtually been defeated on the other fronts at Chania, Rethymnon and Heraklion, the capture of Maleme airfield meant that they were gradually taking the initiative. Despite the thousands of casualties, the German occupation of Crete was now only a matter of time.

In Kandanos

The dusk of Monday 19 May was just beginning to cool down after a very hot day. *Antisyntagmatachis* Charalampos Seiradakis was on his way to Kandanos in a jeep provided by the Greek command. After crossing the coastal road to Maleme where the hidden New Zealanders' shelters could just be seen, at the height of the river Tavronitis they turned left towards Voukolies and soon they were climbing towards Kandanos on the serpentine road through successive gorges. It was a magnificent route and the contrast with the grim prospect of the impending battle could not have been stronger. Passing through the village of Floria, Seiradakis met *Moirarchos* Bitsakis and informed him of his order to resist the Germans. On leaving, he left him a telephone radio set so that they could keep in constant communication with each other.[23]

20 Brigadier General Hargest's reply to Andrew remains historic: 'If you must, you must'.
21 Including the wounded Major General Meindl and other seriously wounded paratroopers.
22 According to New Zealand estimates, the time it took each plane to land, disembark soldiers and take off was only 70 seconds.
23 Seiradakis, *Polemiki ekthesis*, 'I ordered him to leave a guard post, leaving the telephone operator with the portable telephone with which he had been provided on his departure'.

Seiradakis arrived at Kandanos at 8:00 p.m.[24] Although the people were anxious, no one imagined that an attack on Crete would occur any time soon, least of all from the air. The purpose of Seiradakis's hasty arrival was unknown to everyone except for the commander of the *gendarmerie*, *Moirarchos* Archontakis, who had been informed from Chania. The two men had known each other for a long time. After the welcome, a meeting was held to assess the situation.[25] The *gendarmerie* and rural police forces numbered about 200 men with basic weapons but not enough ammunition. They then discussed ways they could implement the order 'to repel paratroopers, reinforce the army sections, and repel enemy landings.' They agreed that an order for the organisation of a militia should be issued immediately. That evening Seiradakis sent out an order calling upon the reserve officers of the province of Selino to report to the Kandanos sub-command at 10:00 a.m. the next morning. The crowd that had gathered outside the command post to learn of developments had begun to thin out. They had learned the purpose of the Greek colonel's arrival and were anxious, but with a strong will to fight the foreign invader.

They needed it as the fateful Tuesday 20 May dawned. The German offensive had just begun, and by 6:30 a.m., hundreds of transport planes had appeared from the west, turning left and heading for Maleme and Chania. The bombing was getting louder and louder. In the distance they could see the gliders descending slowly. Then followed muffled explosions that indicated that the fighting had begun on the northern coast of Western Crete. Seiradakis realised with horror that he did not have the time he needed. He had not slept all night, planning the organisation of the militia. He had asked for blue armbands to be prepared, which the militiamen were to wear according to the instructions.[26] But he had no time for that either. The situation he faced was desperate. He had no regular army and only a few *gendarmerie* forces, he had no time to fully organise the militia, and the number of conscripts was limited.

Additionally, there were not enough weapons and ammunition from Chania was unlikely to arrive on time. On the other hand, he was obliged to take urgent decisions, 'in the spirit of the mandate' he had received from the government. The exceptional circumstances facing Seiradakis made him military commander of Selino. From a strategic point of view, the aim was to relieve the Greek and Allied forces fighting on the Chania Plain. Thus, he decided to create a diversion in the rear of the Germans who were aiming to capture the Maleme airfield. Although he did not know it, at that time his fellow officers at the head of the defence in Rethymnon and Heraklion had successfully followed the same tactics.[27] Seiradakis acted immediately. In his capacity as military commander he decided to mobilise the population of the province and at 7:30 a.m.

24 The following is based on Seiradakis' *Polemiki ekthesis*. Where it is supplemented by other sources these are noted in the footnotes.

25 Participants were *Ypodioikitis* George Bitsakis and *Ypodioikitis* George Mourkogiannis.

26 P. Gyparis, *Iroes kai iroismoi sti Machi tis Kritis* (Athens: privately published, 1955), p.65. 'Instructions for the formation of Militia Guard Units, Ministry of Defence: 'All Militia Guards will wear for distinction on their left arm a ribbon with the national colours', Chania, 5 May 1941, *Archigos epiteleiou* G. Karavitis.

27 *Antisyntagmatarches* Papathanasopoulos and Tzifakis in Heraklion and Rethymnon respectively.

he issued two military instructions to the inhabitants of Selino province. The first was a patriotic rallying call against the foreign invader. The second declared Selino under siege and called on recruited soldiers and inhabitants able to bear arms to report to Kandanos on the same day before sunset.[28]

The next move was to organise the defence at strategic points. For the critical area of Voukolies, which controlled the road to Maleme, Seiradakis telephoned *Lochagos* Maragakis to keep him regularly informed of the movements of German units and promised him 'that he would send a strong detachment within the day'. In the meantime, by 10:00 a.m. on Wednesday morning, 21 May, regular and reserve personnel had begun to assemble in Kandanos after the order that Seiradakis had issued the previous day.[29] It was now noon, when Seiradakis asked everyone to assemble at the church of St Nikolaos next to the *gendarmerie* station, the highest point in Kandanos. It must have been an emotional moment.

Father Stylianos' service in the church of St Nikolaos was brief. All the Seliniots who had gathered in the courtyard were silent to hear what Seiradakis was going to tell them. He was short and clear. As he recorded, 'I pointed out to them the danger of enslavement to the Germans ... and urged them to enlist as militiamen ... The people burst into enthusiastic cheers for the Fatherland and expressed their determination to fight to the last bullet.' Certainly, the excitement of the moment overshadowed any misgivings, although the will of the people of Selino to resist was genuine and in keeping with their age-old traditions. Most men were quick to sign up for the new militia. Seiradakis put *Anthypaspistis* Andreas Papailiakis in charge, with instructions to divide the volunteers into groups. The first detachment of 35 men was ready early in the afternoon and other detachments soon followed.[30] The problem was armament. Although many had brought shotguns with them, others were unarmed. Seiradakis distributed what was in the stores and told them that for more weaponry he was in contact with the headquarters in Chania. There was also the possibility of getting weapons from spoils of the battles.

He was concerned about the possible advance of the Germans from Maleme airport to Voukolies, which was only nine kilometres away. From there, Kandanos was another 20km. Seiradakis did not know at the time that this precise area was the target of the German forces who were quick to exploit the fact that it was unguarded.

After taking Hill 107 on the evening of 20 May, the Germans were gathering forces in the gap west of Tavronitis River to cover their rear towards Voukolies, Kandanos and Paleochora, in the south Libyan Sea. For this purpose, they were to use the infantry of the *gebirgsjäger* on motorcycles and the artillery of *General* Julius Ringel which had begun to land on Wednesday 21 May. The beginning of the Battle of Kandanos was approaching.

28 The texts of both Order 1 and Order 2 are contained in the *Polemiki ekthesis* of Ch. Seiradakis.

29 Seiradakis, *Polemiki ekthesis*. Present were: A. Papailiakis, E. Pallikaris, M. Apostolakis, Labathakis, I. Kalogridis, G. Marmatakis, F. Zevelakis, I. Lazopoulos, I. Seiradakis, Koukoutsakis, G. Papadantonakis, E. Protopapadakis et al.

30 It was led by *Lochias* Kalogridis and the team leaders were *Lochias* Ioannis Lazopoulos and *Lochias* Fotis Choudalis.

The Battle of Floria

On the afternoon of Tuesday 20 May, at 4:00 p.m., Seiradakis had contacted *Moirarchos* Bitsakis in the village of Floria. Although no Germans had appeared by that time, Seiradakis believed that they would not be long in coming and recommended that Bitsakis intensify his surveillance. At the same time, he ordered the Kalogridis detachment to join *Lochagos* Maragakis' group and other villagers who had volunteered to take part in the fighting. Meanwhile, in Maleme, the Germans were having a hard time. As the historian Heinz Richter reports, 'the units of mountain troops who arrived in Crete were under the impression that they had crossed the 'gates of hell' on landing.'[31] They were not wrong.

The defence of the western and southern side of Maleme airfield was the responsibility of *Major* Schätte's unit.[32] A reconnaissance section headed by the young *Leutenant* Horst Heller with two companies had been sent on ahead towards Voukolies. Soon they were confronted by the Greek units.[33] The conflict at Pathakiana was fierce, close and hand-to-hand, with casualties on both sides. *Lochias* Lazopoulos was killed in the battle, fighting heroically.[34] Heller requested the help of the air force and soon fighters appeared and began to fire on the Greek positions. But the enemy was so close that they may have mistakenly fired on their own units.[35] It was just one example of the confusion on the Maleme battlefield.

According to some historians, the confusion was to be further compounded by some information that was received.[36] At noon on Wednesday 21 May, a rumour circulated that a 'ghost regiment' from the southern beach of Paleochora was coming to attack the Germans from the south. The historian I. McD. G. Stewart reports that Student, anxiously awaiting news in Athens, received a message that enemy units were on their way from Paleochora to the Maleme airfield.[37] Richter reports more specifically that at 17:15 rumours circulated that a New Zealand regiment supported by tanks was approaching the German 16th company.[38] As no such regiment existed he calls it 'a

31 Richter, *H Machi tis Kritis*, p.227.

32 Eftimis I. Lambousakis, *To Selino sti Machi tis Kritis* (Chania: privately published, 2021), p.11, and Richter, *H Machi tis Kritis*, p.285. *Major* Schätte's unit consisted of men from the '95th artillery battalion' and the '55th motorcycle battalion'.

33 The Greek units had been reinforced with a machine gun brought by a young lad, Ioannis Fridakis.

34 Seiradakis, *Polemiki ekthesis*, and Lambousakis, *To Selino*, p.11. At the spot where Lazopoulos fell stands his statue.

35 Richter, *H Machi tis Kritis*, p.228.

36 Richter, *H Machi tis Kritis*, pp.228–229. See also Seiradakis, *Polemiki ekthesis* and I. McD. G. Stewart, *The Struggle for Crete, 20 May–1 June 1941: A Story of Lost Opportunity* (Oxford: Oxford University Press, 1991), pp.268–269; also Lambousakis, *To Selino*, p.11. According to Richter, Student never believed the information, while Ringel assumed that the 'ghost regiment' had fled from the southern coast of Crete (Richter, *H Machi tis Kritis*, p.286).

37 Stewart, *Struggle*, p.268. 'Enemy columns approaching on road from Paleochora to the north. Head of column has reached 10km south of the airfield', but then he adds: 'There was of course no column on this road. Partisans in the area were actively engaged with the southern company of paratroopers.'

38 Richter, *H Machi tis Kritis*, p.228.

figment of someone's imagination', and Lamboussakis says that 'its origin remains unknown'.

But Seiradakis offers in his report of the battle a plausible explanation for this confusion. On the morning of Wednesday 21 May, *Tagmatarchis* Kourkoulis, commander of the Greek battalion at Kastelli, had called him on the telephone asking for ammunition. During the time the telephone line was open Seiradakis heard German conversation and laughter and thought that the Germans were listening in on the conversation. This was not strange as 'there was no order, anyone could call and hear any kind of information.' Seiradakis thought it appropriate to pass on an inaccurate piece of information to encourage the battalion but also to mislead the enemy.[39] He replied to Kourkoulis that 'I will send you ammunition and tomorrow I will march with my regiment to Kandanos-Voukolies-Maleme with one of my detachments which I will send from the direction of Deliana-Kolimbari.' It seems that Seiradakis' message was immediately channelled to the German command, which diverted forces from the main front of Maleme in the direction of Selino.

Let us not forget that this was only the second day of the battle and the situation was fluid. What is certain is that two hours after the telephone call a squadron of about 20 German planes flew over the south-western part of the island. They did not, of course, find any New Zealand, or other units, but only a crowd of 1,200 people gathered in Kandanos, which they bombed – fortunately without casualties. For Seiradakis it was proof that, 'the enemy was paying attention to Kandanos as a result of that telephone conversation'. As this is the point at which historians' information converges, it is likely that Seiradakis' deception tactics had an effect and increased the confusion of the German units.

But in Kandanos Seiradakis was troubled. The information about the Germans' advances on Voukolies and the firepower they had at their disposal could have devastating consequences. He could not continue the battle without the agreement of all the inhabitants. So, at sunset on Thursday 22 May, he held a general meeting in front of the school on Kandanos Hill. Everyone gathered with obvious anxiety but they were still determined to resist. Seiradakis explained the situation frankly without hiding anything: he told them about the strength of the enemy, which they all knew, but also about the dangers. 'I invited those assembled to join me in the battle of honour for the resistance of Selino … All of them, without exception, expressed to me their decision to make the last stand in the Kandanian Gorge and that they were indifferent to the destruction of Kandanos.' It was a heroic decision, but it was to have tragic consequences. Immediately afterwards Seiradakis issued a new order of operations designating the steep sides of the Kandanos Gorge as the main line of defence.[40]

Friday 23 May dawned as warm as the previous days. At 10:30 a.m. Seiradakis was informed that a German patrol of about 15 men and two motorcycles had appeared at the Anissaraki Bridge near the gorge. It had met no resistance and had apparently escaped the attention of the guards. But at the first shots, the patrol was forced to turn back

39 'Deception tactics' were in use from the previous war and earlier.

40 The line of defence was defined in the Kandanos Gorge from Xerocampos on the left to the Heights of Nerospilios and Apopigadi on the right.

for reinforcements.[41] It was an opportunity not to be missed. Seiradakis telephoned his troops to cut off the retreat of the German patrol and left immediately for Floria. Soon the outposts that Seiradakis had set up spotted the German patrol retreating to Floria and managed to cut off their escape. At the same time, the *gendarmes* of the Kandanos outpost and several residents were approaching.

The motorcyclists found themselves surrounded. The Greek units attacked the German patrol that had barricaded itself in the houses of the village, and especially in the cafeteria. But there they had no way of escape. According to Seiradakis, 'a fierce battle was then fought between the German detachment and the soldiers ... The battle lasted until the evening'. In the afternoon, the final attack by gendarmes took place, resulting in the death of most of the Germans. Two, however, continued to defend themselves, locked in the building. Seiradakis says, 'I ordered them to surrender but they refused'. Lamboussakis reports that their reply was, 'The Germans do not surrender.'[42] Richter explains that 'they obviously did not trust the assurances of the Greek colonel and preferred to die fighting.'[43] In the end they too were killed. On the night of that bloody day there were at least three Greeks dead. Seiradakis counted 19 German dead[44] and ordered their burial. Among the dead were *Leutenant* Horst Heller and *Unteroffizier* Pickel, both young men. Seiradakis emphasises that, 'I did not find any burning or mutilation on the German corpses.' He was aware that there might be reprisals, and he wanted to prevent them.

There were indeed reprisals, and they were the worst consequence of the Battle of Floria. It was an opportunity for *General* Ringel to issue an order 'threatening to execute any civilians caught carrying weapons ... They were to be taken hostage and in the event of hostile action 10 Greek hostages were to be executed for every dead German.'[45] The hideous cycle of German reprisals had begun at Selino.

The Battle in the Gorge of Kandanos

While the battle in Floria lasted, another Greek group clashed in the village of Mesavlia with a German detachment that was rushing to reinforce their trapped compatriots. The battle was again hand-to-hand and only six Germans survived and were taken prisoner.[46] However, the two battles provided Seiradakis' troops with a lot of spoils. In addition to a radio, they now had 4 machine guns, 22 submachine guns, grenades and a large quantity of ammunition. They would be useful in the battle in the Gorge of Kandanos, though no real match for the firepower of the German Army.

41 Richter, *H Machi tis Kritis*, p.287, reports that no shots were fired but that they returned to Floria to rest.
42 Lambousakis, *To Selino*, p.18.
43 Richter, *H Machi tis Kritis*, p.288.
44 According to Richter it was 12, according to Laboussakis it was 17.
45 Richter, *H Machi tis Kritis*, p.288.
46 They were liberated after the end of the Battle of Crete. There are testimonies (Seiradakis, Lambousakis) that they returned to avenge their captivity.

Indeed, in the previous days the Germans had consolidated the bridgehead at Maleme airfield and had been significantly reinforced with infantry, artillery, small tanks and motorcycles. They were already advancing towards Chania, obliging the Allied forces to retreat. At the same time, a unit was advancing towards the southern coast in the direction of Kandanos. They knew by now that there was no ghost regiment on the Kandanian side but that, 'the guerrilla forces to the west and south were a real threat.'[47] For their part, Freyberg, the commander of the Allied forces, and two New Zealand brigadier generals,[48] having made significant mistakes, were now in a precarious position. Despite the heroic resistance of the New Zealand troops at Galata and Ayia, they were now in danger of being surrounded by the German advance guard. So, Freyberg contacted Middle East headquarters to relocate the troops of 'Creforce' to Egypt.

Seiradakis had returned from Floria late on the night of Friday 23 May. At Kandanos he completed preparations for the battle in the gorge.[49] He placed a group at the entrance with orders to alert him as soon as the German columns appeared and then to fall back to join the rest of the force, leaving the entrance to the canyon free. He set up advanced guard detachments at the large bend in the canyon where the road to Spina turns, and at the site of Nerospilio. He ordered the politician Sergentanis to cover the left of the line at Xerocampos. Before leaving for the front line, he made a telephone appeal to the chairmen of the local communes for more supplies to the gorge from those who had already gone to their villages as the critical moment for the battle was approaching. In all, about 250 armed men had gathered in the gorge.

At 8:30 a.m. on Saturday 24 May, the telephone operator from Floria[50] informed Seiradakis that the first German units had appeared. There was a total was about 1,000 men, many of them on motorcycles.[51] It was a particularly hot day, and the lack of wind made conditions in the gorge unbearable.

At 10:00 a.m. the Germans were approaching. Before they reached the big turn to the gorge they met with a volley of gunfire. It seems that a group of snipers, against Seiradakis' orders, rushed to attack, giving the Germans the opportunity to get off their motorcycles and climb the rocks. The premature attack caused the fighting to get out of control.[52] So the Germans were not taken by surprise and 'the enemy got off their motorcycles, protected their position hastily and the battle began.'[53] The Germans were

47 Richter, *H Machi tis Kritis*, p.229.

48 Edwad Puttick and James Hargest.

49 Ioannis D. Mourellos, *I Machi tis Kritis* (Heraklion: 1950). In p.392 he cites a narrative of *Stratiotis* Marmatakis who took part in the battle.

50 It was Mrs Fragiadaki with whom the conversation was very moving. Seiradakis advised her 'to destroy the telephone and pick up her child.... and flee to Spina to save herself.'

51 Kochylakis, *H epopoiia* p.87. He reports that there was a total of 72 motorcycles with 4 to 5 soldiers each, followed by other units on foot.

52 Kochylakis, *H epopoiia* p.91. Narrated by Manolis Paterakis: 'The mistake was that the Seliniots were in a hurry to shoot and so they achieved nothing. We should have let them go into the gorge and then hit them'.

53 Charalampos Seiradakis, *Polemiki ekthesis apo ti Machi tis Kritis – Machi tis Kandanou, se eidiko afieroma tis efimeridas Chaniotika Nea*, 25 Maiou 2009 (sel. 21 eos 28). Further uncredited quotes in this section are all from Seiradakis' 'Report'.

at a disadvantage as the Cretans fired at them from both sides of the gorge. It seems that they were quite accurate, which impressed the German historian Harald Gilbert, who collected information from soldiers who took part in the battle.[54] Those Cretans who were unarmed supplied the warriors with water and cartridges or carried messages. The same was true of the women of Kandanos and the surrounding villages, of whom Seiradakis says that 'the contribution of the women to the battle was admirable.' The battle continued until late evening.

But it was obvious that the Cretans could not achieve victory over the German units. With the onset of the attack the Germans had called for reinforcements and soon German aircraft were flying over the battlefield making near-vertical bombing runs into the steep gullies of the Kandanos gorge. 'The entire Kandanos basin was covered with powder and smoke'. In the afternoon, another company of motorcyclists arrived, armed with eight mortars. On their arrival the Germans attacked the strong positions of Nevela and Agriomelissa held by the Cretans. As the Cretans' ammunition was running low, they were forced to abandon these positions as soon as it got dark. 'From that moment on it seemed that the battle for the capture of Kandanos had been decided in favour of the Germans because of the fall of these two positions.'

It was crucial to avoid encirclement and to maintain an escape route to Kandanos. Fortunately, by sundown a detachment of *gendarmerie* had arrived to cover the retreat. The next day, Sunday 25 May, began with an artillery bombardment – the Germans had been reinforced during the night by two mountain guns. The noise from the explosions of the guns and mortars was deafening. In contrast, the Cretans had run out of ammunition. Seiradakis found that he could hold out no longer and shortly before noon he gave the order to retreat to the hills around Kandanos. The battle was over.

From the north-western heights they could see the enemy's mechanised units entering Kandanos. The village was empty as all the inhabitants had taken refuge in the hills and surrounding villages. So, on Sunday afternoon the Germans left for Paleochora where they arrived in the evening and barricaded themselves into the old Venetian fortress of Fortezza. After the battle the Germans were angry at the resistance they had met. They had met with fierce fighting in Floria and in the gorge, and on top of this, there was the presence of guerrillas in the battles who did not wear militia insignia, even though the attacks were led by uniformed officers and gendarmes. There were also rumours of mutilation and close fights over dead bodies. Soon reprisals would erupt in Kandanos.

After the battle Seiradakis conferred with his fellow soldiers on a hill east of Kandanos. They made a brief assessment of the battle. A total of 642 men took part in the fights of Floria, Mesavlia and Kandanos Gorge, along with volunteers from the surrounding villages.[55] About 250 had fought in the gorge although reinforcements had arrived during

54 Harald Gilbert, *Das besetzte Kreta 1941–1945* (Ruhpolding: Franz Philipp Rutzen, 2015), vol. 63, p.39. '*Sie waren im Gebirge zumeist hervorragend getarnt und beschossen immer wieder unsere Marschkolonnen. Ich muss anerkennen, das sie selbst auf weite Entfernung hin gut schossen*' ('They were very well camouflaged in the mountains from where they kept firing at our marching columns. I must admit that they shot very well from a long distance').

55 Seiradakis, *Polemiki ekthesis*. 72 gendarmes and field guards, 420 militiamen with military weapons, and 150 civilians with hunting weapons fought in the Kandanos Gorge. The Greek

the battle. Everyone felt proud to have fought the foreign invader but were disappointed that they had failed to stop him. Now they were thinking about the next day and were anxious about their country. The future looked bleak. Everyone was worried about their family and was in a hurry to get back to them. As Seiradakis says, 'I then ordered our warriors to retire to their villages and promised them I would join my fate to theirs.'

He himself departed for the Omalos Plateau and from there to Sfakia, from where he had information that the Greek Government was leaving for Egypt. Although he could have departed with them to the Middle East, he did not. He decided to 'return to the province and share the fate of his fellow warriors, as he had promised them after the battle.'

Seiradakis spent the next two years in the White Mountains, wanted by the Germans. He was in contact with the Greek Government and headquarters in the Middle East, as well as with the first pockets of resistance that began to form in Crete. His family remained in Livadas and he visited them whenever possible. He shared with his compatriots the fate of the painful German occupation that was to last for four long years.

The Destruction of Kandanos

After the German victory, *Generalleutnant* Kurt Student was now the commander of Crete. On 31 May he issued an order authorising harsh reprisals for Cretan resistance without following the formal procedures.[56] The reprisals included executions of people and the destruction of villages.[57] On the morning of 3 June, German units under *Hauptman* Nimber returned to Kandanos, where only a few elderly people were left, and destroyed the houses. Nothing was left standing. Many residents who had taken refuge in the surrounding hills in the hope of eventually returning realised that they no longer had homes to go back to. Matters were made worse by the declaration of Kandanos as a 'no-go zone' and the erection of signs announcing its destruction.[58]

losses are difficult to estimate. Seiradakis reports 15 dead and 18 wounded, but there were more casualties among the civilians. The German forces that took part in the battle were of battalion strength (about 900 men) reinforced with two mountain guns and eight mortars. 191 Germans were reported dead in the three Battles of Floria, Mesaulia and Gorge, and as many again were wounded.

56 Richter, *H Machi tis Kritis*, p.411. Student's order for retaliation states: 'All measures must be taken as soon as possible, bypassing all kinds of formalities and avoiding the voluntary establishment of special courts'. The formalities were a sham since the reprisals were applied before any findings were issued by the German judge Schölz, who undertook to investigate the situation after the battle.

57 The German reprisals began on 2 June 1941 with the mass execution of civilians in the village of Kontomari. The destruction of Kandanos followed the next day, 3 June 1941.

58 A sign read: 'Here stood Kandanos. It was destroyed to atone for the murder of 25 German soldiers'. On the monument erected later a second sign stated: 'For the brutal murder of German paratroopers, alpinists and engineers by men, women, children and priests together because they dared to resist the Great Reich, Kandanos was destroyed on 3 June 1941 and razed to the ground so that it would never be rebuilt again.' A third sign at the exit to Chania

Since then, these signs have become the trademark of Kandanos. But contrary to their grim message, the destruction of the town was not its end. After the war, the inhabitants returned and rebuilt their homes. For the Seliniots, Kandanos conveys a message of resistance and endurance in the face of adversity to this day. Beevor mentions that the Metropolitan of Kydonia and Apokoronas, Agathangelos Xirouchakis, in order to protect the Cretans from reprisals, tried to convince *General* Alexander Andrae, who had replaced Student, that 'with the policy (of retaliation) he would only succeed in causing more bloodshed on both sides.'[59]

* * *

It seems that André agreed, and perhaps other Germans were of the same opinion. Unfortunately, the 'show of force' prevailed during the occupation in the worst possible way. The reprisals continued to be harsh and as a result the acts of resistance multiplied. The vicious cycle of violence and bloodshed continued for the next four years.

With hindsight, some thoughts can be put forward about the Battle of Kandanos and the disasters that followed. We know today that the Battle of Crete was decided in the first days, or even hours, at Maleme airfield and the fateful Hill 107. The Battle of Kandanos was not decisive in the outcome of the struggle for Crete. But if the defence by the New Zealand battalion of Hill 107 had been successful, then the diversion of *Antisyntagmatachis* Seiradakis at Kandanos would have made a positive contribution. Eventually, direct control of the airfield allowed the Germans to receive reinforcements and prevail. They advanced east and forced the Allies to evacuate Crete. To the south, they advanced powerful motorised units that were de facto impossible for the few fighters of Selino to hold back.

In the end, the absence of a regular army and the incomplete organisation of the militia, combined with the deadly battles, made the German retaliation a self-fulfilling prophecy. The hundreds, even thousands, of dead paratroopers aroused in the Germans a desire for revenge that needed only a pretext to manifest itself. They found this in what they considered to be acts of violence by civilians that they did not consider legitimate combatants. But the Cretans had reacted based on their immovable right to self-defence. The German retaliation was harsh. Events such as the destruction of Kandanos and the executions at Kontomari and elsewhere were tragic for the civilian population. The vicious cycle of violence and bloodshed that began with the dropping of the first

read: 'In retaliation of the German soldiers murdered in the rear by armed civilian men and women, Kandanos was destroyed'.

59 Beevor, *Crete*, p.344. Bishop Agathangelos Xirouchakis (1872–1958) from the village of Souri, Chania, followed the priestly life from early on. He had an interest in humanistic studies. He served as a parish priest in St George, Venice, where he obtained a Doctorate in Philosophy. He continued his studies in Vienna, where he stayed for 15 years and published many theological and historical studies. He returned to Chania in 1936 and was ordained bishop. As a religious leader during the Nazi occupation of Crete he did his best to mitigate the suffering of the inhabitants. After the war he helped to avert the civil war in Crete. He remained Bishop of Chania until his death.

paratroopers continued throughout the four-year occupation. The wounds left on the Cretan psyche were to last for decades.

And yet, despite all the traumas, the Cretans never distanced themselves from their basic principles. Their land remained hospitable to all, even to those who once hurt it. Nowhere is this more evident than in the rhyming verse:

> Listen to what Crete ordered to its children's children
> Count the graves of your own
> And of the foreigners
> And light candles. Light a candle to all
> A holy candle and incense
> And if the relatives of the dead foreigners come
> Offer them hospitality.

15

In The Middle East, 1943

The Greek Army in Exile

Charalampos Seiradakis's reminiscences on the British warship *Hedgehog* that escorted them from German-occupied Crete to the Middle East came to an abrupt halt as the ship berthed noisily in the port of Tobruk. It was the morning of 9 May 1943. Ever since the beginning of the war, Tobruk had been a military port, and a camp atmosphere prevailed everywhere as the quay was full of military vehicles, sailors, supplies and ammunition. Although the fighting at El Alamein had ended a year ago, the signs of war were still visible. Trucks and jeeps soon arrived to pick up the recently arrived travellers. The officers Charalampos Seiradakis, Stelios Papaderos and Manolis Papagrigorakis boarded one of them and left immediately for Alexandria, with Cairo as their ultimate destination. They were in a hurry to cross the desert before the unbearable heat of the day set in. Besides, they were ordered to report as soon as possible to the Greek garrison and from there to the headquarters of the general staff of the army. There Seiradakis was to meet his old acquaintance and comrade-in-arms, *Syntagmatarchis* Byron Kapanagiotis,[1] who had recently taken over as minister of military affairs in the Greek Government-in-exile. He was to inform him of the unit he was to take over the very next day.

What situation was Seiradakis going to face in the Middle East? Information from officer friends already in Cairo was confusing and not encouraging. Among these officers was his old comrade-in-arms, *Syntagmatarchis* Pavlis Gyparis, who by the summer of 1942 had been appointed garrison commander in Cairo. The reorganisation of the Greek Army in the Middle East, which was under the auspices of the General Headquarters Middle East, had been undertaken by Deputy Prime Minister Panagiotis Kanellopoulos.[2] The Greek Fleet had already sailed to the ports of Alexandria and Port Said. There were also aspirations to organise a Greek Air Force squadron.

1 *Syntagmatarchis* Byron Karapanagiotis had left the Greek Army after the 1935 Venizelist coup but had been reinstated by the Tsouderos Law. He was a member of the military court at the trial of the 'six' in 1922.

2 Panagiotis Kanellopoulos, *Imerologio katochis, 31 Martiou 1942 – 4 Ianouariou 1945*, Tomos 1 (Athens: Ekdoseis kathimerinis, 2021), (Patras, 1902–1986). Kanellopoulos studied law, philosophy and sociology. In 1942 he became deputy to the exiled government of Tsouderos in Cairo until March 1943. After the war he was prime minister for a short period

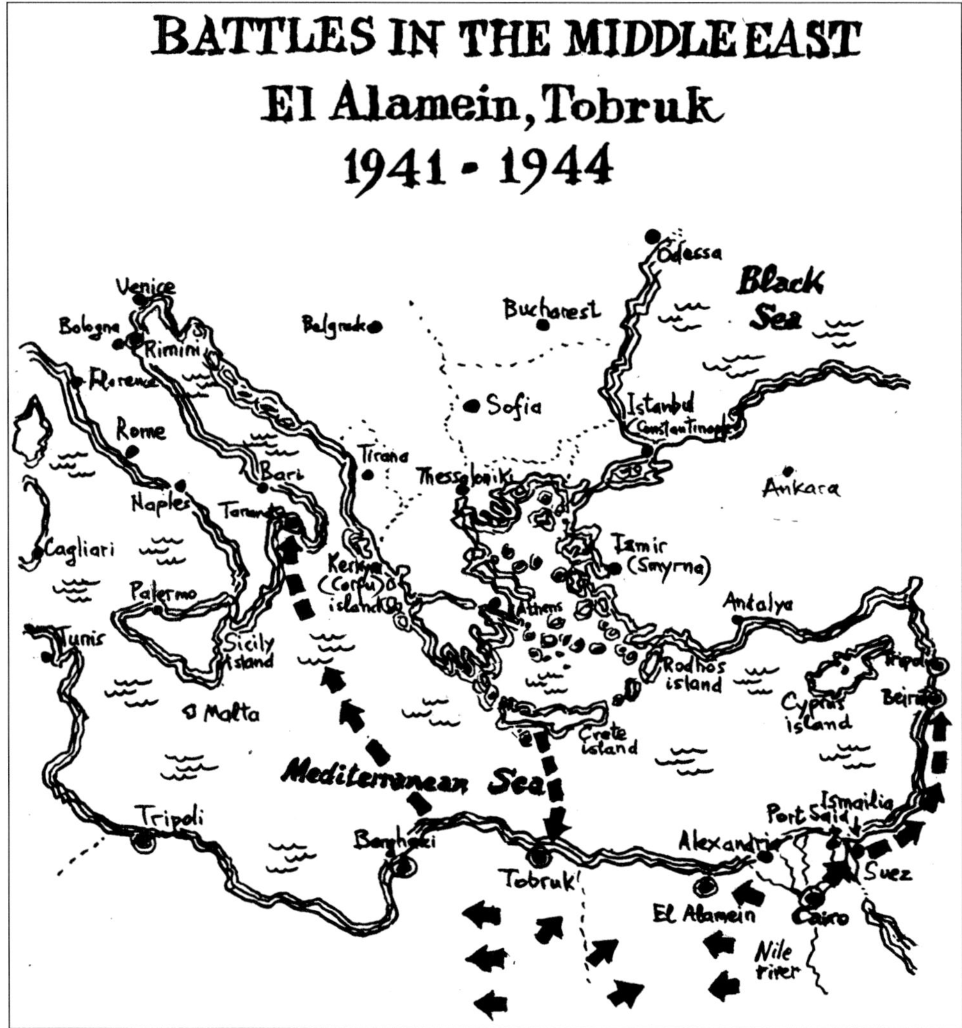

Battles in The Middle East: El Alamein and Tobruk, 1941–1944.

But the army had significant shortcomings. The most immediate was the lack of experienced officers. Fortunately, Prime Minister Tsouderos had provided a solution to this by recalling to the army the experienced officers who had participated in the Venizelist coups of 1933 and 1935. But while for the Venizelists their reinstatement

(1 to 22 November 1945). He succeeded K. Karamanlis as leader of the conservative party (*ERE*). In July 1965 he was sworn in as prime minister for the second time, until the military coup of 21 April 1967. Of his 200 volumes of intellectual work *Istoría tou Evropaïkoú Nou* (*History of the European Mind*) is considered the most important.

was a long-standing demand that rectified an injustice on their behalf, it had displeased several active officers because of changes in the hierarchy. However, it had provided an immediate solution in the staffing of the Greek Army in exile. The second difficulty was recruitment from the Greek community in Egypt as many had avoided conscription. Although Kanellopoulos had remained Vice President and Minister of National Defence for only a year, he had organised a strong army to forward to El Alamein. But he had soon resigned over an episode of mutiny. What exactly had happened to the Greek Army in the Middle East?

The first Greek brigade, commanded by *Syntagmatarchis* Pausanias Katsotas,[3] was sworn in on 20 July 1941, which was 'a day of celebration'.[4] At the same time, a second brigade, commanded by *Syntagmatarchis* Alkiviades Bourdaras, and the General Training and Schools Centre, which was assembling the auxiliary services, began to be organised. The immediate priority of the Middle East government was the participation of the Greek Army in military operations so that Greece would be among the victors when the war ended. However, the Allied staff had misgivings about the battle worthiness of the Greek units, not so much concerning its fighting ability as in relation to the divisive tendencies that had recently been observed. Despite all these misgivings, the Greek first brigade had received orders to advance to the front line of the war.

The First Brigade at El Alamein

As Winston Churchill, the British Prime Minister during most of the Second World War, said succinctly, 'before El Alamein we had no victory, after El Alamein we had no defeat.'[5]

The Allied campaign in the Middle East was not an easy task once Erwin Rommel, a skilled German general whose unorthodox tactics had earned him the title 'Fox of the desert', took over the Axis command.[6]

In April 1941 Rommel had blockaded the British at Tobruk for four months. He captured it in July and from the hills of El Alamein he threatened Alexandria. But then everything went wrong for him. He failed at El Alamein, the United States was preparing for an invasion of West Africa, he was confronted by the new Allied commander, Lieutenant

3 Pausanias Katsotas (1896–1991). *Ypostratigos* of the Greek Army and politician. He fought in the Asia Minor campaign, the Greek Italian War of 1940–1941 and the Battle of El Alamein. He later served as a minister in several governments and as Mayor of Athens.

4 Much of the information on the events of the Middle East is based on the doctoral thesis of Dimitrios Katsikostas, *O Ellinikos Stratos stin Exoria 1941–1944 – Organosi, Syngkrotisi, Polemikes Apostoles kai Kinimata sti Mesi Anatoli*, (Ph.D. thesis, University of Athens, December 2010). This quote from page 62 reflects the pride of the first combat unit of the Greek Army in Exile in the Middle East.

5 One of Winston Churchill's well-known references to the war in the Middle East.

6 In German *Wüstenfuchs*. *General* Erwin Rommel had taken command of the German Seventh Army in the Middle East in February 1940.

General Montgomery,[7] and he himself fell ill and had to leave immediately for treatment in Austria.

In the meantime, the Greek first brigade was ready for battle. In August 1942, Kanellopoulos had convinced Churchill about the participation of Greek forces in the battles of El Alamein.[8] Thus, on 5 August the brigade had advanced to the front. On Sunday 13 September Kanellopoulos had visited the brigade in the desert where he and *Dioikitis* Katsotas received the British commander-in-chief, Bernard Montgomery. 'Monty' appeared 'excited to be able to command a Greek brigade.'[9] The Allied offensive began on 23 October. The fighting continued uninterrupted for over a month under appalling conditions. The heat of the day alternated with freezing temperatures at night. Food was lacking and water was scarce. Ultimately, the fortunes of the war were affected by the absence of Rommel, who had fallen ill.[10] In the tank battle on 2 November, the Allied tanks achieved a decisive victory. Rommel withdrew in tragic circumstances which mainly affected the Italian forces which were left behind and were annihilated. On 24 January 1943 the Eighth Army triumphantly entered Tripoli, Libya.

At the end of November 1942, the Greek first brigade was pursuing the withdrawing enemy. But it had not taken sufficient defence precautions and in an enemy air attack on 9 December it suffered considerable losses.[11] This tragic event was the occasion for political rivalries to resurface. The republicans accused the pro-royalist of being responsible for the inadequate defence, while the monarchists rejected the accusations. Political disputes that had long been going on were back with vengeance. When, in the following days, the brigade was ordered to continue its mission, 10 officers and privates refused to obey, and *Dioikitis* Katsotas had to have them arrested. The event did not go unnoticed by the Allied military command. It understood that there were political factions and lack of discipline in the Greek troops, and it was decided to exclude them from the final attack against Rommel. This marked the end of the first brigade's participation in the El Alamein campaign 'depriving it of the opportunity to participate in the final confrontation and the destruction of the enemy.'[12] By January 1943, the brigade had returned to Lebanon.

7 General Bernard Law Montgomery, later Field Marshal and First Viscount Montgomery of Alamein (1887–1976), commander-in-chief of the Allied forces in North Africa. He had fought as an infantry officer in the First World War and in many battles in the Second World War to date. He became known for his victory at El Alamein.

8 Kanellopoulos, *Imerologio katochis,* Tomos A, p.111. "Churchill told me: 'Your army is very good. We will have several more battles. Enough battles for everyone'"

9 Kanellopoulos, *Imerologio katochis,* Tomos A, p.133. Along with Montgomery, the commander of the Eighth Army, was also A. Hughes, Commander of the British 44th Division.

10 During Rommel's recovery leave his replacement *General* Stumme suffered a heart attack and Rommel had to return urgently to the front, although he was still recovering from illness.

11 Katsikostas, *O Ellinikos Stratos stin Exoria 1941–1944* footnote on pp.147–148. 'Those responsible ... showed criminal indifference'. There were 30 dead (3 officers and 27 soldiers) and 44 wounded.

12 Katsikostas, *O Ellinikos Stratos stin Exoria 1941–1944*, p.150.

Despite its sudden withdrawal from the front, the participation of the Greek Army in the battles of El Alamein was successful. Officers and soldiers alike felt proud to have taken part in the fighting. In a gesture of recognition of the heroic effort of the Greek brigade, the Allied headquarters decorated *Dioikitis* Katsotas and many officers and other ranks.[13]

Military Factions

From 1941 to 1943 many Greek officers and soldiers arrived in Cairo to join the Greek Army in exile. Venizelist officers who had been demobilised after the 1935 coup could now return under the Tsouderos Law. One of these was *Antisyntagmatachis* Charalampos Seiradakis. He had recently arrived in Egypt with a mission to assume command of one of the combat units in the Middle East. He would have liked to have more information about his unit because he had learned that some 'restless elements' belonging to a military organisation had taken the lead in a mutiny four months ago, in March 1943. Who were these people? Soon he will be able to assess the situation up close.

In the Middle East, new balances had been established. Seiradakis soon found that on an operational level there was no problem of cooperation between unit commanders. Most of the pro-royalist officers were disciplined and did not agree with the extreme activities of some of their pro-Metaxas colleagues. For their part, the republican officers, most of them Venizelists, were content to be back in the army and were eager to contribute to the Allied war effort. Thus, common principles and values proved stronger than old rivalries. The need for national unity in wartime for the Allied cause was evident.

But not everyone saw it the same way. The new element in the Greek Army in the Middle East was the strong presence of the left faction. As early as September 1941, *Ypaspistis* Yannis Sallas had founded the *Antifasistiki Stratiotiki Organosi* (the *ASO*, Anti-Fascist Military Organisation) in Palestine[14] which was a 'left-wing political organisation par excellence'. The *ASO* had penetrated the low-ranking officers and soldiers who constituted the 'nervous system of the army'.[15] The aim of the *ASO* was to rally those with a left-wing ideology and soldiers with democratic convictions. From the beginning of 1943 the *ASO* printed the newspaper *Antifasistas*, which was widely circulated in military units. It had considerable influence as it popularised the aims of the organisation and the 'anti-fascist struggle'.[16]

13 Katsikostas, *O Ellinikos Stratos stin Exoria 1941–1944*, p.153. Also decorated were: Pilikas (third battalion, rank unknown), *Anthypaspistis* Apostolidis (first battalion), *Lochias* Voyatzis (engineering company) and *Lochias* Tsolakidis (second battalion).

14 The original structure founded by Sallas was called Communist Military Organisation of the Middle East (CMOMA), which he later renamed ASO.

15 Katsikostas. *O Ellinikos Stratos stin Exoria 1941–1944*, p.68. In the first brigade these committees were organised at company and battalion level. The same in the second brigade and in the General Training and Schools Centre.

16 B. Hatziangelis & L. Rappas, *To Ógdoo Tágma, 1943–1944* (Chania: Rappas, 1994), p.26.

The *ASO* challenged the military hierarchy. It advocated that soldiers were entitled to their own opinion on military matters and anything that deprived them of this right was a fascist tactic. Thus, the designation 'fascist' had become generalised and was a means of political pressure for anyone who did not subscribe to *ASO*'s ideology. Gradually its members disobeyed orders from superiors who disagreed with *ASO* policies, resulting in less discipline and a loss of prestige for army officers. Although the *ASO* was mainly targeting pro-Metaxas officers, it would soon clash with the Venizelists too. For the *ASO* these were 'old democrats' who had rejoined the army to regain the positions they had lost following the coup d'état of 1935. As it turned out, the *ASO* aimed at the regime that would take power in Greece after the war.

At the other extreme were the right-wing officers, enthusiasts of dictator Metaxas' regime. Although they were in the minority, they were still able to influence the situation in the army.

They too had post-war ambitions.[17] They made no secret of the fact that they envisaged the restoration of the King after the war with the support of the Greek Army in exile. For this reason, they did not look kindly on the return of democratic officers to the army and tried to instead promote their own staff to the upper echelons. In the field they had adopted the tactic of mass resignations. Whenever they observed provocative actions by *ASO*, they pushed their officers to resign collectively. However, the policy of mass resignations had become a problem for the Allied Middle East headquarters. Although they invoked reasons of military order to justify their action, the result was further lack of discipline and corrosion of military discipline of the army. In his one year as minister of military affairs, Panagiotis Kanellopoulos had pursued a policy of balancing political trends. He believed that a stable rapprochement between Venizelist and moderate pro-royal officers was possible. But at the same time, he had advocated the right of the conscripts to express themselves freely, which *ASO* had exploited to push its own line. Kanellopoulos had appointed Venizelist officers to combat units, and pro-royalists to staff positions.[18] In practice, it turned out that this policy had reinforced the phenomenon of indiscipline. The danger that acts of disobedience could break out at any moment was imminent. Only one excuse was needed for them to explode.

First Mutiny in the Army

Syntagmatarchis Georgios Hadjistavris was a dynamic officer of the Greek Army.[19] He had rejoined the army with the Tsouderos Law and had taken command of the fifth

17 Katsikostas. *O Ellinikos Stratos stin Exoria 1941–1944*, p.175, n. 42. Their organisation, 'Nemesi' (Nemesis), was founded in autumn 1941. It included, among others, officers Maraveas, Vassos, Kortzas, Vagenas, Antoniou and Kosmopoulos.

18 The creation of a division for the unified command of the two brigades was assigned to the monarchist *Ypostratigos* Christos Zygouris to balance the assignment of the two brigades to the Venizelists *Syntagmatarchis* P. Katsotas and *Syntagmatarchis* E. Bourdaras (November 1942).

19 *Syntagmatarchis* G. Hadjistavris was a republican officer with leftist ideology who had retired after the 1935 coup. The same was true for *Tagmatarchis* H. Stavroulakis and the

battalion of the second brigade, whose commander was *Syntagmatarchis* Alkiviadis Bourdaras,[20] who aspired to make it the second Greek combat unit in the Middle East. But most of its staff were penetrated by the *ASO* which was thus able to pursue its policies, often with the tacit cooperation of like-minded officers.

One of them was Chadjistavris. He tolerated and even supported insubordinate behaviour because it ensured smooth cooperation with his soldiers with whom he shared similar ideology. This tacit cooperation caused fury in the pro-royalist camp who submitted a report against him to the minister of military affairs Kanellopoulos. When Kanellopoulos returned from a difficult mission in London in February 1943 he found the report on his desk. He had to act.

Kanellopoulos had already realised that the policy of equal distances was not working and wanted to revise it. So, on 25 February he asked Chadjistavris to report to Cairo. Chadjistavris refused and brigade commander Bourdaras balked because he feared 'unpleasant consequences' in his units.[21] Only three days earlier a group of monarchist officers in his brigade had submitted a collective resignation. To prevent the worst, on 28 February Kanellopoulos travelled in person from Cairo to the camp near Beirut and asked to see Hadjistavris. He was informed that, 'with the consent of his most hot-blooded soldiers he had been barricaded in his battalion.' The fifth battalion, with the support of the other two battalions, had mutinied! The mutiny was supported by *ASO*, which declared that it would not accept solutions directed against it.[22]

On 2 March Chadjistavris went to see Kanellopoulos with an escort of 50 armed soldiers. He told him that the coup in the fifth battalion had a 'political character' and asked for no less than a reshuffle of the government. At the same time, the mutiny had extended to the first brigade that had fought in El Alamein. It was on a training exercise in Tripoli, Lebanon, when armed *ASO* soldiers ousted *Dioikitis* Katsotas and an *ASO anthypaspistis* took over command.[23] Pro-royalist officers reacted and 38 of them collectively resigned, but the mutineers placed them under arrest. Eventually the command of the two rebel Greek units was taken over by British officers and discipline was restored – albeit temporarily.[24]

Kanellopoulos' position after his mission to London had weakened and the *ASO* was quick to take advantage of it. It bypassed the Greek administration in Cairo and

commander of the second brigade Ep. Bourdaras. Kanellopoulos knew Chatzistavris and reports that he had met him in Beirut on 16 April 1942. *Imerologio katochis,* Tomos A, p.38.

20 *Syntagmatarchis* A. Bourdaras, *Stratigos* Kammenos, *Antisyntagmatachis* Ch. Seiradakis and others were among those who had fled to Karlovo, Bulgaria, following the Venizelist coup in 1935.

21 *Imerologio katochis,* Tomos A', p.375.

22 Hatziangelis & Rappas, *To ogdoo tagma*, pp.38 et seq. The letter to commander Bourdaras states: 'the partial mobilisation which took place for *Syntagmatarchis* Chadjistavris will become general of the Brigade if the fascists ever dare to make serious decisions or if they want to replace you. Signed: *ASO*.'

23 Katsikostas. *O Ellinikos Stratos stin Exoria 1941–1944*, p.189, n. 92. It was the reservist *Ypolochagos* A. Mamalakis. A meeting of the ASO was held on 27 February, which was also attended by the reservist *Ypolochagos* N. Christakos and S. Papadopoulos.

24 Hatziangelis & Rappas, *To ogdoo tagma.*, p.47.

submitted a memorandum to the British high command proposing terms for the peaceful resolution of the mutiny. The Middle East general staff chose to accept them to calm the situation.

The terms were: a government reshuffle, return of the battalion commanders to their units; punishment of the officers who had collectively resigned; removal of the extreme right-wing officers to camps; replacement of the commander of the second brigade, Bourdaras.[25] The officers who had resigned tried to excuse their action on the grounds that their military honour had been undermined and they preferred not to return to the army under present circumstances. Not because of disobedience, as they were accused, but because they would not join a leftist insurrectionary coup.

In the circumstances, it was the *ASO* that felt vindicated, and the outcome of the mutiny meant that it could impose its political line. Thus, the wartime show of defiance was charged to Kanellopoulos who on 5 March resigned. Many were quick to support him, such as the *Frourarchos* Pavlis Gyparis, who showed that he appreciated his work in the army.[26] Of the Greek combat units in the Middle East, only the *Ieros Lochos* (sacred company) of *Syntagmatarchis* Lakis Tsigantes had remained unaffected by political controversy.[27] A few days later, on 14 March, Prime Minister Tsouderos and King George II arrived in Cairo and reshuffled the government. The new faces came from the democratic camp, which was thought to be in a better position to control the situation.[28]

The March 1943 mutiny was a turning point for the Greek Army in exile in the Middle East. For the first time, the rivalries between the extreme elements of the army were openly expressed. They affected moderate officers, both pro-royalists and Venizelists. Gradually, a broader consensus began to emerge among them as they realised that not only the army's combat worthiness but also the preservation of the democratic regime in Greece after the war was at stake.

Calm Before the Storm

At noon on 9 May 1943, Charalampos Seiradakis and two other Greek officers were crossing the Libyan desert and heading straight for Cairo via Alexandria. Along the road through the sand dunes, one could see damaged cars and the few scattered buildings which were still standing. Now and then they overtook a loaded camel or a jeep in a cloud of dust. The heat was unbearable, and the hot air hit them in the face. They had

25 *Syntagmatarchis* Katsotas remained commander of the first brigade.

26 Kanellopoulos, *Imerologio katochis,* Tomos, p.33.

27 The character of *Syntagmatarchis* L. Tsigantes played a decisive role in this. The action of *Ieros Lochos*, perhaps the most active Greek unit in the Middle East, is not examined here.

28 Prime Minister M. Tsouderos also took over the Ministry of Foreign Affairs, while Georgios Roussos became vice president. Vyron Karapanagiotis succeeded him in the Ministry of Military Affairs, with Sophocles Venizelos, who had just returned from America, as Deputy Minister of the Navy. Themistocles Sofoulis was appointed Minister of Welfare, Stylianos Dimitrakakis Minister of Justice and Labour, and Kyriakos Varvaressos Minister of Finance. Chief of Air Force was *Yponavarchos* Petros Voulgaris and of the Fleet *Navarchos* Konstantinos Alexandris.

passed Alexandria and still needed two more hours to reach Cairo, they finally arrived late in the afternoon.

Seiradakis presented himself at the garrison where his old acquaintance and comrade-in-arms Pavlis Gyparis was waiting for him. He informed him of everything about the coup in the two brigades, about the infiltration of the leftist *ASO* into the troops, about the internment of the pro-Metaxas officers in the Lebanese camps, and above all about the new government. The new person was Sophocles Venizelos, who had been appointed deputy minister, but it was possible that he would soon become prime minister in place of Tsouderos. Their well-known minister of military affairs, Karapanagiotis, had been given the difficult task of imposing discipline on the army and sending it back to the front. In this area, he did not deviate from the policy of his predecessor Kanellopoulos: the formation of a reliable army with a balancing of forces.

The new mission of Seiradakis was not easy. He was to become commander of the fifth battalion of the second brigade – with *Tagmatarchis* George Detorakis as second in command – the battalion where the previous mutiny had broken out. In a short while he had discussed everything with Gyparis. Immediately afterwards it was his turn to see Karapanagiotis at the Ministry of Military Affairs. He told him more or less the same things. Karapanagiotis assured him that he would be conciliatory, avoiding extreme solutions. He was optimistic and relied on the new unit commanders, many of whom were experienced officers of republican leanings. The message to Seiradakis was that they should do everything they could to make the army battle ready. It was dusk when the jeep left again with Seiradakis, alone this time, bound for Lebanon and his new unit. They would arrive at dawn.

From 9 May onwards, *Syntagmatarchis* Ioannis Bayetis had taken over as the new commander of the 'left' second brigade, with *Syntagmatarchis* Evangelos Pappas in the first brigade.[29] For the time being, both brigades were calm. However, the *ASO* was suspicious of the new commanders who enthusiastically engaged in the military preparation of their units.[30] At the beginning of May 1943, the second brigade was on the move again. Except for the fifth battalion commanded by Seiradakis which was in Damascus, Syria, the other units were constantly on the move. This policy of constant movement was intended to keep the units in action, although the difficult weather conditions created discomfort and tendencies to disobedience. Desertions were frequent.

Seiradakis and Bayetis had known each other for a long time and had a mutual respect. From the first days the commanders had agreed on the tactics they would follow to avoid any new mutiny. Seiradakis tried from the beginning to gain the trust of his soldiers

29 The new brigade commanders Pappas and Bayetis were moderate democratic officers. In the second brigade the staff officer was *Tagmatarchis* Ath. Geramanis, the sixth battalion was commanded by *Antisyntagmatachis* Kallioris and the seventh battalion by *Tagmatarchis* Od. Papamandelos.

30 Tassos Sakellaropoulos, *Oi enoples dynameis. Symmachies kai dichasmoi sti Mesi Anatoli, 1941–1944* sto Istoria tou Neou Ellinismou 1700–2000, 8os tomos: *H Empolemi Ellada 1940–1949 (Alvaniko Epos, Katochi kai Antistasi, Emfylios)*, (Athens, Ellinika Grammata, 2004), tomos C, (Vivliorama, Athens, 2007), p.174. For *ASO* the commander was a kind of supervisor who would co-decide with the soldiers.

and non-commissioned officers with a stern but fair attitude that was inherent in his character. He kept an exact and equal distance from all factions. But it was not an easy task since, according to reports, the fifth battalion was 'a potential destabilising factor as those described as 'anarchists' exceeded 150 men.'[31] However, in the summer of 1943 there was optimism that with the looming Allied victory the units would soon depart to liberate the homeland.

But despite the apparent calm, the rivalries had not disappeared. It would only take the lighting of a fuse to bring them back to the surface. The new commanders soon realised that the rivalry between the left *ASO* and the pro-Metaxas monarchists had not stopped even for a moment.

The Storm Breaks, a Second Mutiny

The new mutinous episode began, as in March, in the second brigade. On 15 May 1943, pro-royalist soldiers had accused the battalion doctor, Mavrogenis, of being biased in favour of the leftists of the *ASO* and asked for his removal. *Dioikitis* Bayetis refused because the unit needed a good doctor, and the incident ended. Soon two pro-royalist officers asked for the replacement of *Tagmatarchis* Stavroulakis on the grounds that he was biased in favour of *ASO*. This time Bayetis listened and replaced Stavroulakis, but at the same time referred the two instigators for questioning. The fever was rising.

Shortly afterwards, *ASO* made a show of strength to the 'left' fifth battalion of Seiradakis. At the end of May, some pro-royalist soldiers, who had received orders from Camp Merj Uyum in Lebanon, deserted. Seiradakis referred them to a military tribunal, which, however, in the spirit of leniency, sentenced them to a short imprisonment which was only partially enforced. The *ASO* sought revenge. When it learned that two pro-royalist officers would be joining the fifth battalion, which would reduce *ASO* influence, it 'amended the roll, putting the new commander, *Syntagmatarchis* Seiradakis, in a delicate position and finally cancelled the order.'[32] It was a warning from the *ASO* not to change the political balance in the second brigade.

Despite all these incidents, discipline prevailed. But on 2 June the commander of the sixth battalion imposed on a deserter a 'severe imprisonment' in a prison which was notorious for inhumane conditions. Six soldiers, members of the *ASO*, protested strongly and when *Dioikitis* Bayetis called them to report they ran away to their unit. To avoid further incidents Bayetis himself went to the sixth battalion the next day and persuaded them to board the car and return to the brigade command post. The fatality happened on the way. Apparently 'a nod from the driver was interpreted as a sign that the men of the following military detachment intended to execute them or take them

31 Katsikostas. *O Ellinikos Stratos stin Exoria 1941–1944*, p.226. Reported by *Antisyntagmatachis* Manidakis who was aware of the situation as he had been the commander for a short time after the March mutiny.

32 Katsikostas. *O Ellinikos Stratos stin Exoria 1941–1944*, p.228.

to prison.'[33] Terrified, the six soldiers escaped and hid while the soldiers ran to arrest them. A shot was heard, and a soldier named Papastergiou was mortally wounded.[34] The soldiers arrested two of the six who escaped, while the other three fled and disappeared.

Near the incident was the fifth battalion that was conducting exercises. *Dioikitis* Seiradakis realised the critical nature of the situation when he heard the shot, and his soldiers were angered. He ordered his units to regroup but only three companies obeyed while two others under *ASO* pressure armed themselves and headed for the brigade command post. *Anthypaspistis* Constantine Fountoulakis' unit was one of those that obeyed. In his handwritten report to Seiradakis after the incident he stated: 'when the battalion gathered, I took my company and moved towards the camp. You, Commander, ordered me to rush immediately to the fleeing soldiers wherever they were going and to exert all my influence to bring them back ... Based on this order, I left and reached the brigade.'[35] The timely arrival of Fountoulakis at the brigade saved *Dioikitis* Bayetis from certain death. As he was trying to calm things down some of the mutinous members of the *ASO* stabbed him. Fortunately, on Seiradakis' orders, they got him to the infirmary of the fifth battalion and managed to save his life.

Again, the second brigade was in a state of mutiny. The armed soldiers isolated the pro-monarchists and would have executed them if at the critical moment Seiradakis had not appeared and, through a combination of threats and appeals to their honour, imposed order. According to historian Dimitrios Katsikostas: 'the intervention of Seiradakis, who made the mutineers face up to their responsibilities, limited the frenzy that had been provoked and finally succeeded in making the voice of reason prevail among the excited.'[36] However, more violence followed. Wanting to avenge the death of the unfortunate soldier, some men executed *Lochias* Glotsos, whom they thought had shot him. The two deaths made the situation even worse.

It was the last thing the new Minister of Military Affairs Karapanagiotis expected. He was at nearby Beirut when he was informed of the events and rushed to the camp on 7 June to take measures against the new mutiny. The two rebel battalions, the fifth and sixth, were to be disarmed and disbanded as combat units. Soon a British armoured division surrounded them, and the Greek soldiers were locked up in camps. The conclusion of the interrogations was that the main culprit for the incidents was the *ASO* which had urged the soldiers into disobedience. At the same time responsibility was also attributed to the pro-royalists who had caused the desertion. The commander of the second brigade, Bayetis, who had just escaped with his life, was accused of failing to anticipate the events of June.

33 Katsikostas. *O Ellinikos Stratos stin Exoria 1941–1944*, p.229.

34 Katsikostas. *O Ellinikos Stratos stin Exoria 1941–1944*, p.236. It has not been possible to ascertain who fired the shot. The British report notes: 'shots were fired and the men of the detachment wounded a soldier'. At the Court-Martial held later, again no answer was given as to who fired first.

35 Handwritten Memo by *Anthypaspistis* Fountoulakis Konstantinos. (Military archive of Charalampos Seiradakis), Document reprinted in Appendix II.

36 Katsikostas. *O Ellinikos Stratos stin Exoria 1941–1944*, p.235, where he quotes D. Karavaselas 'On information of the facts in the Middle East', Archive GES/DIS/F.805 A/G/D/2.

But the accusation was largely unfair. Lack of discipline and disobedience had deeply scarred the second brigade and especially the 'left' fifth battalion. The command entrusted to Seiradakis proved de facto impossible. Despite his efforts to make it combat ready and even though he did not receive criticism himself, it was not possible for him to bring order, either through an appeal to honour, or with patriotic exhortations. After only two months of command in the Greek Army in the Middle East, Charalampos Seiradakis had to give up the command of the fifth battalion, but he was soon returning to Cairo to take up a new assignment.

Consequences

The mutiny of the second brigade, however, offered a new opportunity to the government. Minister Karapanagiotis called on the pro-royalist officers who did not agree with the pro-Metaxas extremists to re-join the army. The minister's appeal was supported by *Syntagmatarchis* Lakis Tsigantes, who led the *Ieros Lochos* (sacred company). No mutinous incidents had occurred in his unit, even though he had officers from all political factions serving with him.

Tsigantes had issued a patriotic call for everyone to join his unit as ordinary soldiers. The response was immediate. Pro-royal and republican army officers – to which he himself belonged – declared their participation as rank-and-file soldiers and the result was the formation of the most formidable Greek unit in the Middle East, which distinguished itself in the battles and in the liberation of the Greek islands of the Aegean. Tsigantes was thus able to prove that the organisation of a fighting unit that had not been corroded by political ideologies was possible.

After the preliminary enquiry into the June mutiny, 67 junior officers and privates of the second brigade were brought before the military court in October 1943. The court was presided over by *Syntagmatarchis* Lakis Tsigantes and imposed severe sentences. What was not specified was who was responsible for the shooting that killed a soldier and triggered the bloody events that followed. Nor was it possible for the trial to calm political rivalries. The underlying causes that had led to two insurrectionary movements remained alive and waiting for the opportunity to emerge again.

The worst effect of the mutinies was that they had prevented the participation of the Greek Army in the operations of the Second World War. In July 1943 the Allies were achieving victories everywhere and the first landing of troops in Sicily had just taken place, where Greek units were also scheduled to have taken part. This participation was de facto cancelled. As General Warner told Panagiotis Kanellopoulos in Cairo on 21 July, 'if it had not been for the trouble in the Greek Army in March, a Greek section would have taken part in the Sicilian landing.'[37]

37 Kanellopoulos, *Imerologio katochis,* Tomos B, p.102.

16

The Destruction of the Three Villages

Karlovo – Thessaloniki – Chania

Charalampos Seiradakis had already spent over a year in exile in Karlovo, Bulgaria, after the failed Venizelist movement of 1935, when he learned that he would soon be able to return home. In November 1936 he had reunited with his beloved wife Fani and his four daughters in Thessaloniki. At 36 years old Fani was a beautiful woman despite all the hardships. Their two eldest daughters, Eugenia and Maria, were 11 and 10 years old. The two youngest, Elizabeth (Veta) and Helen-Ellas (Lilly), were 4 and 2 years old respectively. While Seiradakis was in exile in Karlovo, his family lived in the house of Fani's mother in Thessaloniki. But they would not stay there for long. As the terms of the amnesty stipulated that returning officers had to live away from the military units in Athens and Thessaloniki, the family had to leave for Crete.

It was November 1936 when the Seiradakis family had arrived after a long journey to their ancestral village of Livadas in Selino, Western Crete. For his fellow countrymen, Charalampos was the heroic battle-ravaged officer who had taken part in countless battles. His father, Joseph, the heroic Kountourossifis, was no longer alive, but his mother Eugenia, who was of advanced age, welcomed them with affection. The family home was situated on a hill overlooking the gorge of Agia Irini and the valley of the Agieriniotis River. It looked like an eagle's nest. They did not stay long as they soon moved to Chania.

Seiradakis immediately felt comfortable in the city of his youth. Chania was no longer the capital of the Autonomous Cretan State where he had worked and participated in the revolution in Therisso 32 years ago. But it remained the capital of Crete and a democratic and cosmopolitan city. Although the medieval centre had not changed much, Chania had expanded into new neighbourhoods and had almost doubled in population. Seiradakis began to operate in Chania circles with the prestige of a military man who had fought and taken part in the recent Venizelist coup of 1935. Chania was also still mourning the death of Eleftherios Venizelos a year earlier, on 18 March 1936.

His public funeral had taken place in Chania on the day of the Greek national day, 25 March. The people of Chania considered him, more than anyone else, their own man and felt orphaned without him.

Seiradakis opened himself to the democratic world of the city, which was made up mainly, but not only, of officers. He met the old chieftains and his fellow warrior Pavlis Gyparis who was more active than ever. He reconnected with his old friend from the French front, Andreas Gyparakis, who had stood by Eleftherios Venizelos until his last breath.[1] During a visit to Chania he met Emmanuel Tsouderos, who had been governor of the Bank of Greece since the years of Venizelos' last prime ministerial term. Seiradakis' daughters were enrolled in the city's schools and continued their studies. Seiradakis and his family spread their wings in Chania.

Occupied Crete

Meanwhile the drums of war were again sounding in Europe. The dictatorial regimes of Hitler and Mussolini made no secret of their expansionist and warlike intentions. Not even 20 years had passed since the huge loss of life in the First World War and the European civil war was about to enter its second and most destructive phase.

Greece did not escape from this raging torrent. On 28 October 1940, Mussolini, unprovoked, had invaded Greece from the mountains of Albania. Ioannis Metaxas' 'No' to Italy's attack led to epic victories in the Epirus mountains and Greece's first heroic victory of the Allies against the Axis forces. Seiradakis could not help but see the irony of history. The traditional Germanophile, Ioannis Metaxas, had now become an Anglophile. Not only had he turned against the Axis, but he was in the precarious position of fighting against the Germans. Finally, April 1941 had found mainland Greece under double occupation and a month later it would be the turn of Crete, and from 1 June 1941, Crete also found itself under German occupation. Nowhere could one feel safe. Seiradakis was already known to the Germans from his action in the Hellenocretan Legion during First World War I in Lorraine and the Dardanelles.

He had recently caused them significant losses at the Battle of Kandanos where he had delayed the advance of German *fallschirmjäge*r. They knew that Seiradakis was escaping to the Selino Mountains where he had set up a radio communication network and was helping fugitive British, Australians and New Zealanders to escape to the Middle East. The intelligence network was particularly active in the three villages of Selino, Moni, Livadas and Koustogerako. Because of their geographical position in the mountains leading through gorges to small ports opposite the coast of North Africa, such as Sougia and Tripiti, it was difficult for the Germans to control them completely.

The three villages of Selino had long been in the Germans' sights. The German military command in Chania had long ago decided to destroy them and for this purpose had assigned a low-ranking Gestapo military man, *Oberfeldwebel* Hans Wachter, who spoke Greek, to organise a raid on the villages.[2] Wachter was known in the East Selino region for his cruelty, and he had created an atmosphere of terror. Gradually the men of the

1 Gyparakis, *Anamniseis*.

2 Penelope Ntountoulaki, *I Mnimi kai I Stachti, Apo ti Machi tis Kritis mechri tin Apeleftherosi,* tomos VI (Chania: Nomarchiaki Aftodioikisi Chanion, Maios 2009), pp.106 et seq.

villages in the White Mountains no longer stayed in their homes but spent the night in winter caves high in the mountains. They visited their families only in secret at night, bringing food and goods from the town to their relatives. In the three villages, and especially in Livadas, there were now only old people, women and small children.

Raid on Selino

The rumours of an impending raid against the three villages became increasingly frequent in the spring of 1943. At that time Seiradakis had received an order from the Middle East general headquarters to go to Cairo to take command of a battalion in the Greek Army in exile. He had contacted two other Greek officers and, together with fugitive British, Australians and New Zealanders, had left Tripiti for Tobruk, Libya, on 8 May 1943.

Seiradakis was as worried as everyone else about the fate of the villages and his family. His relatives in Livadas reassured him that they would take care of his wife and four girls and he should not worry. At the beginning of September 1943, the information had circulated in Livadas that the German attack on the three villages was imminent.

Manolis Seiradakis and his two brothers, Michalis and Dimitris, were beloved cousins of Charalampos and good fighters. As soon as Manolis learned of the impending attack, he alerted Fani that she and the children had to leave Livadas at once because the Germans knew her and she was in danger. A journey to Chania through the Cretan mountains during the occupation was not an easy task. Apart from difficulties in moving through poorly maintained roads, there were roadblocks everywhere.

On 25 September 1943 Manolis found two donkeys that would take them to Kandanos. On one they loaded as many things as they could and the two younger girls, Veta and Lili, were to ride on the other one. Fani and her eldest daughter Eugenia, then 17 years old, would walk the five hours to Kandanos accompanied by Manolis. From there on they would take the bus to Chania. But their second-born daughter Mary, who had just turned 16, would not join them. Two months before, she had been hit in the knee and the wound would not heal. They needed a third donkey, but there was not one available. Fani did not want to leave her daughter behind alone, but Manolis promised her that the next day he would personally accompany Mary to Kandanos and from there to Chania. So, Fani accepted. On the morning of 28 September, Fani, Eugenia, Veta and Lilly took an old bus and followed the road through the gorge where the battle with the Germans had taken place two years before. In the evening, they were able to rest in Chania. But not Fani, who anxiously waited for Manolis to bring Mary the next day. If the family was not all together, Fani could not relax.

Livadas is Burning

Livadas was awakened at dawn on 29 September by the buzzing of war planes. At first they thought they were British, but soon the sirens convinced them that they were German

Stukas. The planes, after circling over the village, came in near-vertically, shooting at the houses. The first ones had already begun to burn, and the women and children ran in terror to shelter in the surrounding houses. The village men up in the mountains watched on without being able to offer any help. The attack on the three villages had begun.

After half an hour of bombing and while the planes continued their attacks on the villages of Moni and Koustogerako, German units appeared from the slopes and surrounded the three villages simultaneously.[3] In Livadas, apart from the women and children, there were only two old men left, Ioannis Papaderos and Ioannis Seiradakis or Michalogiannis, who were killed almost immediately after shooting the soldiers who entered their houses.[4] The Germans soon set Livadas on fire. They rounded up the women and children of the village, about 60 of them, locked them up on the upper floor of an empty house and put guards outside.[5] The basement of the house was smaller and communicated with the upper floor by a *lebarta,* a trap door with a ladder leading down.

The women and children who had been imprisoned could see thick smoke from their houses that were on fire. They spent the night huddled in their room. When later they heard the planes panic set in. The women and children thought that they could escape by taking refuge in the basement, which of course was not the case as the floor would have swallowed them all up. However, out of instinct, the younger children rushed to the elevator and began to roll down the inner staircase to the bottom 'like a human chain'.

A guard appeared at the basement window and, thinking there was a group escape, he fired – fortunately it was not an automatic weapon but a single shot weapon. As the eyewitness Dimitris Seiradakis reports, 'I remember Amalia Tsouris, 14 years old, who fell down with an open wound on her head, and my cousin Mary Seiradaki, the daughter of Charalampos, 16 years old, who was wounded in the arm and chest.'[6]

There was more panic. Those who were coming down the stairs began to turn and go back up, taking with them the children who had been injured. Two young girls, Eugenia Seiradaki, Mary's first cousin, and Irini Seiradaki, the mother of little Dimitri, came down the stairs again with the injured Mary and knocked on the front window. Another guard opened the door and, at the sight of the injured girl, let them run across and fetch medicine for the wounded.[7]

3 Ntountoulaki, *I Mnimi kai I Stachti,* tomos VI, p.110, testimony of Dimitris Seiradakis.

4 War Special Services Department, bulletin C, number 42, January 1944: 'The tragedy of the Seiradakis family had another victim, John Seiradakis, aged 75, whose death was heroic… The old man remained in his home and, having previously succeeded in killing the lieutenant at the head of the German detachment and mortally wounding two other soldiers, he was killed after he had exhausted his last cartridge'. (Military archive of Ch. Seiradakis)

5 Ntountoulaki, *I Mnimi kai I Stachti,* tomos VI, p.101, testimony of Eugenia Seiradaki-Xirouchaki, sister of Mary.

6 Ntountoulaki, *I Mnimi kai I Stachti,* testimony of Eugenia Xirouchaki-Seiradaki and Eugenia Seiradakis, her first cousin (tomos VI, p.104), of D. Seiradakis (p.112) and of Georgios Tsouris (p.122).

7 Ntountoulaki, *I Mnimi kai I Stachti,* tomos VI, p.122, Testimony of Georgios Tsouris.

The Murder of Mary

The next morning, orders were given to take all the women and children to the port of Sougia, which was about an hour's walk. The injured Mary, who could hardly walk, was supported by her cousin Eugenia. But once they had proceeded 300m and reached the Keithe Vrisi, a water fountain next to the village church, it became obvious that Mary could not continue.

At that moment loaded mules were crossing the road. The guard who had earlier allowed them to dress the wounds, upon seeing the injured Mary, untied an animal to carry her to Sougia. His action was noticed by another guard, and he refused to let him do it. The two soldiers argued, and a fight ensued between them. The second guard was more aggressive and he pushed the other down, causing him to hit his head so he could not move for a while. Taking advantage of this momentary weakness, the second guard shot the wounded Mary.[8]

Everyone was stunned. For Mary's cousin Eugenia, who had been carrying her until a moment before, it was an experience that would haunt her for the rest of her life.

The End of the Three Villages

Soon the group of women and children made their way to Sougia. Mary's aunt, the mother of her cousin Eugenia, was trying to find her daughter and niece. It was from her daughter that she learned of Mary's tragic end. How was she to break the news to her mother Fani, who had left the day before and was waiting for her daughter in Chania?

The women and children of Livadas, Koustogerako and Moni spent the night in an open fenced area near the beach and the next day they were taken by boat to Paleochora and from there to the prison of Agia. Fortunately, they did not stay there for long; the city authorities soon intervened, especially the Metropolitan Agathangelos Xirouchakis, whose personality commanded respect from everyone. Throughout the occupation, he had been very active in humanitarian issues. Through his intercession, within a few days all the women and children were released from prison. However, the three villages were declared restricted areas, and it was not possible for anyone to approach them during the entire occupation. The destruction of Livadas was such that even after the war it was never rebuilt as before. The heyday of the olive grove in Livadas was over. Seventy years later, the house where Charalampos Seiradakis grew up still lay in ruins.

Fani Seiradaki could never get over the loss of her daughter. Perhaps she herself felt responsible for not being able to take her with her when they left. Her sisters, the older Eugenia and the younger Veta and Lili, also lived with the pain of their lost sister.

8 *War Special Services Department*, Bulletin C, Number 42, January 1944, p.14: 'During the bombing of the village of Livadas, Miss Seiradaki, aged 16, was wounded. On the way she was exhausted and fell unconscious. Her escort wanted to bring her up on horseback … a quarrel broke out between two Germans, with the result that the escort was overpowered and shot the unconscious Seiradaki.' (Military Archive of Ch. Seiradakis)

The news of the murder of his daughter felt like a lightning bolt to Charalambos Seiradakis. Her loss came at a time when his military life was on shaky ground. Not two months had passed since the fifth battalion that he commanded had ceased to exist as a combat unit following the leftist rebellion.

In Cairo, where he had been transferred, he closely followed the developments of the war and especially the efforts to form a war-ready Greek Army. Perhaps with the new government-in-exile, which was republican in its majority, there were better chances of this. Would they have more success, or would all be lost in the fractious politics that had poisoned the exiled Greek Army?

17

Recruitment and Screening Centre, 1944

Cairo 1943

After the mutiny in his battalion, Charalampos Seiradakis was transferred for a short time to Cairo where he tried to build a new life for himself. He was in constant contact with the Ministry of Military Affairs, while at the same time discovering the bustling capital of Egypt where a thriving and large Greek community had flourished for over a century. To this had been added from the beginning of the war the political staff of the Greek Government in exile and over 500 officers. They all met in well-known Cairo hotels,[1] haunts where they learned what was happening at home, news of the war, news of their families, and of course exchanged views – often with the familiar passion – about the tragic events that had brought the Greek Army in the Middle East into such a desperate situation.

Seiradakis and most officers in the Middle East were concerned about future political and military developments in Greece. The most decisive influence on the political life of the country had been brought by the establishment of the left-leaning National Liberation Front (*EAM*) in 1943 as a popular resistance movement, and the Greek People's Liberation Army (*ELAS*) as the military arm of *EAM*. It was becoming clear that what was at stake after the war was to be the form of government, as the *EAM* and *ELAS* were controlled by the Communist Party of Greece (*KKE*). Seiradakis, having experienced the backsliding of the royal institution in pre-war Greece, remained opposed to the return of the King after the war. At the same time, however, he was concerned about the position of *EAM* as it was becoming clear that it was promoting the establishment of a communist regime. The whole of Greek society, and especially the body of officers, was concerned about this issue.

1 One of these haunts was *Shepheard's*, a large old Cairo hotel which many Greeks and foreigners frequented. Another was the *Iris*, where Charalampos Seiradakis had stayed and was on friendly terms with the owner, H. Sarafis. He maintained correspondence with him even after the war.

For the time being, what took priority in the Middle East was the fate of the Greek Army and the government-in-exile. Seiradakis' friend and old comrade-in-arms Pavlis Gyparis, with his rough but straightforward character, *Frourarchos* in Cairo until recently, had similar anxieties which he expressed in his familiar way. So did his old acquaintance Byron Karapanagiotis, whom Seiradakis rarely saw, since he was – but for how much longer? – minister of military affairs in the Tsouderos government. In Cairo, Seiradakis also had the opportunity to get to know better Sophocles Venizelos, son of Eleftherios, who had recently arrived from America and aspired to play a leading role in political life after the war. In discussions with him, Venizelos did not rule out working together in the Liberal Party.

The association with other moderate officers in Cairo inevitably led to greater understanding. Seiradakis found that most of his colleagues were imbued with the military ethos and patriotism beyond political beliefs. It was the policy that had been successfully implemented by Seiradakis' acquaintance from the 1935 coup, *Syntagmatarchis* Lakis Tsigantes. At no time did the political convictions of the *Ierolochitets*, men of the 'sacred company', constitute an obstacle to their military operations. Should other Greek units in the Middle East also head in this direction?

Recruitment and Screening Centre

In the months that followed the July 1943 mutiny, a new effort was made to reorganise the Greek Army. The new chief of the general staff, *Syntagmatarchis* Eustathios Liosis, established the Ismailia Training Centre (*KEI*)[2] under the command of *Syntagmatarchis* Thrasyvoulos Tsakalotos. In December the General Training Centre and School were also reorganised. There was a need for a new centre for hosting and training new recruits and at the end of November 1943 it established the Recruitment and Screening Centre. Command of the new Centre was assigned to *Antisyntagmatachis* Charalampos Seiradakis.[3]

New recruits had to adapt and train in the conditions of the Middle East. Those who came to enlist were volunteers who had fled from occupied Greece and their journey was often a risky affair.[4] It was thus crucial that they felt comfortable within a strictly military but also welcoming atmosphere. In this respect Seiradakis was the appropriate commander. He had a paternal manner about him and welcomed the recruits with

2 The *KEI* was established in September 1943 as Centre for the Preparation and Training of Officers of Kabrit (*CPEAK*) in Lebanon.

3 Information on the new centre derives mainly from Seiradakis' Diary of Recruitment and Screening Centre, S.O. Book 135, Code 28-72-0 (the cover page is shown in Appendix II). On the staffing and administration of the Centre, Seiradakis reports: 'By Army General Staff Order No. 18579/D.O.S. the above Centre is established, and the following are assigned: *Antisyntagmatachis* Charalambos Seiradakis, *Tagmatarchis* nel Konstantinos Athanasiou, *Lochagos* Stephanou, Moirarchos Stellakis, *Anthypaspistis* Nakas, et cetera (61 names in total)'. With K. Athanasiou, Seiradakis had worked during the mutiny of the fifth battalion three months earlier.

4 Sakellaropoulos, *To soma ton Ellinon Axiomatikon*, pp.314–315.

understanding and care, but also with strict discipline.[5] The camp was in the middle of the desert, not far from the fourth battalion and the city of Ismailia. It was in constant communication with the training centre (KEI) and with trucks and jeeps provided by the Allied command.

A few days after assuming his new tasks, Seiradakis began receiving the arrival of groups of new recruits. Their reception and accommodation in the desert camp required meticulous preparation. Seiradakis' care for the new men is evident from the entries in his diary. On December 14 he reported: 'tomorrow evening 85 soldiers will arrive from Cyprus ... 16/12, 16:00: I have inspected the tents and found that they were worn and ordered new ones.'[6] Two weeks later, on 31 December, came another 600 Samiot conscripts who had fled to the Middle East after the German capture of the island. From these, four new infantry battalions were formed to be incorporated into the second brigade, which was to become war-ready again.

March 29, 1944, was an important day for Charalampos Seiradakis. There are two entries in his diary. The first one concerns the death of his daughter Mary six months earlier, on 29 September 1943. He organised a memorial service in her memory and in his diary he noted: 'The entire Centre attended with the officers.' It would have been a moving event where each of the attendees would have let his thoughts fly to his own loved ones who suffered at home.[7]

The second entry was alarming: 'in the evening, proclamations were made in favour of *ASO* by unknown persons.'[8] It was an event that was a precursor to what was to follow. Just two days later, Seiradakis notes: 'In the 4th battalion, a group event is organised for reconciliation and cooperation between *EAM* and the government. I went to Cairo and reported to Minister Karapanagiotis and Minister Sophocles Venizelos'. This had been preceded by the formation in Greece of the left-leaning 'Political Committee for National Liberation' (known by the initials of its Greek name *PEEA*),[9] or 'Government of

5 Nikos K. Christakos, *Gramma apo to syntrofo (Dimokratikoi Agones 1941–49)*, (Athens: privately published, 1985), p.29, states: 'Commander of fifth battalion Seiradakis often addressed his soldiers as 'my children'.

6 Seiradakis, *Diary*: Concern for the new recruits was constant as evidenced in Seiradakis *Diary*. Page 3: 'Every Wednesday and Friday 3–4 p.m. lectures by the sergeant major in the Officers' Hall'. Regarding personal cleanliness, he notes on 26/12: 'every Wednesday and Sunday at 9 a.m. linen pick-up'. Also on recruits' language training and on 10 January, he proposes to 'extend English lessons to the privates'. On the day of the national holiday 25 March, he notes: 'flag-raising at a Centre meeting and speeches on our national day, comparison of the pre–21 era with the present. Exchange of views with the new recruits'. The last remark is important as Seiradakis wished to have close contact with his soldiers, especially in the light of the mutiny three months before.

7 Seiradakis, *Diary*: 27 March 1944. Moving report on the death of his daughter Mary: 'I went to Ismailia with Vardis to get items for the memorial of those who died in Moni, Livadas and Koustogerako on 29 September 1943, in Kandanos and all Selino during the occupation of Crete. I went to the 4th battalion to meet with priest Chairetis for the memorial of Mary Seiradaki'.

8 ASO: Anti-Fascist Military Organisation.

9 On 10 March 1944, left-leaning politicians and resistance leaders met in Koryschades, a mountain village in central Greece at the initiative of *EAM*. They appointed a National

the Mountain', which had a direct impact on the government-in-exile in the Middle East and especially on the Greek Army. The left *ASO* immediately mobilised for the formation of a government of national unity in Cairo with a view to committing the Greek Government-in-exile to recognise the institutional role of the *PEEA*. At the same time, the *ASO* wanted to create a left-wing bridge in the Middle East that would recognise the leading role of *EAM/ELAS* in the resistance.[10]

The Greek Government in Cairo was, of course, aware of the establishment of the *PEEA*, but for about two weeks it preferred to ignore it without making an announcement.[11] It was Tsouderos' usual tactics of letting the situation drag on before making a stand. The *ASO*, however, interpreted the government's silence on the establishment of the *PEEA* as a provocation and decided to act.

Third Mutiny in the Army

At the combat level the first brigade had been reinforced with new units[12] and in October it made a positive impression on the Allied exercises. The Greek military presence in Egypt had increased: the army numbered about 22,000 men, the navy 8,500 and the air force 4,000, a considerable force, but one that had not been of much use in the Allied forces for its size. But with the beginning of 1944 the General Headquarters of the Middle East offered the Greek troops a new opportunity.

One Greek unit left for Italy as a convoy, while the remaining units took part in a new Allied exercise before they too were sent to the front. The departure was set for early April 1944. But by mid-March there was already a general feeling that something was not going well, as information about new conspiratorial movements was pouring in. In the preceding months, the *ASO* had pursued a low-key policy so as not to interfere with participation in Allied operations. But Tsouderos' delaying attitude on the issue of the *PEEA* led the *ASO* leadership to launch a new mutiny to put pressure on the Cairo government.

The mutiny occurred on 31 March 1944. A committee of 13 officers of the first brigade, members of the *ASO*, presented themselves to Prime Minister Tsouderos with political demands. They requested the formation of a government of national unity, with the 'government of the mountain' of *PEEA* as its main component, and the simple participation of the Cairo government-in-exile. At the same time, they submitted a memorandum of their positions which they communicated to the delegations of Great Britain, France, the United States and the Soviet Union. The previous day a speech by Minister of the Navy Sophocles Venizelos, had been made on Cairo radio, in which he referred to the

Council which was to function as a transitional government known as *PEEA*, or 'government of the mountain'.

10 Sakellaropoulos, *To soma ton Ellinon Axiomatikon*, p.342.

11 Sakellaropoulos, *To soma ton Ellinon Axiomatikon*, p.342. During the celebration of 25 March in Alexandria, several units had declared themselves in favour of the PEEA.

12 The *Deftero Syntagma Pyrovolikou* (Second Artillery Regiment) and the *Proto Syntagma Tethorakismenon* (First Armoured Car Regiment).

intention of the government-in-exile to participate in a single government of all parties and organisations.[13]

It was one of the few times that the usually calm Tsouderos reacted angrily. He told them that the Cairo government was in contact with the *PEEA* and that an announcement would soon be made, but he would not accept military officers leaving for war making political requests to the prime minister. At first, he dismissed them but later ordered that they be locked up in the garrison. Four days after the *ASO* officers' stand, on 3 April, the first brigade encamped near Cairo. It was there that the next move was made. Soldiers and junior officers of *ASO* arrested their unit officers and occupied the camp 'symbolically', as they declared, for 24 hours to establish a 'revolutionary status'. The next day they declared to the commander, *Syntagmatarchis* Pappas, that once they had made their demands clear, they would stop the revolutionary activity.

In the second artillery regiment, the commander faced a similar situation. He assembled his unit and asked those who supported the 'government of the mountain' of the *PEEA* to come out of the lines: 18 officers and 260 armed men members of the *ASO* declared themselves to be with the *PEEA* and came out of the ranks. But instead of being disarmed and isolated, they marched out of the camp with their weapons and proceeded to occupy the Greek garrison in Cairo. There they released the officers who had been arrested by Tsouderos and detained several high officers at the Greek Army headquarters. It was a botched attempt by *ASO* to impose its policy by force on the high military command.

The British military authorities were nervously monitoring the situation but had not intervened until that moment. However, the occupation of the headquarters convinced them to act. A British military contingent took back the garrison and the Greek Army headquarters and proceeded to arrest 14 senior officers whom they suspected of being accomplices to these events.[14] The arrest of the officers was a reaction by the British authorities to the failure of the Greek military leadership to prevent a new mutiny after the two previous ones. They felt that after the removal of the pro-monarchist officers a year earlier, the republicans ought to have prevented or at least been aware of a new coup. But recent movements showed the opposite. On the other hand, other units, such as the seventh infantry battalion,[15] the General Training Centre and Schools[16] and the second transport company, were unaffected by the new mutiny.

On 6 April the General Headquarters of the Middle East cancelled the transfer of the first brigade to Italy. They would no longer participate in the Allied invasion of Sicily. It was a sad moment when more than 1,500 Greek soldiers who had already

13 Sakellaropoulos, *To soma ton Ellinon Axiomatikon*, p.343.

14 The arrested officers were: Kallergis, Stefanakos, Hadjistavris, Vratsafolis, Konstas, Stavroulakis, Angelis, Petrakis and seven members of the Cairo National Liberation League (with left *EAM* orientation). A few days later the British relieved the Minister of Military affairs, B. Karapanagiotis, of his duties.

15 The seventh battalion did not participate in any riotous incidents and formed the base of the Third Greek Mountain Brigade (*3rd EOT*) which took part in the Italy campaign, in Rimini.

16 Part of it was the Recruitment and Screening Centre, which was commanded by Ch. Seiradakis.

boarded the ships bound for Sicily were forced to disembark. They were disarmed and isolated in a camp controlled by British troops. The remaining Greek units considered that the way their comrades were treated was disgraceful, and some took up battle positions. The British preferred to avoid bloodshed and left the rebel units stranded, 'fenced in' without food and water, waiting for them to surrender. And so it happened. After 18 days in isolation, in miserable conditions under the hot sun and deeply embittered, the mutineers of the first brigade surrendered, and the mutiny ended ingloriously on 24 April.

This also marked the humiliating end of a brigade that had fought and distinguished itself in the battles of El Alamein. This time it had ruled itself out of the final battle. For many other Greek soldiers, such as the eighth battalion,[17] the 'fenced in' confinement ordeal would continue for several more months until their final return to Greece.

Mutiny at the Recruitment and Screening Centre

By 6 April Seiradakis had developed a high fever that would not go away.[18] But daily activities in the camp continued normally despite the rumours of a new mutiny and the commander had to be on his feet. Visits by British officers had become more frequent. On 8 April the liaison officer Captain Campbell arrived at the camp and asked Seiradakis to prepare a reception for 474 recruits. It seems more likely he just wanted to ascertain the situation there. The next morning Colonel Green arrived with sad news.[19] He informed Seiradakis that due to the mutiny in the 1st Brigade and the navy, the British military leadership in the Middle East had taken over the command of the Greek Army. It must have been a hard time for Seiradakis and his entire unit to lose command of the Centre, isolated as they were in the middle of the hot desert of Ismailia.

After Green's departure, there was unrest in the Centre. Day after day, Seiradakis records the uneasy scenes that unfolded in the desert camp. *ASO* intensified its efforts to mobilise its members through protest movements, while Seiradakis and his officers were struggling to maintain discipline and avoid conflict. On 11 April, *Anthypaspistis* Mouzourakis reported to Seiradakis 'about incidents of soldiers of the fourth battalion.'[20] It was Easter Week; the British officer Colonel Green was constantly visiting the camp and information was pouring in from various sources about incidents of mutiny in Cairo.

17 Hatziangelis & Rappas, *To Ógdoo Tágma.*

18 Seiradakis, *Diary*, pp.23 et seq.

19 Seiradakis, *Diary*, p.24. '10 April 1944. At 11.30 a.m. Colonel Green arrives at my tent and hands me a personal order from the Chief General of Middle East that he takes command of the Greek Army with *Syntagmatarchis* Liosis as Chief of Staff and recommends adherence to military duties and avoiding the involvement of the army in politics'.

20 The 4th battalion was stationed near the Recruitment and Screening Centre, not far from Ismailia. The penetration of the *ASO* in the 4th battalion was considerable and its members very active.

Sunday 16 April 1944, Easter Day, in the desert of Ismailia. Traditional Easter songs from the homeland and lamb cooked on the spit offered a respite to soldiers and officers who, for the time being at least, seemed to forget their political rivalries.[21]

But on Tuesday, 18 April, it all started again. Several neighbouring units had already mutinied and there was information about irregular transfers of weapons. As Seiradakis notes 'officers and privates prepared a memorandum of protest against Prime Minister Sophocles Venizelos'. If Seiradakis received the memorandum, he would have to forward it to the government, embarrassing thus the new Prime Minister Sophocles Venizelos, who had just taken office and was already facing mutiny. He felt that the best solution was not to receive it at all. Behind the scenes he passed on the information that the consequences for the Centre would be disastrous, and he would not accept it.[22] The *ASO* members of his unit seemed to be convinced and did not insist. For the time being at least. But it was difficult to have a similar success in persuading the 4th battalion where the *ASO* was more aggressive.

As expected, the next day a committee of the 4th battalion came to submit a memorandum protesting the arrests in the 1st brigade battalion and asked him to forward it to the government. Seiradakis explained that their request was 'inappropriate' and that in the present circumstances a political protest would do more harm than good. The committee again appeared to be convinced and did not insist.[23] But it was clear that Seiradakis was now in the crosshairs of the *ASO* and they intended to try again. Worse still, the pressure to submit political memos by the Centre had become known to the British command.

With all this the irritation had intensified in the isolated camp in the desert. The situation became even more tense when Captain Campbell notified them that they were no longer allowed to go shopping in neighbouring Ismailia, but that the British commissariat would bring supplies to them.[24]

Soon the British officer came back with another strict order. Those who had led the political protest were to be isolated in another camp. Seiradakis took the opportunity to point out to Campbell that the Recruitment and Screening Centre had not submitted any such memo and therefore there was no need to isolate anyone. But the order had to be carried out. Seiradakis succeeded at least in getting those who were removed not to go to an isolated camp, but to be transferred to the General Training Centre and School. Thus, on 24 April a group of junior officers and privates boarded vehicles and left for Ismailia.[25]

21 Seiradakis, *Diary*, p.25. Seiradakis noted, 'despite my high fever and exhaustion, I go out to greet the men. I wish them a good Easter and crack the egg – fever 40.2.'

22 Seiradakis, *Diary*, p.25.

23 Seiradakis, *Diary*, p.25. It appears, however, that the memo of the 4th battalion was eventually submitted through another channel.

24 Seiradakis, *Diary*, p.26. 'Campbell issued a verbal order forbidding going shopping in Ismailia, Kassassin, et cetera, we will give a note for the NAFI to shop for us.'

25 Seiradakis, *Diary*, p.28, These were: Moirarchos E. Stellakis, *Lochagos* T. Kavadias, *Lochagos* E. Triantafillidis, *Stratiotis* Petros Pilitsis, *Anthypaspistis* A. Kokkalis, Engineer G. Beltsos, Engineer G. Gumas.

On 29 April Seiradakis was ordered to urgently go to the General Training Centre and School for a meeting with *Dioikitis* Tsakalotos and other officers. It was the moment that *ASO* had been waiting to take revenge. A group of *ASO* members of the 4th battalion took advantage of Seiradakis' absence and came to the camp at night to lure those who had hitherto remained uninvolved into a mutiny. When the next day the usually pragmatic Seiradakis was informed of what had happened in his absence he noted in his diary: 'Things have taken a bad turn.'[26] The British were quick to notice the mutiny in the Centre by the *ASO* of the 4th battalion. They quickly surrounded the camp and announced that the next day they would separate the soldiers. Those who sided with *EAM* would be isolated in a special camp. The prospect was grim. So, during the night and despite the measures taken, a group of about 100 mutineers escaped back to the 4th battalion camp. Not for long, though, as they were chased and soon captured by a British armoured squadron.[27] Seiradakis hurried back to his unit to prevent the worst, but could he save his Centre?

On the morning of May Day at the Recruitment and Screening Centre, the members of the ASO 'removed the crown from their hats, putting badges with the insignia of *ELAS* [the military unit of the leftist *EAM*]. Moral blackmail was being carried out on all officers and soldiers.' Seiradakis described the events: 'At noon, the *Anthypaspistis* of the Centre Frantzis comes to my tent and tells me that from that moment on he also joins *ELAS* and urges me to follow him – he was drunk. I thwart him and he says that he, as the abbot of the Centre, will lead it under *ELAS*.'[28]

At 3 o'clock Seiradakis called a general meeting at the Centre and asked everyone directly the question: 'Who wants to go with the *ELAS*?' Most of them said 'Yes, they did'.[29] Colonel Green, who was watching from a distance, 'not wanting to cause any trouble, boarded a car and left'. The British officer probably wanted to avoid a bloody incident and risk his life, the fate another colleague had suffered a few days earlier when he had been involved in an altercation with insurgents.

At the end of that terrible day, May Day 1944, Seiradakis convened his unit for a roll call. Only 4 officers and 16 privates answered.[30] The Recruitment and Screening Centre followed the fate of most Greek units in the Middle East. It would continue to under operate for a few more months until the gradual return home of those who had remained. The end of the war was near.

26 Seiradakis, *Diary*, p.28. What followed in the centre is set out in the text.
27 Seiradakis, *Diary*, p.29. The camp of the 4th battalion was also surrounded by armoured vehicles with machine guns.
28 Seiradakis, *Diary*, p.29.
29 Report to the Ministry of Military Affairs, Cairo, ref. 275, 7 May 1944. 'I report that following known events, the treasurer of our unit, on his departure, took with him all the books of management including the Barclays bank book. On 30 April there was a balance of 14,500 Egyptian pounds … We are already unable to make any transactions'. (Military archive of Charalampos Seiradakis)
30 These officers were: Seiradakis, Athanasiou, Iliades and Pandidis.

Mutiny in the Navy

Up to then the navy had distanced itself from the incidents that had occurred in the army. This time, however, in the wake of the government's silence on the establishment of the *PEEA*, the ships' crews were also getting agitated. To calm the spirits, the commander of the fleet, *Yponavarchos* Alexandris, had issued a daily order on 3 April stating that the government was in contact with the *PEEA* and that there would be a statement soon – as there was, but to no avail. The following day groups of rebellious sailors occupied the Alexandria naval garrison, the Naval Cadet School and the 'Elli' camp, while another group calling itself the 'Central Committee of the Struggle' occupied the auxiliary ship *Hephaestus*. Soon the stand-off had extended to a large part of the Greek Fleet.

But if for the Allies the Greek land units had only a relative importance, with the navy things were different. For the British, the Greek Navy, which they had recently reinforced with some of their own warships, was vital for dominance in the Mediterranean. In response to the refusal of the Greek warships to sail to carry out naval exercises, the commander of the British Fleet, Vice Admiral Rowlings, demanded on 8 April that the action that already undermined 18 of the 27 ships in the Greek Fleet be stopped. In response, the mutineers banned the ships from sailing.

On 16 April Admiral Cunningham[31] called the new Prime Minister Sophocles Venizelos, who had taken office only two days before, and the fleet Commander Alexandris, and made a dramatic statement: if the mutiny of the crews was not ended, the Greek Fleet would be sunk.

The British ultimatum was putting suffocating pressure on the new prime minister, Venizelos, who immediately called political leaders Panagiotis Kanellopoulos and Georgios Papandreou to a meeting – the latter had just arrived in Cairo on 19 April. They agreed that the mutiny in the fleet had to be suppressed immediately with Greek forces. The next day, the new fleet commander, *Antinavarchos* Petros Voulgaris, formed a 300-man boarding party.[32] On the night of 23 April, three groups in a commando operation boarded the ships and recaptured the corvette *Apostolis* and the destroyers *Ierax* and *Sachtouris*. Soon five other rebel warships in Alexandria surrendered and the mutineers were disbanded. The ships that were anchored at the ports of Port Said and Malta were surrendered on 25 April.[33] The naval mutiny had been crushed, but the price was heavy: 9 dead and 40 wounded – more loss of blood in the civil conflicts of the Middle East.

The mutiny in the army, as was to be expected, had direct effects on the leadership of the Greek Army and the government-in-exile. By 6 April, when the brigade's mission to

31 Admiral Cunningham was known for the Battle of Crete when he rescued around 20,000 troops from the south coast and returned them to Egypt. When asked if the operation to rescue soldiers was worth the loss of ships he had replied: 'Naval trustworthiness takes dozens of years to build, but it is destroyed in very few.'

32 Kanellopoulos, *Imerologio katochis,* Tomos 2, p.185. One section was commanded by *Lochagos* Skoufopoulos, another by Commander Toumbas and the third by Commander Kyris.

33 A. C. Carr, *Thorikto Averof.* This historic battleship was among those that had surrendered

Italy was cancelled, the chief of the general staff of the Middle East, Major General Paget, had blamed Karapanagiotis, for 'negligently contributing to the outbreak of mutiny' and demanded that he resign. By 11 April, King George II had arrived in Cairo. His first move was to name the new Prime Minister, Sophocles Venizelos. It was the end of an era for Emmanuel Tsouderos, who had served as prime minister for four years under difficult circumstances. But Venizelos' office term would not last long. Only 10 days after the suppression of the mutiny, on 24 April, he was forced to resign, and the King entrusted the formation of a new government to centrist politician Georgios Papandreou. London was particularly concerned with the Greek situation in the Middle East. The constant mutinies in the army, the endless debates and intrigues, and above all the inability to form a stable government had paralysed the Greek factor.

The Lebanon Conference

There had to be a solution to the Greek problem. To this end, the British looked favourably on holding a conference with the participation of all the Greek political forces, including the left *EAM/ELAS*, which represented the *PEEA*, the 'government of the mountain'. The conference took place at the Bois de Boulogne hotel in the Lebanese mountains between 17 and 19 May 1944, under the code name of Conference D. Under the chairmanship of Georgios Papandreou, 25 representatives from all factions participated: the Cairo government, old political parties, resistance organisations of Zervas and *EAM/ELAS*, as well as some military personalities representing nationalist organisations.[34]

It was the first time that such a heterogeneous political combination would decide the post-war developments in Greece. Despite tensions, the congress maintained a spirit of mutual understanding and on 19 May an agreement was reached which was called the 'National Contract'. It was decided to set up a government of national unity in which, for the first time, representatives of the communist organisations would participate. It was also agreed to reform the armed forces and to condemn the military mutinies in the Middle East. This meant that the insurgents of recent mutinies would not have access to the new Greek Army. It was also agreed that civil conflicts would cease, and that resistance organisations would be brought under the authority of the government.[35]

34 Kanellopoulos, *Imerologio katochis,* Tomos B', p.200. Among the politicians in Cairo were G. Papandreou as president, P. Kanellopoulos, S. Venizelos, and Exidaris. Old political parties were represented by K. Redis, G. Vassiliadis, A. Mylonas, I. Sofianopoulos, G. Kartalis, D. Lontos, S. Theotokis, G. Sakkalis and F. Dragoumis. From the Zervas resistance group participated: K. Pyromaglou, S. Metaxas and B. Metaxas. From *EAM/ELAS* participated: A. Svolos, M. Porphyrogenis, S. Sarafis, A. Angelopoulos, D. Stratis and N. Askoutsis. Representatives of army organisations were General K. Ventiris (new Chief of Staff) and *Antisyntagmatachis* Stathatos. The drafting of the conclusions of the congress was undertaken by Kanellopoulos, Londos, Rentis and Svolos.

35 The cabinet was formed of: P. Kanellopoulos Minister of Finance and Reconstruction; Th. Tsatsos Minister of Justice; D. Lontos Minister of Welfare; G. Kartalis Minister of Press; S. Theotokis Minister of Nutrition; G. Vassiliadis Minister of Merchant Marine; and K. Rentis, Minister without portfolio.

There were initially doubts regarding the consent of the *PEEA*, as it took a long time to be confirmed by the *EAM/ELAS* headquarters in the mountains. Its consent came finally on 8 June and a new government was formed with Georgios Papandreou as Prime Minister.

The *EAM/ELAS* ministers were sworn in three months later, on 4 September and the new government was finally complete.[36] It was an event of historic importance, as Kanellopoulos stressed at the first meeting of the cabinet under the presidency of Georgios Papandreou. But developments in the following months did not confirm this optimistic outlook as the new ministers of *EAM/ELAS* soon broke off their cooperation with the government.

At the same time the developments of the war moved fast. The Axis forces were withdrawing on all fronts and soon the occupation troops would leave Greece. The Greek Government could no longer remain in Cairo. On 7 September 1944 it left for Naples, which was now free, with the prospect of returning to Greece as soon as conditions permitted. The day of liberation that everyone was awaiting would not be long in coming.

Tríti Ellinikí Oreiní Taxiarchía

With the formation of the government of Georgios Papandreou and the removal of the minister Karapanagiotis, the reorganisation of the army accelerated. The new unit was called *Tríti Ellinikí Oreiní Taxiarchía* (*3i EOT*. Third Greek Mountain Brigade).[37]

On 7 August, after intensive training in Tripoli, Lebanon, the *3i EOT* was ready to board the ships and depart for the port of Taranto where it would participate in the battles in Italy. Even at the last moment, the Greek Army was ready to contribute to the Allied effort. The force consisted of 213 officers, 70 non-commissioned officers and 3,084 soldiers. Many of those who came from the first brigade would recall that four months before they had been in the same situation. They had boarded the ships when suddenly they were told to disembark because a mutiny had broken out – the third in less than a year.

In early September, *Dioikitis* Tsakalotos and the *3i EOT* were ordered to advance to the front line.[38] The Greek units were once again placed under the command of the

36 The *EAM/ELAS* Ministers were: A. Svolos Minister of Finance (to whom Kanellopoulos handed over); A. Angelopoulos deputy Finance Minister; H. Tsirimokos Minister of National Economy; N. Askoutsis Minister of Transport; Zeugos Minister of Agriculture. Kanellopoulos, *Imerologio katochis*, Tomos B', p.262.

37 The *3i EOT* brigade included a headquarters company, four infantry battalions, two field artillery regiments and auxiliary services. *Syntagmatarchis* Thrasybulus Tsakalotos was appointed as commander with *Syntagmatarchis* Nikolaos Papadopoulos as second in command.

38 Katsikostas, *O Ellinikos Stratos stin Exoria 1941–1944*, p.372, n. 217. 'The insecurity of the Greek staff even for the 'legitimate' brigade, after 3 years of suffering, was reflected in the agony of *Syntagmatarchis* Liosis who 'only became calm when he saw it boarded'.' (Operations Report III EOT, p.2, F.810/3/3).

old familiar New Zealand General Freyberg – the same man who had fought in May 1941 at the Battle of Crete and a year later with the Greek soldiers of the first brigade at El Alamein.

Although Italy had capitulated on 3 September 1943, the German forces put up a fierce resistance on Italian soil and the Allied advance to the north of the country was slow and deadly. The German defensive line, the Gothic Line, on the southern and eastern side of the Apennine mountains between Florence and Arezzo reached as far as Rimini. There they had reinforced their lines to avoid being outflanked from the sea. The *3i EOT* was ordered to break through the German defences and enter the town. The fighting was bloody and lasted four days. In a final offensive the Greek forces captured the airfield and on 21 September they raised the Greek flag on the town hall of Rimini. The victory was a great one, but it came at considerable human cost: 6 officers and 79 soldiers killed, 17 officers and 184 soldiers wounded.[39]

Rimini was the first victory of the Greek Army in the Second World War after the victories of Albania and the successful participation of the first brigade in the battle of El Alamein. In the two preceding years, the Greek Army, although it had been prepared to take an active part in the war, was neutralised by political rivalries and constant rebellions. Thus, its contribution to the final Allied victory was more symbolic than substantial. But the Battle of Rimini demonstrated that the Greek Army had never ceased to be combat ready and that, had it been pushed to the front before its cohesion was eroded, it would have made a significant contribution to the whole Allied effort.

* * *

On 13 June 1944, Charalampos Seiradakis was put on automatic retirement due to his age.[40] Two months later he was awarded, together with *Syntagmatarchis* Elias Kaligiannis, the Medal of Exceptional Deeds because 'each of them showed exceptional willingness and zeal.'[41] It was another distinction after a military career of 33 years and continuous participation in battles and struggles. But again, his retirement would be temporary. As the fighting in Crete continued, Seiradakis was recalled to the ranks of the army five months later, on 28 November 1944. By a decision of the special units' command, he was assigned to the headquarters of the Crete military unit.[42] He was anxious to return home.

39 Among the wounded at Rimini was Evangelos Kourakos, the future husband of the younger daughter of Charalampos Seiradakis, Lilly. He served for many years as Deputy Governor of the Bank of Greece.

40 He was 58 years old. Cf. Circular of the Ministry of Military Affairs, no. 111394/4532, no. 40, p.3. Cairo, 17 June 1944. (Charalampos Seiradakis military archive)

41 Ref. No. 117762/2769, circular no. 72. Signed. G. Papandreou. (Military archive of Charalampos Seiradakis) reprinted in Appendix II.

42 Structure of Special Units, 1st Office, no. 187, progress sheet no. 60. (Charalampos Seiradakis military archive)

On 29 August 1944, 10 Cretan officers and civilians had addressed a request to prime minister George Papandreou in Cairo.[43] In it they stated that the clashes with the German Army in Crete 'have taken the form of a real battle ... and it is impossible to remain inactive. We request ... that you allow us to go to Crete to join the fight.' Their request was accepted but they had to wait another three months. Finally, the departure from the port of Alexandria took place at the end of November and a total of 54 people, most of them military officers, sailed for Heraklion in Crete.

For Seiradakis, the period of a year and a half he had spent in Egypt left him with mixed feelings. He felt that he had done everything possible to organise war-ready units. But both the 'left' fifth battalion and the Recruitment and Screening Centre that he had commanded were eventually disbanded by politicking and factions in the army.

All this caused him sadness and anger, and he was not the only one who felt this way. The reflections of most military and political leaders who had lived through the events in the Middle East at close quarters were published in numerous memoirs in the years that followed. Academics and researchers have analysed them, and continue to do so, for the reasons that led to the disparagement of the Greek war effort. Even 80 years later, the conflicts in the army in exile in the Middle East remain a divisive issue.

When he returned to Greece, Seiradakis realised that there was a risk of new civil strife. A few days after his arrival, the bloody *Dekemvriana* riots erupted in Athens, intensifying political fanaticism. Although Seiradakis did not rule out future involvement in politics – his discussions with Sophocles Venizelos had piqued his interest – he felt that the time had not yet come for him to make that decision. What he felt was the urgent need to contribute to alleviate the humanitarian crisis plaguing devastated Crete. He kept receiving messages that the situation in Selino was desperate. He also longed to be reunited with his beloved Fani and his daughters. He wanted to share with them the pain of the loss of their unfortunate Mary, also a victim of the atrocities during the occupation. On board the ship that was taking him back to his beloved Crete, he counted the hours until he could meet them again.

43 Letter of 29 August 1944 to the President of the Greek Government. Signed: *Stratigos* A. Skoulas, *Syntagmatarchis* I. Kaligiannis, *Syntagmatarchis* I N. Papadakis, *Syntagmatarchis* Ch. Seiradakis, *Syntagmatarchis* A. Papadakis, Officer A. Volanis, Doctor I. Mountakis, Doctor I. Paizis, Bank clerk I. Yemenakis, and Officer Badouvas. Source: military archive of Charalampos Seiradakis.

18

Prefect in Chania, 1947

Back Home

On 29 November 1944 the ship that had sailed the day before from Alexandria was sailing into the port of Heraklion. More than 50 soldiers and civilians who returned home after years of forced exile in the Middle East disembarked from the ship in an atmosphere of general excitement. Among them was *Syntagmatarchis* Charalampos Seiradakis.[1] In the devastated city the signs of war were evident and the wounds of the occupation of the previous four years were still fresh.

Although he was approaching 60, Seiradakis still felt vigorous and full of energy. But he was haunted by the recent past. He could not get out of his mind the successive mutinies that had taken place in the Middle East. Even more so the calamity that had befallen his village, Livadas, and his family. Now the time had come to find them again, to reunite with his beloved Fani and his three daughters who were now grown up. For the moment, however, he could not go to Chania to meet them. He had to wait in Heraklion. Chania had not yet been liberated. What had happened?

When the occupation troops left Athens on 12 October 1944 and were gradually retreating from the rest of Greece, the German units that had remained in Crete found themselves blockaded on the island. There was no way to escape and in the death throes of the Third Reich no one was able to decide their fate. Thus, by the autumn of 1944, German garrisons from all over the island, fully armed, had begun to assemble in Chania in a perimeter of about 30 kilometres from Souda Bay in the east to Maleme in the west. Within it were crowded around 15,000 German officers and soldiers under *Oberst* Bendack with a significant firepower capable of mounting a strong defence. Outside the zone, British troops had surrounded the Germans, while local resistance groups made sporadic attacks on them.

It was a very unusual situation indeed. While the rest of Greece and Crete itself were celebrating the end of the war, Chania was in a state of peculiar occupation. Although entry and exit were controlled by German patrols, communication was relatively easy

1 Middle East Special Units March Sheet with serial no. 60 of 28 XI 1944. By General Staff Order of 24/12/1944 he was assigned to the Military Command of Crete, Heraklion. (Military archive of Charalampos Seiradakis)

in the bewildered city. Bishop Agathangelos Xirouchakis had played an important role in normalising this paradoxical situation. Now he had to mediate again for the smooth departure of the Germans without bloodshed.

Yet a dangerous nervousness prevailed everywhere. The people of Chania were anxious for the Germans to leave so that they could finally feel free, but Bendack did not want to surrender before the British had secured ships to take them to Germany. The British waited for orders while they negotiated with Bishop Agathangelos and with Bendack. Often there were isolated attacks. Thus, the winter months of 1944 and 1945 passed without any decision being taken.[2] However, all sides showed restraint. A characteristic example was that on the day the war ended, Greeks and British had celebrated the Allied victory at the Chania Club on Bolaris Street, while German soldiers patrolled outside.

The people of Chania lived through this strange time with bitter feelings. After four years of occupation, the city was full of ruins from the bombings of May 1941. This peculiar situation in Chania would last until 12 June 1945, when the last German soldier left the city and the Chaniots could finally breathe freely.[3]

Humanitarian Aid

The consequences of the occupation in Crete were disastrous. The land was left uncultivated. Many villages were deserted and people suffered from shortages of basic goods. There was a danger that in winter people would starve. The United Nations Relief and Works Agency had already been activated,[4] and the first supplies had begun to arrive in the port of Heraklion. However, a distribution network was needed to channel the aid to the countryside, especially to the more remote villages in the mountains. It was urgent because the first snow had begun to fall on Psiloritis and Madares mountains. Soon the Greek allied aid service of Heraklion was set up and appointed coordinators for each prefecture.

Charalampos Seiradakis was appointed coordinator for the prefecture of Chania.[5] The question that immediately arose was which place was most suitable for the collection and distribution of humanitarian aid. In the devastated Chania there were not many

2 Stavros G. Vlontakis, *"Ochyra thesis Kritis". Chroniko germanikis katochis sta Chania apo Oktovri 1944 kai tis agglogermanikis apo Maio os Ioulio 1945* (Athens: privately published, 1976).

3 Georgios Kavvos, *Germano-italiki katochi kai antistasi Kritis 1941–1945* (Heraklion: privately published, 1991), p.823.

4 The United Nations Relief and Rehabilitation Administration (UNRRA) was established on 9 November 1943 in Washington, DC, by 44 countries to provide humanitarian aid to states devastated by World War II.

5 Order of the Military Command of Crete, no. 735: Infantry *Syntagmatarchis* Ch. Seiradakis as general supervisor for the receipt and dispatch of food, clothing et cetera for the province of Selino … and in parallel for the province of Sfakia. Since these arrangements are being made by the Red Cross, it should decide with the ICRC office in Heraklion office to achieve the above. N. Papadakis, *Ypostratigos*. (Military Archive of Charalampos Seiradakis)

options. Only the courtyard of the ABEA olive mill, just outside the western walls of the old town, could meet the needs of such a large-scale operation. Although the factory had been destroyed by bombing, there was still plenty of storage and parking space for trucks.

In the organisation of a network for the distribution of humanitarian aid in the prefecture of Chania, Seiradakis found many supporters. First, *Syntagmatarchis* Christos Tzifakis, who was with him when he returned from the Middle East and been appointed general commander of Crete. Also, his old acquaintance and fellow warrior *Syntagmatarchis* Pavlis Gyparis, who had taken over as *frourarchos* in Chania. Of course, Gyparis had other concerns – trying to control the leftist movement in Chania which, like the rest of Greece, had embarked on an attempt to seize power. Although open conflict had not yet broken out, Gyparis had organised a militia battalion to maintain control of the area. He did, however, provide Seiradakis with the trucks he had asked for and jeeps to move his staff. The Crete military command also gave him two military assistants.[6]

The support that Seiradakis found from his family was also important. His nephews Michalis, Manolis and Dimitris Seiradakis, as well as several people from his mother's family, Georgiakakis, offered to help either as truck drivers or as distributors in the villages of Selino. Even more unexpected was the support he found from the British archaeologist and member of the Greek humanitarian aid committee, Mercy Money-Coutts, who had experience in Crete as an archaeologist, and spoke Greek with 'an impeccable Anglo-Cretan accent' and knew people and situations. Mercy proved to be an invaluable support. She proved to have organisational skills, endurance for arduous journeys, but also empathy towards the downtrodden villagers. Many of them waited anxiously for her to arrive by jeep.

Of course, she would not have made it alone if she had not had Michael Seiradakis, one of Charalambos' favourite nephews, as her driver. The constant deliveries of UNRRA lasted for over a year and as expected, Mercy and Michael's relationship was not limited to their work. Early in 1946 they told Uncle Charalampos that they intended to marry and asked for his blessing. They proved to be a loving couple who lived together in old age.

Livadas and Kandanos

As soon as he had arrived in Heraklion, Seiradakis had informed Fani that he would soon be back in Chania. But not immediately, as Seiradakis was known to the Germans and however relaxed the controls at the entrances to the city, he was in danger of being arrested. So, he had departed in a jeep for Selino to make an initial assessment of the help the place needed. When he arrived in Livadas he was confronted with a picture of

6 Order of the Military Command of Crete, no. 80, 7 January 1945. 'Due to service needs, *Anthypaspistis* G. Belivanakis G. and *Stratiotis* S. Tsouchlarakis are assigned on food distribution duty in Selino and Kissamos. Signed: *Archigos Epiteleiou* E. Kelaidis.' (Military archive of Charalampos Seiradakis)

devastation – his village no longer existed. Nevertheless, Livadas would somehow try to come back to life. Several families had returned and were rebuilding their homes, although the village would never live as before, and besides, people were increasingly flocking to the cities. The urbanisation that characterised post-war Greece was bringing more villagers to Chania – and more Chaniots to Athens.

The next day Seiradakis climbed up to Koustogerako where he found his beloved cousins from his mother's side. It too was destroyed, although the houses there could be rebuilt relatively easily. In the jeep he continued his tour of Selino. He went to Moni, went down to Sougia, Rodovani, Kampanos, Lakkoi, Sempronas, Kakodiki. Last he left Kandanos. The place where he had first fired a rifle at the enemy, had gone to school, had fought Turks and Germans, now lay in ruins. Of all the major villages it had suffered the most damage because of the resistance he himself had put up to the Germans three years before.

Seiradakis noticed the signs the Germans had engraved justifying their heinous act. 'In atonement for the Germans killed from the rear' was written on one of them. No, it was not from the rear! The battle had been fought in a straight line, face to face, and that he knew better than anyone. So be it. What was important at that moment was humanitarian aid in the villages. He headed for the Gorge of Kandanos where the battle had taken place and from there, through the snow-covered Madares mountains, he went down to the main village of Apokoronas, Vamos. There he was to meet the next day with Tzifakis, Gyparis and other city officials to plan their next moves.

When he returned to Heraklion in early February, he submitted a memorandum to the military commander of Crete and Bishop Agathangelos Xirouchakis.[7] In it he analysed the needs in the destroyed villages of Western Crete, stressing that it was urgent to speed up the distribution to avoid a humanitarian crisis. In the following months Seiradakis faced the difficult task of coordinating humanitarian aid in the prefecture of Chania. Apart from the roads and general infrastructure, which were in a deplorable state, few of the government logistics services were functioning satisfactorily. Most of them had become disorganised during the occupation. The only positive aspect was the ABEA warehouses, which provided a satisfactory solution for the collection, storage and distribution of humanitarian aid.

Seiradakis had to deal with a myriad of problems. A typical example is the report of the community of Therisso in April 1945.[8] Its president complained that the 2,400 inhabitants had difficulty in receiving aid and had asked 'not to take the telegram of the prefect into account' but to channel the aid from another direction.[9] As was eventu-

7 Report of 8 February 1945 to the Military Commander in Crete, Ch. Tzifakis, and Mons. Bishop Agathangelos: On the distribution of clothing and medicines in the burnt villages. Please make available the items of clothing, footwear and medicines mentioned in writing to all the burnt villages of the prefecture of Chania without exception, which the Red Cross in Chania has a list … as the winter has set in hard and the people need them. (Military archive of Charalampos Seiradakis)

8 Ref. No. 115. Report from President of Therisso to Ch. Seiradakis, 14 April 1945. (Charalampos Seiradakis military archive)

9 The Prefect of Chania at that time was K. Christakis, from Ierapetra.

ally done. Another request came from the village of Plemeniana, whose few inhabitants felt 'side-lined in respective distributions' and needed the bare necessities – food and clothing. Seiradakis notes in his own handwriting that he arranged for help for 'three families, 18 people.'[10] His archive is rife with similar requests, all of which were urgent. At the same time, he oversaw the student ratios in the schools. A circular of the educational district of Crete mentions that Seiradakis as vice president of 'our Committee of Municipal School Boards of Crete ... should have all assistance and information.'[11]

A Wedding

Finally, in June 1945 the last German soldier had left Chania and so Charalampos Seiradakis was able to return to his city. After two years of separation, he was reunited with his beloved family. Fani was thrilled. Their two youngest daughters, Veta and Lilly, had just started high school. Although they were saddened by the loss of the late Mary, Charalampos and Fani Seiradakis now had the joy of an impending marriage before them.

Their eldest daughter Eugenia, or Loula, had been engaged a year ago to Michael Xirouchakis, a tall and kind man for whom Fani had heard many good words. When Michael's older sister, Kiki Kassimatis, had come one Sunday the previous February to ask Eugenia to marry on behalf of her brother, Fani had told her to wait until her husband returned from the Middle East. Fani made no secret from her joy. She had taken a liking to her future son-in-law and had received good information about the family of the merchant Nikolaos Xirouchakis. He had married his two daughters, Kiki and Artemis, and had a good name in Chania society.[12]

The wedding took place in the house of the new couple on the road to Chalepa in front of the sea. Not that there was any problem with having the wedding in the church, but it was customary at the time in Chania for the priest to go to the house and have the religious wedding there. In fact, the wedding of Michalis and Eugenia Xirouchakis was blessed by the Bishop of Chania himself, Agathangelos, who was the uncle of the bride. Along with the relatives of the couple, many friends of the two families had come. First and foremost was *Capetanios* Pavlis Gyparis who rushed to congratulate the daughter of his old friend and fellow warrior Seiradakis. With him was Christos Tzifakis and many battle-scarred military men. Many of the Seiradakis family from Livadas had also come to honour their uncle. The wedding of Michalis and Loula was a happy one. They had two sons and lived together lovingly for the rest of their lives.

10 Plemeniana 7 November 1945. Personal letter signed by, E. Archontakis, M. Stavrianoudakis, Chatzidakis. (Personal archive of Charalampos Seiradakis)

11 Ref. No. 78. 8th Educational Region, Committee of Student Meetings, Chania, 10 December 1945. Inspector General I. Zacharioudakis. (Personal archive of Charalampos Seiradakis)

12 Kiki had married the chemist engineer, Minas Kassimatis. Artemis had married the doctor, Vassilis Georgilas.

Political Developments

The weaknesses observed in the administrative services in Crete were directly related to the political instability prevailing in Athens. For many years after the liberation, no government could be established. After the departure of the Germans, the government of Georgios Papandreou was unable to control the situation. During the occupation, *EAM/ELAS* had gained a broad popular base, and the bloody clashes of December 1944 in Athens had a painful impact on the divided Greek society. It took a reinforced British military presence and the arrival of Churchill himself on Christmas Day to defuse the situation. A new government under Nikolaos Plastiras negotiated the Varkiza Agreement with *EAM/ELAS* on 12 February 1945, but this too did not lead to a permanent solution.[13]

The elections of 31 March 1946, from which the left-wing parties abstained, led to a generally accepted government under Panagiotis Poulitsas with the participation of Sophocles Venizelos, Georgios Papandreou and Panagiotis Kanellopoulos. But this did not last long either. Finally, a new government under the Chairman of the Popular Party, Konstantinos Tsaldaris, organised the referendum of 1 September 1946 which decided the regime issue. This was followed by the restoration of kingship in Greece and the return of King George II three weeks later.[14] But his return was not long in triggering a new reaction by *EAM/ELAS*, which initially manifested itself in sporadic attacks in the countryside and soon escalated into a civil conflict that was to last for almost three years, until 1949.

With the return of Constantine Tsaldaris from the United States in January 1947 and the union of the Dodecanese islands with Greece, a new coalition government was formed under Demetrios Maximos. However, the civil war was already having a devastating effect on the country, especially in the countryside. On 12 March 1947 the President of the United States had announced the 'Truman Doctrine', and with it, the United States replaced Great Britain in its supportive role in Greece. The world had entered the era of the Cold War.

It was not long before the 'Marshall Plan' followed, by which the United States channelled enormous financial and technical aid to the reconstruction of Europe. Although the Marshall Plan did not solve the accumulated problems all at once, it was the beginning of the economic development of Western Europe that continued for the next decades. In Greece, the effect of American aid was manifold, but the most immediate was the intensification of the war effort against the communist offensive. At the same time, it financed reconstruction, infrastructure and public administration.

13 It was the Varkiza Agreement in the aftermath of the Yalta Conference of 4–11 February 1945, or the 'agreement of the percentages', as it became known. The Soviet Union had given up its ambitions in Greece and Great Britain had given up its ambitions in Eastern Europe.

14 King George II returned to Greece on 27 September 1946 after the referendum of 1 September 1946, which decided by 69 percent in favour of the reinstitution of the King. King George II died seven months after his return, on 1 April 1947, and was succeeded by his younger brother as King Pavlos I.

At the beginning of 1947 the political situation in the country remained volatile. The military conflicts between the national Greek Army and the 'Democratic Army of Greece', as communist *ELAS* had renamed itself, had now spread throughout the country. On 1 April 1947, King Pavlos I succeeded his brother George II, who died suddenly, on the throne. In the whirlwind of the civil war, in August 1947, the leaders of the two rival parties, Constantinos Tsaldaris of the Popular Party and Themistocles Sophoulis of the Liberals, formed a united government.[15] However, the now elderly Sophoulis died five months later and was replaced by the vice president Alexandros Diomedes. The civil conflict ended in 1949 with a victory for the national army. This was followed by two elections, in 1950 and 1951, which produced governments of Sophocles Venizelos and Nikolaos Plastiras. Greece's membership of the North Atlantic Treaty Organisation, or NATO, was then ratified, which established the structure of the post-war world.[16] Soon afterwards the new constitution was implemented.[17] New elections were held on 16 November 1952, with a majority system, which was won by a wide margin by retired General turned politician Alexandros Papagos. After his death in 1955, Konstantinos Karamanlis became prime minister for the first time, opening a new chapter in modern Greek history.

Prefect

In October 1944 Sophocles Venizelos returned to Athens with the aim of entering politics for the Liberal Party. Seiradakis was among those he trusted, and he had proposed to him to be on the candidates' list for Chania. Seiradakis was positive although at the time he was still busy with humanitarian aid in the prefecture of Chania. Fortunately, after tireless efforts, the rural distributions had been on track and requests from even the most remote villages were being met without complaints. Thus, Seiradakis began to seriously consider his participation in political life.

The proposal did not take long to come. In the elections of 31 March 1946, Sophocles Venizelos formed the National Political Union[18] and asked Charalampos Seiradakis to stand as a candidate in Chania.[19] Seiradakis had accepted and entered enthusiastically the election campaign, touring the villages of Selino that were his electoral base.

15 Spyros Markezinis, *Politiki istoria tis neoteras Ellados* (Athens: Papyros, 1968), vol. D', p.327. The government of Th. Sofoulis with Al. Diomidis as vice president, established a war council, in which K. Tsalderis, Sof. Venizelos, P. Kanellopoulos and Sp. Markezinis participated. *Stratigos* Alexandros Papagos was appointed to command of the army.

16 NATO: North Atlantic Treaty Organisation. A post-WWII international organisations included in the Bretton Woods Agreement of December 1944 that also created the International Monetary Fund (IMF), the World Bank and the Organisation for Economic Cooperation and Development (OECD).

17 The 1952 Constitution was in force until the military coup of 21 April 1967.

18 It was a coalition of the Democratic Socialist Party of G. Papandeou, the Venizelist Liberal Party of Sophocles Venizelos, and the National Unionist Party.

19 The other candidates in Chania were: Manousos Voloudakis, Polychronis Polychronidis, Georgios Sarris, Pavlos Gyparis, and Konstantinos Mitsotakis.

However, the candidacy in Selino was also being contested by other politicians, so Seiradakis soon discovered the usual intra-party rivalries.[20] He was not prepared for this. In the end Venizelos intervened in favour of Seiradakis who remained on the ballot, but the candidate who was contesting the position on the Venizelos ballot joined the rival Sofoulis combination, so the votes were split. Venizelos' party was deprived of two seats and one of them was that of Seiradakis. In a letter to Sophocles Venizelos, Seiradakis explained that, 'as I predicted, we had the formation of a second party, the spread of slander that you are supposedly royalist, and thus the votes of Selino were split.'[21] Seiradakis' first experience in politics was not successful. However, Pavlis Gyparis had been elected to Parliament for Chania on the same ballot paper.

At the beginning of 1947 during the civil war that had erupted the previous year there were no military forces in Chania. Most of them had been sent to the mountains of Vitsi and Gramos, in Northern Greece. In Chania and the surrounding villages there were unrest and violent incidents. Several attacks by gangs were reported. The militia organised by Pavlis Gyparis was not sufficient and he had asked for the help of regular army units. At the same time, Seiradakis was approached to become *Nomarch* of Chania. The erratic conditions of the civil war and the attacks on the villages demanded special handling and the experienced Seiradakis was considered more than suitable for the task.[22] Seiradakis took office as *Nomarch* of Chania on 12 March 1947. Coincidentally, it was the same day that the Truman Doctrine was announced. But Seiradakis' new mission did not bode well as terrorism in the Cretan countryside was growing by the day.

The resistance against the Axis in Crete had taken a different turn from the rest of Greece. Firstly, the two largest Cretan resistance organisations had signed agreements with each other in 1943 and 1944 to avoid civil strife.[23] Thus, there was some optimism that Crete would avoid the worst.

However, this seemed less likely in the spring of 1947 as attacks on the villages became more frequent. The telegrams exchanged between the military and administrative authorities report several violent incidents. *Nomarch* Seiradakis and *Frourarchos* Gyparis coordinated their efforts to deal with the situation.[24] Gyparis took control of the army and the *gendarmerie*, while the commander-in-chief Tzifakis together with the

20 The rival candidate was Emmanuel Baklatzis, from the neighbouring village of Moni.

21 Letter of Seiradakis to Sofoklis Venizelos, Chania 8 April 1946. S. Venizelos replied to this letter on 21 April 1946. Source: Personal archive Charalampos Seiradakis.

22 Ministry of the Interior, no. 17244, 10 March 1947. 'We inform you that by Royal Decree of 28 February 1947 … you have been appointed Prefect of Chania. Signed: Minister Georgios Papandreou'. (Personal archive of Charalampos Seiradakis.)

23 On 7 November 1943 an agreement was signed in Therisso between the resistance organisations *EOK* (National Organisation of Crete) and *EAM* (National Liberation Front). The agreement was negotiated and signed on the side of *EOK* by Nikolas Skoulas and Konstantinos Mitsotakis, and on the side of *EAM* by Miltiadis Porphyroghenis and Emmanuel Mandakas. The Therisso Agreement was confirmed and supplemented by the Tromarissa Agreement which was signed on 15 September 1944 by K. Mitsotakis for *EOK*, and by G. Vlantas for *EAM*.

24 Fortress Commander in Chania Pavlis Gyparis had undertaken to neutralise the attacks in the villages, alongside his parliamentary duties.

Nomarchs Seiradakis, Xylouris and Nathenas tried to normalise the situation by gentler means. Thus, in April there was relative calm. The prefects put pressure on Minister Sophocles Venizelos to speed up the passage of a law granting general amnesty in Crete. At the same time, they suggested that he should declare martial law in Chania and Lassithi, with the agreement of the deputies, and seek new recruitments in Rethymnon and Heraklion.

But the measures were delayed and things got worse. Organised gangs were targeting the island's infrastructure, mainly roads and bridges, and cutting telephone communications. On 24 May Seiradakis reported that the Kandanos *gendarmerie* sub-command had been attacked. A feeling of insecurity had begun to prevail again in long-suffering Selino. On 31 May there was a deadly fight in the village of Kakodiki, near Kandanos, and on 10 June people broke into the offices of the TTT public utility company in Kalyves, near Chania, and cut the telephone lines.[25] Even from the island of Gavdos in the southern sea there was a report of an attack on the gendarmerie station. On 26 June Seiradakis told Tzifakis that 'the Minister of Justice should understand that if we had amnesty in time Crete would be quiet.'[26] It was a sensitive issue due to the civil unrest, but Sophocles Venizelos did propose a draught law providing for amnesty for offences committed up to 28 May 1945. However, the delay of it entering into force did not help to normalise the situation.

Furthermore, in June the attacks extended to Kissamos in Western Crete. A politically motivated murder became the starting point for a family feud in the surrounding villages. Throughout Crete, gangs were active in the countryside under the pretext of leftist ideology. One such group, led by a man named Plakiotakis, was wiped out on 27 June in the village of Emporou, near Heraklion. At the beginning of July, *Nomarch* of Rethymnon Charalampos Xylouris announced that the armed men of Gyparis had succeeded in eliminating the notorious gang of Yannis Podias which had had 120 armed men. With ferocity it had become the terror of the region while Podias himself was known for controversial activities during the occupation.[27] The gangs of Pappas, Roukounakis and Kaparakis suffered the same fate as Podias. Often, however, after the extermination of one gang a new one appeared.

On 1 August 1947, Seiradakis sent two reports to Sophocles Venizelos on the situation in the prefecture of Chania.[28] In the second, which is longer, he noted that in most

25 Telephone, Telegraph and Telecommunication services. TTT services were important because it was the only means of communication at a time when telecommunications technology was not fully developed.

26 Letter of Ch. Seiradakis to General Commander Christos Tzifakis, Chania, 26 June 1947. (Personal archive of Charalampos Seiradakis)

27 Beevor, *Crete*, p.485. Beevor states that 'Yiannis Podias … had the traditional barbaric end of an outlaw'. Podias was in the service of Chieftain Manolis Bandouvas in Heraklion but then turned against him. Cf 8 July 1947, Digital archive of the National Foundation 'Eleftherios K. Venizelos' (file 015). Prefect of Rethymnon Ch. Xylouris requests Sof Venizelos pensions for victims of Podias' gang.

28 Digital archive of the National Foundation 'Eleftherios K. Venizelos'. Reports on 31 July 1947 and 1 August 1947 of Prefect of Chania Ch. Seiradakis to Sofoklis Venizelos,

provinces the inhabitants felt 'anxiety and insecurity'. Only in Selino was there some improvement because the gangs feared 'family reprisals'. At the same time, there was dissatisfaction with the inaction of politicians in Chania. In his opinion, the politicians of the Liberal Party in Chania ought to leave the city and visit the villages. 'I think that … they ought to go out into the countryside, even with army escort, and guide the people, encourage them and, if necessary, take charge of them.' Of course, the Chania deputies had their own political agendas and the prefect's remark did not go down well with some of them. As for dealing with the attacks in the villages, Seiradakis asked, 'that the infantry battalion should not leave the prefecture of Chania. It is the official representation of the state, and it is mainly on it and on the men of Mr Gyparis that the people are pinning their hopes'.

Sophocles Venizelos must have considered the remarks of Seiradakis, especially the exhortations to the members of his party in Chania. As he noted in his reply, 'I wish to achieve absolute calm throughout the island as soon as possible and I ask all friends who can contribute to this to do their utmost.'[29] The reference to his party's deputies in Chania was indirect but clear.

An American Visit to Crete

The disasters of the occupation could not be dealt with within a year. Shortages of basic food, medicine and clothing persisted, and US aid to Crete, alongside UNRRA assistance, was crucial.

At the beginning of August 1947, the first cargo of 4,000 tons of wheat arrived in Heraklion to be distributed on the island. On this occasion, a group of Americans with the head of the American aid mission to Greece, A. Woodward, Director M. Mac Ghee and the journalist, Robert Conway, visited Heraklion. It was their first visit to Crete. They obviously wanted to see for themselves how well the administration and distribution of American aid on the island was being managed and distributed. The prefects of Heraklion Nathenas, Rethymnon Xylouris and Chania Seiradakis, together with Tzifakis, commander-in-chief, were there to receive them.

Judging by the speeches and what was reported after the visit, it must have been quite successful. Not only for the Cretans who welcomed their guests with warm hospitality, but also for the American officials who noted the effective management of the aid. Seiradakis addressed the foreign visitors with words that allowed for no misunderstanding. 'The martyred people of Crete … did not lose their faith for a moment and soon after their liberation they were engaged in the struggle for their reconstruction.'[30] This

Vice President of the Government, on the deterioration in his prefecture and overall situation in the countryside.

29 Digital archive of the National Foundation, 'Eleftherios K. Venizelos: 23 August 1947, reply letter of Sof. Venizelos to Prefect of Chania Ch. Seiradakis.'

30 Address of Char. Seiradakis to A. Woodward, Chief of the American Assistance Mission to Greece. Heraklion, 22 August 1947. (Personal archive of Charalampos Seiradakis)

was exactly what the American officials wanted to hear. The will of a people who had suffered the horrors of the occupation to work and recreate.

Two days later Robert Conway published an article in an American newspaper which was reprinted and translated in the Cretan press.[31] Entitled 'Crete – fighting the Reds, asking for food, not weapons', it focuses on the food problem of Crete in connection with the ongoing civil war. The text is interesting as it reflects the atmosphere in those difficult days.

> The Greek civil war, the deterioration of the economy and the shortage of food are also affecting the largest of the Greek islands. But what they need most is not weapons or ammunition, but food and building materials... Manolis Badouvas is the leader of the Cretan resistance... Another great leader of Crete is Charalampos Seiradakis, Prefect of Chania. He is more categorical about the great needs of the island. [he concluded with] Here there is an estimated dozen communist gangs of about 20 well-armed guerrillas roaming around Crete. They surprise villages, carry out rapid attacks on military outposts, blow up bridges and undermine roads.

The picture painted by the American journalist was accurate. He describes a people who have the will and the strength to recover from the disasters of the occupation but is prevented by violent civil conflict. His conclusion was that Crete deserved the help that the Americans were offering and that it was being managed properly and effectively. It was an optimistic message for the future of Crete.

Resurgence and Repression

The observant Conway was not wrong about the activity of the guerrilla groups. As early as the beginning of August, attacks on the villages of Crete had been revived. Throughout the prefecture of Chania, regular army and armed guerrillas were clashing.[32] The same was true in the prefectures of Heraklion and Rethymnon, where the fighting was even more violent. On 4 August chief Commander Tzifakis urgently returned from Athens to Heraklion with *Syntagmatarchis* Thrasymvoulos Tsakalotos and called a meeting with *Syntagmatarchis* Gyparis, brothers Manolis and Giannis Badouvas, and the three prefects.[33] They unanimously decided to undertake new operations to deal with the attacks of the gangs in the countryside. The initiative was taken by the Badouvas brothers in the prefecture of Heraklion and the omnipresent Pavlis

31 The text is reproduced from a newspaper clipping in the personal archive of Char. Seiradakis. The article was published in August 1947, but it is unclear in which newspaper.

32 Report from Ch. Seiradakis to commander-in-chief in Crete Ch. Tzifakis, 3 August 1947. (Personal archive of Charalampos Seiradakis)

33 Digital archive of the National Foundation 'Eleftherios K. Venizelos', file 015. 'Letter from the chief in command Ch. Tzifakis to Sofoklis Venizelos on the state of operations in the prefecture of Chania and the on the activities of national state forces and the armed bands,' 5 August 1947.

Gyparis in Rethymnon and Chania. Three weeks later Tzifakis could inform Sophocles Venizelos that the development of public order in Crete was 'satisfactory'.[34] But it was the last letter he sent him. In the following days the Sophoulis government decided to replace him.

By September the military conflicts in Crete had entered their final phase. Seiradakis gives us important information about them in a report dated 9 September 1947.[35] He stated that 'the situation is improving. After the decimation of the Bandourogiannis gang and the killing of its leader, the declared bandit Rozakis was also eliminated by the men of Mr Gyparis in the Apokoronas region'. Seiradakis' observations on the elimination and low morale of the guerrilla groups signalled the weakening of their activity in the Cretan countryside.

In the autumn of 1947, the civil war was calming down in Crete, in contrast to the rest of Greece where it was developing into a full-on conflict. The tactic of the communist 'democratic army' to instigate battles against the national army throughout 1948 did not manifest itself in any area of Crete. On the contrary, the guerrilla armed bands on the island were gradually disarmed and the civil war progressively ended. With hindsight, the agreements signed in Therisso and Tromarissa during the occupation had brought the desired result. At least Crete had been spared the worst of the suffering that the civil war had brought to the rest of Greece.

Citizen

But the political balance had already changed. The main effort of the new government was the military operations against the communist 'democratic army' in Central and Northern Greece. In Chania, the position of chief commander of Crete was now held by Emmanuel Baklatzis who had replaced Christos Tzifakis.[36] Although an outspoken Venizelist, like Seiradakis, relations between the two men were not the best after their recent contest during the previous year's elections. Baklatzis soon promoted Nikos Birakis, a lawyer with resistance activities and contacts in political circles, to the post of Prefect of Chania. This marked the end of Charalampos Seiradakis' career as Prefect of Chania. He had served for about a year during a turbulent period marked by attacks in the countryside and an urgent humanitarian crisis. He contributed positively to both, and

34 Digital archive of the National Foundation 'Eleftherios K. Venizelos: 'Letter from the commander in chied in Crete, Ch. Tzifakis to Sofoklis Venizelos on the state of public order in Crete in each prefecture,' 21 August 1947. (Personal archive of Charalampos Seiradakis)

35 Digital archive of the National Foundation 'Eleftherios K. Venizelos'. Letter of Ch. Seiradakis to Ch. Tzifakis, Chania, 9 September 1947. (Personal archive of Charalampos Seiradakis)

36 Emmanuel Baklatzis was from the village of Moni, next to Livadas, which was also destroyed during the German attack of 1943. He was a lawyer in Chania and served as a Member of Parliament from 1950 to 1963, initially with the *EPEK* of N. Plastiras, and then with the Union of the Centre. In the 1960s he edited the newspaper *Athinaiki.*

his tenure was generally considered a success. He now had time to turn his attention to his family and to Livadas where the situation remained harsh.

There, too, he continued to be active. Even before he became prefect, he participated in the provincial road committee of the prefecture of Chania and promoted road construction in Eastern Selino.[37] He also participated in the Court of Auditors that administered the regional fund of the Chania rural police.[38]

Soon he began to accept invitations to speak at events organised by the committee for national education as well as at institutions and associations.[39] At the same time, he continued to have intensive contacts with Sophocles Venizelos and the party, although he did not stand as a candidate in any further elections. However, his stay in Chania would soon come to an end, as Seiradakis was considering moving to Athens with his entire family.

37 Special fund for provincial roads in the prefecture of Chania. Road: Prasses – Kambanou – Sougia. See Ministry of Public Works, no. pr. 30938, Athens 3 June 1949. (Personal archive of Charalampos Seiradakis)

38 Court of Auditors, excerpt no. 1199 of 1948, and 57 of 1949. (Personal archive of Charalampos Seiradakis)

39 National Enlightenment Committee, no. 45519. Speech at the 'Ceremony of awarding diplomas of gratitude to the families of the fallen', 8 March and 5 April 1949. (Personal archive of Charalampos Seiradakis)

Epilogue

Seven years after settling in Chania, the Seiradakis family decided to move to Athens. The occasion was the enrolment of the youngest daughter Helen-Ellas, or Lilly, at the University of Athens Law School and the family did not want to leave her alone. But there were also other reasons. Seiradakis had not been included on the Liberal Party's electoral list and at 66 years of age he was not in the mood to engage in intra-party intrigues. Moreover, life in Athens offered new interests.

So, in the summer of 1952 the family moved to Athens, to Ano Patissia, which was then a green suburb. The courtyard had a garden full of rose bushes that stirred new emotions in the aged Seiradakis. Yet he was anything but isolated. He intensified his contacts not only with his extended family to which he had become a beloved mentor, but also with old comrades-in-arms and politicians. With his beloved Fani, everyday life was calm and so different from the adventures of the past. The air connection to Chania now allowed the family of his eldest daughter Eugenia, or Loula, with her husband Michalis Xirouchakis and two grandchildren to visit more regularly. It was then that I, the younger grandson, began to get to know my grandfather better. I was present at the discussions when old comrades-in-arms came to visit him, and there were many such comrades and visits. I remember Sophocles Venizelos, Professor Tomadakis, fellow officer Gregorakis, who was also a putschist in '35, and so many others.

Every year on 14 July Charalampos Seiradakis was a guest at the French Embassy who did not forget the participation of the *Clan Crétois* in the battles of Lorraine and Gallipoli. In May 1961, the Pancretan Union had invited Seiradakis to deliver a historic speech at the church of St Nicholas of Kandanos. Twenty years had already passed since he had led the heroic battle against the Germans in the martyred town. The following year had seen the celebration of the 50th anniversary of the Greek victory at Bizani, Ioannina. In the front row behind King Pavlos I was Charalampos Seiradakis along with other veteran *Bizanomachoi* who had liberated Ioannina and all of Epirus. Also present were his fellow fighters Pavlis Gyparis and his nephew Andreas Gyparakis. Moving moments. In 1963 I remember my grandfather's sadness when Sophocles Venizelos died suddenly, just before the elections. It was a significant loss that shook the Venizelist world.

In 1964 a trip to Lemnos was unforgettable for everyone. The young godson of Seiradakis, Lakis Davrados, was a doctor in Myrina and had invited his godfather to visit him. Along with his beloved Fani, grandpa Charalampos had taken me with him. Lemnos certainly brought back memories to Seiradakis of the First World War, from 49 years earlier, when the port of Moudros was a base for the British in the Gallipoli campaign. It was there that he had made his first flight with the British pilot. Grandfather Seiradakis' war memories had impressed the 14-year-old grandson who, during the summer in Lemnos, had received a foretaste of the magic of the Aegean islands. Three years later, the dictatorship of the colonels of 21 April was a painful experience for Seiradakis. Apart from its extreme right-wing character, he felt that the irreverent impertinence of the leaders was an insult to his military dignity.

As the years went by, the health of the tough Seiradakis began to fail. In the winter of 1970, he became weak and had to be hospitalised. His heart could not take it. At the age of 84 and after a life rich in action and adventures, Charalampos Seiradakis passed away on September 20, 1970.

Three days later, two funerals were held simultaneously at the first cemetery of Athens. A crowd of people accompanied two personalities of the Venizelist world to their final resting place. Saddened Livadians and beloved relatives had come to pay tribute to Charalampos Seiradakis. A little further away, loved ones were bidding farewell to Alexander Othonaios, another pillar of Venizelism. One world was leaving; a new one was coming.

Europe, Middle East, N. Africa After the Second World War

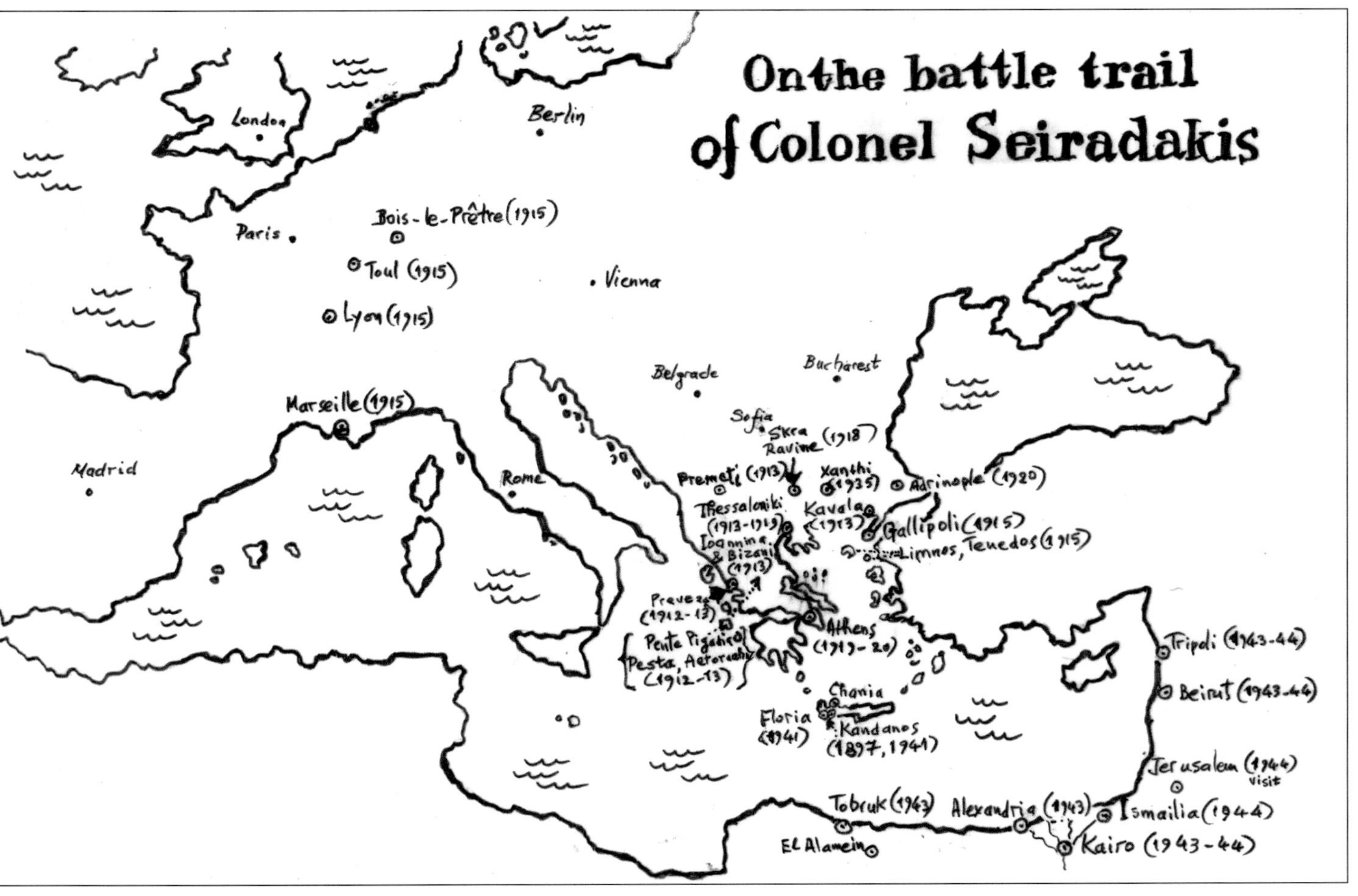

On The Battle Trail of Colonel Seiradakis

Appendix I

Excerpts from the 'Memorandum of the Revolutionary Assembly'

Therisso, 22 May 1905 (Papadakis Printing House)

The text in Greek

ΚΥΡΙΕ Γ. ΠΡΟΞΕΝΕ,
Η κατηγορηματική απόφασις των Προστατίδων Δυνάμεων όπως μη επιτρέψωσι υπό τας ενεστώσας περιστάσεις την Ένωσιν της Κρήτης μετά του Βασιλείου της Ελλάδος πληροί.

οδύνης την καρδίαν πάντων των Κρητών … Ουδέποτε διανοηθέντες να στρέψωμεν τα όπλα ημών κατά των Προστατίδων Δυνάμεων, από της ευμενείας των οποίων εξηρτήσαμεν ανέκαθεν την οριστικήν πλήρωσιν των εθνικών μας πόθων, υπόχρεοι είμεθα να κύψωμεν και πάλιν προ της νέας αποφάσεως αυτών …

Το εθνικόν αίσθημα του Κρητικού λαού είναι τοσούτον ανεπτυγμένον, η παράτασις δε του προσωρινού καθεστώτος ήρχισε τοσούτον να ανησυχεί την εθνικήν των κατοίκων συνείδησιν ώστε ο διορισμός τοιούτου διακεκριμένου ξένου κυβερνήτου δεν ημπορεί παρά να εξεγείρει ολόκληρον τον κρητικόν λαόν τοσούτον βαθέως ώστε να μην είναι δυνατή καταστολήτης εξεγέρσεως αυτού άλλη παρ' εκείνην την οποίαν ηδύνατο να επιτύχει άκαμπτος υλική βία …

Τούτων ούτως εχόντων πρόδηλον είναι ότι αδύνατον αποβαίνει εις ημάς να ανεχθώμεν την επί πλέον παράτασιν τοιούτου καθεστώτος. Αλλ' ούτε δύναται να ζητηθή η θεραπεία της καταστάσεως εις απλήν μεταρρύθισιν του καταστατικού χάρτου, όπως ούτος αποβεί συμφωνότερος προς το εθνικόν πνεύμα των Κρητών και εις την παροχήν ελευθερίας περί την επιβολήν και μεταρρύθμισιν των φορολογικών βαρών …

Πεποίθαμεν ότι εκτιμούντες την μέχρι τούδε δράσιν ημών εν σχέσει προς την τήρησιν της Δημοσίας τάξεως θέλετε αναγνωρίσει όλην την ειλικρίνειαν ήτις εμπνέει πάσας τας σχετικάς ημών προσπαθείας …

Καθ' όν χρόνον οι πέριξ ημών λαοί οδεύουσι μετά ταχύτητος εις την οδόν της προόδου, αι προστάτιδες Μ. Δυνάμεις δεν θα θελήσωσι βεβαίως ποτέ να καταδικάσωσι τον Κρητικόν λαόν όπως βιοί έστω και προσωρινώς υπό καθεστώς, όπερ δεν επιτρέπει εις αυτόν να επιτελέσει κανέν γενναίον βήμα προόδου.

Ο Πρόεδρος της Συνελεύσεως *Ι. Παπαγιαννάκης*
Ο Γραμματεύς *Κ. Μάνος*

The text in French:

MONSIEUR LE CONSUL GENERAL,
La décision catégorique des Puissances Protectrices de ne pas permettre dans les conjonctures actuelles l'annexion de l'ile au royaume de la Grèce, remplit de douleur le cœur de tous les Crétois ...

N'ayant jamais songé de porter nos armes contre les Puissances Protectrices de la bienveillance desquelles nous avons toujours fait dépendre l'accomplissement définitif de nos vœux nationaux, nous sommes obligés de nous incliner de nous encore devant leur nouvelle décision ...

Le sentiment national du peuple Crétois est tellement développé et la prolongation du régime provisoire actuel a tellement commencé à inquiéter la conscience nationale des habitants, que la nomination d'un administrateur étranger ne peut que soulever tout le peuple Crétois dans une telle mesure qu'aucune autre répression de son soulèvement ne serait possible que celle que pourrait amener une force matérielle inexorable, en le brisant sans pitié ...

Il est évident qu'il nous est impossible de supporter plus longtemps un tel régime. Mais il est de même impossible de chercher le redressement de la situation dans un simple remaniement de la constitution pour que celle-ci devienne plus conforme à l'esprit national des Crétois et dans la concession de la liberté d'imposition ...

Nous sommes convaincus qu'appréciant nos efforts pour le maintien de l'ordre nous reconnaitre toute la sincérité qui inspire nos efforts, ainsi que leur efficacité ...

A l'époque ou les peuples autour de nous marchent avec rapidité dans la route du progrès, les grandes Puissances Protectrices ne voudront jamais condamner le peuple Crétois de vivre, même provisoirement, sous un régime qui ne lui permet guère de faire un seul pas de véritable progrès ...

Le Président de l'Assemblée I. Papayannakis
Le Secrétaire C. Manos

The text in English

MISTER CONSUL GENERAL,
The categorical decision of the Protecting Powers not to allow under the present circumstances the union of Crete with the Kingdom of Greece fills the hearts of all Cretans with anguish …

Having never thought of turning our arms against the Protecting Powers, from whose benevolence we have always derived the definitive fulfilment of our national desires, we are obliged to bow again before their new decision …

The national feeling of the Cretan people is so well developed, and the prolongation of the temporary regime has begun to so alarm the national conscience of the inhabitants that the appointment of such a distinguished foreign governor cannot but upset the whole Cretan people so deeply that it is impossible to suppress their rebellion other than in ways which could be achieved by rigid material force …

Having said this, it is obvious that it is impossible for us to tolerate the prolongation of such a regime. Nor can we ask for the situation to be remedied by a simple reform of the charter, so that it is more in keeping with the national spirit of the Cretans and the freedom to impose and reform the tax burden …

We trust that those of you who appreciate our action in relation to the maintenance of law and order will recognise the sincerity which inspires all our efforts in this regard …

As long as the people around us are moving rapidly along the road of progress, the Protecting Powers will certainly never want to condemn the Cretan people to live, even temporarily, under a regime which does not allow them to take any brave step forward.

The President of the Assembly *I. Papagiannakis*
The Secretary *K. Manos*

Appendix II

Selected Documents from the Personal and Military Archives of Charalampos Seiradakis

Medals/Decorations Awarded

1. Medal of the Greek-Turkish War 1912–1913
2. Medal of the Greek-Bulgarian War 1913
3. Medal of Military Merit, 17 April 1917
4. Medal of the Inter-Allied Struggle 1914–1918
5. French War Cross, 1915
6. Exceptional Deeds Medal, Cairo, 12 October 1944
7. Moral reward during the Battle of Crete, 9 June 1948

Medals from the French Army

1. Médaille commémorative d'Orient avec inscription *'Dardanelles'.*

2. Médaille commémorative Française de la Guerre 1914 – 1918 avec barrette *'Engagé volontaire'.*

3. *SIRADAKIS Charalambos ... né en 1886 au village Livada ... Adjudant d'infanterie de l'armée française (No. Mle 29498), colonel d'infanterie de l'armée grecque, e. r. Vice-Président de la ligue des volontaires Hellènes dans l'armée française, ex préfet de la Canée, ... a servi à la Légion Étrangère du 26 février au 15 aout 1915. Il a pris part aux combats en Lorraine avec le 346e régiment d'infanterie. Il a reçu de ses chefs les meilleurs éloges. Pendant la campagne contre la Turquie il a fait preuve dans des circonstances difficiles d'une belle conduite aux combats du 6 – 7 aout 1915. Ténédos, le 15 aout 1915, le chef de bataillon J. Romieu.*

   (SIRADAKIS Charalambos ... born in Livadas in 1886 ... Lieutenant in the French Army (No. 29498), Colonel of the Greek Army, Vice President of the

Association of Greek volunteers in the French Army, former Prefect of Chania … served in the Foreign Legion from 26 February to 15 August 1915. He took part in the battles of Lorraine with the 346th infantry regiment. He received the highest praise from his superiors. During the campaign against Turkey he fought well under difficult conditions in the battles from 6 to 7 August 1915. Tenedos, 15 August 1915, *Major* J. Romieu)

4. Recommendation for promotion to Commander of *6e Compagnie, 346e Régiment d'Infanterie* (*RI*) Bon. Dewillée, with the agreement of Commander of *346e CP Lieutenant Colonel* Gillot, 17 June 1915 (to *1er Étranger*, Marseille):

   Avis du Lt Colonel Gillot le 346e Régiment d'Infanterie. Les sergents Siradakis et Yannakakis peuvent faire deux bons adjudants, ils sont braves, énergiques et ont fait leurs preuves. Je transmets aux Lieutenant Gyparis avec avis favorable. Le 17 juin 1915, signé Gillot, 346e Régiment d'Infanterie.

   (It is the opinion of Colonel Gillot of the 346th Infantry Regiment. Sergeants Siradakis and Giannakakis will make good adjutants, they are brave, active and have proven their worth. I forward this to Lieutenant Gyparis with a positive recommendation. June 17, 1915,

   signed Gillot, 346th Infantry Regiment.)

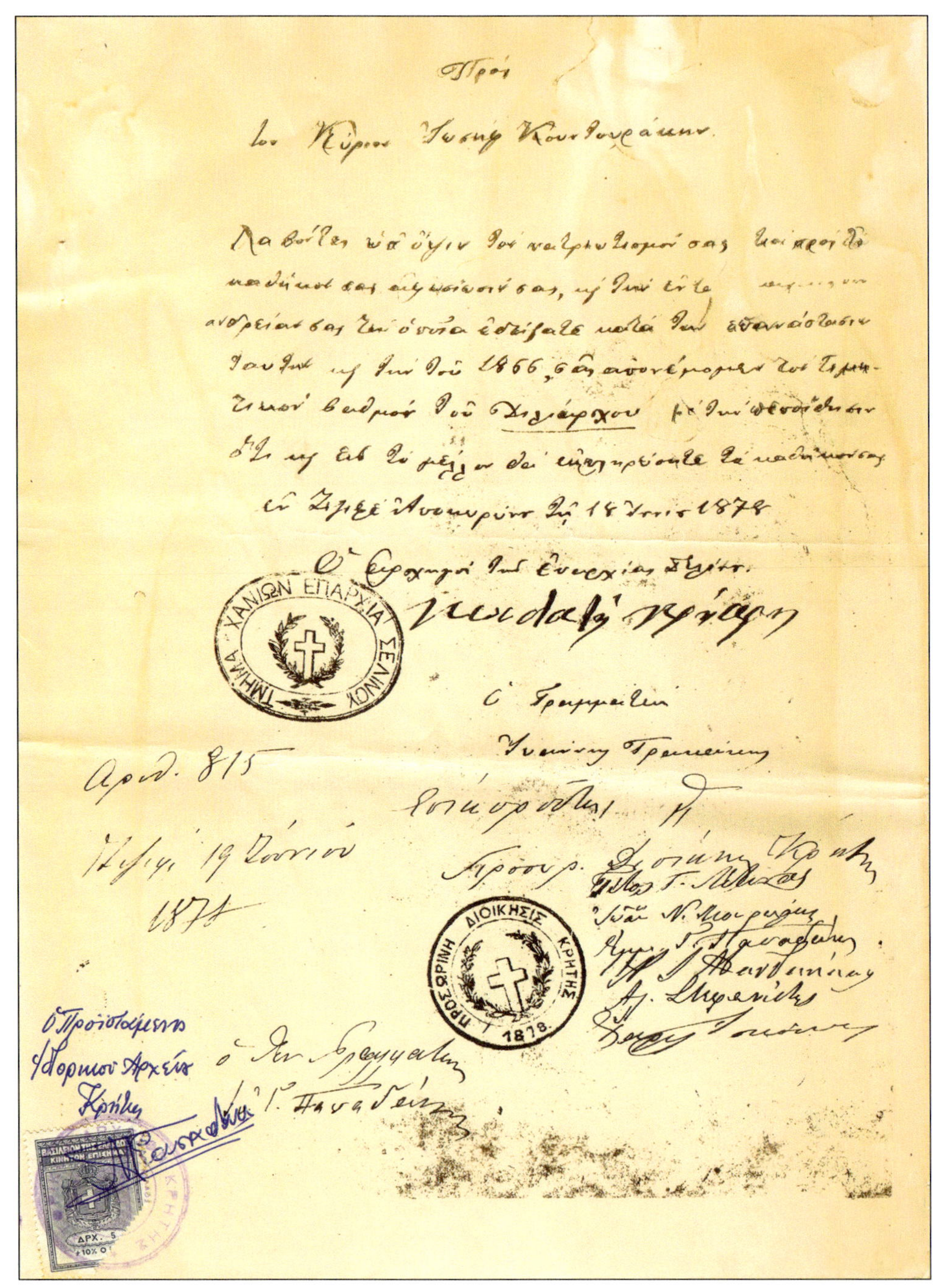
ΤΜΗΜΑ ΧΑΝΙΩΝ ΕΠΑΡΧΙΑ ΣΕΛΙΝΟΥ

Αριθ. 815

19 Ιουνίου 1878

ΠΡΟΣΩΡΙΝΗ ΔΙΟΙΚΗΣΙΣ ΚΡΗΤΗΣ 1878

Joseph Seiradakis, or Koudourossifis, is awarded the rank of Chiliarchos for his heroism in successive Cretan revolts, 14 June 1878.

ΓΕΝΕΑΛΟΓΙΚΟ ΔΕΝΤΡΟ
Τῶν Σειράδων

ΡΙΖΑ καί ΚΛΑΔΟΙ
τοῦ Δημήτρη Σειραδάκι

Ἡ ρίζα τῆς οἰκογενείας, κατά τον ἀείμνηστο θειο μας Χαράλαμπο Σειραδάκι, ἔχει τὴν καταγωγή ἀπό τὸ γένος τῶν Σκορδυλῶν, ὁ γενάρχης τῶν ὁποίων μέ τό ὄνομα Μαρίνος ἦτο ἕνας ἀπό τά δώδεκα ἀρχοντόπουλα τοῦ Βυζαντίου. Οὗτος ἐγκατεστάθη στὴν Κρήτη τό δωδέκατο μ. Χριστόν αἰῶνα ἐπί Ἀλεξίου Κομνηνοῦ τοῦ Ϛ'. (βλέπε νέα παγκόσμια ἐγκυκλοπαίδεια τῆς μορφωτικῆς ἑταιρείας, τόμος 25-26 στή σελίδα 401.)

Ἕνα μέλος τῆς οἰκογενείας αὐτῆς τῶν Σκορδυλῶν, μέ τό ὄνομα Γιάννης, κατώκησε στό χωριό Ἅη-Γιάννη τῶν Σφακίων. Λόγω τῆς ἀρχοντικῆς του ἐμφανίσεως, ἀπεκαλεῖτο ἀπό τούς ἀηγιανιῶτες, καλόσειρος, αὐτός πρέπει νἆναι ἀπό καλή σειρά, ἔλεγαν, καί ἀπό τότε ἐπῆρε τό ἐπώνυμο Σειρὰς καί ὡς συνηθίζεται στὴν Κρήτη τό Σειρᾶς ἔγινε Σειραδάκις.

Τό 16° περίπου αἰῶνα ὁ Γιάννης Σειραδάκις ἦλθε καί κατώκησε στό Λειβαδᾶ-Σελίνου

Κατά τόν ἀείμνηστο δέ θεῖο μας Ἐμμανουήλ Βαρδῆ Σειραδάκι καί ἀπό τίς σημειώσεις του «Οἰκογενειακαί ἀναμνήσεις » πού ἄφησε; γράφει:

Genealogical tree of the Seiradakis family, composed by Strategos Dimitrios Seiradakis, 1962.

Εμμ. Βαρ. τοῦ Σειραδάκη

1

Οἰκογενειακαί ἀναμνήσεις.

Ἡ οἰκογένεια «Σειρᾶς»

τό οἰκογενειακόν ὄνομα "Σειρᾶς" ἤ
Σειραδάκης δέν εἶναι τό ἀρχικόν ὄνομα τῆς οἰκογενείας μας. Διότι ὁ ἀρχι-
κός γεννήτωρ τῆς οἰκογενείας τῶν Σειράδων, ὁρμηθείς ἐκ Θολετροῦ τῶν Σφακίων
καί ἐγκατασταθείς εἰς Θηβαδά τοῦ
Σαχάνου, πρό 400 ἐτῶν περίπου, ἀποτέ-
λει μέρος τῆς οἰκογενείας τῶν "Καρα-
ραίνων" μιᾶς τῶν ἰσχυροτέρων οἰκο-
γενειῶν τῶν Σφακίων. Οἱ ἐν Σφακίοις
ἀπόγονοι τῆς οἰκογενείας ταύτης ἐνα-
βρύνονται καί ἀναγάγουσι τήν κα-
ταγωγήν αὐτῶν εἰς ρίζαν τῶν Βυζαν-
τινῶν Αὐτοκρατόρων, ἀλλ' ἡ τοιαύτη αὐτῶν ὑψηλοφροσύνη μή βεβαιουμένη
διά θετικῶν ἀποδείξεων δέν εἶναι

—//—

Personal genealogical note written by Mayor of Chania Emmanuel Seiradakis, 1960.

Φλώρινα 22/10/913.

Φίλτατέ μου κ. Σειραδάκη.

Ἔλαβον τὴν ἐπιστολήν Σας, καὶ Σᾶς ζητῶ συγγνώμην διὰ τὴν βραδύτητα τῆς παρούσης μου, ὁ σκοπὸς τῆς παρούσης μου εἶναι, ὅπως Σᾶς συγχαρῶ, διὰ τὴν γενναιότητα καὶ αὐτοθυσίαν, ἣν ἔδειξεν ὁ ἀγαπητός Σας υἱός εἰς ὅλας τὰς μάχας, τιμήσας τὴν τε πατρίδα καὶ γονεῖς, καὶ ἀποσπάσας τὸν θαυμασμὸν τῶν τε ἀνωτέρων του, συναδέλφων καὶ κατωτέρων, καὶ δικαίως ἡ ὑπηρεσία διὰ τὰς ἐξόχους ὑπηρεσίας τοῦ τετιμημένου υἱοῦ Σας ἐπρότεινε, ὅπως τῷ χορηγηθῇ τὸ παράσημον τῆς ἀνδρείας

This and next page: First Balkan War Letter from Ypolochagos D. Konstantinidis to Joseph Seiradakis, father of Charalampos, 22 October 1913.

First Balkan War. List of officers of the Anexartito Syntagma Kriton (Independent Regiment of Cretans), handwritten note by Charalampos Seiradakis, Chania, September 1912.

Personal letter from Lochagos B. Mountakis to Ch. Seiradakis, Ioannina, 26 March 1963

C.E.O.

Ier Régiment Entrager

L'Adjudant Siradakis Charalambos servi à la Légion Etrangère du 26 Février au I5 Août I9I5. Il a pris part aux combats en Lorraine avec le 346ème Règiment d'Infanterie. Il a reçu de ses chefs les meilleurs éloges.

Dans la campagne contre la Turquie il a eu dans des circonstances difficiles une belle conduite aux combats du 7 Août I9I5.

Ténédos, le I5 Août I9I5

LE CHEF DE BATAILLON

I. ROMIEU

Pour la copie certifiée conforme.
Le Sécr. Général de la Ligue
des Volontaires Hellènes 1914-18.

LIGUE DES VOLONTAIRES HELLÈNES DE L'ARMÉE FRANÇAISE 1914-1918 ATHÈNES

First World War. French military document on the participation of Adjutant Charalampos Seiradakis in Lorraine and Gallipoli expeditions, 15 August 1915.

ΣΥΝΔΕΣΜΟΣ ΕΛΛΗΝΩΝ ΕΘΕΛΟΝΤΩΝ
ΓΑΛΛΙΚΟΥ ΣΤΡΑΤΟΥ
ΟΔΟΣ ΓΕΩΡ. ΓΕΝΝΑΔΙΟΥ 7 - ΤΗΛ. 620.389

ΕΠΙΤΙΜΟΣ ΠΡΟΕΔΡΟΣ
Ο Κος ΠΡΕΣΒΕΥΤΗΣ ΤΗΣ ΓΑΛΛΙΑΣ
ΕΝ ΕΛΛΑΔΙ

'Αριθ. Πρωτ. 12/1-1-61

LIGUE DES VOLONTAIRES HELLÈNES
DANS L'ARMÉE FRANÇAISE
7, RUE DU GEOR. GENADIOU

PRÉSIDENT D' HONNEUR
Mr L' AMBASSADEUR DE FRANCE
EN GRÈCE

'Αθῆναι, Athenes, 16 [illegible] 1960

A Monsieur le Colonel

J. A r n o u l d

Attaché Militaire, Naval et de l' Air auprès

l' Ambassade de France en Grèce

Monsieur le Colonel,

Nous avons l'honneur de vous prier de vouloir bien proposer afin que les Messieurs ci-dessous soient nommés par le Gouvernement de la V République, Chevaliers de la Légion d' Honneur, croyant qu'ils sont dignes de cette honneur et tenant compte de leur grande et constante fidélité à l'égard de la France:

1) Paul GYPARIS, Colonel e.r., ex-deputé, Lieutenant dans l' Armée Française, ex Président de notre Ligue et Président d'honneur de la même Ligue.

2) Charalambos SIRADAKIS, Colonel e.r., Adjudant dans l' Armée Française, ex-Préfet, et ex Surveillant de la Croix-Rouge Internationale. Vice-Président de la Ligue des Volontaires Hellères dans l' Armée Française.

3) André GYPARAKIS, Lt.-Colonel, e.r. Membre du Conseil d' Administration de notre Ligue. Conseiller Municipal d' Athènes.

4) Constantin GIANNAGAKIS. Lt .-Colonel, e.r., Ex-Adhudant d' Infanterie dans l' Armée Françaises. Membre du Conseil d' Administration de notre Ligue et ex-surveillant de la Croix Rouge Internationale.

5) Palos PAPADONICOLAOS, Lt-Colonel e.r. Membre du Conseil d' Administration. Ex-surveillant de la Croix Rouge Internationale.

Ci-inclus élements des proposés et copie des ordres des autorités françaises.

Veuillez agréer, Monsieur le Colonel, l'assurance de notre considération distinguée.

POUR LE CONSEIL D' ADMINISTRATION

First World War. Proposal of Colonel J. Arnould to name as Chevalliers de la Legion d'Honneur officers of the Hellenocretan Legion, 16 July 1960.

Avis du Chef de Bon Dewillée commt le 6e Bon du 346e.

En raison de l'extension que va prendre le clan Crétois lors de sa réorganisation prochaine aux Dardanelles ,le Lieutenant Gyparis prend ses précautions pour compléter les cadres de l'unité dont le commandement lui sera confié et pour fournir au besoin,à d'autres unités grecques, des sous-officiers énergiques et éprouvés.

Les avis successifs des chefs militaires français sous lesquels sert actuellement le lieutenant Gyparis,ont une grande importance,car c'est sur ces avis que se basera le gouvernement hellène pour conférer des grades réguliers ,dans l'armée grecque,à ceux qui s'en sont montrés dignes.

Je demande ,en conséquence,qu'on transmette ,avec avis favorabl les propositions pour le grade d'adjutant concernant les SergentsSIRADAKI Ces Sous-officiers sont de braves et énergiques soldats,fiers d'aller combattre aux Dardanelles aux côtés de leurs frères d'armes franç Je n'ai eu qu' à me louer d'eux en particulier,et de tout le clan crétois en général.

Le 17 Juin 1915 DEWILLEE.

Avis du Lt.Colonel Gillotcomt le 346e Regt d'Infanterie.

Les sergents Siradakis et Yannacakis peuvent faire deux bons adjutants ,ils sont braves,énergiques et ont fait leurs preuves.je transmet la demande du Lieut. Gyparis avec avis favorable.

Le 17 Juin 1915

(signé) GILLOT. Sceau du 346e Reg. d'Infanterie.

Transmets avec avis ~~favorable~~ conforme .

17 Juin 1915 Le Commandant de la 145e Brigade d'Infanterie Chef de Secteur,Signature illisible (L.S.)

73 Div.

Transmis avec avis favorable.

Transmons au Général Commandant en Chef pour être adressé au dépot du 1er Etranger,à Lyon, sur lequel est dirigé le detachement crétois.

N° 7626
.au 9 / 4 le 20 Juin 1915
P.O. le Chef d'Etat major

Signature illisible
(Sceau de la 73e Division

Q.G. 18 Juin 1915
Le Gal Cdt. le 73e Div.

Signature illisible.

Sceau : Grand Quartier Général des Armées

arrivée le 21 Juin 1915
N° du Répertoire 127/8
Remise au P.

Pour copie certifié conforme.
Le prototype est gardé à mon archive (clan Greco-Cretois).
Tenedos 25-7-1915 Le Chef du clan Crétois P. Gyparis

Paul Gyparis
Lieutenant d'Infanteri

This and next page: First World War. Opinion of Major Dewillée on the promotion of Ch. Seiradakis and K. Giannakakis as sous-lieutenants in the French Army, 17 June 1915.

ΜΕΤΑΦΡΑΣΙΣ ΕΚ ΤΟΥ ΓΑΛΛΙΚΟΥ

Γνωμάτευσις τοῦ Ταγματάρχου DEWILLEE, Διοικητοῦ τοῦ 6ου Τ/τος τοῦ 346 Συν/τος.

Λόγῳ τῶν διαστάσεων τά ὁποίας θά λάβῃ ἡ Κρητική Φάλαγξ (Κλάν) μετά τήν προσεχῆ ἀναδιοργάνωσίν της εἰς τά Δαρδανέλλια, ὁ ὑπολοχαγός Γύπαρης λαμβάνει προφυλακτικά μέτρα διά νά συμπληρώσῃ τά στελέχη τῆς μονάδος, τῆς ὁποίας θά τοῦ ἀνατεθῆ ἡ Διοίκησις, καί διά νά ἐφοδιάσῃ ἐν ἀνάγκῃ, ἄλλας Ἑλληνικάς μονάδας μέ ὑπαξιωματικούς δραστηρίους καί δοκιμασμένους.

Αἱ διαδοχικαί γνωματεύσεις τῶν Γάλλων Στρατιωτικῶν Ἀρχηγῶν ὑπό τούς ὁποίους ὑπηρετεῖ νῦν ὁ ὑπολοχαγός Γύπαρης, εἶναι μεγάλης σπουδαιότητος, διότι βάσει τῶν γνωματεύσεων τούτων θά στηριχθῆ ἡ Ἑλληνική Κυβέρνησις διά νά ἀπονείμῃ τακτικούς βαθμούς εἰς τόν Ἑλληνικόν Στρατόν, εἰς ὅσους ἀπέδειξαν ὅτι εἶναι ἄξιοι τούτων.

Συνεπῶς αἰτοῦμαι ὅπως διαβιβασθοῦν, μέ εὐνοϊκήν γνωμάτευσιν, αἱ προτάσεις διά τόν βαθμόν τοῦ Ἀνθυπασπιστοῦ, αἱ ἀφορῶσαι τούς Λοχίας Σιραδάκην Χαράλαμπο καί Γιαννακάκην. Οἱ ὑπαξιωματικοί οὗτοι εἶναι γενναῖοι καί δραστήριοι στρατιῶται, ὑπερήφανοι νά μεταβοῦν καί πολεμήσουν εἰς τά Δαρδανέλλια, παρά τό πλευρό τῶν ἐν ὅπλοις Γάλλων ἀδελφῶν των. Εἶμαι ἰδιαιτέρως ἱκανοποιημένος ἐκ τούτων, καί γενικῶς ἐξ ὅλης τῆς Κρητικῆς φάλαγγος.

τῇ 17 Ἰουνίου 1915
Ὑπογρ. DEWILLEE

Γνωμάτευσις τοῦ Ἀντ/χου ΖΙΛΟ, Δ/του τοῦ 346 Συν/τος Πεζικοῦ :

Οἱ λοχίαι Σιραδάκης καί Γιαννακάκης δύνανται νά εἶναι καλοί ἀνθυπασπισταί εἶναι γενναῖοι, δραστήριοι καί δοκιμασμένοι. Διαβιβάζω τήν αἴτησιν τοῦ Ὑπ/γοῦ Γύπαρη μέ γνωμάτευσιν εὐνοϊκήν.

τῇ 17 Ἰουνίου 1915. Ὑπογρ. ΖΙΛΟ Σφραγίς

Διαβιβάζεται μετά εὐνοϊκῆς γνωματεύσεως, τῇ 17 Ἰουνίου 1915 Ὁ Διοικητής τῆς 145 Ταξιαρχίας Πεζικοῦ. Τομεάρχης. Ὑπογραφή Σφραγίς

73η Μεραρχία. Διαβιβάζεται μετά εὐνοϊκῆς γνωματεύσεως. Διαβιβάζεται πρός τόν Ἀρχιστράτηγον ἵνα ἀποσταλῇ εἰς τό ἔμπεδον τοῦ 1ου τῶν Ξένων, ἐν Λυῶν εἰς τό ὁποῖον κατευθύνεται ἡ Κρητική Φάλαγξ. Γεν. Ἀρχ. τῇ 18 Ἰουνίου 1915 Ὁ Διοικητής τῆς 73ης Μεραρχίας. Ὑπογραφή δυσανάγνωστος.

Ἀριθ. 7626. Τῇ 9/4 τῇ 20 Ἰουνίου 1915. Ε.Ο. Ὁ Ἐπιτελάρχης. Ὑπογρ. Δυσανάγν
Σφραγίς.

Σφραγίς. = Μέγα Γενικόν Ἀρχηγεῖον Στρατιῶν. Ἄφιξις τῇ 21η Ἰουνίου 1915
Ἀριθ. Πρωτ. 127/8
Παρεδόθη εἰ Ρ

LIGUE DES VOLONTAIRES HELLÈNES DANS L'ARMÉE FRANÇAISE 1914-1918 ATHÈNES

Διά τὴν ἀκρίβειαν τῆς μεταφράσεως
ὁ Γεν. Γραμματεύς·

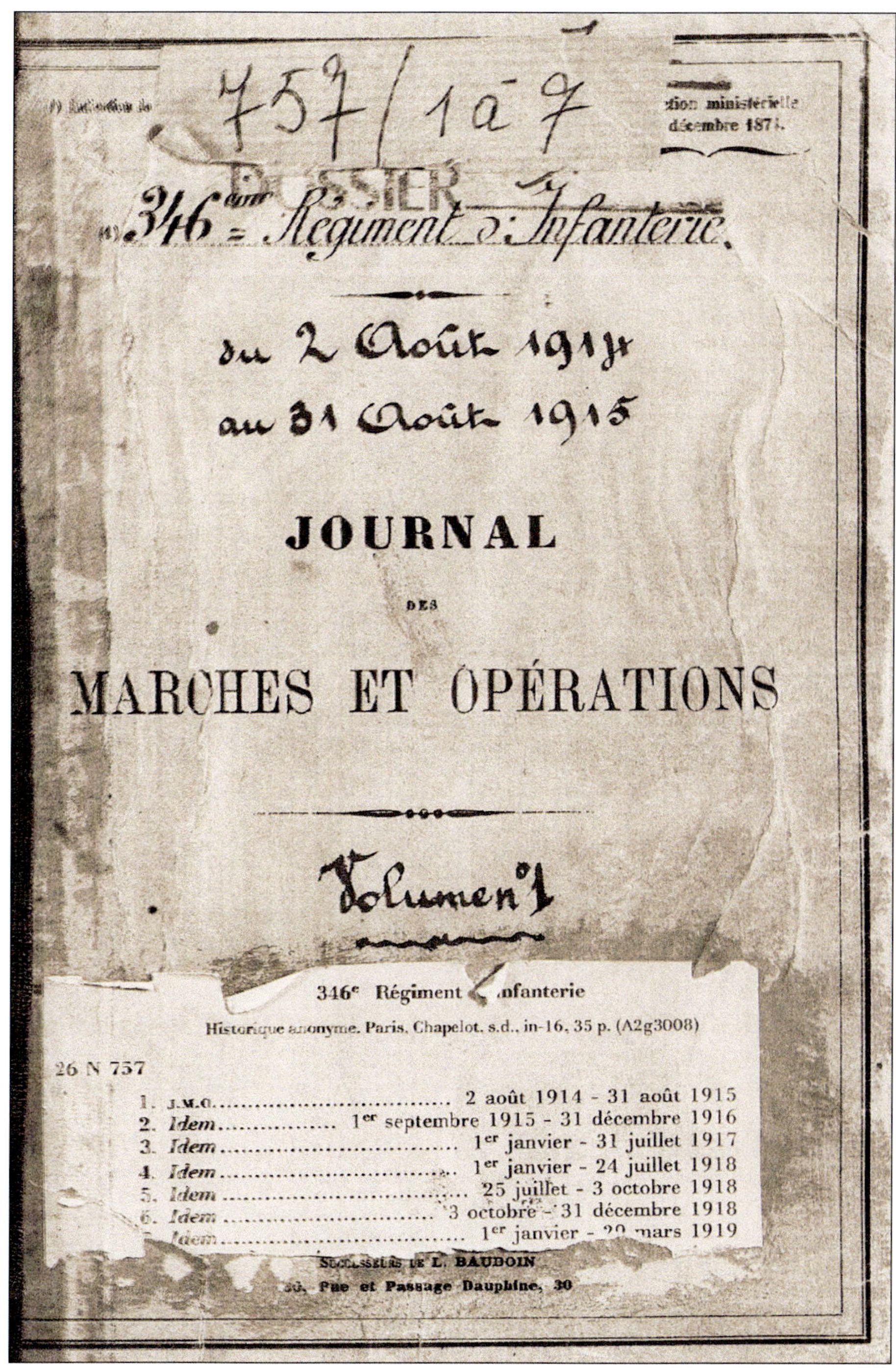

757/1a 7

DOSSIER

346ème Régiment d'Infanterie

du 2 Août 1914
au 31 Août 1915

JOURNAL

DES

MARCHES ET OPÉRATIONS

Volume 1

346e Régiment d'Infanterie

Historique anonyme. Paris, Chapelot, s.d., in-16, 35 p. (A2g3008)

26 N 757

1. J.M.O. .... 2 août 1914 - 31 août 1915
2. *Idem* .... 1er septembre 1915 - 31 décembre 1916
3. *Idem* .... 1er janvier - 31 juillet 1917
4. *Idem* .... 1er janvier - 24 juillet 1918
5. *Idem* .... 25 juillet - 3 octobre 1918
6. *Idem* .... 3 octobre - 31 décembre 1918
7. *Idem* .... 1er janvier - 20 mars 1919

Successeurs de L. Baudoin
30, Rue et Passage Dauphine, 30

First World War. Campaign diary of the 346e Régiment d'Infanterie, to which the Hellenocretan Legion was attached, 2/6/2014 to 31/8/1915.

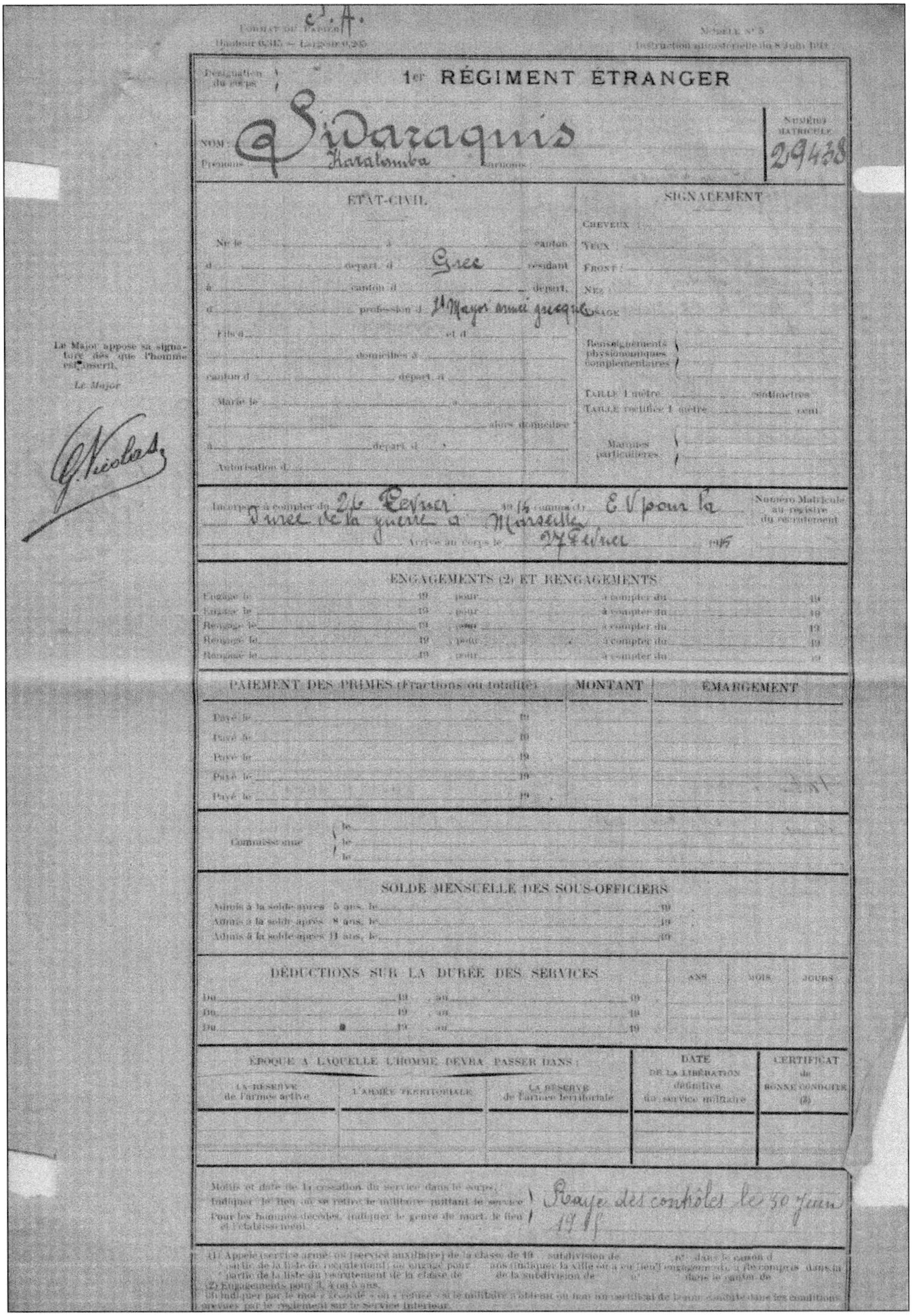

1er RÉGIMENT ÉTRANGER

NOM : Sidaraquis

Prénoms Haralamba

Numéro matricule 29438

ÉTAT-CIVIL

SIGNALEMENT

Grec

profession d' Major armée grecque

Incorporé à compter du 26 Février 1915 comme (1) E.V pour la Durée de la guerre à Marseille

Arrivé au corps le 27 Février 1915

ENGAGEMENTS (2) ET RENGAGEMENTS

PAIEMENT DES PRIMES (Fractions ou totalité) | MONTANT | ÉMARGEMENT

SOLDE MENSUELLE DES SOUS-OFFICIERS

DÉDUCTIONS SUR LA DURÉE DES SERVICES

Rayé des contrôles le 30 juin 1915

First World War. Registration of Charalampos Seiradakis (as Sidaraquis Haralambe) in the Légion Étrangère, February 1915.

Vence 8-5-35.

Αγαπητέ μου κ. Σειραδάκη

This and next page: Letter of Strategos Nikolaos Plastiras to Tagmatarchis Charalampos Seiradakis, 8 May 1935.

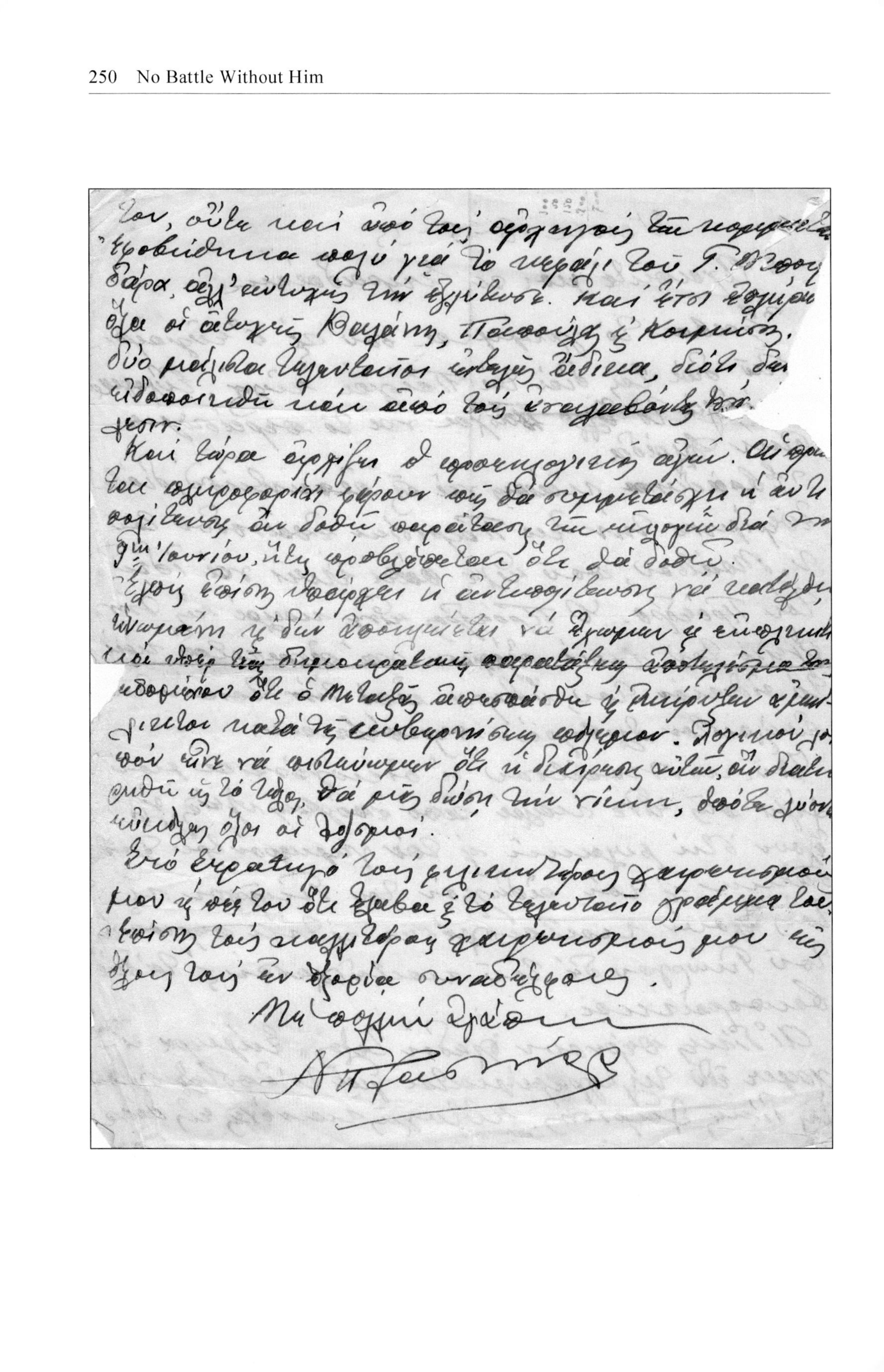

Με πολλή αγάπη

ΕΚΘΕΣΙΣ

**Δράσεως τοῦ Συν/ρχου πεζικοῦ Σειραδάκη Χαραλ.
κατὰ τὴν μάχην τῆς Κρήτης ἀπὸ 20-30/5/41**

Κατὰ τὴν κάθοδον τῆς Α.Μ. τοῦ Βασιλέως καὶ τῆς Κυβερνήσεως εἰς τὴν Κρήτην τὸν Ἀπρίλιον τοῦ 1941 ὁ ἐν περιλήψει ἀναφερόμενος ἀξιωματικὸς εὑρίσκετε εἰς τὴν κατάστασιν τῆς αὐτεπαγγέλτου ἀποστρατείας εἰς ἣν ἐτέθη διότι μετέσχε τοῦ κινήματος τῆς 1ης Μαρτίου 1935. Ἐπὶ τῆς καταστάσεως αὐτῆς ἀνεκλήθη κατόπιν τοῦ ὑπ'ἀριθ. 3013/41 Α.Ν. καὶ ἀνετέθη εἰς αὐτὸν ἡ ὀργάνωσις καὶ ἐκτέλεσις λόχων ἐξ ἐφέδρων ὁπλιτῶν διὰ τὴν ἀπόκρουσιν τῶν ἀλεξιπτωτιστῶν εἰς τὴν Ἐπαρχίαν Σελίνου.

Διὰ Σέλινον ἀνεχώρησεν τὴν 19ην Μαΐου 1941 συνεπείᾳ τῆς ὑπ' ἀριθμ.21 Δ.Π. τοῦ Ὑπ.Στρατιωτικῶν ἡ δὲ πτῶσις τῶν ἀλεξιπτωτιστῶν ἤρχισεν εἰς τὴν περιοχὴν τοῦ Νομοῦ Χανίων τὴν 7.15΄΄ ὥραν τῆς ἑπομένης.

Ὁ ὑλικὸς χρόνος ἀπομένως πρὸς ὀργάνωσιν καὶ ἐκτέλεσιν λόχων ἐξ ἐφέδρων διὰ τὴν ἀπόκρουσιν τῶν ἀλεξιπτωτιστῶν ἐμηδενίσθη.

Παρὰ τὸ γεγονὸς αὐτὸ ὁ Συν/ρχης Σειραδάκις Χαραλ. διὰ πρωτοβουλίας ἐξιεπαίνου ἐπεδίωξεν καὶ ἐπέτυχεν τὴν ταχεῖα συγκέντρωσιν σοβαροῦ ἀριθμοῦ ἐθελοντῶν μὲ παντοειδῆ ὁπλισμόν, συμπεριλαμβανομένων καὶ πρωτογόνων κυνηγετικῶν ὅπλων, καὶ μὲ ἐλάχιστα πυρομαχικά.

Διὰ τῆς καλῆς καὶ ἐπικαίρου χρησιμοποιήσεως τῆς δυνάμεως ἐκείνης τῶν ἐθελοντῶν, ἀφοῦ συνεδέθη τηλ/κῶς καὶ μὲ τὶς Βουκολιές ἀπησχόλησε κατὰ τὴν διάρκειαν τῶν ἐπιχειρήσεων πλῆρες Γερμανικὸν τάγμα τοῦ ὁποίου αἱ μὲν εἰς νεκροὺς ἀπώλειαι ἀναβιβάζονται εἰς 15 αἱ δὲ τοιαῦται εἰς τραυματίας δὲν ἐξηκριβώθησαν.

Συνεπείᾳ τῆς τοιαύτης ὑπὸ τὸν Συν/ρχην Π. Σειραδάκιν Χαράλ. ἀντιδράσεως τῶν ἐθελοντῶν καὶ γενικῶς τοῦ πληθυσμοῦ, μηδὲ τῶν γυναικῶν τῆς Ἐπαρχίας ἐξαιρουμένων, ὑπῆρξε ἡ ἐκ θεμελίων κατεδάφισις τῆς κωμοπόλεως Κανδάνου, κατὰ τὴν κατάληψιν τῆς Κρήτης καὶ ὁ ἀθρόος τυφεκισμὸς πολλῶν ἐκ τῶν κατοίκων τῆς Ἐπαρχίας Σελίνου, μεταξὺ τῶ

./.

./.

ὁποίων καί ἡ κόρη του, ὑπό τῶν τύπον ἀντιποίνων, διά τήν συμμετοχήν αὐτῶν εἰς τήν μάχην.

Κατόπιν τούτων προτείνομεν εἰς τό Συμβούλιον τήν εἰς τόν Συν/ρχην Πεζικοῦ ἐ.α. Σειραδάκιν Χαράλαμπον ἀπονομήν τῆς ἀνωτέρω ἠθικῆς ἀμοιβῆς.-

Ἐν Χανίοις τῇ 9 Ἰουνίου 1948

Βεβαιουται τό γνήσιον της ὑπογραφῆς του Ε.Α. Ἀντ/γου Ν. Σκουλα Ἀχιλλέως.-

Χανιά τη 9 Ἰουνίου 1948

Ὁ Διοικητής του Τμήματος

This and previous page: Second World War. Proposal of Antistratigos N. Skoulas for 'moral reward' to Ch. Seiradakis for his participation in the Battle of Crete, Chania, 2 June 1948.

Μ ν η μ ό ν ι ο ν

Πρόλογος: 1) Τά πρό τῆς εἰσβολῆς.

2) 'Ανάθεσις εἰς τούς "Αγγλους τῆς ἐντολῆς τῆς ὀχυρώσεως τῆς Κρήτης.

3) Τρόπος ἀφοπλισμοῦ τῆς Κρήτης.

4) 'Απόφασις τῆς Κυβερνήσεως διά τήν συγκρότησιν πολιτοφυλακῆς καί ἀνάκλησις ἐν ἀποστρατείᾳ 'Αξ/κῶν διά τό ἔργον ἐκπαιδεύσεως καί ὀργανώσεως αὐτῆς.

5) 'Υπάρχουσαι ἐν Κρήτῃ δυνάμεις: α) Βρετανικαί (δύναμις αὐτῶν). β) 'Ελληνικαί καί (δύναμις αὐτῶν.) Σχολή Εὐελπίδων καί 7 τάγματα πολιτοφυλάκων κ.λ.π.

6) Γενική κατάστασις: 'Οπλισμός καί ἠθικόν τοῦ Στρατοῦ.

7) 'Ανάθεσις τῆς 'Αρχιστρατηγίας εἰς τόν Φράϊμπεργκ.-

8) Κάθοδος τῆς 'Ελληνικῆς Κυβερνήσεως.

9) Πληροφορίαι περί εἰσβολῆς.

10) Στρατιωτικόν συμβούλιον ὑπό τήν προεδρείαν Στρατηγοῦ Σκουλᾶ καί χορήγησις Φ.Π.-

11) Προπαρασκευή τῆς μάχης.

20ή Μαΐου.

Εἰσβολή: ΠΛΗΡΟΦΟΡΙΑΙ

12) 'Απόφασις ἐπιστρατεύσεως καί ἔκδοσις διαταγῆς.

13) 'Ιδέα ἐνεργείας. ‹‹ ΑΠΟΦΑΣΕΙΣ ΜΟΥ ΠΕΡΙ ΤΗΣ ΜΑΧ[ΗΣ]

14) Προσέλκησις πολιτοφυλάκων. ΤΡΟΠΟΣ ΠΡΟΣΚΛΗΣΕΩΣ

15) 'Αποστολή προκαλυπτικῶν ἀποσπασμάτων, καί περισυλλογή πληροφοριῶν.

16) 'Επικοινωνία τηλεφωνική μέ Καστέλι καί μετάδοσις πρός γερμανούς ψευδῶν πληροφοριῶν.-

./.

This and next page: Second World War. Military report/memo of Ch. Seiradakis on the Battle of Crete, Chania, 1945.

\- 5 -

ΣΥΜΠΕΡΑΣΜΑΤΑ

1) Καθ'ὅλην τήν διάρκειαν τῆς μάχης τῆς Κρήτης ἀπασχολήσαμεν ἡμεῖς εἰς Κάνδανον ἕνα πλῆρες γερμανικόν Τάγμα καί τό ὁποῖον ἀπεδεκατίσαμεν.

2) 'Από τῆς πρώτης στιγμῆς ὁ ἐχθρός ᾐσθάνετο τήν ἀπειλήν μας ἐκ τῶν νώτων.

3) Κινητοποιήσαντες τούς κατοίκους τῆς 'Επαρχίας Σελίνου, ἀνακουφίσαμεν τόν εἰς τήν πεδιάδα τῶν Χανίων μαχόμενον στρατόν μας.

4) Δέν μᾶς ἐδόθη ὁ ὑλικός χρόνος διά τήν ἐκγύμνασιν καί ὀργάνωσιν τῶν πολιτοφυλάκων καί τά πράγματα μᾶς ἠνάγκασαν νά ἀκολουθήσωμεν τήν παράδοσιν τοῦ Κρητικοῦ λαοῦ νά ἀναθέσωμεν τήν Διοίκησιν πολλῶν ἐκ Τμημάτων μας εἰς πρόσωπα πεπειραμένα καί δυναμικά διά νά φέρουν εἰς πέρας τήν ἀποστολήν των καί τοῦτο ἐλλείψει ἐπαρκῶν ἀξ/κῶν.-

5) Συνεπείᾳ τῆς ἐνεργείας μας ταύτης κατεστράφη ἡ Κάνδανος. Καί ἐπηκολούθησαν αἱ ἐκτελέσεις καί καταστροφαί ὑπό τῶν γερμανῶν, διότι ὁ'αγών δέν ἔληξε μέ τήν μάχην αὐτήν τῆς Κανδάνου, ἀλλ'ἐσυνεχίσθη μέχρι πέρατος τῆς ἀπελευθερώσεως. Ἦτο ὁ τελευταῖος ἀγών τῆς ἐκπνεούσης τότε ἐλευθερίας τῆς 'Ελλάδος, ἀλλά καί τῆς Εὐρώπης.-

6) 'Η Εὐρώπη ὁλόκληρος εἶχεν ὑποκύψει. 'Ολόκληρος ἡ ὑπόλοιπος 'Ελλάς εἶχε καταληφθῆ ἀλλ'ἡ Κρήτη ἐμάχεται καί ἡ Κάνδανος ἀνθίστατο. 'Υπεδουλώθη ἡ Κρήτη εἰς τήν ὑλικήν δύναμιν.- Πάντως τελευταία ὅλων- εἰς τάς μηχανοκινήτους φάλαγγας τοῦ Χίτλερ. Δέν ὑπεδουλώθη ὅμως καί ἡ Κρητική ψυχή.

Εἶμαι βέβαιος πώς ὁ ἱστορικός τοῦ μέλλοντος θά ἀναγνωρίση ὅτι εἰς τούς ἐπικούς αὐτούς ἀγῶνας τῆς Κρήτης ὀφείλεται καί ἡ καθυστέρησις τῆς ἐπιθέσεως τοῦ Χίτλερ κατά τῆς Ρωσσίας ὅπου ὁ βαρύς χειμών συνεπικούρησε τούς Ρώσσους καί τό νά ἀποτύχη τό κατακτητικόν σχέδιόν του. [illegible]

Ἐν Καΐρῳ [illegible] 1945.

Ὁ

Ἀντισυν/χης Πεζ. Σειραδάκης Χαράλαμπος

Πρὸς

Τὸν Ἀντιστράτηγον κ. Σκουλᾶν Ἀχιλλέα

Τέως Στρατιωτικὸν Διοικητὴν Κρήτης

Ἐνταῦθα

[illegible]

Second World War. Military report of Charalampos Seiradakis to Antistratigos N. Skoulas on the Battle of Crete, Cairo 1945.

ΕΦΗΜΕΡΙΣ ΤΗΣ ΚΥΒΕΡΝΗΣΕΩΣ

ΤΟΥ ΒΑΣΙΛΕΙΟΥ ΤΗΣ ΕΛΛΑΔΟΣ

Ἐν Χανίοις τῇ 14η Μαΐου 1941, Τεῦχος Μόνον, Ἀριθμ. φύλλου 161.-

Περιεχόμενα

Β΄ ΔΙΑΤΑΓΜΑ

«Περὶ ἀνακλήσεως καὶ προαγωγῆς Ἀξιωματικῶν ἐξελθόντων διὰ πολιτικοὺς λ-
γους (1).

«Περὶ ἀκυρώσεως Δ/τος διαγραφῆς Ὑποστρατήγου Καφάτου Σόλωνος...... (2).

Β΄ ΔΙΑΤΑΓΜΑ

«Περὶ ἀνακλήσεως καὶ προαγωγῆς Ἀξιωματικῶν ἐξελθόντων διὰ πολιτικοὺς λ-
γους.

ΓΕΩΡΓΙΟΣ Β΄
ΒΑΣΙΛΕΥΣ ΤΩΝ ΕΛΛΗΝΩΝ

Προτάσει τοῦ Ἡμετέρου ἐπὶ τῶν Στρατιωτικῶν Ὑπουργοῦ καὶ ἔχοντες ὑπ᾽ ὄψει τὰς διατάξεις τοῦ ὑπ᾽ ἀριθμ. 3013 Α.Ν. «περὶ ἀποκαταστ-
άσεως Ἀξιωματικῶν ἐξελθόντων τοῦ στρατεύματος διὰ πολιτικοὺς λόγους ἀπ-
φασίσαμεν καὶ διατάσσομεν.

Ἀνακαλοῦμεν

Εἰς τὴν ἐνεργὸν τοῦ Στρατοῦ Ὑπηρεσίαν τοὺς κάτωθι Ἀξιωματικοὺς ἐξελ-
θόντας τοῦ στρατεύματος διὰ πολιτικοὺς λόγους, τοῦ διαρρεύσαντος χρόνου ἀπὸ τῆς ἐξόδου των λογιζομένου ὡς τοιούτου Ὑπηρεσίας δι᾽ ἁπάσας τὰς πε-
πτώσεις πλὴν ἀποδοχῶν.-

Πεζικοῦ

....

12) Ταγματάρχην Σειραδάκην Χαράλ. (α.μ. 10553 γεννηθέντα τ-
1/1/1886.- ....

Πυροβολικοῦ

.... Ἱππικοῦ.......................

Μηχανικοῦ .... Ὑγειονομικοῦ ....

..............Στρατολογίας..................... Ἐλέγχου .

Τοὺς ἀνωτέρω ἐντάσσομεν ἐν τῇ οἵα κατεῖχον σειρᾷ ἀρχαιότητος πρὸ το-
ἔτους 1935 καὶ

Προβιβάζομεν

Τοὺς κάτωθι ἐκ τούτων δικαιουμένους προαγωγῆς ἀφ᾽ ἧς χρονολογίας προήχθ-
σαν νεώτεροι των μόνον ὅσον ἀφορᾷ τὴν ἀρχαιότητα, οὐχὶ δὲ καὶ τὰς ἀποδο-
χὰς ἀνακολούθως.

Πεζικόν

.... Εἰς .. Ἀντισυνταγματάρχας ....

7) Ταγματάρχην Σειραδάκην Χαράλ. ἀπὸ 7/10/1935

....

....

Εἰς τὸν αὐτὸν Ὑπουργὸν ἀνατίθεμεν τὴν δημοσίευσιν καὶ ἐκτέλεσιν τοῦ παρόντος Διατάγματος.-

Ἐν Χανίοις τῇ 12η Μαΐου 1941
ΓΕΩΡΓΙΟΣ Β

Ὁ
Ἐπὶ τῶν Στρατιωτικῶν Ὑπουργὸς
ΕΜΜ. Ι. ΤΣΟΥΔΕΡΟΣ

Ἐθεωρήθη
Διὰ τὴν ἀκρίβειαν τῆς ἀντιγραφῆς

Second World War. Decision of Greek Prime Minister Emmanuel Tsouderos recalling Charalampos Seiradakis to active service in the Army, Chania, 19 May 1941.

872

PERMIT OFFICE
AVAILABLE UNTIL
18 MAY 1945

19 JUL 1944

IDENTIFICATION CARD.

OFFICERS OF
ALLIED FORCES IN THE
MIDDLE EAST

Place of Issue 17. Area
Date 19-7-44
Valid until 18-5-45
Signature of Holder
5738/2/PMEM/5/43

Permit Officer, M.E.F.

Name SIRADAKIS
Haralambos
Nationality Greek
Age 58. Years
Nature of Employment Lieut-Colonel
Place of Employment Roy. Greek Forces
Height 5'-7¾"
Colour of Eyes Brown
Colour of Hair Grey

تذكرة اثبات شخصية

نشهد بأن حامل هذه البطاقة
اسم
هو أحد أعضاء أو عامل التابعين الى
القوات البريطانية أو قوات الحلفاء
فى الشرق الأوسط .

This card is valid only to the date shown. The holder is responsible for its renewal. It must be returned on termination of service or employment; on departure from the Middle East; or on demand.

Second World War. Military identification card of Antisyntagmatachis Charalampos Seiradakis in the Middle East (Officers of the Allied Forces in the Middle East), 19 July 1944.

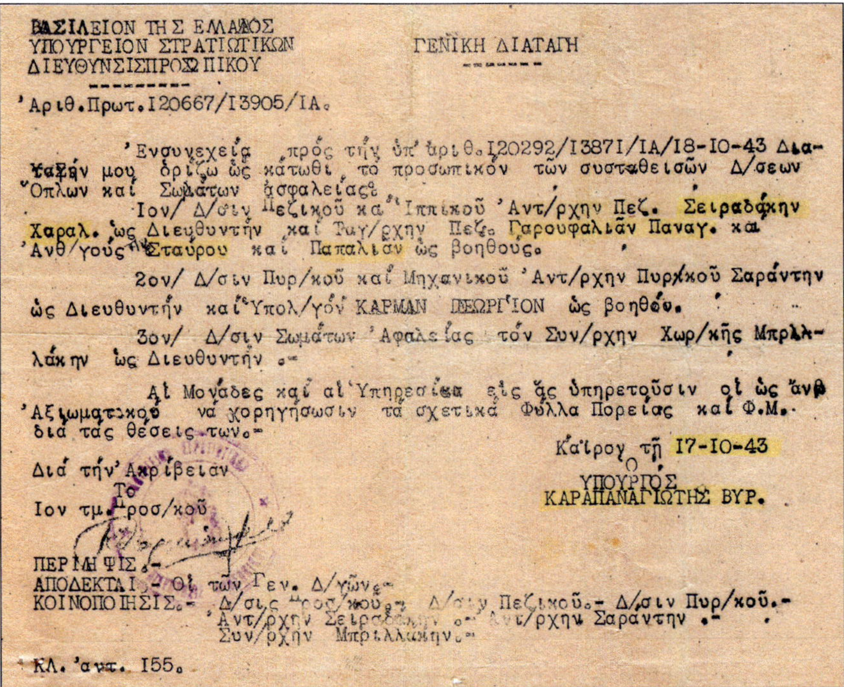

ΒΑΣΙΛΕΙΟΝ ΤΗΣ ΕΛΛΑΔΟΣ
ΥΠΟΥΡΓΕΙΟΝ ΣΤΡΑΤΙΩΤΙΚΩΝ
ΔΙΕΥΘΥΝΣΙΣ ΠΡΟΣΩΠΙΚΟΥ

ΓΕΝΙΚΗ ΔΙΑΤΑΓΗ

Ἀριθ. Πρωτ. 120667/13905/ΙΑ.

Ἐνσυνεχείᾳ πρός τήν ὑπ' ἀριθ. 120292/13871/ΙΑ/18-10-43 Διαταξήν μου ὁρίζω ὡς κάτωθι, τό προσωπικόν τῶν συσταθεισῶν Δ/σεων Ὅπλων καί Σωμάτων ἀσφαλείας.

1ον/ Δ/σιν Πεζικοῦ καί Ἱππικοῦ Ἀντ/ρχην Πεζ. Σειραδάκην Χαραλ. ὡς Διευθυντήν καί Ταγ/ρχην Πεζ. Γαρουφαλιάν Παναγ. καί Ἀνθ/γούς Σταύρου καί Παπαλιάν ὡς βοηθούς.

2ον/ Δ/σιν Πυρ/κοῦ καί Μηχανικοῦ Ἀντ/ρχην Πυρ/κοῦ Σαράντην ὡς Διευθυντήν καί Ὑπολ/γόν ΚΑΡΜΑΝ ΓΕΩΡΓΙΟΝ ὡς βοηθόν.

3ον/ Δ/σιν Σωμάτων Ἀσφαλείας τόν Συν/ρχην Χωρ/κῆς Μπριλλάκην ὡς Διευθυντήν.

Αἱ Μονάδες καί αἱ Ὑπηρεσίαι εἰς ἅς ὑπηρετοῦσιν οἱ ὡς ἄνω Ἀξιωματικοί νά χορηγήσωσιν τά σχετικά Φύλλα Πορείας καί Φ.Μ. διά τάς θέσεις των.

Κάϊρον τῇ 17-10-43

Ο ΥΠΟΥΡΓΟΣ
ΚΑΡΑΠΑΝΑΓΙΩΤΗΣ ΒΥΡ.

Διά τήν ἀκρίβειαν
Τό
1ον τμ. Προσ/κοῦ

ΠΕΡΙΛΗΨΙΣ.-
ΑΠΟΔΕΚΤΑΙ.- Οἱ τῶν Γεν. Δ/νσεων
ΚΟΙΝΟΠΟΙΗΣΙΣ.- Δ/σις Προσ/κοῦ.- Δ/σιν Πεζικοῦ.- Δ/σιν Πυρ/κοῦ.- Ἀντ/ρχην Σειραδάκην.- Ἀντ/ρχην Σαράντην.- Συν/ρχην Μπριλλάκην.-

Κλ. ἀντ. 155.

Second World War. Military order of Greek Minister for Military Affairs B. Karapanagiotis assigning command of the Recruitment and Screening Centre to Ch. Seiradakis, Cairo, 17 October 1943.

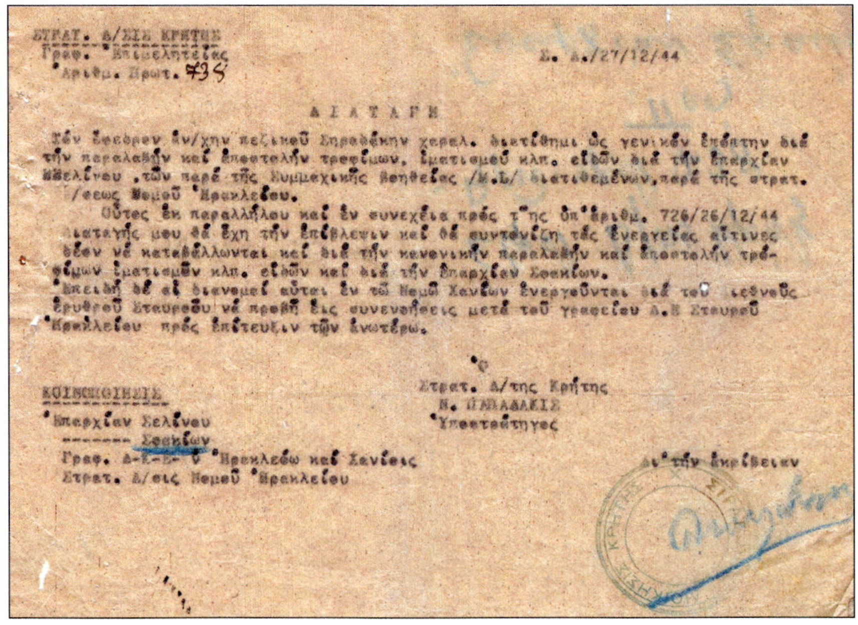

ΣΤΡΑΤ. Δ/ΣΙΣ ΚΡΗΤΗΣ
Γραφ. Ἐπιμελητείας
Ἀριθμ. Πρωτ. 735

Ε. Δ./27/12/44

ΔΙΑΤΑΓΗ

Τόν ἔφεδρον Αν/χην πεζικοῦ Σηραδάκην Χαραλ. διατίθημι ὡς γενικόν ἐπόπτην διά τήν παραλαβήν καί ἀποστολήν τροφίμων, ἱματισμοῦ κλπ. εἰδῶν διά τήν Ἐπαρχίαν Σελίνου, τῶν παρά τῆς Συμμαχικῆς Βοηθείας /M.L/ διατιθεμένων, παρά τῆς Στρατ. Δ/σεως Νομοῦ Ἡρακλείου.

Οὗτος ἐκ παραλλήλου καί ἐν συνεχείᾳ πρός τῆς ὑπ' ἀριθμ. 726/26/12/44 διαταγῆς μου θά ἔχῃ τήν ἐπίβλεψιν καί θά συντονίζῃ τάς ἐνεργείας αἵτινες δέον νά καταβάλλωνται καί διά τήν κανονικήν παραλαβήν καί ἀποστολήν τροφίμων ἱματισμῶν κλπ. εἰδῶν καί διά τήν Ἐπαρχίαν Σφακίων.

Ἐπειδή δέ αἱ διανομαί αὗται ἐν τῷ Νομῷ Χανίων ἐνεργοῦνται διά τοῦ Διεθνοῦς Ἐρυθροῦ Σταυροῦ νά προβῇ εἰς συνεννοήσεις μετά τοῦ γραφείου Δ.Ε. Σταυροῦ Ἡρακλείου πρός ἐπίτευξιν τῶν ἀνωτέρω.

Ο
Στρατ. Δ/της Κρήτης
Ν. ΠΑΠΑΔΑΚΙΣ
Ὑποστράτηγος

ΚΟΙΝΟΠΟΙΗΣΙΣ
Ἐπαρχίαν Σελίνου
------- Σφακίων
Γραφ. Δ.Ε.Σ. ν Ἡρακλείου καί Χανίων
Στρατ. Δ/σεις Νομοῦ Ἡρακλείου

Διά τήν ἀκρίβειαν

Assignment of command for distribution of humanitarian aid in Western Crete to Syntagmatarchis Ch. Seiradakis, 27 December 1944.

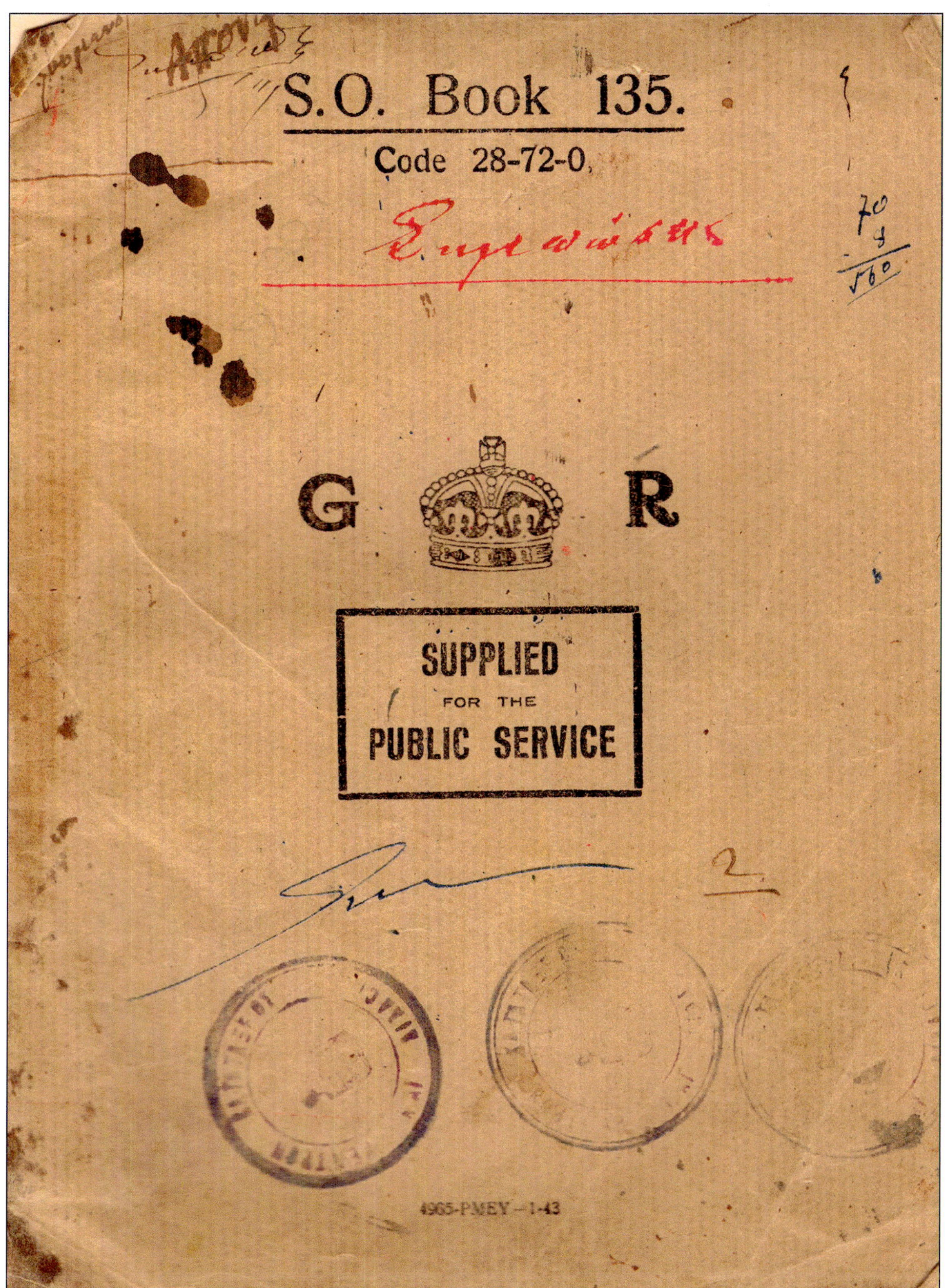

A rare document of the Second World War: the military diary of Ch. Seiradakis, commander of the Recruitment and Screening Centre in Ismailia Desert, Egypt, 1943–1944.

Υπόμνησις
του υπασπιστού Φουντουλάκη Κων/τίνου.

Εις την απολογίαν μου καταθέτω ότι:
όταν εσήμανε το σάλπισμα συγκεντρώσεως επήρα τον Λόχον μου και
διευθύνθην προς τον καταυλισμόν.
όταν διηρχόμην έμπροσθεν του Διοικητηρίου μετά του Λόχου σεις
Κε Διοικητά με επαγγέλατε εις την σκηνήν σας εμέ και τον κ.
Δράκον ενώ ο Λόχος εξηκολούθη να βαδίζη και μας εξηγήσατε
εν ολίγοις τα γενόμενα μας διετάξατε δε να κρατήσωμεν τους
άνδρας του Λόχου εις τον καταυλισμόν του Λόχου.
Κατά το διάστημα αυτό ο Λόχος είχε φθάσει εις τον καταυλισμόν και είχε λύσει τους ζυγούς: όταν έφθασα εγώ μετά του
κ. Δράκου εις τον καταυλισμόν του Λόχου πολλοί στρατιώται ε[illegible]
ντο προς το σάλπισμα και διέταξα τον μεν κ. Δράκον να
ζητήση οδηγίας εγώ δε επιτήθην ίνα συγκρατήσω τους φεύγον[illegible]
ενώ ήρχετο προς την σκηνήν σας ο κ. Δράκος [illegible]
τα μαγαζεία του σάλπισματος όπου ήλθομεν προς σας και
ανέφερα εγώ την διαφορήν των στρατιωτών.
σεις με διετάξατε να σπεύσω αμέσως προς τους φεύγοντας
στρατιώτας να τους ακολουθήσω όπου πάνε και να ασκήσ[illegible]
όλην μου την επιρροήν ίνα τους γυρίσω πίσω αφ' όσον δε
με υπακούουν να φροντίσω πάσει θυσία όπου ίδω ο[illegible]
υπάρχει κίνδυνος να γίνουν επεισόδια να τα αποτρέψω.
Βάσει αυτής της διαταγής σας έφυγα και έφθασα μέχρ[illegible]
Ταξιαρχίας.

Φουντουλάκης

Second World War. Handwritten report of *Anthypaspistis* Konstantinos Fountoulakis to unit commander Ch. Seiradakis on the events of the mutiny in the Middle East, Cairo, 1944.

'Εν Καΐρω τῇ 29 Αὐγούστου 1944

Πρός
τόν Κύριον Πρόεδρον τῆς 'Ελληνικῆς Κυβερνήσεως
'Ενταῦθα

Κύριε Πρόεδρε,-
"Εχωμεν την τιμήν νά Σᾶς γνωρίσωμεν ὅτι πληροφορί
διαφόρων πηγῶν καί δή προερχόμεναι ἐκ ραδιοφωνικῶν ἐκπομ
Λονδίνου καί πλείστων ἀξιοπίστων αὐτοπτῶν μαρτύρων συμπα
ωτῶν μας οἵτινες ἐσχάτως ἔφθασαν ἐκ Κρήτης, φέρουν ὅτι α
συγκρούσεις μεταξύ τῶν κατοίκων τῆς Νήσου καί τῶν ἐκεῖ Σ
τιωτικῶν Γερμανικῶν 'Αρχῶν κατοχῆς, ἔλαβον γενικωτέραν μ
ἐπαναστατικῆς ἐξεγέρσεως, ὥστε νά εὑρίσκωνται περιφέρεια
συγκεκριμένως εἰς τάς 'Επαρχίας Σελίνου καί Μυλοποτάμου
ἔχουν λάβη τήν μορφήν ἀληθοῦς μάχης.-
Κατά τάς συγκρούσεις ταύτας οἱ Γερμανοί ἐφαρμόζου
τάς προσφιλεῖς εἰς αὐτάς μεθόδους χρησιμοποιοῦντες τά γυ
κόπαιδα τῆς Νήσου ὡς ἀσπίδα τῶν ἐπιθετικῶν των ἐλιγμῶν.-
Οὕτως ἡ Κρήτη ὑποστᾶσα ὁλοκληρωτικήν καταστροφήν
κατά τήν κατάληψίν της, καί κατά τήν διάρκειαν τῆς σημερ
σκληρᾶς κατοχῆς, ἐξακολουθεῖ νά ὑφίσταται καί σήμερον κα
χρόνον ἐπίκειται ἡ ἀπελευθέρωσίς της νέας μεγαλειτέρας θ
'Επειδή, Κύριε Πρόεδρε, εἰς στιγμάς κατά τάς ὁποί
ἡ ἰδιαιτέρα μας Πατρίς ἀγωνίζεται τόν θανάσιμον ἀγῶνα κα
τοῦ κατακτητοῦ εἰς τόν ὁποῖον συμμετέχουν καί αὐτά ἀκόμη
γυναικόπαιδα της, μᾶς εἶνε ἀδύνατον νά αἰσθανόμεθα ὅτι π
μένομεν ἀδρανεῖς ἐνῶ τό 'Εθνικόν μας καθῆκον μᾶς ἐπιβάλε
δώσωμεν χεῖρα βοηθείας εἰς τούς ἀγωνιζομένους συμπατριώτ
Διά ταῦτα, παρακαλοῦμεν τήν 'Υμετέραν 'Εξοχότητα
ἐκπρόσωπον τῶν ἐν τῇ Μ.Α. Κρητῶν ὅπως ἀντιλαμβανόμενος κ
ἐκτιμῶν πλήρως τά αἰσθήματα ἡμῶν, προέλθητε εἰς τά ἀναγκ
διαβήματα παρά τῷ "Αγγλω 'Αρχιστρατήγω καί μᾶς ἐπιτρέψη
μεταβῶμεν εἰς Κρήτην διά νά μετάσχωμεν τοῦ ἐκραγέντος ἀγ
ὅστις καί συμβάλλει εἰς τούς γενικωτέρους Στρατιωτικούς
πούς τοῦ Συμμαχικοῦ πολέμου.-
Μέ τήν πεποίθησιν ὅτι θέλομεν τύχη τῆς δεούσης
ὑποστηρίξεως 'Υμῶν [illegible]
[illegible] Διατελοῦμεν μεθ' ὑπολήψεως

(ὑπ.) Σκουλᾶς 'Αχ. ὑποστρ. - Παπαδάκις Νικόλ. ὑποστρ.
Καλιγιάνης Η. συνταγμ.- Βολάνης 'Ανδρ. σμήναρχο
Σειραδάκις Χ. συνταγμ.- Μουντάκης Ιωάν. ἰατρός
Παπαδάκης Α. συνταγμ.- Παΐζης 'Ιωάν. ἰατρός
Γεμενάκης Ι. τραπ.ὑπάλ- Μπαντουβᾶς ἰδιώτης

Second World War. Memo request of Greek officers in the Middle East to return and continue fighting in Greece, 29 August 1944.

Κ Ρ Η Τ Η - Π Ο Λ Ε Μ Ω Ν Τ Α Σ - Τ Ο Υ Σ Ε Ρ Υ Θ Ρ Ο Υ Σ
Ζ Η Τ Ο Υ Ν Τ Ρ Ο Φ Ε Σ , Ο Χ Ι Ο Π Λ Α......

Ὑπό Ροβέρτου Κονγουέη.

ΧΑΝΙΑ-ΚΡΗΤΗΣ- 24 Αὐγούστου 1947.

Ὁ Ἑλληνικός ἐμφύλιος πόλεμος, ἡ χειροτέρευσις τῶν οἰκονομικῶν καί ὁ περιορισμός τῶν τροφίμων ὑφίσταται καί εἰς τήν μεγίστην τῶν Ἑλληνικῶν Νήσων τό αὐτό μέ τήν Ἠπειρωτικήν Ἑλλάδα, μία ἐπίσκεψις μᾶς τό διαπιστώνει.

Ἐκεῖνο ὅμως τό ὁποῖον οἱ Κρῆτες ἔχουν μεγαλειτέραν ἀνάγκην δέν εἶναι τά ὅπλα οὔτε τά πυρομαχικά οὔτε καί τά στρατεύματα, ἀλλά τρόφιμα καί οἰκοδομικόν ὑλικόν.

Νοιώθουν τούς ἑαυτούς των ἱκανούς ν'ἀντιμετωπίσουν τούς ἀντάρτας. Ἡ καλιτέρα των προστασία ἐναντίον αὐτῶν εἶναι οἱ ἐθνικισταί ἀντάρται πού παρεκλήθησαν καί ὁπλίσθησαν παρά τῆς Βασιλικῆς Κυβερνήσεως καί κηνυγοῦν τούς ἐρυθρούς.

ΑΡΧΗΓΟΣ ΤΗΣ ΚΡΗΤΗΣ - ΕΝΑΣ ΗΡΩΣ ΤΟΥ ΠΟΛΕΜΟΥ.

Ὁ Μανώλης Μπαντουβᾶς εἶναι ὁ ἀρχηγός τῆς Κρητικῆς ἀντιστάσεως. Εἶναι ἕνας μπαρουτοβαμμένος ἀρχηγός πού ἔγινε θρυλλική φυσιογνωμία μέ τούς ἀγῶνες του ἐναντίον τῶν Γερμανῶν εἰς τήν Κρήτην.

Τό ἐνδιαφέρον του ὅμως σήμερον εἶναι πιό μεγάλο γιά τροφές παρά ὁ ἀγών του ἐναντίον τῶν κουμμουνιστῶν.

Ἕνας ἄλλος ἐπίσης μεγάλως ἀρχηγός τῆς Κρήτης εἶναι καί ὁ Χαράλαμπος Σειραδάκης Νομάρχης Χανίων. Αὐτός εἶναι πιό κατηγορηματικός πάνω στῆς μεγάλες ἀνάγκες τῆς Νήσου. Ἐδήλωσε μάλιστα ὅτι ἡ σημερινή ἔλλειψις τροφίμων εἶναι μεγαλειτέρα ὅλων τῶν μετά τήν ἀπελευθέρωσιν ἐποχῶν καί ἡ ἐπακολουθοῦσα ἐξ αὐτῆς δυσαρέσκεια βοειθεῖ τούς κουμμουνιστάς. Ἐρωτηθείς δέ γιά το'τί προτιμᾶ καί τί ἔχει περσσότερον ἀνάγκην, ὅπλα, 'Αμερικανικά στρατεύματα, ἤ τρόφιμα καί οἰκοδομικά ὑλικά. -ἀπήντησεν ἀδίστακτα..ΕΕΕΕΑ Τ Ρ Ο Φ Ι Μ Α.

Ο Ι Κ Ρ Η Τ Ε Σ Ε Ι Ν Ε Δ Η Μ Ο Κ Ρ Α Τ Α Ι
Ο Χ Ι Κ Ο Υ Μ Μ Ο Υ Ν Ι Σ Τ Α Ι.....

Ἐδῶ ὑπάρχει μιά ὑπολογίσημος δωδεκάς κουμμουνιστικῶν συμμοριῶν ἀπό εἰκοσαρία περίπου ἄνδρες καλά ὁπλισμένων ἀνταρτῶν περιπλανωμένων ἀνά τήν Κρήτην. Αἰφνηδιάζουν Χωριά ἐνεργοῦν ταχείας ἐπιθέσεις ἐναντίον στρατιωτικῶν φυλακίων, ἀνατινάσσουν γεφύρας καί ὑπονομεύουν δρόμους. Τά τέσσαρα πέμπτα τῶν Κρητῶν ἐψήφησαν κατά τῆς ἐπαναφορᾶς τοῦ Βασιλέως κατά τό πρόσφατον Δημοψήφισμα.

Αὐτοί εἶναι Δημοκρατικοί ἀλλ'ὄχι κουμουνισταί. Ἡ Κρήτη μεγάλως ὑπέφερε κατά τόν πόλεμον. Πολλά ἀπό τά Χωριά καί τάς πόλεις της εἶναι τόσο ἐρειπωμένα πού μόνον στήν Πωλωνία μπορεῖ κανείς νά τά δῆ.

Διά τήν μετάφρασιν

Article of American journalist Robert Conway (in Greek translation) on the political situation and the management of US assistance in Crete, Greece, 24 August 1947.

Bibliography

Books

Anon., *Historique du 346e Régiment d'Infanterie* (Paris: Librairie Chapelot, n.d.)

Anon, *Dépôt des 2e et 3e Régiments de Marche du 1er Étranger*, Marseille, 26 février 1915

AA. VV., *Venezia e la difesa del Levante da Lepanto a Candia 1570–1670*, exhibition catalogue (Venice: Arsenale, 1986)

Alexakis, Ioannis S., *O protos stratos tis Kritis: I kritiki politofylaki,* (Athens: privately published, 1969), text in Greek

Androulakis, Yannis, *I ekpaidefsi stin Kriti* (Chania: privately published, 1990), text in Greek

Beevor, Antony, *Kriti, I Machi kai I Antistasi* (Athens: Govostis Publications, 2004). Originally published in English: *The Battle and the Resistance* (London: John Murray, 1991)

Bujac, Colonel Jean Léopold Emile Bujac, *Les campagnes de l'armée hellénique*, (Paris: Charles-Lavauzelle & Cie, 1930)

Carr, John C., *Thorikto Averof – Keravnos sto Aigaio* (Athens: Psychogios, 2015). Originally published in English: *RHNS Averof: Thunder in the Aegean* (London: Pen & Sword Maritime, 2014)

Christakos, Nikos K., *Gramma apo to syntrofo (Dimokratikoi Agones 1941–49)*, (Athens: privately published, 1985), text in Greek

Christidis, Vasilios, *The Conquest of Crete by the Arabs (ca. 824): A Turning Point in the Struggle between Byzantium and Islam* (Athens: Academy of Athens, 1984)

Clark, Alan: *The Fall of Crete* (London: Anthony Blond, 1962)

Czubak, Nicolas, *Les batailles du saillant de Saint-Mihiel 1914–1918* (Hellecourt: L'Est Républicain, 2017)

Dafnis, Gregorios, *I Ellas metaxy dyo polemon, 1923–1940* (Athens: Icarus, 1974), text in Greek

Damer, Sean & Frazer, Ian: *On the Run: ANZAC Escape and Evasion in Enemy-Occupied Crete*, (London: Penguin, 2007)

Daskarolis, Ioannis V., *Dimokratika Tagmata. Oi « praitorianoi » tis B' Ellinikis Dimokratias, 1923–1926* (Athens: Papazisis Publications, 2019), text in Greek

Davis, Wes: *Epichirisi "Ariadni": O mystikos polemos gia ti sotiria tis Kritis apo tous Nazi* (Athens: Patakis, 2014) text in Greek

Dertilis, George: *Epta polemoi, tesseris emfylioi, epta ptochefseis, 1821–2016* (Athens: Polis, 2016) text in Greek

Diamantopoulos, Thanasis, *I diki ton 'Exi'. Ethnikos dichasmos kai i korifosi tou. Exilasmos i dikastikos fonos?* (Athens: Patakis Publications, 2022), text in Greek

Drakontaeidis, Philippos D. (ed.), *Christos Karagiannis, I istoria enos stratioti: Mia synglonistiki maryria gia tis ellinikes ekstrateies (1918–1922)* Athens: Khedros, 2013), text in Greek

Drakontaeidis, Philippos D. (ed.), *Konstantinos X. Nider – Campaign in Ukrania, January – May 1919* (Athens: Kedros, 2015), text in Greek

Franchet d'Espèrey, Louis Félix Marie François, *L'épopée de l'Armée d'Orient* (Paris: Payot, 1920)

Fromkin, David: *A Peace to End All Peace: The Fall of the Ottoman Empire and the Creation of the Modern Middle East* (New York: First Owl Book Editions, 2001)

Gallant, Thomas, W.: *Brief Histories – Modern Greece* (Oxford: Oxford University Press, 2001)

George, Prince of Greece, *Anamniseis ek Kritis 1898–1906,* (Athens: 'G. Rodis' Brothers' Printing Office, 1959) text in Greek

Geanakoplos, Deno John, *Constantinople and the West* (The University of Wisconsin Press, 1989)

Gerolymatos, André: *Emphylios – Ellada 1943–1949, Enas diethnis polemos* (Athens: Dioptra, 2018) text in Greek

Giannakopoulos, Konstantinos I., *Vizantini Anatoli kai Latiniki Dysi* (Athens: Bibliopoleion of Estia, 1966), text in Greek

Gilbert, Harald, *Das besetzte Kreta 1941–1945* (Ruhpolding: Franz Philipp Rutzen, 2015), text in German

Grundon, Imogen, *Rash Adventurer: A life of John Pendlebury* (London: I.B. Tauris, 2007)

Gyparakis, Andreas, *Anamniseis apo ti genia mou* (Athens: privately published, 1978) text in Greek

Gyparis, Pavlos, *Iroes kai iroismoi sti Machi tis Kritis* (Athens: privately published,1955), text in Greek

Hall, Richard C., *The Balkan Wars 1912–1913: Prelude to the First World War* (New York: Routledge, 2000)

Hatziangelis, Vangelis & Rappas, Lambis, *To ogdoo tagma. Pos kai giati kai apo poious dialythikan oi Ellinikes Enoples Dynameis sti Mesi Anatoli (1943–1944)* (Chania: Rappa Publications, 1994), text in Greek

Hutchison, Thomas Setzer, *An American Soldier under the Greek Flag at Bezanie: A Thrilling Story of the Siege of Bezanie by the Greek Army, in Epirus, During the War in the Balkans* (Nashville, TN: Greek-American Publishing, 1913)

Kakouri, Athena, *Ta dyo vita* (Athens: Kapon Publications, 2016) text in Greek

Kalliataki Mertikopoulou, Callia: *Ellinikos alytrotismos kai othomanikes metarrythmiseis* (Athens: Estia, 1988), text in Greek

Kalyvas, Stathis N., *Katastrophes kai thriamvoi,* (Athens: Papadopoulos Publications, 2015), text in Greek

Kalyvas, Stathis & Marantzidis, Nikos, *Emphylia Pathi* (Athens: Metaixmio, 2015), text in Greek

Kanellopoulos, Panagiotis, *Imerologio katochis, 31 Martiou 1942 – 4 Ianouariou 1945* (Tomos A kai B) (Athina, Ekdoseis kathimerinis, 2021), text in Greek

Katiforis, Panagiotis, *H Elliniki Amyna sti Machi tis Kritis* (Athens: Ariston Books, 2017, first edition 1950), text in Greek

Kavvos, Georgios, *Germano-italiki katochi kai antistasi Kritis 1941–1945* (Heraklion: privately published? 1991)

Kochylakis, Yannis, *H epopoiia tis Machis tis Kritis kai tis Ethnikis Antistasis* (Athens: Smyrniotakis, 1993), text in Greek

Koukounas, Demosthenes, *H Kriti ypo katochi* (Athens: Ariston Books, 2013), text in Greek

Lambousakis, Eftimis I., *To Selino sti Machi tis Kritis* (Chania: privately published, 2021), text in Greek (the cover page reads: Ekdosi: Eftychiou I. Lambousaki, Chania 2021)

Larentzakis, George, *Oi Tourkokrites kai to Kritiko zitima* (Chania: Erisma, 2015), Greek text

Llewellyn-Smith, Michael, *Venizelos, The Making of a Greek Statesman, 1864–1914*, volume I (Oxford: Oxford University Press, 2021)

Llewellyn-Smith, Michael, *Ionian Vision: Greece in Asia Minor 1919–1922* (London: Hurst & Co., 1998)

McDevitt, Jim, *My Escape from Crete* (Auckland, New Zealand: privately published, 2002)

MacDonald, Callum: *The Lost Battle: Crete 1941* (London: Pan MacMillan, 1993)

Machairidis, Christos: *Mikrasiatiki tragodia*, tomoi A and B (Chania: Erisma, 2015) text in Greek

MacGillivray, J. Alexander, *Minotaur: Sir Arthur Evans and the Archaeology of the Minoan Myth* (London: Jonathan Cape, 2000)

Malessis, Dimitris, *Itta, Thriamvos, Katastrophi. O Stratos sto Elliniko Kratos apo to 1898 eos to 1922* (Athens: Ekdoseis To Vima, 2022), text in Greek

Manousakas, Manousos: *H Kritiki logotechnia kata tin epochi tis Venetokratias* (Thessaloniki: Aristotle University, 1965), text in Greek

Manousakas, Manolis: *Istorika gegonota, synoikies kai ktiria tis polis ton Chanion* (Chania: Erisma, 2021), text in Greek

Manousakis, Giorgis, *Kritikes epanastaseis 1821–1905* (Chania: Ethniko Idrima Erevnon kai Meleton 'Elefterios Venizelos', 2004), text in Greek

Mantran, Robert (dir.), *Histoire de l'Empire Ottoman*, sous la direction de Robert Mantran (Paris: Fayard, 1989)

Markezinis, Spyros V., *Politiki istoria tis neoteras Ellados*, 4 tomoi (Athens: Papyros, 1968)

Mayrogordatos, George T., *1915, O Ethnikos Dichasmos* (Athens: Patakis, 2015), text in Greek

Mayrogordatos, George T., *Meta to 1922, I paratasi tou dichasmou* (Athens: Patakis, 2017), text in Greek

Michaelidis, Iakovos: *To kinima tis Ethnikis Amynis,* (Thessaloniki: University Studio Press, 2015) text in Greek

Mourellos, Ioannis D., *Istoria tis Kritis,* 4 volumes (Heraklion: Printing House 'Eleftheras Skepseos', 1931–1934), text in Greek

Mourellos, Ioannis D., *I Machi tis Kritis* (Heraklion: 1950), text in Greek

Ntountoulaki Penelope I., *I Mnimi kai I Stachti VI, Apo ti Machi tis Kritis mechri tin Apeleftherosi,* tomos VI (Chania: Nomarchiaki Aftodioikisi Chanion, Maios 2009), text in Greek

Palmer, Alan: *Twilight of the Habsburgs* (New York: Grove Pr, 1994)

Panagiotakis, Georgios: *Dokoumenta apo ti Machi kai tin Antistasi tis Kritis, 1941–1945* (Heraklion: G. Dekoratis, 2000), trilingual text

Papadakis, Nikolaos Emm (Papadis): *Eleftherios Venizelos, O Anthropos, o Igetis,* tomoi A & B (Athens: Estia, 2017), text in Greek

Ploumidis, Spyridon, *I 'Sidira' Dekaetia. Oi ethnikoi polemoi tis Ellados (1912–1922)* (Athens: Minos, 2022), text in Greek

Richter, Heinz A., *H Machi tis Kritis,* (Athens: Govostis Publications, 201). Originally published in German: *Operation Merkur: Die Eroberung der Insel Kreta im Mai 1941* (Ruhpolding: Franz Philipp Rutzen, 2011)

Rizas, Sotiris, *To telos tis Megalis Ideas,* (Athina, Kastaniotis, 2015), text in Greek

Rouyer, Bruno, *Avoir 20 ans au Bois-le-Prêtre, septembre 1914 – juillet 2015* (Haroué: Gerard Louis Editeur, 2015)

Satrazanis, Antonis, *Oi treis Galloi archistratigoi tis 'Stratias tis Anatolis' sti Thessaloniki: Maurice Paul Emmanuel Sarrail, Marie Louis Adolphe Guillaumat kai Louis Felix Marie Francois Franchet d'Esperey* (Thessaloniki: University Studio Press, 2015), text in Greek

Seiradakis, Charalampos, *Military Diary, Recruitment and Screening Centre, S.O. Book135, Code 28-72-0 (Supplied for Public Service), Ismailia, 1944.*

Simms, Brendan: *Europe: The Struggle for Supremacy, from 1453 to the Present* (London: Penguin, 2014)

Spanakis, Stergios C., *Poleis kai choria tis Kritis sto perasma ton aionon* (Heraklion: Detorakis, 1991), text in Greek

Stewart, Ian McD. G., *The Struggle for Crete, 20 May – 1 June 1941: A Story of Lost Opportunity* (Oxford: Oxford University Press, 1991)

Stavrinou, Miranda, *I Aggliki politiki kai to Kritiko Zitima,* (Athens: Domos Publications, 1986), text in Greek

Thomas, David A.: *Crete 1941: The Battle at Sea* (London: German, 1972)

Tomadakis, Vassilios (ed.), *Ioannou D. Kondylaki Agnosta Apomnimonevmata (1905) apo ti symmerochi tou stin Kritiki Epanastasi tou 1897* (Athens: Kardamitsas Publications, 2002), text in Greek

Tritos, Michael, *I apeleftherosi tou Metsovou (31 Oktovriou 1912)* (Ioannina: privately published, 2012) text in Greek

Tuchman, Barbara W., *The Guns of August* (New York: Ballantine Books, 1994)

Tzanes Bounialis, Marinos, *O Kritikos Polemos (1645–1669)* (Athens: Stigmi, 1995), text in Greek. (NB, Earlier editions by Agathangelos Xirouchakis, N. Nenedakis and I. Politis)

Vardinogiannis, Vardis, *I antistasi sto Selino*, (Athens: Themelio, 1988), text in Greek

Veremis, Thanos: *Eleftherios Venizelos: O oramatistis tou efiktou* (Athens, Metaichmio, 2017), text in Greek

Veremis, Thanos, *Oi epemvaseis tou stratou stin elliniki politiki, 1916–1936* (Athens: Alexandria Publications, 2018), text in Greek

Vlontakis, Stavros C., *H "Ochyra thesis Kritis". Chroniko germanikis katochis sta Chania apo Oktovri 1944 kai tis agglogermanikis apo Maio os Ioulio 1945* (Athens: privately published, 1976) text in Greek

Xirouchakis, Charis, *ABEA 1889–2019: Chania kai ABEA – Mia koini poreia,* (text: Charis Xirouchakis, editorial coordination: Kyriakos Naxakis, illustration: Gisis Papageorgiou), Chania: Chania Cooperative Bank of Chania, 2019) text in Greek and English

Zampelios, Spyridon, *Kritikoi gamoi. Anekdoton epeisodion tis kritikis istorias epi Veneton (1570)* (Athens: Printshop Vretos Valettas, 1883), text in Greek

Chapters and Articles

Kallivretakis, Leonidas F., 'Imerologion ekstrateias 1912–1913. Odoiporikes kai polemikes simeioseis Ipirou – Makedonias – Thrakis tou ethelonti Konsti I. Kapidakis" in *Istor* 2, 1990. text in Greek

Maris, A. M., 'O protos taktikos stratos tis Kritis – I Kritiki Politofylaki, i exelixi tis kai i polemiki drasitis' in the *Etisia Ekdosi Dimou Chanion* (Chania: Municipal Library of Chania, 1978), pp.14–21, text in Greek

Sakellaropoulos, Tasos, *Oi enoples dynameis. Symmachies kai dichasmoi sti Mesi Anatoli, 1941–1944* sto Istoria tou Neou Ellinismou 1700–2000, 8os tomos: *H EMPOLEMI ELLADA 1940–1949 (Alvaniko Epos, Katochi kai Antistasi, Emfylios*), (Athens: Ellinika Grammata, 2004), text in Greek

Sakellaropoulos, Tasos, *To soma ton Ellinon Axiomatikon ston polemo kai tin politiki, 1940–1945*, sto *Istoria tis Ellados tou 20ou aiona,* tomos 3, (Athens: Vivliorama, 2007), text in Greek

Seiradakis, Charalampos, *Polemiki ekthesis apo ti Machi tis Kritis – Machi tis Kandanou,* a special report to the newspaper *Chaniotika Nea*, 25 May 2009, pp.21–28. text in Greek

Other Sources

Decrees of the Tsouderos government: A.N. 3013/9-5-1941 'Peri apokatastseos Axiomatikon kai Anthypaspiston exelthonton tou stratevmatos dia politikous logous' & A.N. 3058/27-6-1941 'Peri ermineftikon diataxeon ton arthron 1 & 2 tou A.N. 3013/9-5-1941' (text in Greek)

Electronic Resources

Anon, Dépôt des 2e et 3e Régiments de Marche du 1er Étranger, Marseille, 26 février 1915.

Venizelosarchives.gr – Digital Archive of the National Foundation for Research and Studies 'Eleftherios K. Venizelos'

www.haniotika-nea.gr/21-fevrouariou-1913-i-simvoli-ton-kriton-stin-apeleftherosi-ton-ioanninon/

Kamenopoulos, Sotiris, '21 Fevrouariou 1913: I symvoli ton Kriton stin apeleftherosi ton Ioanninon' in *Chaniotika Nea*, 23/2/2016

www.history-point.gr/21i-fevroyarioy-1913-oi-kritikoi-ki-enas-amerikanos-stratiotis-stin-ipeiro

Karkanis, Georgios, '*I syngkrotisi kai I drasi tou Kritikou Foititikou 'Ierou Lochou' kata tous Valkanikous polemous 1912–1913'*, stin istoselida www..eriande.elemedu.upatras.gr/eriande/synedria/synedrio4/practika1/karkanis.htm

Katsikostas, Dimitrios, *O Ellinikos Stratos stin Exoria 1941–1944 – Organosi, Syngkrotisi, Polemikes Apostoles kai Kinimata sti Mesi Anatoli*, (PhD Thesis), (Athens: EKPA, December 2010) https://thesis.ekt.gr/thesisBookReader/id/25448#page/ 1/mode/2up (in Greek)

Mayrogonatos, E., *Oi Krites stous Valkanikous polemous*, https://epikimaxikilkis1913.blogspot.com/2015/04/blog-post_35.html

Papailiaki, Niki, *H Machi tis Kandanou, Maios 1941*, file:///C:/Users/Admin/Downloads/62205634-1.pdf and journal *Approaches*

Online forum

www.greatwarforum.org/topic/234339-greek-infantry-at-gallipoli/

Online encyclopedia: el.wikipedia.org

Online historical archive: SanSimera.gr

Online archives: Venizelosarchives.gr